Women, America, and Movement

Women, America, and Movement

Narratives of Relocation

Edited by
Susan L. Roberson

University of Missouri Press
Columbia and London

Library of Congress Cataloging-in-Publication Data

Women, America, and movement : narratives of relocation / edited by
Susan L. Roberson.
     p.   cm.
   Includes bibliographical references and index.
   ISBN 0-8262-1176-3 (alk. paper)
   1. American fiction—Women authors—History and criticism.
2. Women and literature—United States—History.   3. Emigration and
immigration in literature.   4. Frontier and pioneer life in
literature.   5. Migration, Internal, in literature.   6. Immigrants
in literature.   7. Exiles in literature.   8. Narration (Rhetoric)
9. Home in literature.   I. Roberson, Susan L., 1950–   .
PS374.W6W66   1998
810.9'9287—dc21   98-6619
                                                            CIP

⊗™ This paper meets the requirements of the
American National Standard for Permanence of Paper
for Printed Library Materials, Z39.48, 1984.

Designer: Stephanie Foley
Typesetter: BookComp, Inc.
Printer and binder: Edwards Brothers, Inc.
Typefaces: Americana and ITC Giovanni
Frontispiece: photo courtesy of the Roberson family

For credits, see page 291.

This book is dedicated to

the memory of my grandmothers,
Rena Rose Roberson and Jane Petty Taylor,

my mother-in-law, Bettye Knowles Moon,

and my mother, Margaret Taylor Roberson

—all women who dared to find a home on the road

Contents

III.
Dislocations

IV.
Geographies of the Self

Women, America, and Movement

Narratives of Relocation and Dislocation

An Introduction

SUSAN ROBERSON

A Story

In 1925 my grandmother, a young wife with the first of her five children, migrated with her husband and her father's family from Oklahoma to southeast New Mexico. Like many other folks, they went in search of better opportunities, of land that would provide a better livelihood than the marginal land of Oklahoma, soon to dry up in the dust bowl. With thirty thousand acres of land made available by the newly opened irrigation system in the Pecos Valley, they hoped to enjoy a prosperity they had not experienced as farm workers in Oklahoma. Typical of many migrants, they went as a group, an extended family, to an area already occupied by at least one other household of Robersons. By 1925 my grandparents had already made an initial incursion into the Pecos Valley, but because my grandmother had insisted on being close to her mother when her first baby was born, they had returned to Oklahoma. Thus the great migration of 1925, a three-day trek by Model T, was really the second one for my young grandparents. Nor would it be the last move they made. Between 1925 and 1942, they moved from one farm to another sharecropping and back to Oklahoma for a two-year interlude before they were able to buy their own farm in Otis, New Mexico. My records indicate eight moves in seventeen years, a move approximately every two years. My records indicate as well that the expected prosperity was a long time coming. Yet their story of kinship ties, multiple moves, and delayed prosperity is not much different from that of millions of other families who have pulled up stakes in search of greener pastures.[1]

1. I want to thank Judith Roberson Smith, Freddie Rose Newton, Clara Jo

I base this brief narrative on recollections of family stories and vague memories, for all who remain now are the children and grandchildren of the migrants of '25. My grandmother, like many women, left no written documents of that journey. The only "text" that marks this journey is a black-and-white photograph, itself a part of the family's collective memory. Taken on a chilly November day, for the family had first to finish the Oklahoma harvest, the photograph captures a breakfast or lunch stop in a draw or ravine below the road where the car sat. Framed by the horizontal lines of the landscape and marked by the blankness of the women's faces, the photo tells a story of the tensions between the barrenness and immensity of the landscape and the intimacy of the gaze. For the women stare not at the vastness of space or their venture but at the figure of the photographer. Like the picture itself, their gazes are centered on the familiar, the familial. By focusing on each other, the women and the photographer create a place of value—the family setting, the photograph, the body, that place where their gazes meet—that arrests the flow of time and the mobility of movement, a place "haunted" by memory that asks us to read its meaning. The location, the text, of this picture is then not so much the high plains as it is the body of the group, the family that makes a place out of space. As Michel de Certeau says, "Places are fragmentary and inward-turning histories, pasts that others are not allowed to read, accumulated times that can be unfolded but like stories held in reserve, remaining in an enigmatic state, symbolizations encysted in the pain or pleasure of the body."[2] It is on such enigmatic sites that we must try to read the silent story of my grandparents' migration, a story that leaves unsaid that which we as second- and third-generation gazers want to know, want to hear.

What did that move mean to the women in the picture? What did the move mean to my grandmother, a new wife and mother? Surely relocating to New Mexico entailed more than packing up the car and moving to a new home. How did she respond to the new environment? Was it stifling

Hughes, and Joe Rose for graciously and enthusiastically sharing their memories and stories with me. Thanks also to Judith Smith for giving me a copy of that remarkable photograph of the Rose and Roberson migrants, which appears at the beginning of this introduction. I would also like to thank Jacqueline Doyle and Caroline Gebhard, who read drafts of this introduction and provided useful suggestions for revision.
2. Michel de Certeau, *The Practice of Everyday Life*, trans. Steven F. Rendall (Berkeley and Los Angeles: University of California Press, 1984), 108. See also p. 117 of de Certeau; and Yi-Fu Tuan, *Space and Place: The Perspective of Experience* (Minneapolis: University of Minnesota Press, 1977), 12, for more discussion on the differences between place and space.

or freeing? Were the traumas of relocation meliorated by her extended family? Was she able to bring most of her belongings with her or was she forced to leave a great many behind? Was she too in search of a better life or was she captured by love to share her husband's dream? Or was there some impulse, some agitation in the blood, that compelled this family group to pack up and hit the road? Perhaps so, for even after they achieved some degree of prosperity, my grandmother was likely to hop on a Greyhound bus to celebrate family graduations, weddings, and births. So although her interest in going was connected to her large family, perhaps she also needed some space, some motion, some means of temporary escape from the everyday routines of life. Even after she was placed in a nursing home, and before she became really helpless, my grandmother would try to cajole visitors into driving her away. Yet even as her life was marked by migrations and motion, my memories of her are tied to place, to the farm in New Mexico I visited nearly every summer for fourteen years, until my own moves interrupted those visits. More specifically, I remember her in the kitchen, apron about her middle, preparing food for the swarms of grandchildren, who, like me, spent summers with her.

Movement, place, relocation: These are events in the everyday lives of women, like my grandmother, who took their moves for granted, who did not write stories or memoirs or journals about their migrations or how they affected their lives. That is why reading the narratives of women who did write of their own life experiences or who imagined the travels and places in the lives of their characters strikes a chord of interest in us. To read the narratives of movement, like those discussed in this volume, brings us back to reveries of our own experiences, to our past, for migrations and movements drive our history, our histories, and contribute to the construction of our (American) character. As a nation and as individuals we have been called to the open road, to new hopes and new freedoms connected with new places, places which, however, were not always as new, free, or unoccupied as we may have imagined or wished. For complicit with the call to the open road is a myth that presupposes an empty wilderness for those lately come to this continent to take and claim. At the beginning of our history, when Michel Chevalier remarked on the restlessness of the American, he ignored the other "Americans" who were very much rooted to place: "[The American] has no root in the soil, he has no feeling of reverence, and love for the natal spot and the paternal roof; he is always disposed to emigrate, always ready to start in the first steamer that comes along, from the place where he had but just now landed." Even so, much of our literature celebrates with Chevalier the locomotive agitation that seems so much a part of the American experience. Walt Whitman showed us the way "to landscapes of continents and the public road." Huck Finn chose to light out for the Indian territories rather than return to civilization. And Jack Kerouac and his buddies made frantic runs across the nation, "leaving confusion and nonsense behind and performing our one and noble function of the time, *move.*" Movement, then, is as much a part of our literature as it is a part of our lives.[3]

But the canonized narratives of the national impulse tell only a part of the story, for by and large they have been the narratives of, by, and about men. Since the first colonists landed on the east coast and since the first Europeans intruded on native lands, American women's lives have also been disrupted and affected by relocation and dislocation. Lacking the means, time, or encouragement to write about their relocations and dislocations, women like my grandmother had to improvise their lives as they lived them, to face changes in plan and expectation caused by geographic dislocation with "ambiguity, uncertainty, or simple lack of knowledge" in "ways that are usually passed over in silence." Some women have had to face the added task of finding their way in a new culture or a new language, of balancing their lives in the "contact zone" where "disparate cultures meet, clash, and grapple with each other," or of being displaced by the colonization of their lands. Even so, we do have a number of narratives written by women who have recorded and imagined experiences of cultural displacement, immigration, migration, and emigration. To some extent they tell stories similar to those by men, of new lands, of hardship, promise, and adjustment. But to examine women's narratives of movement is to discover more than the "M-factor" of the American character—"movement, migration, mobility"—with a slightly feminine angle. It is to discover the traumas, the costs, and the rewards of movement, migration, and displacement that accrue to women and the texts they write because of their gender and their gendered situation in life. It is also to consider the intersections between movement and the feminine, for as Frances Bartkowski observes, "The critique of femininity, itself a contested cultural space, has taught us to recognize the mobility, plasticity, and mimicry involved in becoming a woman."[4] To read the text

---

3. Michel Chevalier, *Society, Manners, and Politics in the United States: Letters on North America*, trans. T. G. Bradford from the 3d Paris ed., Boston 1839, reprint Research and Social Works Series no. 352, New York: Burt Franklin, 1969, 286; Walt Whitman, *Leaves of Grass*, ed. Harold W. Blodgett and Sculley Bradley (New York: W. W. Norton, 1965), 83; Jack Kerouac, *On the Road* (New York: Penguin Books, 1955), 133.

4. Renato Rosaldo, *Culture and Truth: The Remaking of Social Analysis* (Boston: Beacon Press, 1989), 92, 91; Mary Louise Pratt, *Imperial Eyes: Travel Writing and*

of a mobile or displaced woman often requires us to probe behind and between the lines of texts, to listen to her silences and to decode subverted, subversive messages, to be ourselves explorers, uncovering and discovering the story of her migrations and dislocations and of the self shaped and revealed in the venturing forth.

To listen to these narratives at the end of this century has particular relevance, for if anything the rate of migration and immigration has accelerated and in all likelihood will continue to do so. Our borders have become porous, and daily we are asked to reconsider the national constitution, what constitutes the American character and way of life as well as the laws that constitute our national agenda. Indeed, the elasticity and permeability of the many borders and boundaries that have defined or tried to define our lives is global and not restricted to any one nation-state. Homi Bhabha reminds us that "in the *fin de siècle,* we find ourselves in the moment of transit where space and time cross to produce complex figures of difference and identity. . . . For there is a sense of disorientation, a disturbance of direction . . . an exploratory, restless movement." People are moving faster and in greater numbers than ever before.[5] Technology has assisted migration and movement, facilitating journeys that a century ago would have been daunting if not virtually impossible. In fact, one almost need not leave home to travel through space, cyberspace, or the networks of the world via the World Wide Web. And while here in America it may seem that franchises and chain restaurants have homogenized our world, technological and social change can have a dizzying, vertiginous effect even on the geographically stationary.

The Politics of Location

The importance of place in an individual's life has long been recognized by a variety of thinkers and writers, including the poet Adrienne Rich, who writes in several places about "the politics of location." In "Blood Bread, and Poetry" she tells us that she writes from and imagines herself from

---

Transculturation (London: Routledge, 1992), 4; George Pierson, "The M-Factor in American History," in *The Character of Americans,* rev. ed., ed. Michael McGiffert (Homewood, Ill.: Dorsey Press, 1970), 121; Francis Bartkowski, *Travelers, Immigrants, Inmates: Essays in Estrangement* (Minneapolis: University of Minnesota Press, 1995), 111.

5. Homi K. Bhabha, *The Location of Culture* (London: Routledge, 1994), 1; see Deepika Bahri's essay in this collection, "Always Becoming: Narratives of Nation and Self in Bharati Mukherjee's *Jasmine.*"

a historical context, a time and place that went into the making of her character and her poetry. She calls this context, which is both historical and individual, "location." She writes, "My personal world view . . . was not original with me, but was, rather, my untutored and half-conscious rendering of the facts of blood and bread, the social and political forces of my time and place." What she suggests are ontological and epistemological groundings in location, that who we are and how we look at and come to know the world are to a large degree fashioned by the world, by the time and space of our particular locations. But she takes the meaning of location to mean more than just geographic and historical contexts, for she speaks of the body as a location from which she writes and of poetry, politics, and her own position "as a lesbian-feminist poet and writer" as locations, as places where she discovers and defines herself, where she finds herself to be one of the "dispossessed" and fragmented.[6] These locations, she further suggests, are gendered and colored; they are not the gender- and race-neutral positions she had at one time supposed them to be. At the same time that Rich comes to realize how "locations" are determined, defined, and controlled by a gendered and colored group— white males—she realizes that women and people of color also shape and define their own locations against and beyond patriarchal, hegemonic legacies.

Making these observations from her position as a political, lesbian poet in 1984, Rich has opened for us new spaces, new locations, of intellectual and imaginative journeyings. We have come to realize with Rich that location is individual and particular rather than transparent and essentializing. We have also come to see that location is porous and relational, that the borders we once thought to be stable are fluid, unfixed, contested. Alison Blunt and Gillian Rose in the introduction to their book, *Writing Women and Space*, assert that "feminists plotting the politics of location imagine 'an insistent, simultaneous, nonsynchronous process, characterized by multiple locations': a space that is fragmented, multidimensional, contradictory, and provisional." And Doreen Massey contends that space is "constructed out of social relations" and is hence a dynamic rather than static site of power and signification. "Such a way of conceptualizing the spatial," she argues, "inherently implies the existence in the lived world of a simultaneous multiplicity of spaces. . . ." Much of the work being done with colonialist, post-colonialist, and transnational literatures and

6. Adrienne Rich, "Blood, Bread, and Poetry: The Location of the Poet," in *Adrienne Rich's Poetry and Prose*, ed. Barbara Charlesworth Gelpi and Albert Gelpi (New York: W. W. Norton, 1993), 242, 249, 245, 252.

issues are premised on these kinds of assumptions about multiple and multidimensional locations, politics, and poetries (literatures).[7]

These same assumptions have also opened up new ways of viewing other spaces. Not only have we come to realize the impact of locations of terrain and nationhood, power and knowledge on literature and the discourses of various genres, but also we have come to understand that writing is itself a location, a site for the construction of further spaces of power and knowledge, spaces that are also gendered. The metaphoric and real connection between the colonization of geographic spaces and the colonization of intellectual and sexual spaces has prompted some feminists like Rich and bell hooks to decry the fragmenting, alienating, and marginalizing of their position and to call for a radical resistance. hooks writes: "As a radical standpoint, perspective, position, 'the politics of location' necessarily calls those of us who would participate in the formation of counter-hegemonic cultural practice to identify the spaces where we begin the process of re-vision." For hooks those spaces are the homeplace and the margins, both sites of resistance and political struggle.[8]

"The politics of location" further asks us to consider not only how sexuality is a space that can be colonized or how women's sexual vulnerability and spatial movement can complicate each other, but how gender itself affects our experience of space. Tradition and circumstance have long influenced the ways men and women experience space or location and movement through space. In large part, the difference between men and women's experience of space and mobility is constructed and learned. Shirley Ardener argued in 1981 that "the 'social map' of patriarchy created 'ground rules' for the behavior of men and women, and that the gender roles and relations of patriarchy constructed some spaces as 'feminine' and others as 'masculine' and thus allocated certain kinds of (gendered) activities to certain (gendered) places. Gender difference was thus seen as inscribing spatial difference." Not surprisingly, the spaces allocated to women were and are still generally the private spaces of the home and family.[9]

7. Alison Blunt and Gillian Rose, introduction to *Writing Women and Space: Colonial and Postcolonial Geographies* (New York: Guilford Press, 1994), 7; Doreen Massey, *Space, Place, and Gender* (Minneapolis: University of Minnesota Press, 1994), 2–3.

8. bell hooks, *Yearning: Race, Gender, and Cultural Politics* (Boston: South End Press, 1990), 145.

9. Quoted in Blunt and Rose, *Writing Women and Space*, 1; see Gillian Rose, *Feminism and Geography: The Limits of Geographical Knowledge* (Minneapolis: University of Minnesota Press, 1993), 22–28, for a discussion of some findings about women's movement through time and space.

Though Ardener's point can be deconstructed in terms of class and race, it is corroborated by other social scientists who have found that women experience mobility and movement through time and space differently than do men, in large part because of constraints placed on them by patriarchy and their traditional roles as wives and mothers. Iris Young argues this point in "Throwing Like a Girl," where she contends that a woman's experience of her body as "a *thing* at the same time that she experiences it as a capacity" contributes to inhibited and ambiguous motility and mobility. Furthermore, Elizabeth Hampsten, in her study of midwestern working women's diaries, contends that women describe the landscape and place differently than men do. For Hampsten's women, place has more to do with other people than with cartographic location and "has other boundaries than topography"—dangers, fearful elements, cold, drought, disease, madness, death. And in her look at imperializing travel writing, Mary Louise Pratt finds that unlike men, who write about their encounters with the terrain and indigenous cultures, women travelers tend to describe "the indoor world" of domestic spaces and to make their "territorial claim" on the "private space, a personal, room-sized empire."[10]

What Rich has shown us, among so many other things, is that when we talk about people, politics, and poetry, we must add to the categories of race, class, gender, and sexuality the category of location, of positionings in time and place. What the authors of this collection will show us is that movement—journeying, relocation, dislocation—adds yet another dimension to our discussions of identity, poetry, and politics. At the same time that the authors consider the role of place and of "the politics of location" in the lives and stories of women writers and characters, they also configure a new discourse and a new politics, a "politics of *re*location."

Mappings

Adrienne Rich relates a game of positioning she used to play as a child. When she and a girlfriend would write letters to each other, they would address their letters with ever widening points of reference—city, state, country, continent—until they at last located themselves in "The Solar

---

10. Iris Marion Young, "Throwing Like a Girl: A Phenomenology of Feminine Body Comportment, Motility, and Spatiality," in her *Throwing Like a Girl and Other Essays in Feminist Philosophy and Social Theory* (Bloomington: Indiana University Press, 1990), 147; Elizabeth Hampsten, *Read This Only to Yourself: The Private Writings of Midwestern Women, 1880–1910* (Bloomington: Indiana University Press, 1982), 40; Pratt, *Imperial Eyes*, 159–60.

System" and "The Universe." Though the map by which she located herself expanded concentrically into "the infinite unknown," she was herself stable, at the center of her universe, sure at least of *where* she was.[11] When, however, the center becomes decentered, when a person is mobile and migratory or displaced from traditional lands and cultures, the task of locating and finding oneself is more complicated than the simple concentering Rich's youthful map would suggest. Likewise, the various maps by which the migrant locates herself are complicated by the very dynamics and instability of her positionings. Rather than assuredly finding herself at the center, the journeying woman often finds herself in the margins, the borderlands between cartographic, political, poetic, and psychic lines that likewise become destabilized, porous, redrawn with her relocations.

We all make maps and plot our lives cartographically. As Helen Buss argues in her look at Canadian women's autobiographies, "mapping can be seen metaphorically as joining the activities of self-knowledge and knowledge of the world. Language 'maps' both the self and the coexistent world." The maps we make are of various kinds, but the most primary are the cognitive maps by which we locate ourselves and negotiate movement through space. Roger Downs and David Stea define cognitive mapping as a process by which we locate, navigate, find our way: "*Cognitive mapping* is an abstraction covering those cognitive or mental abilities that enable us to collect, organize, store, recall, and manipulate information about the spatial environment." Thus, I have a mental map composed of images, landmarks, and other clues that enables me to drive around town to my usual haunts—the university, the grocery store, my children's schools—without really thinking about what I'm doing. As Downs and Stea further point out, a "*cognitive map* is a *product*—a person's organized representation of some part of the spatial environment." A cognitive map is something that I make up to represent the way I see or react to my environment; it is not necessarily accurate, for it is a "representation," nor is it the only map that can be composed of that space. But this map of my own making provides a reference by which I locate myself—find out *where* I am and *who* I am—for "in some very fundamental but inexpressible way, our own self-identity is inextricably bound up with knowledge of the spatial environment. . . . [The] sense of place is essential to any ordering of our lives."[12]

11. Adrienne Rich, "Notes toward a Politics of Location," in *Blood, Bread, and Poetry: Selected Prose 1979–1985* (New York: W. W. Norton, 1986), 211–12.
12. Helen M. Buss, *Mapping Our Selves: Canadian Women's Autobiography in English* (Montreal: McGill–Queen's University Press, 1993), 9; Roger M. Downs

What happens, then, when one is unsure of the environment, gets lost, displaced, or disoriented? Kevin Lynch notes "the sense of anxiety and even terror" that accompanies geographic dislocation: "The very word 'lost' in our language means much more than simple geographical uncertainty; it carries overtones of utter disaster." As Lynch recognizes, there is more at stake than geographic dislocation and the reprocessing of the mental, cognitive maps to help us make our way through new environments. At stake as well are security, personal identity, and the "ordering of our lives." Just as the mobile individual must reprocess maps of geographic wayfinding, sometimes on a daily basis, so she must reprocess maps that define, orient, and locate the self. As the map of geographic location becomes a dynamic, kinetic map of relocation, so too the map of the journeying self is involved in a fluctuating and dynamic reprocessing, reordering, and redefining of the self. And if, as Foucault suggests, cartographic maps are implements and representations of knowledge, power, and discourse, then they too become fluctuant, destabilized, decentered, ambiguous with movement through the spatial environment. Though maps have been historically "graphic tools of colonization," Rosi Braidotti suggests that "nomadic cartographies need to be redrafted constantly; as such they are structurally opposed to fixity and therefore to rapacious appropriation." Perhaps with these more "nomadic cartographies" women, who have been mapped and colonized, can assert new powers and discourses derived from a new knowledge of "the nonfixity of boundaries."[13]

The Politics of Relocation

Spatial movement thus invites a remapping of the various spaces, lines, borders, definitions, and names that define or attempt to define our lives and our stories. It invites us to consider a "politics of relocation" that is more kinetic and destabilized than Rich's paradigm of location, and to find

and David Stea, *Maps in Minds: Reflections on Cognitive Mapping* (New York: Harper and Row, 1977), 6, 27.

13. Kevin Lynch, *The Image of the City* (Cambridge: Technology Press and Harvard University Press, 1960), 4; Michel Foucault, *Power/Knowledge: Selected Interviews and Other Writings, 1972–1977,* ed. Colin Gordon (New York: Pantheon Books, 1980), 69–70; see also J. B. Harley, "Maps, Knowledge, and Power," in *The Iconography of Landscape: Essays on the Symbolic Representation, Design, and Use of Past Environments,* ed. Denis Cosgrove and Stephen Daniels (Cambridge: Cambridge University Press, 1988), 277–312; Blunt and Rose, *Writing Women and Space,* 9; Rosi Braidotti, *Nomadic Subjects: Embodiment and Sexual Difference in Contemporary Feminist Theory* (New York: Columbia University Press, 1994), 35–36.

new locations that give way with each journey. If as Noel Arnaud writes, "I am the space where I am," then with each relocation one must reconsider the "I am." And if, to quote Gaston Bachelard, "words . . . are little houses," then the journeying woman both carries her words with her and she reconstructs a new house of words with each new domestic structure. From learning the idioms of place to learning a new language, migrants find themselves straddling and mixing the discourses that mark specific places and themselves, as strangers or members of the community. Indeed, those who experience "life on the hyphen," like "Hispanic-Americans" and "Asian-Americans," may find with Gustavo Pérez Firmat that they are "nilingual"—homeless in two languages.[14]

The dislocation of discursive as well as geographic markers of self may also explain why the narratives of relocation are to some extent experimental or fragmented, giving voice to a self in process rather than a self in situ. Indeed, like the journeys they recount, the narratives are themselves both sites and journeys of exploration and discovery, engaging the author in a dynamic experience that leads to new understandings, to new corners of the self, crossing, extending, and breaking graphic boundaries. Likewise, the social, spiritual, and political houses in which we reside, by which we map our relational locations, are translocated and transformed with geographic journeying. Certainly the nomadic life resists "settling into socially coded modes of thought and behavior" and designates a "creative sort of becoming." Though Rosi Braidotti is here thinking of intellectual nomadism, her assessment of the effects of wandering, of crossing over or residing in the borderlands of many kinds of terrain, points to new ecologies of the self and of "critical consciousness."[15]

For some women adventuring and living in the margins, the "in-between spaces" are frightening and cause a vertiginous unbalancing of life and self. Finding oneself "in the moment of transit where space and time cross to produce complex figures of difference and identity" can cause, as Homi Bhabha recognizes, "a sense of disorientation, a disturbance of direction." But it can also mark exploration, progress, and promise, for spaciousness and the power to move are "closely associated with the sense of being free." Thus, some women experience adventuring and living in the borderlands as exhilarating and freeing. The difference in experiences has to do in large part with individual personality, with the degree of choice in relocation

14. Quoted in Gaston Bachelard, *The Poetics of Space,* trans. Maria Jolas (Boston: Beacon Press, 1964), 137, 147; Gustavo Pérez Firmat, "The Facts of Life on the Hyphen: Reflections on Hispanic American Identity," in a talk delivered at Auburn University, Auburn, Ala., May 5, 1997.
15. Braidotti, *Nomadic Subjects,* 5–6, 5.

decisions, and with factors related to class, race, and language as well as gender. bell hooks writes that moving "out of one's place," politically, to the margins, to sites of "radical possibility" is "difficult yet necessary. It is not a 'safe' place. One is always at risk." Speaking of more geographic and cultural boundaries, Gloria Anzaldúa writes that "Living on borders and in margins, keeping intact one's shifting and multiple identity and integrity, is like trying to swim in a new element, an 'alien' element." For the immigrant, exile, or refugee, living in diasporic border zones multiplies identities, loyalties, voices, and violence, making the diaspora a site of hybridity and of alienation. Moreover, extending geographic boundaries does not always mean that other boundaries that encircle our lives are also pushed or cut, for, as Norma Alarcón finds, "the 'invitation' to cross over, when it is extended, does not ameliorate the lot of women of color," who too often find themselves outside the boundaries of privilege and prosperity.[16]

Moving, whether one takes on the task of moving to "sites of radical possibility" or just to another town, unbalances the *ecology of the self.* All people experience some degree of self-concept change, some degree of cultural, political, poetic change, in conjunction with geographic journeying. Travel "not only provide[s] information about the world; [it] provide[s] information about the self" in transit who observes and learns from her experiences. There is a very real connection between our physical movement and our sense of self, for the experiences and trials of the road shape our perspectives of other peoples and places and of ourselves. Moreover, according to Merleau-Ponty, "It is the body in its orientation toward and action upon and within its surroundings that constitutes the initial meaning-giving act." What Merleau-Ponty suggests is that knowledge and identity, epistemology and ontology, are tied to the position of the bodied self in relation to its environment and that with physical movement they are reprocessed.[17]

16. Bhabha, *Location of Culture,* 1; Tuan, *Space and Place,* 52; hooks, *Yearning,* 145, 149; Gloria Anzaldúa, *Borderlands/La Frontera: The New Mestiza* (San Francisco: Spinsters/Aunt Lute, 1987), 1; see Smadar Lavie and Ted Swedenburg's introduction to *Displacement, Diaspora, and Geographies of Identity* (Durham: Duke University Press, 1996), 14–18; Norma Alarcón, "Traddutora, Traditora: A Paradigmatic Figure of Chicana Feminism," in *Scattered Hegemonies: Postmodernity and Transnational Feminist Practices,* ed. Inderpal Grewal and Caren Kaplan (Minneapolis: University of Minnesota Press, 1994), 129.
17. Stefan E. Hormuth, *The Ecology of the Self: Relocation and Self-Concept Change* (Cambridge: Cambridge University Press, 1990), 1–2; Eric J. Leed, *The Mind of the Traveler: From Gilgamesh to Global Tourism* (New York: Basic Books, 1991), 72; Merleau-Ponty summarized in Young, "Throwing Like a Girl," 147.

For a woman these identifications and understandings are complicated by her gendered position. For one thing, women have been traditionally already marginalized, already forced into "exile" and estrangement by their society, by patriarchal, hegemonic politics. Indeed, as Toril Moi points out, woman is herself considered a "frontier"—"if patriarchy sees woman as occupying a marginal position within the symbolic order, then it can construe them as the *limit* or border-line of that order. . . . woman will then come to represent the necessary frontier between man and chaos." Estrangement, exile, and liminality seem to have been "built into the female condition," and geographic displacement may aggravate that estrangement and sense of foreignness that women already experience, especially women who have been additionally marginalized by class, race, and ethnicity. Even women who move within the circle of corporate America, following husbands or fathers from city to city, find themselves alone on a kind of behavioral and locational frontier that is negotiated for their menfolk by the company, the team, the profession, but is not negotiated for them.[18]

At issue as well is women's degree of choice in relocating. Some women really have no choice, compelled as they are by economic need or political displacement to migrate. Other women, no doubt like my grandmother, willingly follow their husband's or father's dream of prosperity to another location, hoping likewise to better their situation. Even so, to the extent that they are captured by love and silent in the relinquishment of their own hopes and dreams, they are complicit in their own displacement. For some of these women the dream turns to nightmare, and, as Annette Kolodny finds, the female captivity narrative provides a literary vehicle through which women can "safely confront the often unhappy experiences of their . . . migration," mediating the distress of a displacement often forced upon them. Even under the best circumstances, women tend to relinquish control and autonomy when it comes to pulling up stakes and moving. In her study of contemporary women involved in relocation, psychologist Audrey McCollum comments that "for women . . . there are obstacles against making wise and responsible choices about moving.

18. Toril Moi, "Feminist, Female, Feminine," in *The Feminist Reader: Essays in Gender and the Politics of Literary Criticism,* ed. Catherine Belsey and Jane Moore (Houndmills, Basingstoke, Hampshire: Macmillan Education, Ltd., 1989), 127; Jane Marcus, "Alibis and Legends: The Ethics of Elsewhereness, Gender and Estrangement," in *Women's Writing in Exile,* ed. Mary Jane Broe and Angela Ingram (Chapel Hill: University of North Carolina Press, 1989), 276. I owe the last insight to my mother-in-law, Bettye Knowles Moon, who followed her husband, Wally Moon, on the baseball circuit.

Aspects of feminine psychology—a tendency to merge with loved ones, contradictory states of both helplessness and power in their sense of self—may cause women's choices to be more illusory than real."[19]

Finally, women, more than men, have traditionally been associated with home, family, and domestic duties, with sessility rather than mobility. After all, women are themselves a site, a home, the child's first place. And, as Julia Kristeva remarks, "the biological fate that causes us to be the *site* of the species chains us to *space: home,* native soil, motherland." Because of her anatomical and mythic associations with home and safe enclosures, woman has also been "chain[ed]" or enclosed within the home and the private sphere of her maternity. This fate can make one feel secure, connected to one's past and origins, but it can also create anxieties about enclosure and confinement. Home is thus a place of ambiguous meaning, an ideal one attempts to return to or recreate with each relocation or an imprisonment from which one attempts to flee. For many women like bell hooks the "homeplace [can be] that space where we return for renewal and self-recovery, where we can heal our wounds and become whole." But for other women the maternal home is a place from which to escape: Gloria Anzaldúa writes that she had to "leave the source, the mother, disengage from my family, *mi tierra, mi gente. . . .* I had to leave home so I could find myself." Even if one adopts Anzaldúa's resolution to escape the homeplace and carry home on her back, in turtle-like fashion, the task of constructing or deconstructing the location(s) and meaning(s) of home and family often falls to women. Women who settle in a new domain face the task of making a home out of the new place, of re-creating in the new place the atmosphere of the familiar home or of putting her own stamp on the environment and taking control of it, "imprinting qualities of self in the dwelling." Women who relocate also often face the task of maintaining contact with family and friends left behind. If, as Nancy Chodorow maintains, "feminine personality comes to define itself in relation and connection to other people," then geographic and interpersonal disconnection can threaten one's sense of self. Indeed, many women who relocate experience feelings of failure, grief, and loss, which they attempt to assuage with retained contact with the homeplaces and people left behind. The frequent letters geographically mobile women wrote in the early nineteenth century, Carroll Smith-

19. Annette Kolodny, *The Land before Her: Fantasy and Experience of the American Frontiers, 1630–1860* (Chapel Hill: University of North Carolina Press, 1984), 34; Audrey T. McCollum, *The Trauma of Moving: Psychological Issues for Women* (Newbury Park, Calif.: Sage Publications, 1990), 21–22.

Rosenberg finds, "provided an important sense of continuity in a rapidly changing society."[20]

More tenuously, some women may construct "mobile" homes, disassembling their families or raising their children on the road, forging new liaisons between the frontier and the domestic, the mobile and the stationary, the fluctuant and the stable. Though mobility may become the site of a truer "home," it is an uncanny home, and the woman exile is an uncanny figure who "rejects her role as representation of home" and mother and becomes herself a "mobile home." Moreover, "home," that region of comfort and protection that is truly a "symbol of self," is not simply or always a domestic place, but a space—political, poetic, and personal—mediated between the private and the public, between traditionally gendered definitions of self and roles, between the stasis of place and the dynamics of movement. Thus "to be unhomed is not [necessarily] to be homeless," for new sites of knowledge, power, and creativity emerge in the narratives of the "unhomed" where traditional lines and boundaries are crossed, extended, subverted, fragmented. Even so, "homelessness hurts."[21]

Mapping the Narratives of Relocation

The texts of displacement written by women and about women's experiences constitute the terrains that the authors of this collection map out and explore, discovering new ways of reading women's narratives and women's lives. Adding the axis of geographic relocation to our critical consciousness, the essays invite us to reposition ourselves hermeneutically, to consider a new ethnography, and to initiate new conversations about displacement,

20. See Leed, *Mind of the Traveler*, 4, for a definition of *sessility;* Julia Kristeva, *Nations without Nationalism*, trans. Leon S. Roudiez (New York: Columbia University Press, 1993), 33–34; for more about home as a site of female imprisonment, see Sandra M. Gilbert and Susan Gubar, *The Madwoman in the Attic: The Woman Writer and the Nineteenth-Century Literary Imagination* (New Haven: Yale University Press, 1979), 83–92; hooks, *Yearning*, 49; Anzaldúa, *Borderlands/La Frontera*, 16; McCollum, *Trauma of Moving*, 99; Nancy J. Chodorow, *Feminism and Psychoanalytic Theory* (New Haven: Yale University Press, 1989), 45; Carroll Smith-Rosenberg, "The Female World of Love and Ritual: Relations between Women in Nineteenth-Century America," in *The American Family in Social-Historical Perspective*, 2d ed., ed. Michael Gordon (New York: St. Martin's Press, 1978), 340.

21. Marcus, "Alibis and Legends," 272–73; Roberta M. Feldman, "Settlement-Identity: Psychological Bonds with Home Places in a Mobile Society" *Environment and Behavior* 22 (March 1990): 184; Bhabha, *Location of Culture*, 9; Marcus, "Alibis and Legends," 275.

migration, and journeying, and the costs or rewards that accrue to women in transit.

The essays collected here represent a wide range of experiences, real and imagined, and a wide range of personal and critical perspectives. Just as the traveling woman must map out new terrains, so the authors have had to map out what is still a largely unexplored and diverse terrain. The authors have reached no consensus except that relocation makes some sort of impact or effect on women. Some of the essays chart stories and lives in which women experience movement as expansive and freeing; others find that the costs and sacrifices demanded of the migrating woman are too great to bear and to ask. Indeed, escaping geographic fixity does not guarantee victory over all of the other boundaries and cartographies that hold and define us.

Despite the range of the essays, they coalesce around issues of politics, poetry (narrative), and self-identity that Adrienne Rich identified as elements of a "politics of location," or as we would have it, a politics of relocation. Many of the authors are concerned with political issues of race, class, and sexual economics and their impact on migratory women, finding that ideology is itself a space to be traversed and negotiated along with more physical boundaries of space and place. The authors of the collection explore the pernicious effects of racism and racist politics on Asian immigrants, black Americans, and Native Americans and their attempts to relocate themselves, to journey freely, to regain ancestral lands. They examine the exploitation of migrants from Appalachia and of women newly arrived in the New World or the big city and the sexism that relegates women to wives, mothers, sexual objects. And they investigate the uneasy position of the exile who finds herself outside of America. The authors of this collection are also interested in examining what happens to narrative structure when authors or their characters cross geographic boundaries, how women writers negotiate geographical transfer in their texts, how the text itself becomes a place, a geography where one finds oneself. They are interested in language, in the play between different languages and discourses and how language marks and confines the migrant. Finally, all of the authors of this collection are concerned with the impact of migration, movement, and dislocation on the identity of women, their senses of self and their roles in family, home, and social life, how women are often forced to straddle the in-betweenness of gendered expectations, and how they are often asked to find a new home—on the frontier, in foster homes of their own devising, in traveling, and in return to homes of the past.

I

Boundaries and Border Crossings

Exile, Depatriation, and Constance Fenimore Woolson's Traveling Regionalism

PETER CACCAVARI

In a letter she wrote as a young girl to a friend who was about to be married and then live in Europe, Constance Fenimore Woolson touched on issues that would preoccupy her writing life throughout her adulthood: exile, travel, place, freedom, art, patriarchy, and depatriation:

> To Miss Flora Payne, afterwards, Mrs. William C. Whitney.
> "Seems to me if *I* had a friend in exile across the ocean"—In *exile!* I wish I could be in "exile" too, if I could visit the most beautiful and famous places the world can show! You are the most fortunate young lady I know, and ought to be the *happiest.* I envy you to that extent that the tenth commandment makes me shudder, for although I am willing to settle down after thirty years are told, I do not care to be forced into quiescence yet awhile.[1]

For the young Woolson, exile appears not to be a lonely state but one that offers freedom through mobility. For her, exile represents a desire for place—not a single, fixed, familiar place but many, sequential, unfamiliar places. She wants not to "settle down" for thirty years, and yet the enviable state she is describing is made possible by her friend's marriage, her settling down. It is clearly not her friend's marriage that is the object of longing for Woolson; it is the apparent freedom and reconfiguration of attachment to place(s) that the marriage allows. Indeed, Woolson's letter demonstrates an early attempt at envisioning a depatriation of both place and subjectivity. She thinks that through expatriation she will gain a fresh

---

1. Clare Benedict, ed., *Constance Fenimore Woolson* (London: Ellis, [1932]), 16–17.

look at the world, giving her a different perspective on her own land when she returns to it in quiescence. The young Woolson also thinks that even in marriage exile will escape the boundaries of patriarchy. Yet Woolson would come to see that such an exile could be possible without marriage, that the gendered obligations of husband and family actually prevent such exile from coming to fruition, and that even when achieved, exile involves conditions that are anything but enviable.

Even today Woolson as a writer is in exile, little known despite success in her own day. A self-enforced exile from home and nation both within the United States and abroad, she sought as well to distance herself from cultural and gendered constraints upon her writing and life. Known, when she is thought of at all, as a regionalist, Woolson wrote about a variety of places where she had lived or visited, including the Great Lakes (*Castle Nowhere*, 1875), the South (*Rodman the Keeper: Southern Sketches*, 1880), and Italy (*The Front Yard and Other Italian Stories*, 1895, and *Dorothy and Other Italian Stories*, 1896). However, while regionalism is usually predicated on belonging to one particular place in some self-contained and highly demarcated construction of "authenticity," Woolson achieved something quite different: she created a permeable regionalism that brings into question the very ideas of regional and national, national and international, local and global, inside and outside, private and public, participant and observer. Rather than writing a regionalism about *becoming-in-place*, she developed a kind of regionalism based on *becoming-through-placings*. Like Frantz Fanon, who wrote, "In the world through which I travel, I am endlessly creating myself,"[2] Woolson used travel to both create herself over and over again and to depict characters made anew by place, placement, and re-placement. The self-creations reflected in Woolson's "traveling regionalism" are, however, conflicted with the tension between the potential for unprecedented freedom (political, social, economic, and geographic) for women in the late nineteenth century and the constraints of domestic ideology that, while in the process of being critiqued and dismantled, still held powerful sway over women.

Indeed, it is the cultural conflation of woman and home that makes Woolson's brand of regionalism so radical and so conservative, so expansive and so located. As Jane Marcus points out, "A woman exile is, in addi-

---

2. Constance Fenimore Woolson, *Dorothy and Other Italian Stories* (New York: Harper and Brothers, 1896); *The Front Yard and Other Italian Stories* (New York: Harper and Brothers, 1895); *Rodman the Keeper: Southern Sketches* (1880; reprint, New York: Garrett Press, 1969). Subsequent citations will appear parenthetically in the text. Frantz Fanon, *Black Skin, White Masks*, trans. Charles Lam Markmann (New York: Grove Press, 1967), 229.

tion, an uncanny figure, in Freud's formulation, for her very body means home and hearth, the womb/home of humankind. If she is homeless, lost, wandering, where are we, her daughters and sons?"[3] Woolson was a contradiction of woman's role in domestic ideology because of her professional status as writer, her "homelessness" in travel, and her unmarried and childless state. She attempted to exchange her womb/home identity as woman for a mind/movement identity that sought to re-create woman through intellectual depatriation, forsaking fatherlands and exploring borderlands. Even so, Woolson could not eradicate the pull of domestic ideology and fashion herself as a subject of unrestrained freedom. Her life and her fiction became contested domains where home and world, rootedness and transience, vied for dominance. Although Woolson wanted to deconstruct the binary oppositions of home/exile, wife/writer, and womb/mind, she was ultimately unable to get beyond these oppositions, and so found herself and her art between them.

A logical extension of the relationship between woman and home is the relationship between exile and nation. Looking at the Modernist women who would be the successors of Woolson and her generation, Shari Benstock recognizes that women often experience an internal exile:

> For women, the definition of patriarchy already assumes the reality of expatriate *in patria*; for women, this expatriation is internalized, experienced as an exclusion imposed from the outside and lived from the inside in such a way that the separation of outside from inside, patriarchal dicta from female decorum, cannot be easily distinguished.

Woolson did not have to wait until she traveled to Europe to experience exile; this was the stuff of her everyday life in the United States. As Benstock goes on to say of woman, as did Marcus about the womb and home, "Her very body is the 'native land' on which patriarchy stakes its claims."[4]

Similarly, Cheryl Torsney locates Woolson in a state of betweenness historically and psychologically. Torsney conjectures that part of the explanation for Woolson's literary neglect since her death is that "she comes of age as a writer just after the heyday of domestic fiction . . . and dies in 1894 just before the maturation of the New Woman. Thus, her professional career

3. Jane Marcus, "Alibis and Legends: The Ethics of Elsewhereness, Gender, and Estrangement," in *Women's Writing in Exile,* ed. Mary Lynn Broe and Angela Ingram (Chapel Hill: University of North Carolina Press, 1989), 272–73.
4. Shari Benstock, "Expatriate Modernism: Writing on the Cultural Rim," in *Women's Writing in Exile,* ed. Mary Lynn Broe and Angela Ingram (Chapel Hill: University of North Carolina Press, 1989), 20, 26.

is interposed between two periods when women wrote from positions of secure identity and power." It was this period "between the weakening of the bonds of womanhood and the freedom of the New Woman" when "local color writing comes to the fore." Like the period, Woolson herself was caught between bonds and freedom, in the complicated interplay of bonds both constrictive and expansive, of freedoms both liberating and debilitating. As Torsney observes, Woolson's characters "often take on Woolson's own fragmented identity, rehearsing both her transitional generational position and her individual history of family disaster and exile. Woolson's artist-heroines can neither entirely align themselves with the Cult of True Womanhood nor fully reject their upbringing . . . and become New Women."[5] It is thus between bonds and freedom, between home and exile, that Woolson and her characters create a traveling region-alism that is neither here nor there, yet also both here and there. Woolson portrays regions as places where cultures and ideologies meet and blend in ways that make identity—both regional and individual—ambivalent and unsettled. Part of this blending and ambivalence comes from a confusion of outside and inside, of internal exile; but part also comes from Woolson's taking stock of her situation, of assuming agency, and reconstructing a place, or rather, a series of places, from which she can speak in exile. She would find a way to transform expatriation through depatriation. And yet, even this achievement would be incomplete, caught between two worlds as she was.

Woolson's traveling regionalism initially developed out of the transi-tion from her stories set in the Great Lakes region to those set in the South during Reconstruction and the migration of Northerners to the South following the Civil War. Often known collectively by Southerners as "carpetbaggers" (a term deriving from the belief that a person can be identified by place), these transplants began an unprecedented mobility to settled parts of the United States, breaking down regional coherence and creating a decentered sense of place. Woolson's writing of this period, itself a kind of literary carpetbagging, reflected this mobility and confluence.

In her story, "Old Gardiston," in *Rodman the Keeper*, the narrator refers to "double-faced, conscienceless whites" who "were sometimes emigrant Northerners, sometimes renegade Southerners, but always rascals" (116). The narrator intends "double-faced" to mean duplicity with its usual pejorative implications, but it is also an apt description for the Janus-like literary carpetbagging that Woolson engages in, embodying multiple

5. Cheryl B. Torsney, *Constance Fenimore Woolson: The Grief of Artistry* (Athens: University of Georgia Press, 1989), 7, 8, 33.

identities, resulting in a variety of complications and contradictions. In a letter to Paul Hamilton Hayne, she speaks of her Southern stories: "I have tried to 'put myself in their place,' and at least to be fair." Whereas the typical regionalist is supposedly already "there," Woolson must "put" herself in that place. And yet, she does not thereby become *of* that place in a nativist sense. Instead, she engages in a cultural alibi that positions her both here and elsewhere, constructing multiple levels of place and identity that replace the carpetbagger's image of deceit with ambiguity and decenteredness.[6]

Reconstruction taught Woolson much about a changing sense of place. Judith Kinsolving, a Southern woman who is the focus of Woolson's story, "In the Cotton Country," has lost everything in the Civil War and tells the story's northern-born narrator: "I do not know anything certainly any more, for my world has been torn asunder, and I am uprooted and lost. No, you can not help me, no one can help me. I can not adjust myself to the new order of things; I can not fit myself in new soil; the fibers are broken."[7] While much regional fiction exhibited a rooted sense of place and mourned, like Kinsolving, its disintegration in a modern mobile culture, Woolson took the rootlessness to be a part of her contemporary condition. She saw it as an opportunity for self-reconstruction.

Many of the stories in *Rodman the Keeper*, like "Old Gardiston" and "In the Cotton Country," deal with dislocation caused by war and internal (that is, domestic) exile caused by a civil war. The images of dislocation and dividedness (and reconciliation) exemplify Woolson's sense of regionalism and gender as she attempts to create new spaces and new selves by crossing distances and chasms, trying to bring exiles to a new home. Kinsolving experiences a profound sense of loss—of home, region, nation, and identity—as someone who has been depatriated from the United States through secession, depatriated from the Confederate States of America through surrender, and repatriated to the United States. In her concluding dialogue Kinsolving says, "I will abide in my own country" (148), and we are left wondering which country she is talking about,

6. Jay B. Hubbell, "Some New Letters of Constance Fenimore Woolson," *New England Quarterly* 14 (1941): 731; Jane Marcus discusses alibi in the context of exile in a very different way than I do here, but it is worth noting that she wants to keep the deceitful and criminal connotations of alibi in literary criticism as a reminder of when scholars usurp the voice of others disingenuously and act in bad faith, both outside and inside feminist scholarship.

7. Constance Fenimore Woolson, "In the Cotton Country," in *Women Artists, Women Exiles: "Miss Grief" and Other Stories*, ed. Joan Myers Weimer (New Brunswick: Rutgers University Press, 1988), 147. Subsequent citations will appear parenthetically in the text.

thinking perhaps that ultimately she is referring to the new country of her reconstructed self.

Writing about her Southern fiction, Fred Lewis Pattee called Woolson "an unlocalized soul," who, unlike other American regionalists, was "bounded each by a single horizon," but, "like Henry James, was rooted nowhere." As a refinement of Pattee's idea, I would suggest that Woolson is a *polylocalized* soul—someone who is in some sense "native" to a number of places, not by birth or even duration of habitation, but by observation and imagination. In part, she sought the reconstruction of place through and in writing. She wrote Henry James in 1883: "Well—that is my feeling with regard to your writings; they are my true country, my real home. And nothing else ever is fully—try as I may to think so."[8]

It was not only James's writings, however, in which Woolson found a home; her own provided one too. The title of her story, "Castle Nowhere," is a telling image of both her own rootlessness and her dwelling in/on her fiction. In that story, a man who has committed murder goes off with his older sister to a remote part of the head of Lake Michigan. With them they have brought a foundling child whom the man raises as his own. In that place the man comes to be known as Fog, his sister as Shadow, and the girl as Silver. To feed and clothe them, he periodically sets a beacon for ships lost in storms to follow into reefs so that the vessels are destroyed, the crews killed, and their supplies washed up on shore for the family's use. After a time Shadow dies. Into this wilderness wanders an explorer, Jarvis Waring, who uncovers Fog's past, and eventually marries Silver. Fog dies, and Waring and Silver leave Castle Nowhere, which goes to ruins and falls into the lake.

Joan Myers Weimer identifies this story as a justification of regionalism and its particularization of locale and culture:

> Woolson also entertained and rejected the possibility of being "nowhere" rather than one particular "somewhere"—a possibility that challenges the basis of regionalist writing. "Nowhere" is outside geography, history, religion, society, and culture. There, sinful father and innocent daughter can live happily together until "somebody"—a potential suitor for the daughter—invades, bringing with him a variety of cultural "somewheres" that eventually destroy "nowhere."

8. Fred Lewis Pattee, "Constance Fenimore Woolson and the South," *South Atlantic Quarterly* 38 (1939): 131; Leon Edel, ed., *Henry James: Letters*, vol. 3, 1883–1895 (Cambridge: Harvard University Press, Belknap Press, 1980), 551.

Woolson's project in "Castle Nowhere" is similar to that in "In the Cotton Country"; both affirm the portrayal of locale within the regionalist tradition while at the same time engaging in a reconstruction of place in a modern sense. "Castle Nowhere" opens narratively in the present remarking about the past: "Not many years ago the shore bordering the head of Lake Michigan . . . was a wilderness unexplored. It is a wilderness still. . . ."[9] Although it may be a wilderness still, it is not as remote as it once was, and we are to understand that it is part of a vanishing frontier. Not only does the castle become "nowhere," but the wilderness itself is becoming "nowhere" as well. Indeed, regionalism is not beyond the reach of the outside, which inevitably breaks into its pristine landscape.

Moreover, the gender issues that Woolson's story raises demonstrate the hold of patriarchy even in remote places. Silver is handed off from Fog to Waring and is portrayed as utterly malleable in the hands of both men. Starting life as a homeless foundling, then taken to a place that is no place, she will finally be taken away by Waring, it is presumed, to what is supposed to be her rightful place, as the angel of a house somewhere rather than a castle nowhere. Silver is supposed to be an exile who is in some ways being returned home by Waring, and yet, we cannot help but see her as returning to the same exile, simply in a different location. She is repatriated in terms of returning to "civilization," but she has never been away from patriarchs. This would be the last time Woolson did not interrogate the cultural assumptions and contradictions implicit in marriage plots and domesticity. In her later fiction marriage would appear, to take an image from "Castle Nowhere," as the deceptive beacon, as "a false light" (44) where women's vessels are dashed on the reefs and men collect for their own benefit the remains that drift ashore.

The home that does arise, however, out of "Castle Nowhere" is the home that writing provides Woolson. Her admiration for James's work was a writer's admiration, her appreciation for James's fiction a validation of her own seriousness as a writer. Yet her questioning of identity and relation to place made her question, as well, James's understanding of these issues. In a letter to James, she tells him: "But if you had never left the banks of the Maumee, you would still have been, dumbly, an 'alienated American' (I suppose you have no idea where the Maumee is!)." Moreover, as a literary carpetbagger, Woolson found her regional doubleness as a Northerner in

9. Joan Myers Weimer, ed., *Women Artists, Women Exiles: "Miss Grief" and Other Stories* (New Brunswick: Rutgers University Press, 1988), xxviii; Constance Fenimore Woolson, "Castle Nowhere," in *Women Artists*, ed. Weimer, 25. Subsequent citations will appear parenthetically in the text.

the South already compounded into a plurality by her identity with New England and the Great Lakes. By the time Woolson went to live in Europe, especially Italy, she had developed a plurality of identities rooted in region and gender in her writing. Weimer observes of this aspect of Woolson's life and writing: "Her psychological doubleness—anguished and amused, home-rooted and restless—was underlined by her complicated dual national identities—a Northerner in the South, an American in Europe. She transforms these facts of her life into the insights of her fiction."[10] I agree with Weimer but would push the "complicated" nature of Woolson's national identities further, saying that her identity, even as a Northerner, is at least dual—born in New Hampshire and having lived in Ohio—and that from that point on there is compounding of identities rather than merely dualities. Indeed, Woolson's polylocalism and ambivalence emerge out of a sense of multiple identity rather than an organic unity lost or idealized, making her traveling regionalism permeable and fluid.

In "The 'Mechanics' of Fluids" Luce Irigaray observes that metonymy is "closely allied to fluids" and helps to characterize women's sexuality. This characterization, according to Irigaray, applies to women's discourse as well. "Woman never speaks the same way. What she emits is flowing, fluctuating. *Blurring.*" Boundaries are not fixed but permeable: "Fluid—like that other, inside/outside of philosophical discourse—is, by nature, unstable." Similarly, Woolson destabilizes regions and cultures, blurring sectional and community boundaries, undermining insider/outsider distinctions, creating a metonymic regionalism that emphasizes connection and intersection. Irigaray's framework relates to Benstock's ideas about exile and expatriation. Women's sexuality and discourse may blur boundaries between inside and outside, but so does the internalization of patriarchal assumptions about women and home. The multiplicity of women's identities that Irigaray has spent much time examining—"this sex which is not one"—is, for Benstock, the basis for understanding Modernism, women, and exile: "The standard definitions of the terms *expatriate* and *exile* suggest the cultural assumptions of coextensive self-identity, of coherent subjectivity, of the singular 'I' that Modernism so ruthlessly questions."[11] Just as Benstock rewrites the definitions of *expatriate* and *exile* to reflect women Modernists' experience, Woolson did her own rewriting of *expatriate* and *exile* earlier, in part by rewriting the singular *I* and the regionalism that accompanied it into a serial *I* and a regionalism that reflected the cycles

10. Edel, *James,* 527; Weimer, *Women Artists,* xxiii.
11. Luce Irigaray, *This Sex Which Is Not One,* trans. Catherine Porter (Ithaca: Cornell University Press, 1985), 110, 112; Benstock, "Expatriate Modernism," 23.

of dislocation and relocation that increasingly were becoming the norm of life in the United States.

James Clifford's concept of "traveling cultures" can shed some light on Woolson's traveling regionalism. He writes that "I'm trying to sketch a comparative cultural studies approach to specific histories, tactics, everyday practices of dwelling *and* traveling: traveling-in-dwelling, dwelling-in-traveling." Woolson's work and life exemplify Clifford's notion of "dwelling-in-traveling." Like the fluidity that Irigaray says destabilizes the inside/outside of philosophical discourse, or like the disintegration of inside/outside boundaries of internal and internalized exile under patriarchy that Benstock observes, Clifford seeks to blur the participant/observer distinctions of ethnography. "In the history of twentieth-century anthropology, 'informants' first appear as natives; they emerge as travelers. In fact, . . . they are specific mixtures of the two roles."[12] The relation of Woolson's fiction to ethnography would make a valuable study all its own. While Woolson is not self-consciously acting as an ethnographer, her work addresses such ethnographic issues as the constructions of native, informant, and authenticity.

The regionalist is typically seen as the "native," the one born to a place and culture and fluent in the local knowledge. But writing about a region also makes the native an informant and threatens the authenticity of the report. The regionalist as chronicler of a region becomes, then, something of a hybrid, both a native and an informant, one whose reliability is and is not in question. Woolson alludes to the complexity of regionalist writing in her story "In Venice" from *The Front Yard and Other Italian Stories.* An American, Claudia Marcy, observes that "these Venetians of to-day . . . do not appreciate in the least their wonderful water-city—scarcely know what it is." According to Miss Marcy, an outsider can best observe what is actually there, what to the insider is invisible. Another American, Elizabeth Lenox, replies: "They don't study 'Venice' because they are Venice—isn't that it?" (241). For Mrs. Lenox, the Venetians' immediacy and immersion in place makes them the more authentic precisely because they do not observe. Woolson negotiates between both these stances, and, like Clifford, dwells on the specific mixtures of the two roles, making the informant one who lives between and among different cultures.

Not only does the role of informant reveal aspects of Woolson's regionalism, it also shows the part that gender plays in that regionalism. While the subject position of the native is the privileged position of the regionalist,

12. James Clifford, "Traveling Cultures," in *Cultural Studies,* ed. Lawrence Grossberg, Cary Nelson, and Paula A. Treichler (New York: Routledge, 1992), 108, 97.

the woman traveler is an uncanny figure who has abandoned her "sphere," who has transgressed by crossing the threshold of home into a world that is supposedly not her own. Traditionally men have been allowed to move freely between the public and the private without the permeability of these spheres threatening their identities. But when a woman engages in physical and cultural mobility, she becomes an informant, someone who ceases to be the pristine native, the angel in the house, without, however, quite becoming a traveler, a "man" of the world. Either way, if she stays at home or goes out into the world, she is an exile, banished culturally if not geographically. And just as homelessness makes a woman an uncanny figure, so narrative, the work of the mind and not of the womb, exiles her from traditional female identifications. Thus, woman is like the Venetian who is most Venetian in silence. Woolson, however, wanted to legitimize women's use of narrative without quite relinquishing home and the feminine. As informant, she sought to create a na(rra)tive that moves frequently (if not freely) across boundaries and borders, even if she could not fully free herself from the ideology she critiqued.

Woolson addresses the issue of the exiled woman writer in "At the Château of Corinne" from *Dorothy and Other Italian Stories*. In this story, Katharine Winthrop, an American widow living on Lake Leman (Lake Geneva) in Switzerland, visits Coppet, the house in which lived the exiled Madame de Staël, who wrote *Corinne, or Italy* (1807). Visiting Coppet with her is another American, John Ford, who has some very definite ideas about women and narrative. When Katharine calls Madame de Staël "a woman of genius," John replies:

> "A woman of genius! And what is the very term but a stigma! No woman is so proclaimed by the great brazen tongue of the Public unless she has thrown away her birthright of womanly seclusion for the miserable mess of pottage called 'fame.' "
> "The seclusion of a convent? or a prison?"
> "Neither. Of a home." (263)

Katharine is a poet and so has much at stake in this discussion under Madame de Staël's roof. She says to John, "You dislike literary women very much," to which he responds, "I pity them" (264). When Katharine asks John to comment on her book of poetry, he notes that "the distinguishing feature of the volume" is "a certain sort of daring. This is its essential, unpardonable sin." Such a woman who dares in this way is a "poor mistaken sibyl"—literally an uncanny figure (268). The act of narration itself, for John, makes a woman an exile from her proper sphere of domesticity. She becomes a witchlike figure, with all the ostracism and power that such a figure embodies, someone both repugnant and fearsome. The sibyl is a sage, but as a woman she must be seen as lonely and deformed. John's patriarchal gaze can only frame women in dualities: home or exile, womb or mind.[13]

The talk about home in the exile's house resonates on a number of levels. John tells Katharine and the others of their party that "Madame de Staël detested the country; to the last, Coppet remained to her a dreary exile" (262). It was a house but not a home; Madame de Staël was a woman but not feminine. In John's view, narrative itself, which unfeminized Madame de Staël, threatens to do the same to Katharine. As informants, Madame de Staël and Katharine dwell in two worlds, and between two worlds, the private and public worlds. In John's eyes, narrative in the hands of women exchanges a home for a prison-house of language. For Katharine, however, home is a prison, a place with impermeable borders, where a person is one thing and not any other. The château of Coppet makes a stark contrast to another castle, the Castle Nowhere, showing how far Woolson had come in delineating the complexities and contradiction of home and exile, captivity and freedom.

At the turning point in the story when Katharine and John are once again at Coppet, this time professing a love for each other that hinges on Katharine's economic dependence—she has lost her fortune—and her renunciation of narrative. Speaking again of her book of poetry, Katharine asks John: "But you do not forgive the book?" He responds: "I will forget it instead. You will write no more" (285). Katharine concedes, and the story ends with their return to John's home in the United States as man and wife.

The images in the final few paragraphs are dense: "In the library of Mr. John Ford, near New York, there hangs in the place of honor a water-color sketch of an old yellow château. Beneath it, ranged by themselves, are all the works of that eloquent authoress and noble woman, Madame de Staël" (287). The château of exile is contrasted to the American home. The public character of Madame de Staël is contrasted to the private setting of

13. Elizabeth Barrett Browning's *Aurora Leigh* (1857) has a scene between Romney and Aurora in book 2 that is very similar to the scene between John and Katharine in terms of women's relationship to art in general, and the woman artist as witch in particular. For a discussion of "At the Château of Corinne" and *Aurora Leigh*, see Torsney, *Constance Fenimore Woolson*, 97, 104, 106–7. For a discussion of *Aurora Leigh*, especially the scene between Romney and Aurora, in the context of Italy, *Corinne*, and gender, see Sandra M. Gilbert, "From *Patria* to *Matria*: Elizabeth Barrett Browning's Risorgimento," *PMLA* 99 (1984): 196–98, 201–2.

the library. It is clear that although the narrator calls Madame de Staël a "noble woman," we are to understand that as a technical term, referring to her aristocratic origins. From John's perspective, Katharine is the truly noble woman for she has renounced narrative and public life. As Cheryl Torsney points out, it is in this house "that both Katharine, metaphorically, and Mme de Staël, literally, are brought into line."[14] The narratives of Madame de Staël have been contained, her works "ranged by themselves," as Katharine has been contained in this home-turned-prison. In fact, Katharine loses all power of narration, for in this scene she is not heard from at all; she is silenced, and the library, with its knowledge and narrative, is identified with John, who is the legitimate guardian of narrative. The "home" is to be Katharine's, although the "house" is John's; Katharine resumes her traditional place and role, and will be only an observer of Madame de Staël's narrative achievements (if she ever opens those books again), not a participant in narrative herself. Katharine's repatriation has re-placed an exile of words with a homecoming of silence.

Even though her heroine returns to a traditional and confining home, one of Woolson's goals was to reconstruct home and narrative as compatible for the woman writer. In the letter to Henry James where Woolson says that his writings are "my true country, my real home," she explicitly conflates home and narrative. However, this narrative home is James's writing, not her own. Again, the man is the guardian of narrative: the "home" is Woolson's, but the narrative "house" is James's. Although Katharine is not Woolson, Katharine is a warning of the allure that home has for women, including Woolson, and its potential to silence them. Despite Katharine's repatriation—both physical and patriarchal—and Woolson's gendered displacement in this letter to James, in her own works Woolson asserts the right of claiming narrative for women, making her own words both her home and house.

In another letter to James, this one written in 1882 in Dresden, Woolson noted that she had been thirteen years "without a home," and talked about being an American abroad:

> But I suppose there never was a woman so ill fitted to do without a home as I am. . . . Like a poor old bird shut up in a cage, who tries to make a nest out of two wisps of straw. Or the beaver I saw in the Zoological Gardens here, who had constructed a most pathetic little dam out of a few poor fragments of old boughs. I stood and looked at that beaver a long time. He is an American—as I am?[15]

14. Torsney, *Constance Fenimore Woolson*, 95.
15. Edel, *James*, 539, 540.

This passage invokes several of Woolson's frequent themes—homes, boundaries, and the nature of being American. We can see Woolson's anxiety of exile, fearing the loss of national identity and home. She wonders whether she is any longer an American and considers her homes abroad akin to the beaver's "most pathetic little dam." She seems to feel much like John's portrayal of Madame de Staël at Coppet, viewing her own expatriation as "a dreary exile." Rather than the home being a prison, as Katharine initially feared, this letter imagines exile to be a prison, a cage. Her greatest freedom seemed at times to be her greatest confinement, indicating her own ambivalence about her position as a woman exile. She feels an anxiety of depatriation, not in a gendered sense, but in a nationalistic one, wondering aloud if she is still an American.

Indeed, when she wrote James, "But I suppose there never was a woman so ill fitted to do without a home as I am," she indicated that women are especially in need of homes. She had written to him earlier that year about the death of a parent: "A daughter feels it more than a son, of course, because her life is so limited, bounded by home-love. . . ."[16] The Victorian image of the home-bound woman is evident here. Yet Woolson is able to both imagine and resist that image by expanding the private sphere of the home in both her writing and her life by moving home from place to place, thus lessening its confinement and pushing back its boundaries. It is no coincidence that the death of her father opened the way to her move from Cleveland to Florida and that the death of her mother allowed her the chance to live in Europe. The death of her parents, while making her emotional reactions painful because of "home-love," made her less bound, less limited by home. Moreover, Woolson did not exchange her parent's home for a husband's home, remaining single all her life. By dwelling-in-traveling, Woolson was able to create greater freedom for herself than she would have had in a more conventional Victorian life as a woman. In the childhood letter Woolson wrote to her friend Flora, who was about to be married, she did not see Flora's marriage as an impediment to the exile Woolson so longed for; as an adult who at last came to experience that exile, she realized that marriage and home were not compatible with the freedom that exile represented for her. No doubt she feared becoming like Katharine, a woman writer silenced by home-love. Yet she regretted not having a home. While the price Katharine paid for a home was too high for Woolson, its appeal never seemed to fade. In her life, she felt the elegiac loss of place depicted in regional fiction, even as she was forging a more modern sense of transition and mobility.

16. Ibid., 536.

Woolson used images of boundaries to explore her ambivalence about home. As the narrator of "In the Cotton Country" comes upon Judith Kinsolving's house, the former comments that there is no fence around the house: "Take away the fence from a house, and you take away its respectability; it becomes at once an outlaw" (136). In "The Front Yard," Prudence Wilkin, a New Hampshire woman transplanted to Assisi, Italy, when she marries an Italian, Antonio Guadagni, is quickly widowed and spends the next sixteen years taking care of his large and largely ungrateful family. Despite her poverty and exhaustion, what she wants most in the world is a proper front yard. She scrimps and saves so that she can remove the pig shed in front of her house and replace it with

> a nice straight path going down to the front gate, set in a new paling fence; along the sides currant bushes; and in the open spaces to the right and left a big flowerin' shrub—snowballs, or Missouri currant; near the house a clump of matrimony, perhaps; and in the flower beds on each side of the path bachelor's-buttons, Chiny-asters, lady's slippers, and pinks; the edges bordered with box. (16)

In the two stories, fences define both a sense of home as a place within and a sense of the alien without. In keeping with the traditional and gendered separation of the private and public spheres, these fences seek to maintain a purity of place. In "In the Cotton Country," this endeavor is unsuccessful; the fence has been destroyed, the South defeated, and the Northerners have come. In "The Front Yard," Prudence finally gets her front yard, which, thanks to three American women, is successful in creating a pure place for her. Not only does she physically re-create a corner of New England in her Italian home, but she maintains her cultural identity as well. She considers the Italian language to be "simply lunatic English, English spoiled" (8). Of her stepson, whom she calls "Jo Vanny" rather than Giovanni, she says: " 'He's sort of American, anyhow.' It was the highest praise she could give" (18). Despite her sixteen years in Italy, Prudence is resolutely American, a cultural purity maintained, like her Missouri currants within the yard fence. In this way, Prudence is also like the beaver in the Dresden zoo, fenced in, building a "home" in that boundary that is reminiscent of its indigenous place, but surrounded by foreign environs.

And yet, Prudence is not meant to be a paragon of cultural virtue. Her distaste for everything Italian and refusal to assimilate in any manner, paralleled by the Italians' dislike of her American qualities and habits, shows two cultures in a stand-off. Home is both sanctuary and prison, both a remembrance of things past and, like the beaver's in the Dresden zoo, "a most pathetic little dam" constructed from "a few poor fragments of old boughs." Whereas Torsney argues that Prudence's sacrifice "is not that of self to a generalized and all-consuming love of family,"[17] attempting to show that Prudence is not a traditional domestic woman-as-martyr, it strikes me that her sacrifice is indeed that of self-renunciation, but, as with Prudence's xenophobia, it is not a trait Woolson wants emulated. Woolson is criticizing Prudence's attempt at repatriation in exile, with its fierce, immobile regionalism and its acceptance of patriarchal values (indicated by her caring for her husband's family and the "matrimony" flowers she plants in her front yard).

In "A Pink Villa," also from *The Front Yard and Other Italian Stories,* young Eva Churchill, who was born in the United States but has lived in Italy for fifteen of her nearly eighteen years, falls in love with David Rod, an American from Florida. Although she has lived most of her life in Italy, she has been protected by her mother "like a hot-house flower" (124). The pink villa, Italian in design but housing Americans and keeping American culture intact abroad, is the hothouse. As with Prudence's front yard or the beaver at the Dresden zoo, we have another image of a boundary keeping its inhabitants from contact with the outside and creating an artificial atmosphere for them within.

With Eva's marriage to David, it seems that Woolson will break down boundaries, will free her heroine from the house that keeps her from the outside world and from herself. Indeed, David, derided for being a "backwoodsman" (117) without refinement and called "Signor Ra" (125) after the Egyptian god of the sun, seems to be the catalyst for Eva's journey to the naturalness of the Florida wilderness. Eva, the hothouse flower, is being recalled to the unmediated sun. Thus, her going with David, while still within the context of marriage and its restraints, offers the hope of greater freedom with a broader horizon. And yet, any notion of "nativeness" or even "nature" is immediately called into question. Eva may be returning to her "native" country, but Florida is by no means her native land. David may be the outdoors type, but he is cultivating the land, not letting it remain in any kind of natural state. Eva and David will make a home, not find one. Eva appears to be following in the footsteps of Katharine; hers would seem to be an act of repatriation, a returning to the United States after having been married. But here the home becomes as big as the wilderness, appearing to be physically without boundaries, while still maintaining the cultural boundaries that home has come to represent.

17. Torsney, *Constance Fenimore Woolson,* 149.

"A Transplanted Boy" from *Dorothy and Other Italian Stories* is perhaps Woolson's most explicit and most complex examination of home, exile, and depatriation. In that story, an American mother, Violet Roscoe, and her son, Maso, live in Pisa. Her actual name is Violet Coe (Mrs. Thomas Ross Coe) but people changed it in conversation to "Roscoe," and Maso's name has been Italianized from Thomas. On their own, with little money since her husband's death six months after Maso's birth, Violet and Maso live in Pisa and "had often followed a nomadic life for a while when funds were low . . ." (87). A devoted mother, Violet is also fiercely independent, and rather than return to New Hampshire where her husband's family lives and from which her meager finances come, she prefers to do as she pleases. She forsakes the New England sense of duty that Prudence Guadagni feels and lives her life on her own terms. Her exile is not dreary: "I have a better time abroad than I do at home . . ." (74). Their lives have been one of dwelling-in-traveling, making a home not so much in a place as among themselves in a private but distinctly undomestic sphere (both in terms of household and nationality). Like Eva Churchill, Violet makes a home rather than finds one. Unlike Eva, and much like Woolson herself, she does so on her own.

But Violet becomes ill, and for her health she must go north, leaving Maso with a tutor. When the tutor abruptly leaves, Maso does not send his mother the tutor's letter about his departure. Rather than disrupt his mother's recuperation, Maso tries to live on his own until he becomes increasingly destitute and ill. At last, Violet returns and finds Maso. The story ends with their return to New Hampshire, home of her brother-in-law, Reuben Coe:

> A month later Mr. Reuben J. Coe, of Coesville, New Hampshire, said to his brother David: "That foolish wife of Tom's is coming home at last. In spite of every effort on my part, she has made ducks and drakes of almost all her money."
> "Is that why she is coming back?"
> "No; thinks it will be better for the boy. But I'm afraid it's too late for that." (121)

Reuben Coe finds Violet to be a "foolish wife" who has denied both her nation and her womanly responsibilities, but it seems that he is uneasy that the boy has lived abroad in an untraditional domestic arrangement. Concern for Maso's health may inform Coe's comment, but it seems that Coe and Woolson are also concerned with issues of identity.

Indeed, when the destitute boy turned to the U.S. consul in Leghorn for help, Woolson brings these issues of identity to the fore. The consul, a Michigan man named Maclean, does not immediately recognize Maso as an American: "And of what nation are you?" he asks (102). Moreover, because Maso has had no formal education, he does not even recognize that the day of his encounter with the consul, the Fourth of July, is a celebration of American independence and national identity. Learning of Maso's nomadic history, the consul says: "I see—one of the expatriated class" (105). Perhaps this is why it may be "too late" for Maso, not that he was so desperately ill but that he has become too thoroughly Italianized. It is just this ambiguity on which the meaning of the story hinges. Entitled "A Transplanted Boy," it very obviously suggests that Maso is an American "transplanted" in Italy. That is certainly Reuben Coe's understanding. However, the title could also suggest that Maso is transplanted when he returns to the United States. He is a hybrid, a new creation, who is as American as he is Italian. Woolson's line about the beaver in the Dresden zoo—"He is an American—as I am?"—is as applicable to Maso as to herself, for while he continually thinks of himself as an American, much of his situation points to his being polylocalized in a way that defies neat categorization.

In an article disparaging Woolson, Robert White raises two important issues relevant to Woolson's Italian stories. First, White asserts that Woolson "was never an expatriate, in the twentieth-century sense of the term, but she seems to have enjoyed keenly her succession of *outre-mer* years." White does not go on to explain why Woolson is not an expatriate in the Modernist sense, but Benstock clarifies this point. According to Benstock, "Female Modernists were expatriated (if this term is even applicable) differently than their male counterparts," and she places this difference at the site of gender. She goes on to assert that even "[t]he definitions of *exile* and *expatriate* were different for men and women. . . ."[18] White is correct that Woolson was not an expatriate in the *male* twentieth-century sense of the term; she was much closer to the *female* one. As the traveling in her life increased, the obligations to home decreased, and her depiction of these locales reflected a new relationship between dweller and place. It is precisely the "succession" that White notes that made Woolson's expatriation an extension of her regional writing set in the United States,

18. Robert L. White, "Cultural Ambivalence in Constance Fenimore Woolson's Italian Tales," reprint in *Critical Essays on Constance Fenimore Woolson*, ed. Cheryl Torsney (New York: G. K. Hall, 1992), 133; Benstock, "Expatriate Modernism," 23.

the kind of metonymy and fluidity that Irigaray saw as characteristic of women's ways of knowing and narrating.

In her expatriation, Woolson explored the idea of repatriation as a gendered event. In "At the Château of Corinne," Katharine is returned to the United States as John's wife. No longer an expatriate, she is also no longer a writer, and Katharine returns to her homeland replacing exile with home, narrative with silence. Eva of "A Pink Villa" likewise returns to the United States as a wife, and although their home seems to be an expression of a belonging that is constructed by the two of them rather than received from society and imposed on the woman, we are left with doubt as to whether Eva will find as much freedom as her physically boundless home would seem to promise. Finding her fullest self-expression in exile and a succession of homes, Violet of "A Transplanted Boy" remakes the idea of home into a family without a husband, a home without permanence. Unlike Woolson, Violet expresses no regrets for having chosen an unconventional lifestyle, even if her return for Maso's sake may arise from such a regret. Violet's forced return to the United States and a brother-in-law (the law of the husband) makes her defeat as devastating as Katharine's, with the significant exception that Violet is aware of her confinement, of being homeward bound.

Woolson was concerned with the idea of self-consciousness as an aspect of the expatriate experience. In her notebooks Woolson had written an idea for a story: "An American who has lived so long abroad that he is almost de-nationalized, and *conscious of it fully*; which makes him an original figure."[19] In a sense this expatriate would become a depatriate, decentering national identity and bringing to its logical conclusion in the form of dwelling-in-traveling abroad the traveling regionalism begun in the United States. Woolson compounds this depatriation, moreover, with gender as she attempts in her writings and in her life to free herself of the patriarchal country of letters and culture. Despite her declaration to James that she found her "true country, [her] real home" in his writings, she was aware of the dangers of women finding their homes in men's houses and fictions, of the dangers of patriation and repatriation, and so she tried to become a depatriate, with mixed results and feelings.

The second point in White's article which has important implications for the study of Woolson's Italian stories derives from his title, "Cultural Ambivalence in Constance Fenimore Woolson's Italian Tales." White argues that, despite her stated love for Italy as a country, Woolson actually had conflicted attitudes about the people and culture. White erroneously

19. Benedict, *Woolson*, 138. Emphasis is in the original text.

reads Woolson's characters as espousing Woolson's own views. Moreover, White misplaces the location of this cultural ambivalence, characterizing it as xenophobia. Rather, Woolson's cultural ambivalence lies in her position as a woman within American culture in the last half of the nineteenth century, caught between the Cult of the True Woman and the New Woman. Her portrayals of home and exile, marriage and independence, reflect this ambivalence. In addition, she delineated in her fiction the ambivalence of culture itself, how it is not unitary or fragmented but, like Irigaray's representation of women's psychology and discourse, plural. Even representing certain historical/social periods as being defined by ideas called the "Cult of the True Woman" and the "New Woman" is a falsely homogenizing schematic that Woolson would have recognized as erasing the multiplicity of voices that formed those periods; for her, regionalism embodied pluralities that defied easy categorization.

While dwelling-in-traveling proved beneficial for Woolson's writing, it was a strain on her life. She wrote, "I should like to turn into a peak when I die, to be a beautiful purple mountain, which would please the tired, sad eyes of thousands of human beings for ages." Her image of death is one of place, not movement. James recognized this desire for home, for placement, and when she died he wrote to John Hay in 1894: "The only image I can evoke that interposes at all is that of the blest Roman cemetery that she positively *desired*—I mean in her extreme love of it—and of her intensely consenting and more than reconciled rest under the Roman sky. *Requiescat.*"[20] The quiescence that Woolson so wished to put off as a girl writing to her friend Flora had come at last. Whether it was forced or embraced may never be known, and the ambiguity of her end is a fitting emblem of the conflicting forces of home and exile that characterized her life.

20. Ibid., xvi; Edel, *James,* 460.

"Colored Biscuits"

Reconstructing Whiteness and the Boundaries of "Home" in Kaye Gibbons's *Ellen Foster*

GIAVANNA MUNAFO

Whether they are able to enact it as a lived practice or not, many white folks active in anti-racist struggle today are able to acknowledge that all whites (as well as everyone else within white supremacist culture) have learned to over-value "whiteness" even as they simultaneously learn to devalue blackness. They understand the need, at least intellectually, to alter their thinking. Central to this process of unlearning white supremacist attitudes and values is the deconstruction of the category "whiteness."

—bell hooks,
Black Looks: Race and Representation

There's a truth that I am desperate to make you understand: race is not the same as family. In fact, "race" betrays family, if family does not betray "race."

—Mab Segrest,
Memoir of a Race Traitor

Ellen Foster tracks the plight of a young female protagonist besieged by an alcoholic, abusive father and the pressures of economic as well as emotional privation. The novel opens by turning expectations regarding domesticity and familial relations upside down. Gibbons's astonishing first line—"When I was little I would think of ways to kill my daddy"—bludgeons the daddy's-little-girl prototype so dear to portraits of idealized families. The text works against the fine grain of highly palatable but distorted visions of domestic life and family dynamics. As Veronica Makowski claims, "*Ellen Foster* is Gibbons's attempt to rewrite the saga of the American hero by changing 'him' to 'her' and to rewrite the southern female bildungsroman by changing its privileged, sheltered, upper-class heroine to a poor, abused outcast." In addition, unlike much recent work of the "new South,"[1] Gibbons's first novel makes racial identity and American racism central concerns. *Ellen Foster* displays the racial exigency of concepts like "home" and "family" and reveals that race, and specifically racism, have been erased from the scene in primer-esque editions of the American Dream.

While engaging in explicit and compelling examinations of blackness, Gibbons also conducts a sustained interrogation of the whiteness typically exempted from consideration in investigations of race (where race typically means any race other than white). For the economically and emotionally impoverished Ellen Foster, whiteness constitutes her one saving grace, the privilege that makes her better than nothing and separates her from her black school friend Starletta's brand of marginality. The line demarcating black from white is starkly drawn by Ellen's family where racial and economic liminality destabilize home life. Ellen's father makes what little money they have by selling liquor to the black men with whom he associates—a transgression of the color line that Ellen's maternal grandmother accents by repeatedly hurling the epithet "nigger" at her white son-in-law. Thus, Gibbons establishes the major tensions underlying Ellen's domestic and familial world as both complex and incendiary.

Ellen's mother's death sets the girl's quest in motion, leaving her alone with a father whose alcoholic brutality turns to incestuous assault. Ellen's struggle to escape this dangerous and demoralizing home life leads her into a journey both psychic and material: she must simultaneously reconstruct the figurative and literal dimensions of "home." The stories that Ellen relates chart this journey, which includes significant encounters with six different homes: her school friend Starletta's, where she finds a haven when her father first attacks her; her aunt Betsy's, where her pursuit of long-term asylum results in a comforting but brief two-day hiatus; her sympathetic art teacher's, where school officials, having discovered physical evidence of abuse, temporarily house her; her grandmother's, where the state, after

1. Kaye Gibbons, *Ellen Foster* (New York: Vintage Books, 1987), 1. Subsequent citations will be made parenthetically in the text. Veronica Makowski, " 'The Only Hard Part Was the Food': Recipes for Self-Nurture in Kaye Gibbons's Novels," *Southern Quarterly* 30 (Winter–Spring 1992): 103; Pearl K. Bell, "Southern Discomfort," *The New Republic* 198 (February 29, 1988): 40.

terminating her father's custody and removing her from the art teacher's home, places her; her co-worker Mavis's, where, while living with her grandmother, she spies on scenes of domestic stability; and her aunt Nadine's, where, after her grandmother dies, she stays until being thrown out on Christmas Eve.

During this last, miserable leg of her journey, Ellen asks her cousin about "that woman with all the girls lined up by her" in the church pew and learns that "they are the Foster family and that lady would take in anything from orphans to stray cats" (98–99). Desperate for a home that offers the kind of order and contentment she reads in this scene, Ellen immediately determines to become a member of the "Foster family." Her misreading of descriptor for family name underscores Gibbons's persistent antagonism toward naturalized conceptions of "family." When Ellen does become a member of the town's foster home, she begins signing her school papers "Ellen Foster," inscribing both her childish naïveté and one of the novel's most pressing concerns.

Gibbons insists that familial and domestic reconstitution are both necessary and possible. The location of the foster home, "way on the other side of school," at first renders it out of reach, while its context renders it off-limits: as her cousin puts it, the Fosters live "between the nigger church and Porter's store" (114). This place, Ellen's ultimate home, is sandwiched, that is, between the very racial difference and economic exchange that the housing practices of Ellen's maternal family and white community obsessively disavow. Nonetheless, Ellen trudges the full, cold distance and tells the woman who answers the door, "I mean to be here" (115). Here, at the final turning point in Ellen's narrative, Gibbons depicts a woman-child who's taken her life by the reins, in part out of necessity, in part out of the will to change.

Although the novel accents the import of Ellen's material triumphs (managing to eat enough, dress adequately, save money, and, ultimately, find a new home), a far less tangible achievement—the attempt to reconstruct her own whiteness—crowns her development. Ellen must endeavor to reconstitute her own lived experience of white female racial identity, engendering, as much as possible, a white female self capable of interrupting complicity in white supremacy.

Complicity and Resistance

Gibbons figures her young white protagonist's search for home and family as continuous with and dependent upon her attempts to revise the racial, and sexual, ideologies they underwrite. Ellen's inheritance includes the assumption of an essential difference between white people and black people, and it insures that she will approach even the most mundane aspects of daily life engaged in practices that maintain and bolster white racial superiority. When she refuses to eat a biscuit her black friend Starletta offers her because it is a "colored biscuit," Ellen reifies the essential difference between these worlds, echoing white supremacy's double-edged habit of insuring its authority and, at the same time, its invisibility via normative status.

"Biscuits," for Ellen, remain part and parcel of her domestic and familial world—an implicitly white terrain—and become "colored biscuits" once removed from that context. Her assignment of the racial marker "colored" exposes the unspoken, unmarked qualifier always already attendant, in Ellen's world, to "biscuits": white. In her study of contemporary American white women's experiences of and relations to racial identity, Ruth Frankenberg explores the process by which "whiteness comes to be an unmarked or neutral category, whereas other cultures are specifically marked 'cultural.'" Her interviewees tend to understand whiteness as no culture, formless, and invisible ("bland" and "blah"), and their attempts to particularize this nothingness consistently summon comparisons "based on color, the linking of white culture with white objects—clichéd white bread and mayonnaise" (199).[2] Taking the tendency of these white women to liken themselves to white bread as one marker of white, female racial identity, Ellen's designation of the biscuit Starletta offers her as "colored," like her refusal to eat it, embodies the ideological boundaries that arise out of white racial anxiety. The color line excludes and polices others and otherness in order to bolster a whiteness that threatens to dissipate into nothingness.

Gibbons's narrative traces Ellen's progress along a route of increasing racial consciousness, moving from her specification of the biscuits Starletta's mother makes as "colored" (and, therefore, inedible to her) and her comment that the sweater Starletta's mother and father give her "does not look colored at all" (and, therefore, can be worn by her), to her recognition that such distinctions denigrate by measuring against implicit white normativity and superiority (32). Gibbons registers this change explicitly; near the end of the novel, Ellen asks her "new Mamma" to "make a fuss over how pretty Starletta is. But not the kind of fuss that says you sure are pretty to be colored. The kind that says you sure are pretty and that is all. The other

2. Ruth Frankenberg, *White Women, Race Matters: The Social Construction of Whiteness* (Minneapolis: University of Minnesota Press, 1993), 197, 199.

way does not count" (123). While, on the one hand, this "conversion" can appear contrived, Gibbons aggressively critiques the exploitive aspect of Ellen's relationship to the novel's black families and characters. In so doing, she exposes the complex of resistance and complicity inherent in her young white protagonist's nascent antiracism.

Gibbons inevitably scripts both her heroine's subversive resistance and her inescapable complicity.[3] The novel opens with Ellen's confession that, in the past, she imagined her father's death. The form that this confession takes reveals the dynamics of both racial division and of the gendered domestic order in which Ellen flounders. "When they [the rescue squad] come in the house," fantasizes Ellen, "I'm all in a state of shock and just don't know how to act what with two colored boys heaving my dead daddy onto a roller cot" (1). In the world of her imagination, as in the everyday world of her actual life, Ellen's precarious racial, sexual, and domestic situations converge. The phrase "colored boys" at once summons the battles of the civil rights movement and their failure in this small, rural community, while Ellen's vigilance against transgressions of the color line rings out in the semantics of a racialized "they" entering her domestic space. Further, the moment of trespass figured here elucidates Ellen's sexual vulnerability.

This vulnerability surfaces more explicitly later in the novel, but Gibbons introduces it in this portrait of Ellen surrounded by men who have invaded her home (a domestic space traditionally gendered female and representative of the female body) and who, literally, support the man who, we later learn, exercises his masculine authority as well as his parental privilege by sexually assaulting her. In the logic of dreams, Ellen's fantasy figures both the wish of her father's death fulfilled and the condensation and displacement of her attendant anxieties.[4] The reverie Ellen entertains here—and with which Gibbons chooses to open the novel—condenses fears of both maternal and paternal abandonment, of domestic instability, of racial disorder, and of sexual vulnerability into a complex image of trespass and invasion. Following the lead of a racist community and culture, Ellen displaces these anxieties, figuring them, not as the products of her

---

3. I am indebted to Caroline Rody here, whose analysis of another white, female, antiracist narrative, *Wide Sargasso Sea*, suggestively addresses this point. Concerned with the contours of what she calls "daughterist" literature, Rody explores white feminist and antiracist or anticolonialist revolt against systems of white supremacist patrimony. See her "Burning Down the House: The Revisionary Paradigm of Jean Rhys's *Wide Sargasso Sea*," in *Famous Last Words: Changes in Gender and Narrative Closure*, ed. Alison Booth (Charlottesville: University Press of Virginia, 1993).

4. See Sigmund Freud, *On Dreams* (London: W. W. Norton, 1952), 76.

mother's disability and father's malfeasance, but as the result of a volatile color line. Further, the rhetoric of black men "coming" in her "house," as she puts it, lends to the scene the specter of sexual and racial trespass made one. This confluence—accented by summoning the especially incendiary interracial coupling of a white woman and a black man—establishes the narrative's insistence on the contingency of Ellen's sexual and racial negotiations. It is in the context of Ellen's struggle to achieve domestic and familial stability that Gibbons most powerfully demonstrates this contingency.

Ellen buys into the equation her grandmother posits between depravity and blackness. Attempting to salvage some shred of paternal affinity, the child lays the blame for her father's criminality and cruelty on his affiliation with blackness. Thus, instead of figuring the attendants of her fantasy as allies—insofar as they remove her abusive father—she imagines them as agents of disruption and as threats to her own racial and sexual purity.

Still on the first page of the novel, Gibbons stresses the impact Ellen's father's actual death has upon the status of their home. "Next thing I know," Ellen tells us, "he's in the ground and the house is rented out to a family of four" (1). Ellen has no home to call her own. Immediately following this recollection, as the narrative shifts to the present, we learn that her home situation has, since then, radically changed:

> I live in a clean brick house. . . . Two years ago I did not have much of anything. Not that I live in the lap of luxury now but I am proud for the schoolbus to pick me up here every morning. My stylish well-groomed self standing in the front yard with the grass green and the hedge bushes square. (2)

Gibbons stresses the significance of superficial control of the domestic environment, often turning Ellen's attention to the pleasures of such control. The fact that, in her new home, "[e]verything matches" and "is all so neat and clean" enthralls Ellen (5). She embraces order as a corrective to disorder and espouses cleanliness as a corrective to filth, both literally and metaphorically.

Ellen's materialistic impulses derive from both actual neediness and what Gibbons exposes as a familial and cultural consumerism. The novel explores the impact and limitations of the latter while documenting the extent and implications of the former. Dressed warmly in winter, with regularly washed hair, Ellen cherishes the emblems of care and nurturance her foster home provides, truly amazed, after so much deprivation, that, after eating an egg sandwich with "mayonnaise on both sides" for breakfast, she can actually choose to fix herself another for lunch (2). Thus provisioned with a glimpse of Ellen's present-tense, orderly, and stable domestic situation, we lurch quickly back and forth with Ellen as she recalls the journey she has taken, beginning with its inception in flight from her violent, abusive biological home.

"Shaking Itself to Death": Hearth and Home Undone

Gibbons provides a parable of parenting, one that Ellen relies upon after her mother's death, to gauge prospective "new mamas":

> When the beans were ready to eat she would let me help pick. Weeds do not bear fruit. She would give me a example of a bean that is grown to hold in one hand while I picked with the other. If I was not sure if a particular bean was at the right stage I could hold up my example of a bean to that bean in question and know. (49)

Providing her with the tools to judge ripe from unripe, good from bad, Ellen's mother laid down a path for her daughter to follow in life. As Ellen says, "I just worked the trail my mama left," and her struggle to find a home and a new mama continue this effort to reconstruct the "one season" of her mother's wellness during which she enjoyed such nurturance and care (49).

The model her mother provides contains lessons as much about fighting cultural and, consequently, racial turf wars as about discerning ripe from unripe. As in her subsequent novels, Gibbons recounts the plight of a white woman who "marries down" and incurs the wrath and rejection of her wealthy family. The physical and emotional deterioration such displacement induces contributes to Ellen's eventual homelessness. While Gibbons's attention merely skims the mother's story, it reveals how her choices shape Ellen's life. Ellen inherits from her mother the impulse to transgress restrictive social codes. Crossing the class line, in this case, entails crossing the color line, however unwittingly. For when Ellen's mother marries across class lines she enters a world where the color line so determinedly policed in her community of birth wavers and shifts erratically. Without the complementary schism of radical economic disparity, racial divisions become far more unruly and, in some ways, far more threatening.

While Gibbons's portrait of Ellen's father and his "colored buddies" suggests some measure of interracial congeniality, the author situates this integrationist cameo in the context of commercial exchange, alcoholism, and sexual violence (25). "Missah Bill," as they call him, sells liquor to the black men with whom he drinks to excess. As the retention of formal address indicates, even among drinking buddies the distinction between white supplier and black consumer remains. On the other hand, the homosocial bonding in which Ellen's father and his black companions engage finds its support in shared socioeconomic alienation (one source of his retreat into alcoholism) and the compensatory sexual dominance they assume and enact. Ellen, whose racist essentialism rings out in her reference to the "pack of colored men" from whom she hides, tells us she "always walked in wide circles around [her father]"—a marking of distance from both his sexual rapacity and his racial transgressiveness (25). The novel scrutinizes Ellen's predicament and responses, charting the complex relations between racial, economic, and sexual ideologies and practices. Gibbons's portrait of Ellen as sexual prey and of the racial and economic contexts out of which her situation arises initiate Ellen's quest for a new home and family and her corresponding struggle to reconfigure her own racial and sexual positioning.

Ellen is "just about ripe" according to one of her daddy's "colored" friends who cautions, "[y]ou gots to git em when they is still soff when you mashum" (37). Like a sweet potato, Ellen is to be harvested and mashed for consumption.[5] Sensing danger, she hides in the closet and explains,

> What else do you do when your house is run over by colored men drinking whiskey and singing and your daddy is worse than them all put together?
>
> You pray to God they forget about you and the sweet young things that are soff when you mashum and how good it feels when she is pressed up by you. You get out before one can wake up from being passed out on the floor. You get out before they start to dream about the honey pie and the sugar plums. (37)

Venturing out from her hiding place, Ellen attempts to escape from the house, but her flight is interrupted by her father's drunken sexual assault. Gibbons shapes Ellen's narrative here so that the past-tense experience and the present-tense relating of it merge: "Get away from me he does not listen to me but touches his hands harder on me" (38). Breaking from him, she races away from the abuse her home has come to represent and towards Starletta's house, toward, as she says, "the smoke coming out of the chimney against the night sky" (38).

5. I owe the sweet potato comparison to Angela Gilchrist, a student in the seminar on Toni Morrison's novels I taught at the University of Virginia during the spring of 1994.

This paradigmatic image of hearth and home, writ large against the night sky, beckons Ellen away from her "natural" home and toward a newly reconstituted one. She runs, in part, from the blackness signified by her father and his buddies—the racial difference that essentialist white supremacy equates with both lasciviousness and violence. This is not to say that her father and his cohorts are not lascivious and violent, but the novel displays the fallacy of an implicit connection between such "evil" and race, literal blackness. Significantly, Ellen runs from one "black" scene to another here, from blackness as evil to blackness as haven. The former frighteningly threatens to undermine her whiteness (marker of both racial and sexual "purity"), while the latter provides both the necessary reification of that whiteness and a context in which to begin reevaluating it.

As the narrative progresses, Ellen's concept of "home" and all of that term's seemingly immutable qualities undergo gradual but, ultimately, radical revision. While her indoctrination into whiteness has taught her that her father's association with black men constitutes his evilness, she discovers that he is "worse than them all put together" and that his "evil" retreats "back into his self" (38). If her home consists of him, she concludes, it cannot house her any longer.

Gibbons closes the scene of Ellen's flight with the child wondering "what the world has come to," and, indeed, her world has come to pieces in ways both tragic and, at the same time, potentially fruitful. Against the supposed fixity of domestic order Gibbons asserts its fragility and constructedness. Describing the general state of affairs in her home at the time of her mother's death, Ellen says, "[e]verything was so wrong like somebody had knocked something loose and my family was shaking itself to death. Some wild ride broke and the one in charge strolled off and let us spin and shake and fly off the rail" (2). On the verge of disillusionment, Ellen both appeals to a higher power and registers its absence; she believes in the cosmic glue that supposedly binds families together while, at the same time, she knows that no such "natural" bonds exist in her family.

Similarly, in flight from her biological home and toward the smoking chimney that signifies haven, Ellen reports, "I gather my head and all that is spinning and flying out from me" (38). This image of barely contained disintegration—which suggests how profoundly Ellen's sense of self depends upon the state of her domestic and familial relations— closes the chapter. Acutely aware that "the one in charge" has jumped ship, Ellen attempts to take the wheel, as it were, and keep her life from "shaking itself to death."

Policing Bloodlines

Willing to stay at Starletta's house only one night, Ellen turns to her mother's sister, Betsy, for shelter from her father's abuse. In selecting this new home, Ellen resorts to a set of acceptable criteria heavy on superficial elements and sadly light on more sustaining ones: a bathtub is important, as is a "nice house," one with "flowers growed all up on the mailbox" (40–41). Superficial comforts abound at Aunt Betsy's; they shop and buy Ellen a dress and "more little things than [she] can think of," like "a pair of gloves with a sequin cat sewed across the hands" that she "cannot play in" but "are good to look at" (41). Gibbons further stresses the feebleness of the visit's emotional substance: Ellen entertains herself by bathing, "[l]ooking in dresser drawers," and "[f]ingering the what-nots," while her aunt "spends right much time on the couch looking at magazines with stars in them" (41). Fresh from her father's abusive hold, Aunt Betsy's plush consumerism pampers Ellen's sorely bruised sensibilities.

However, Ellen eventually comes to deride Betsy's consumerism. Having just delivered the news of Betsy's mother's death, Ellen responds to her aunt's "so near Christmas" scathingly: "I was dying my own self," she explains, "to tell her well Betsy why don't you just see if the undertaking driver will stop and let you shop a minute on the way to the grave?" (90). The contrast between Ellen's initial embrace and eventual rejection of Betsy's consumer-driven, superficial existence mimics the contrast between her original insistence, vis-à-vis her black coworker Mavis's family, that she "only wanted one [a home] white and with a little more money" and her ultimate realization that economic and racial demarcations cannot insure domestic and familial stability or happiness (67). Betsy's whiteness and her economic stability, at least as much as her aunthood, preselect her as appropriate guardian, just as blackness and poverty render Starletta's family inappropriate—despite Betsy's blatant insensitivity to Ellen's situation and Starletta's family's explicitly rendered concern for her well-being and its readiness to intervene. Ellen's formulation of an acceptable home as "white and with a little more money" (more, that is, than the impoverished homes of the black families she encounters) reflects both the racial homogeneity of "family" and an overdetermined correlation between racial identity and economic status.

Ellen's foray into Betsy's posh domesticity is short-lived, and she returns to her own home reluctantly, determined to evade her father's attempts to "grab and swat" (43). But, despite Ellen's heroic stab at self-protection and her persistent effort to stay "home," school officials discover physical evidence of abuse and initiate Ellen's next series of relocations. Ultimately, the school's intervention results in a court decision that grants her grandmother legal custody, placing Ellen once more, and more permanently, in the care of her maternal family.

Ellen immediately becomes the target of the hatred her grandmother, until now, had reserved for her son-in-law. Class anxiety compels her to label Ellen's daddy "nigger and trash"—his life is marred by business failure, rowdiness, and alcoholism, all marks, when coexistent, of the downward mobility Ellen's mother married into despite (or specifically *to* spite) her mother's wishes. Economic hardship, emotional excess, and substance abuse come to distinguish rich from poor not because these conditions and behaviors are exclusively or even disproportionately the province of the latter, but, rather, because the authority of the former results in part from projecting such destabilizing threats onto the economic and racial others against whom it defines itself.

Although the child strongly resembles her mother (Mavis, significantly, affirms this resemblance [65]), her grandmother insists that she favors her scoundrel father. When Ellen's father dies, her grandmother tells her "make sure you cry more than you did for your mama," legislating through her matriarchal (and economic) authority Ellen's affiliation with paternal (and alienation from maternal) ancestry (69). Holding Ellen responsible for her mother's daughterly infractions, the vindictive woman sends Ellen out to work in the fields. Ellen reports, "I used to play in the fields with Starletta and watch her mama and daddy chop but I never figured it would be me one day"—a subtle but unmistakable glossing of the separate racial spheres overwhelmingly maintained in Ellen's world and reinscribed by her grandmother (63). Ellen's white skin does not spare her field labor because her grandmother equates the girl's previous associations with black people (her father's buddies and her school friend Starletta) with a transgression of the color line so radical it renders Ellen a "nigger," just like her father.

Each gesture further reinforces the separation the woman desperately seeks to impose between herself and the embodiment of her daughter's transgression. Translating class difference into racial difference magnifies its distance from the white self—magnifies, in other words, its otherness—to insure the stability of white, upper-class identity. This attempt to consolidate whiteness is perhaps most obvious when her grandmother ascribes to Ellen the racist clichés attached to black female sexuality. "You laid up all in that house with your daddy's buddies. I'm surprised you don't have some little nigger baby hanging off your titty," she derisively tells Ellen (78). In this last, specifically gendered, maneuver of disassociation, Gibbons's portrait of the old, white mistress summons the not-so-subtle role female sexual "purity" plays in the struggle to define and bolster white racial identity. Constructed in accordance with racist ideology, white women's racial identity—like black women's—finds expression in explicitly sexual terms.

Shut up in a museumlike "torture chamber" of isolationism, Ellen imagines her grandmother's insistence that she is no longer white made literal. Projecting her own racial anxieties and desires onto a handy proxy, she fantasizes "turning [her] buddy Starletta loose" to "have a rampage in one room and out the other" among her grandmother's "what-nots" and "costly items" (62). Unlike the accessories of life with Aunt Betsy, the objects that populate Ellen's new quarters fail to pacify her neediness, even on first encounter. Alienated from use-value and collected as a means of self-aggrandizement, the elaborately turned furniture and ancient vases Ellen curiously ponders enjoy a protectedness only exceeded by that which envelopes her grandmother's own carefully guarded status. "I'll break your little hand if you touch that vase," she warns Ellen, who attests to the seriousness of the threat by confessing that it made her "think how a broke hand might feel" (62).

Ellen's vision of riotous racial other wreaking havoc in the heart of white domestic civility underscores Ellen's ability and willingness to trade in racist clichés, especially under duress regarding her own unstable racial and sexual identity. On the other, the displacement of her own desires in this projection onto Starletta at the same time articulates Ellen's identification with her friend, and it underwrites Ellen's incipient reconfiguring of "home" as not showplace but habitat. Rather than painting the Starletta of Ellen's fantasy rampage "savage," Gibbons's consistently antagonist rendering of Ellen's familial domains figures her disruptive potential as an advantageous, even necessary, corrective. The fact that Ellen imagines her desire fulfilled by Starletta (instead of imagining herself demolishing her grandmother's moneyed, white, female preserve) registers her recognition that the space is racialized, that its sanctity engenders its whiteness and vice versa.

Gibbons similarly interrogates the disjunction between the state's investment in white bloodlines and Ellen's experience of her own biological family when, after the grandmother's death, Aunt Nadine inherits guardianship of the girl. Prior to this state-engineered arrangement, Ellen's only narrated encounter with Nadine takes place in the aftermath of Ellen's mother's death, and Gibbons's portrait of their interaction then provides a telling context for the familial fiasco occasioned by Ellen's eventual placement in Nadine's home. Ellen's initial observations of her mother's sister stress the workings of the color line, exposing both Ellen's own reliance upon racist commonplaces and her aunt's obsessive racial anxiety. Ineptness, a quality Ellen disdains, summons things black when Ellen considers her aunt's inability to efficiently and calmly manage her own sister's funeral. The girl complains that "[Nadine] could not organize a two-car colored funeral so she has herself all worked up over this affair" (14). At the same time, she registers the ludicrousness of Nadine's racial paranoia, explaining, "[w]e have to drive through colored town to get to the [funeral]. . . . My aunt is so glad to be out of colored town. She unlocks her car door because now she feels safe" (19). Both party to and critical of such racial vigilance, Ellen catalogs its preponderance in the world of her family and community.

Nadine's fear of entering "black" spaces signals the vulnerability historically rendered fundamental to the very category "white woman." As Vron Ware demonstrates in *Beyond the Pale*, oppressive ideologies of both race and gender traffic in images like this one of a white woman whose physical proximity to racial others spells racial and sexual danger.[6] Ellen's ruminations about her aunt's profession, which arise as the funeral caravan makes its way through "colored town," emphasize this dangerous proximity. Ellen describes Nadine's fawning attitude toward the undertaker, explicitly noting the connection between such deference and Nadine's "job":

> My aunt is entertaining the smiling man. That is her part-time job. When she is not redecorating or shopping with Dora she demonstrates food slicers in your home.
>
> She will bring her plastic machine into your living room and set the whole business up on a card table. After everybody plays two or three made-up games she lets you in on the Convenience Secret of the Century. She will tell you how much it would run you in the store. If the smiling man has a wife he can expect my aunt and her machine in his living room sometime soon. (17)

The gendered economy charted here has particular implications regarding domestic and familial frameworks. Women prepare the family's food, but men control the means by which that work can be accomplished. Thus, Nadine must broker the "Convenience Secret of the Century" through men to women. In much the same way that children's material requirements and accessories must both appeal to children themselves and to their parents, wives compose Nadine's target market while husbands are the ultimate consumer. Her job entails, as Ellen notes, entertaining men, cajoling them

6. Vron Ware, *Beyond the Pale: White Women, Racism, and History* (New York: Verso, 1992).

into the wide-spirited gesture of providing their wives with tools to lighten the burdens of domestic labor. Ellen's description of Nadine's job relies upon the popular, euphemistic rhetoric of prostitution ("entertaining men"), a correspondence that underscores the sexualized nature of her position in men's homes. As in both Ellen's original home and her Aunt Betsy's (where Gibbons stresses the ornamentalism of women's activities), subservience characterizes wives' relations to husbands, women's relationships to men—female self-interest remains routed through male desire.

Continuing her reverie regarding Nadine's occupation, Ellen links it to the racial anxiety and color line surveillance apparent in Nadine's locking and unlocking of her car door. Passing out of "colored town" and into white neighborhoods, Ellen comments, "[o]h and wouldn't she like to be inside one of these white houses peeling cucumbers in a snap! And she will tell you about how everybody got his money and especially about the doctors. All they do is cheat, gamble, and run around" (19). Nadine's eagerness (as intuited or projected by Ellen) to enter the white domestic space of the houses they pass contrasts markedly with her fear of being removed from the safety of her automobile and exposed to the perceived danger of "colored" neighborhoods. The car figures Nadine's own person/world: locked and inaccessible in response to racial difference, unlocked and accessible in response to racial homogeneity. The sexual connotations of Nadine's locked and unlocked personal space—particularly in the context of the sexualized rhetoric that describes her job—reinforce the intimately related racial ones.

In rejecting black individuals and homes as unfit for even commercial exchange, Nadine reinforces her own racial privilege while disarming the threat of identification posed by the fact that both she and the black communities/individuals she disdains are the objects of white male exploitation. Perhaps even more threatening are the potential sexual and gender-based alliances suggested by the hypothetical incursions into interracial domestic/commercial exchange Nadine so adamantly disavows. "Entertaining" a "smiling [black] man" while engaging in the sisterhood of wives generates a nightmare of miscegenistic affiliation.

The contradiction Gibbons displays here—between Nadine's projection of sexual license onto racial others and her willingness to trade on her own sexuality in commerce with white men—is a central one. White supremacy allows and encourages Nadine to disavow her own libidinal agency in the service of maintaining distinct boundaries between white and nonwhite, pure and impure. White women, in particular, must remain "locked" against a perceived threat to both their whiteness and their supposed chastity. This mechanism obscures the fact that, at the same time, sexism fixes Nadine as sexualized object in relation to men and male-dominated culture. Thus she can both endorse the myth of black hypersexuality (in locking herself off from blackness as an expression of her own sexual and racial purity) and, paradoxically, exploit her own sexuality to negotiate a space in the economic terrain controlled by white men (by unlocking herself to prospective white male customers). This contradiction results directly from the authorizing function whiteness serves in relation to the category "woman."

Having barely initiated her quest for domestic and familial reconstruction, Ellen registers not the complexities of Nadine's racist machinations, but the simple fact of their intrusive, insipid presence. Indeed, as noted, Ellen's own white supremacist inheritance encourages her to participate in Nadine's racist orientation even as she chronicles its obtrusiveness. Later in her journey, however, when Ellen must live with Nadine, she has already encountered the stifling xenophobia of her grandmother's home as well as the alternative domestic and familial models resident in the homes of Starletta, Julia and Roy, and Mavis.

Ellen's brief stay with Aunt Nadine and cousin Dora, and especially the dreadfully disappointing and painful Christmas she spends with them, propels her into the foster care system. At this point in the novel, Gibbons's two alternating narratives converge: the predominantly unhappy story of the events that lead up to Ellen's ultimate rejection of her "natural" family (told in past tense) and the predominantly happy story of her life as a member of the "Foster family" (told in present tense). Gibbons accents the centrality of the racial dynamics operating in the foster home Ellen embraces. Recollections of life at Nadine's interrupt immediate, joyous preparations for Starletta's visit to the "Foster" home, until the narratives collapse into one at the point of Ellen's defection from her family and initiation into a newly constituted foster family. Significantly, while Starletta's visit promises, for Ellen, to resolve all inequities ("then we will all be straight," she says), her "family" Christmas underscores the divisiveness dominating the space demarcated by Ellen's family ties (100).

Like Aunt Betsy, Aunt Nadine proves to be her mother's daughter, a woman consumed by shopping and blind to the tragic circumstances of her niece's life. At Christmas she showers her daughter, Dora, with every gift the child desires, and more, while presenting Ellen, the prototypical poor relation, with one packet of art paper. Her excuse—that Ellen is "so peculiar and hard to buy for"—suggests the more rudimentary motivation for her thoughtlessness: Nadine conceives of Ellen not as a member of her family, not even as another member of her chosen community, but as that which is "peculiar." The grandmother's habit of magnifying the distance between herself and Ellen persists in Nadine's treatment of her ward. Framed by Ellen's eagerness to make Starletta's visit a milestone of bridge-building (afterward she hopes to feel that "the two of us are even"), this familial betrayal ends with Ellen's final severing of conventional family ties (100). When Nadine threatens to evict Ellen from her home on Christmas, the girl flees and presents herself to her "new mama," the woman she's identified in church as a potentially appropriate mother.

In framing Ellen's ultimate break from blood ties with her endeavor to forge a meaningful and lasting connection with Starletta, Gibbons emphasizes Ellen's need to bridge racial divisions as an integral part of the process of home-building she embarks upon as a member of the "Foster" family. This family exists in curious relation to the notions of "family" that Ellen has experienced as so constraining. At once a family and not a family, Ellen's foster home provides many of the elements she deems necessary to an acceptable home, yet it allows for reconstruction, revision, and experimentation. Although she is "not sure if it has ever been done before," Ellen asks permission for her black friend to visit for the weekend (85). And, although none of the biological family members with whom she's lived would permit this blurring of the color line on their property, Ellen's "new mama" says, "sure Starletta can come stay with us" and even offers to "whip up" some hand-towels with an *S* embroidered on them for their guest (99, 100). The fact that her new family welcomes Starletta overjoys Ellen, who deems this revision of "home" groundbreaking, comparing it to declarations of war and the miracle of birth (99).

Gibbons traces the development of Ellen's relation to Starletta, a relation that moves from condescension and proprietariness ("she was mine") to respect and recognition. Starletta takes "a hunk [of birthday cake] with the N part out of [Ellen's] name"—a scriptural exchange that suggests the larger exchange taking place, one in which Ellen begins to substitute humane, empathetic identification for white supremacist distortions. Starletta ingests the *N* from Ellen's name, and the embroidered *S* from Starletta's name remains with Ellen.

The Colored Path

Gibbons specifically locates a conglomerate model of acceptable domesticity in three extrafamilial homes, and she accents their freedom from cruelty and abuse. Significantly, she also stresses these homes' liminal positions vis-à-vis dominant modes of consumer exchange, as well as their relative remove from white supremacist patriarchy. Two of these homes belong to black characters who, as a direct result of racial exploitation, inhabit the extreme low end of the economic terrain charted by the novel. The third home belongs to a markedly eccentric white couple who debunk arbitrary racial as well as sexual divisions (welcoming Starletta into their home and reversing typical gender roles) while waging a battle against the marketplace by growing their own produce organically. Among other things, Ellen learns not that black families are good and white families are bad but, rather, that just as blackness itself does not signal evil, whiteness itself does not signal benevolence, or even sufficiency. While the novel trades, at times, in stereotypes (the black family, especially mother, as source of nurturance and care for the white child) and perpetuates servant/served models of relation between black and white communities or individuals, Gibbons persistently undermines whiteness's claims to authority and ultimately figures Ellen's development as affirming only insofar as it incorporates a resistance to white supremacist ideologies regarding her own identity and its familial and cultural contexts.

Ellen's journey both begins and ends by seeking Starletta. Gibbons opens the chapter following Ellen's father's first sexual assault with Ellen negotiating the terms of her lodging with Starletta's mother. The woman refuses payment and takes the traumatized child into her bed for the night, but Ellen's concern for maintaining racial boundaries compels her to sleep in her coat on top of the covers. Thus, she "cannot say [she] officially slept in the bed" (39). However, when she gets up the next morning, Ellen reports, "I was surprised because it did not feel like I had slept in a colored house" (39). While her experience insists that the terms of essentialist racial differences are inadequate, Ellen remains firmly situated within a sociocultural system that makes access to alternative terms both difficult and threatening. Nonetheless, Ellen intuits that Starletta's home might be a safer, more comforting environment than her own, despite the former's lack of what her white family and world had always identified as necessary prerequisites to acceptable domesticity: running water, private quarters, spotless floorboards. While Ellen continues to subordinate Starletta and her family, relying on the marker "colored" to distinguish their home and community from her own, her experience undermines this practice little by little.

Ellen's encounters with her biological family vitiate any residual faith in blood ties the girl may have harbored after her mother's death and father's abusiveness. Her placements in and observations of extrafamilial homes encourage Ellen to envision "home" beyond the boundaries of "natural" family ties. Ellen's familial experiences equip her to identify elements she does not wish to include in the home she seeks to reconfigure, and her extrafamilial experiences (with Starletta's family, Julia and Roy, and Mavis's home) enable her to identify elements she considers essential to that reconfiguration.

Only willing to seek refuge at Starletta's for occasional brief periods and expelled from her Aunt Betsy's, Ellen remains at home until, as noted, school officials intervene. They place her fate in the hands of the courts and arrange for Ellen to stay with her art teacher, Julia, and Julia's husband, Roy, until custody decisions can be made. This arrangement suits Ellen, who, when told that her teachers "had decided what to do with [her]," responds with relief, "It is about time. . . . Yes Lord it is about time" (45). Soon thereafter, when her father invades the schoolgrounds, exposing himself and yelling that he will "pay for it"—"it" presumably referring to sexual access to his daughter—Julia comforts Ellen and adds, "let's go home" (54). Gibbons stresses that Ellen does consider her teacher's house her *home:* she begins Ellen's next account, "When we got home . . ." (55).

But Gibbons quickly interrupts this amenable domestic arrangement with the news that the court has decided to place Ellen back with her family (55). "I do not believe it," Ellen comments, adding, "It sounds crazy to me because the three of us could pass for a family on the street" (55). Ellen gauges the acceptability of familial relation, at least in part, corporeally. In Starletta's family, for example, she would stick out like the proverbial sore thumb—because of her whiteness. Such a unit decidedly would not "pass for a family on the street." The court, on the other hand, has its own criteria. It upholds the white family as "society's cornerstone," rejecting extrafamilial claims to parental relation (56).

Julia and Roy provide the care and parenting of an appropriate family for Ellen, but Gibbons exposes the ways the state intervenes to police reconstructed families in accordance with its own economic and racial agendas. Julia and Roy, ex-hippie artists and organic farmers in the post-civil-rights-movement South, cannot prevail in their bid for the child against her grandmother's Old South, monied gentility. While Ellen's virulently racist grandmother runs a plantation-like spread, houses black field laborers in "shacks," and "[does] not pay them doodly-squat," Julia and Roy graciously welcome Starletta into their home to celebrate Ellen's birthday (21, 66). Their response to Ellen's friendship with Starletta contrasts markedly with that of Ellen's other teachers who make quite plain that a "colored" friend "would not do" (44). Additionally, Julia and Roy eschew arbitrary gender-driven divisions of labor, Julia holding down a job and Roy remaining home to "do his thing"—garden, cook, and perform housework (48).

Additionally, Gibbons accents the correlation between Ellen's experiences gardening with Julia and Roy and her experiences gardening with her deceased mother. Indeed, it is only while working in the garden with them that Ellen recalls the single happy memory she harbors—the way her mama "liked to work in the cool of the morning" and how she worked the garden trail her mama left (49). It is during her stay with Julia and Roy that Ellen first converts the telling and retelling of that "one season" of happiness (a fantasy) into a reenactment of such pleasure and well-being (a reality). When the child welfare agency selects the aged, solitary blood kin over the eager couple as Ellen's new family, it interrupts this process of regeneration, effectively foreclosing the curative process Gibbons emphatically associates with growing seasons and garden paths. The agency's decision also authorizes the xenophobic dimensions of Ellen's biological family and rejects an alternatively fluid and inclusive familial model. The state re-places Ellen in a "home" constructed on the very grounds of white supremacy and exploitation, hence the thickness of (white) blood wins out.

Ellen observes that the judge—in positing her family as part of "society's cornerstone"—"had us all mixed up with a different group of folks," since her family "never was a Roman pillar but is and always has been a crumbly old brick" (56). Gibbons summons the Eurocentric formula for white purity and supremacy: Greek and Roman civilizations as conglomerate figure for civilization itself, a figuring that invariably measures white superiority against the "uncivilized" cultures of darker peoples. As Ellen's white racial defenses soften, the court attempts to bolster them. Ellen must struggle not only against the indoctrination of her childhood, which enforced white supremacy as her racial privilege (the messages she received from her mother's family, as from the school system and the culture in which it thrived, that blacks "would not do" and that her father's "evil" resulted from his association with blacks), but also against legal and political institutions determined to uphold the color line by insisting upon the inviolability of white bloodlines.

Firmly ensconced within the acceptable bounds of her grandmother's home, Ellen nonetheless discovers a route beyond its racist borders. It is from the vantage point of institutionally enforced familial membership that Ellen initiates her self-consciously articulated quest for an acceptable, not necessarily biological, home and family. Gibbons continues to make racial identity central to Ellen's attempted reconfiguration of these structures. Desperate for companionship and care, Ellen develops an apprenticeship with Mavis, one of the black women with whom she works in the fields while living with her grandmother. Mavis affirms Ellen's resemblance to her deceased mother, enabling the child to resist her grandmother's insistent equating of Ellen with her father. Significantly, her relationship with

Mavis enables Ellen to claim her maternal inheritance while struggling to unlearn the racism of her familial and cultural environments.

Working in the fields with Mavis—like working in the garden with Julia and Roy—reinvents Ellen's one season of happiness in the garden with her mother. Mavis, like Ellen's mother, lays down a path for Ellen to follow, and Ellen, in turn, works the trail Mavis leaves just as she worked her mother's trail. The rows of the fields mimic the paths and trails, both literal and figurative, so prominent throughout the novel. Here, too, Gibbons weaves narratives of familial reconstruction with narratives of racial reconfiguration. The "path" upon which Ellen embarks during her field-work summer becomes the path that leads to her newly constituted vision of the home she desires.

Drawn to the life outside her grandmother's pallid mansion, the child eases her hunger for meaningful, loving family ties by observing Mavis's family at day's end. Ellen, retaining her habit of marking racial difference with the prefix "colored," discovers the "colored path" toward home:

> While I was eavesdropping at the colored house I started a list of all that a family should have. Of course there is the mama and the daddy but if one has to be missing then it is OK if the one left can count for two. But not just anybody can count for more then his or her self.
>
> While I watched Mavis and her family I thought I would bust open if I did not get one of them for my own self. Back then I had not figured out how to go about getting one but I had a feeling it could be got. (67)

The process of denaturalizing family ties essential to Ellen's quest for a new home involves her reconceptualization of home as something one might "get" as opposed to something one simply has. Additionally, as Ellen comes to realize that the models of home available within her extended family do not meet her requirements, she must negotiate the color line, which insists that "colored house[s]" provide not models but antimodels of white homes.

Indeed, Ellen's report (just before moving from her grandmother's house to Nadine's) that "this time this would *not* be home" emerges specifically in the context of the distance, both literal and figurative, from Nadine's to what Ellen has come to call the "colored path" toward "home" (emphasis added, 94). Ellen relinquishes the tenets of "natural" family ties and, consequently, as she puts it, "do[es] not have to feel sad about being here [at Nadine's] in the middle of a place so far from the house at the end of the colored path" (94). The path to which Ellen refers here is, in actuality, the path from her grandmother's estate to the houses of the field laborers with whom Ellen worked all summer. Preparing to leave her grandmother's, Ellen explains,

> I knew I had found a little something on that colored path that I could not name but I said to myself to mark down what you saw tonight because it might come in handy. You mark down how they laugh and how they tell the toddler babies, you better watch out fo them steps. They steep! Mark all that down and see if you can figure out what made you take that trip every night. Then when you are by yourself one day the list you kept might make some sense and then you will know that this is the list you would take to a store if they made such a store and say to the man behind the counter give me this and this and this. And he would hand you back a home. (93–94)

Ellen's conception of the world remains firmly situated within a consumerist rhetoric and logic, and her reliance on the marker "colored" to distinguish one world from another persists. At the same time, the "colored path" and the lessons at its end provide Ellen with a model essential to the progress of her domestic and familial quest, a quest that entails critique of and antagonism toward these very tendencies. A continuation of the "path" laid down by her mother's lessons apropos discerning ripe from unripe, good from bad, the "colored path" comprises both the material means of access to a specific house, Mavis's, and the ideological process of reconstruction Ellen must undergo to achieve the "home" she lacks. Ellen arrives at Nadine's painfully conscious of the fact that her chosen path—the "colored path"—leads elsewhere.

Ellen self-consciously identifies domestic and familial characteristics in direct defiance of both the spoken and the unspoken racial boundaries excluding Starletta's and Mavis's homes from those culturally sanctioned as models or substitutes for her own. It is significant that Julia and Roy's home similarly provides Ellen with crucial exposure to and insight into alternative models, contributing to the conglomerate picture she incrementally sketches of a reconfigured home and family. Gibbons situates Ellen's whiteness as at once inscribed by white supremacist familial and cultural forms and practices and as susceptible to revision.

In closing, the novel equivocates. But does this equivocation derive from Gibbons giving with one hand what she takes away with another or, instead, from constraints that may be inherent in white antiracist fiction? Ellen's indoctrination into white supremacist ideology insures that when she looks at Starletta she sees a stereotype of a "little black girl." Ellen even admits that Starletta "never has said much good or bad to me" (84). The novel can be faulted for this portrait and for its habit of making black characters and homes serviceable vis-à-vis Ellen's tragic tale and heroic advances. But insofar as it reveals the machinations of whiteness that are responsible for this kind of marginalization, Gibbons's novel, far from taking white centrality for granted, persistently strives to undermine it. The narrative struggle is one insistent upon "making room for" Starletta's story. Nonetheless, Starletta remains a narrative absence, a gap. This problem is one built into the very fabric of Gibbons's novelistic challenge here—the entire tale is told from the perspective of an abused, outcast little girl whose ability to empathize with or imagine the subjectivities of others is necessarily constrained. Aside from Ellen, no other character in *Ellen Foster* moves beyond type into fictive personhood. But, importantly, Gibbons makes special claims for Starletta and for Ellen's ability to move beyond the very restrictions at issue here.

Interestingly, while Gibbons makes little or no effort to develop Starletta's character beyond Ellen's caricature-ish portrait, the author admits to having considered and then abandoned the possibility. Discussing the origins of *Ellen Foster,* Gibbons explains that she "began writing a poem from the viewpoint of the black girl who becomes Ellen's best friend, but the story gradually metamorphosed into a novel." In the same interview, she also mentions that, when she began a subsequent novel, *Charms for a New Life,* she had planned to continue the story of the black midwife introduced in *A Cure for Dreams,* but decided that the midwife character in *Charms* "should be white, not black, as originally conceived."[7] The tension apparent in Gibbons's account between the desire to tell a black tale, as it were, and the drive to interrogate white racial identity may be at the heart of *Ellen Foster*'s final uneasiness. In the end Ellen's "triumph"—embodied, as the text insists, in her relation to Starletta—rings slightly tinny.

When Ellen acknowledges that she "came a long way to get here," her "here" is both physical domestic space (the foster home) and ideological space (125). Gibbons's closing emphasis on Ellen's relationship to Starletta and to black people more generally privileges interracial (black/white) resolutions over intraracial (white/white) ones. But because Gibbons has not established adequate grounds for a truly mutual interaction between Ellen and Starletta, Ellen's imagined reunion wherein she and Starletta will finally be "even" is more wishful thinking than likely outcome (100). This problem arises, not because Gibbons mistakes her novel's "real" concern for race relations (as reviewer Ralph C. Wood claims), but because the race relations at the very heart of *Ellen Foster* have as much to

7. Kaye Gibbons, interview by Bob Summer, in *Publishers Weekly* 240 (February 8, 1993), 60, 61.

do with the way " 'race' betrays family" in Ellen's biological family as they
have to do with interracial alliances.[8]

Because the novel ends with a protracted reverie about Starletta, Gibbons signals to us that here is the "here" to which Ellen has traveled all
along. Forty pages sooner, however, Ellen's conception of what family and
race, including whiteness, mean and do not mean crystallizes:

> I wonder to myself am I the same girl who would not drink after Starletta
> two years ago or eat a colored biscuit when I was starved?
> It is the same girl but I am old now I know it is not the germs you cannot
> see that slide off her lips and on to a glass then to your white lips that will
> hurt you or turn you colored. What you had better worry about though is
> the people you know and trusted they would be like you because you were
> all made in the same batch. You need to look over your shoulder at the one
> who is in charge of holding you up and see if that is a knife he has in his
> hand. And it might not be a colored hand. But it is a knife. (85)

These thoughts prompt Ellen to muse, "Sometimes I even think I was cut
out to be colored and I got bleached and sent to the wrong bunch of folks"
(85). As at novel's end, Ellen gropes toward her "here," a destination whose
physical manifestation she has discovered in her foster home but whose
less material dimensions she will continue to explore and reimagine armed
with potentially transformative experiences and realizations. Skin color
does not determine character. Being from the "same batch" does not insure
against cruelty and abandonment. Violence between family members is
far more likely than violence between strangers. The myth of the deranged
racial other is a smoke screen used to obscure the real story of domestic
violence and sexual abuse in white homes. White womanhood, when
sculpted in response to imagined black male sexual aggression, is both
deformed and disabled—convinced that the enemy lies in wait outside,
white women are made helpless against the enemy among them. Here lies
the fertile ground Ellen has both stumbled upon and determinedly sifted
as the basis for her continued growth.

Kaye Gibbons's first novel may not, as its conclusion so much strives to
imply, heal the divisions between Ellen and Starletta (or between Ellen's
and Starletta's worlds), because these divisions have been made both
palpable and hardy by history, culture, and personal trauma. Nonetheless,

8. Ralph C. Wood, "Gumption and Grace in the Novels of Kaye Gibbons," *The
Christian Century* 109 (September 23–30, 1992): 843; Mab Segrest, *Memoir of a
Race Traitor* (Boston: South End Press, 1992), 102.

Ellen Foster reveals the ways in which ordained domestic and familial models are intimately wed to economies of race and gender that, in American culture now as historically, are made and maintained in the service of white supremacist patriarchy. Ellen's physical and conceptual dislocation from her "real" home and family enables her ultimate relocation, both literal and ideological, in a home and family where the possibility of resisting those economies constitutes her real triumph.

Haunting the Borderlands

La Llorona in Sandra Cisneros's "Woman Hollering Creek"

JACQUELINE DOYLE

> *Aiiii aiiii aiiiii*
> She is crying for her dead child
> the lover gone, the lover not yet come:
> Her *grito* splinters the night
> —Gloria Anzaldúa, "My Black *Angelos,*"
> *Borderlands/La Frontera*

"If I were asked what it is I write about," Sandra Cisneros commented in a lecture in 1986, "I would have to say I write about those ghosts inside that haunt me, that will not let me sleep, of that which even memory does not like to mention." Poverty, the unrecorded lives of the powerless, the unheard voices of "thousands of silent women" are some of the ghosts that haunt *The House on Mango Street*, dedicated in two languages "*A las Mujeres*/To the Women." Cisneros's narrator, Esperanza, chronicles the unhappy histories of "the ones who cannot out," women immobilized by poverty, cultural and linguistic barriers, restrictive gender roles, and domestic violence. Gazing out of windows they cannot open, standing in doorways they cannot exit, woman after woman on Mango Street is trapped at the threshold or boundary of a room or house not her own. Marin moons in the doorway, "waiting for a car to stop, a star to fall, someone to change her life." Mamacita "sits all day by the window and plays the Spanish radio show," afraid to go outside because she doesn't speak English. Because Rafaela is young and beautiful, her husband locks her in her room each Tuesday night while he plays dominoes. Minerva comes over each week "black and blue" with the "same story." Sally claims her father "never hits [her] hard," but she marries to escape, only to sit alone in her husband's house "because she is afraid to go outside without his permission." She looks "at the walls, at how neatly their corners meet, the linoleum roses on the floor, the ceiling smooth as wedding cake."[1]

The story of Cleófilas in Cisneros's "Woman Hollering Creek" extends and revises such histories, opening a borderland space where old myths take on new resonance and new forms and where new stories are possible. Haunted by the legendary wail of La Llorona, Cleófilas seeks a language to articulate her own story and the stories of the mute feminine victims of male violence in the newspapers. As Adrienne Rich writes in "Natural Resources," *"we have lived with violence so long"*:

> Am I to go on saying
> for myself, for her
> *This is my body*
> *take and destroy it?*

Reconstituting the "communion of saints" as a community including women, Cisneros transfigures the *grito* of La Llorona, and mines new natural resources for the expectant mother Cleófilas and her sisters and *comadres*. Felice's joyous holler as she and Cleófilas cross Woman Hollering Creek releases new mother tongues. "What kind of talk was that coming from a woman," Cleófilas marvels of her border crossing. "But then again, Felice was like no woman she'd ever met. Can you imagine, when we crossed the *arroyo* she just started yelling like a crazy, she would later say to her father and brothers. Just like that. Who would've thought?"[2]

1. This essay was originally published, in somewhat different form, in *Frontiers: A Journal of Women Studies* 16:1 (1996); a shorter version was presented at the American Literature Association Conference (1994). Special thanks to Ruth Jenkins (California State University, Fresno), Stephen D. Gutierrez (California State University, Hayward), William Howarth (Princeton University), the Frontiers collective, and a very special thanks to Susan Roberson (Auburn University) for their attentive readings of early drafts of the paper.

Sandra Cisneros, "Ghosts and Voices: Writing from Obsession," in "From a Writer's Notebook," *The Americas Review* 15, no. 1 (1987): 73 (see also 72, 76); Cisneros, *The House on Mango Street* (New York: Random House, 1984; New York: Vintage, 1989), 110, 27, 77, 85, 92, 102.

2. Adrienne Rich, "Natural Resources," *The Dream of a Common Language: Poems 1974–1977* (New York: W. W. Norton, 1978), 64–65; Cisneros, "Woman Hollering Creek," in *Woman Hollering Creek and Other Stories* (New York: Random House, 1991), 55–56. Subsequent page numbers from this story will be supplied parenthetically in the text.

In an interview in 1988, Cisneros discussed the difficulties of growing up as a Mexican American woman, "always straddling two countries . . . but not belonging to either culture," "trying to define some middle ground" where revision and reinvention of cultural and sexual roles might be possible, only to be "told you're a traitor to your culture."[3] In *Borderlands/La Frontera* Gloria Anzaldúa constructs her "new *mestiza* identity" in just such a "middle ground" or borderland area, where languages, cultures, religions, and gender identities collide and cross. The "Borderlands," as Anzaldúa defines them, encompass both geographic and psychic spaces, a polyglot interzone that is "physically present wherever two or more cultures edge each other, where people of different races occupy the same territory, where under, lower, middle and upper classes touch, where the space between two individuals shrinks with intimacy."[4] This borderland terrain exists both inside and outside the individual; Anzaldúa maps the competing cultural, national, racial, sexual, and linguistic discourses occupying the spaces within and surrounding the Mexican American woman, even as she undoes the static oppositions that would confine and immobilize her. Moving beyond the "*virgen/puta* (whore) dichotomy," Anzaldúa reconstructs *mestiza* identity as dynamic and multiple (84), the borderlands as a region of constant transition and transformation, where "languages cross-pollinate and are re-vitalized . . . die and are born" (viii). The new *mestiza* speaks "a forked tongue, a variation of two languages" and numerous dialects (55). "She reinterprets history and, using new symbols, she shapes new myths" (82). She remothers herself and refashions her gods to give birth to her own identity.

The issue of "redefining myself or controlling my own destiny or my own sexuality," Cisneros said in an interview, is the "ghost I'm still wrestling with." In the stories in *Woman Hollering Creek*, Cisneros reshapes the myths that define Chicana identity, conjuring the ghostly apparitions of what Anzaldúa calls "Our Mothers": La Virgen de Guadalupe, La Malinche, La Llorona (30–31). Norma Alarcón compellingly argues that these highly charged "symbolic figures" have been used as "reference point[s] not only for controlling, interpreting, or visualizing women" in Mexican American culture, "but also to wage a domestic battle of

3. Pilar E. Rodríguez Aranda, "On the Solitary Fate of Being Mexican, Female, Wicked and Thirty-three: An Interview with Writer Sandra Cisneros," *The Americas Review* 18, no. 1 (1990): 65–66.
4. Gloria Anzaldúa, *Borderlands/La Frontera: The New Mestiza* (San Francisco: Spinsters/Aunt Lute, 1987), vii. Subsequent page numbers will appear parenthetically in the text.

stifling proportions."[5] Cisneros reenters the "quiet war" zone defined by Esperanza in *The House on Mango Street* to chart the interstices and in-betweens of the borderlands, to remap symbolic maternal landscapes, and to open a protean space where La Llorona's ghostly wail is replaced by "a voice all [her] own," a "high, silver voice" that calls Cleófilas to a new spiritual birth (51). If Octavio Paz famously defined Mexicans as "the sons of *la Malinche*," Cisneros surveys the possibilities for the daughters of La Llorona.[6]

"Woman Hollering Creek" charts psychological, linguistic, and spiritual border crossings. The story appropriately begins on a literal threshold and a literal border. Don Serafín grants Juan Pedro Martínez Sánchez "permission" to take his daughter Cleófilas Enriqueta DeLeón Hernández "as his bride, across her father's threshold, over several miles of dirt road and several miles of paved, over one border and beyond to a town *en el otro lado*—on the other side . . ." (43). Cleófilas crosses these physical boundaries only within the confines of a patriarchal economy where she is permitted to exchange residence in her father's house for residence in her husband's, to exchange a town on one side of the border for a town much like it on the other. Trapped with her abusive husband in Seguín, Texas, Cleófilas thinks of Mexico: "The town of gossips. The town of dust and despair. Which she has traded for this town of gossips. This town of dust, despair" (50).

To reach this residence north of the border, Juan Pedro drove Cleófilas over yet another significant border or crossing point, the bridge spanning La Gritona, the creek behind his house. "The natives only knew the *arroyo* one crossed on the way to San Antonio, and then once again on the way back, was called Woman Hollering, a name no one from these parts

5. Aranda, "On the Solitary Fate," 67; Norma Alarcón, "Chicana's Feminist Literature: A Re-vision through Malintzin/or Malintzin: Putting Flesh Back on the Object," in *This Bridge Called My Back: Writings by Radical Women of Color*, ed. Cherríe Moraga and Gloria Anzaldúa (Watertown: Persephone Press, 1982), 182, 189 n. 1. For further significant rereadings of La Malinche and La Llorona, see Emma Pérez, "Sexuality and Discourse: Notes from a Chicana Survivor," *Chicana Critical Issues*, ed. Norma Alarcón et al. (Berkeley: Third Woman Press, 1993), esp. 53–56; Cordelia Candelaria, "La Malinche, Feminist Prototype," *Frontiers* 5, no. 2 (1980): 1–6; and Candelaria, "Letting *La Llorona* Go, or Re/reading History's Tender Mercies," *Heresies* 7, no. 3 (1993): 111–15.

6. "I have begun my own quiet war," announces Esperanza, "Simple. Sure. I am one who leaves the table like a man, without putting back the chair or picking up the plate." Cisneros, *House*, 89; see Octavio Paz, *The Labyrinth of Solitude: Life and Thought in Mexico*, trans. Lysander Kemp (New York: Grove Press, 1961), chap. 4.

questioned, little less understood" (46). As a newlywed crossing the bridge, Cleófilas wondered whether "pain or rage" inspired the woman's "holler," but laughed too at the "funny name for a creek so pretty and full of happily ever after" (46). The "orchid of blood" from her first split lip replaces her bridal bouquet and girlish dreams of "happily ever after" (47, 43). Now she sits each day "by the creek's edge," with one child by her side and one in her womb, confined at this boundary line just beyond the back threshold of Juan Pedro's house, because "there is no place to go" (43, 53, 51).

The creek's mysterious name, and perhaps her own situation, reminds Cleófilas of another unhappy wife and mother confined to the banks of a river: "Is it La Llorona, the weeping woman? La Llorona, who drowned her own children. Perhaps La Llorona is the one they named the creek after, she thinks, remembering all the stories she learned as a child" (51). A folk tale told for centuries in Mexico and the Southwest, "La Llorona" survives today in many forms. In one common version, a proud young girl marries above her station and is so enraged when her husband takes a mistress of his own class that she drowns their children in the river. Stricken by grief when she is unable to retrieve them, La Llorona dies on the river's edge. But the villagers to this day hear a voice in the wind and the water— "Aaaaiiiii . . . my children. Where are my children?"—and see a wailing apparition in white walking up and down the riverbank after dark.[7] The story of "La Llorona" often ends with a warning to children to stay indoors at night, for outside they may fall into her clutches. Cleófilas's neighbors tell her to stay away from the creek, "Don't go out there after dark, *mi'jita*. Stay near the house. . . . You'll catch a fright wandering about in the dark, and then you'll see how right we were" (51).

Immersed in romance novels and the *telenovelas*, Cleófilas is initiated into a culture of weeping women, the tale of "La Llorona" retold in countless ways around her. She is imaginatively stirred by the *telenovela María de Nadie* without noticing the parallels to La Llorona's story in the "poor Argentine country girl who had the ill fortune of falling in love" with the son of her wealthy employer (52). Cleófilas's own life begins to resemble La Llorona's as she decodes and erases evidence of her husband's infidelities: "A doubt. Slender as a hair. A washed cup set back on the shelf wrong-side-up. Her lipstick, and body talc, and hairbrush

7. In another common version, her children have been born out of wedlock, and her rage is provoked by her lover's pending marriage. See Candelaria, "Letting *La Llorona* Go," 112–13; and José E. Limón, "La Llorona, the Third Legend of Greater Mexico: Cultural Symbols, Women, and the Political Unconscious," in *Between Borders: Essays on Mexicana/Chicana History*, ed. Adelaida R. Del Castillo (Encino, Calif.: Floricanto Press, 1990), 399–432.

all arranged in the bathroom a different way. No. Her imagination. The house the same as always. Nothing" (50). Janice Radway suggests that romance novels with their "fairy tale" endings appeal to a "deep-seated sense of betrayal" in their readers; "life has not given them all it once promised." Looking for the "great love of [her] life" and to move up in the world, Cleófilas has crossed the border to find a life "like a *telenovela*, only now the episodes got sadder and sadder" (44, 45, 52). The names of her two widowed neighbors, Dolores and Soledad, suggest "pain" and "solitude": the tears of La Llorona and of the Mater Dolorosa.[8] Anzaldúa exposes the "institutionalized oppression" in the Church's use of La Virgen "to make us docile and enduring," and the exploitation of La Llorona "to make us a long-suffering people" (31). So Cleófilas, dreaming of romance and marriage, absorbs the message of fidelity and suffering from religion, society, and popular culture. In the words of her favorite *telenovela* in Mexico, *Tú o Nadie:* "You or no one. Because to suffer for love is good. The pain all sweet somehow in the end" (45). She is marked doubly by the romances that enthrall her when her husband throws a book—"*her* book, a love story by Corín Telado"—across the room and raises "a hot welt across [her] cheek" (52).

La Llorona weeps, Anzaldúa observes, because there are no other options in her culture. "Wailing is the Indian, Mexican and Chicana woman's feeble protest when she has no other recourse" (33). Octavio Paz notoriously interpreted all of the "Mexican representations of Maternity" as essentially "passive figures": the Blessed Virgin signifying "pure receptivity"; Cortés's Indian mistress La Malinche/La Chingada signifying the raped mother; and La Llorona signifying "the 'long-suffering Mexican mother' we celebrate on the tenth of May." Paz did not explore the contradictions implicit in celebrating on Mother's Day a mother who murders her own children, however. Nor did he release these figures from the immobilizing *virgen/puta* opposition that elevates La Llorona as a Mexican Mater Dolorosa while it debases her as a *mujer mala* akin to La Malinche. As Cordelia Candelaria has recently argued, "the *Llorona* legend begs for reconsideration and possible recuperation." Candelaria's poem "La Llorona: Portrait by the River" opens, *"La luz es todo: light is crucial."* The "light" in which this ghostly foremother is seen determines our perspective:

8. Janice A. Radway, "Women Read the Romance: The Interaction of Text and Context," in *Feminist Literary Theory: A Reader*, 2d ed., ed. Mary Eagleton (Cambridge: Blackwell, 1996), 201; on the cult surrounding the *Mater Dolorosa* ("Our Lady of Sorrows")—the Virgin as Pietà, mother grieving her dead son—see Marina Warner, *Alone of All Her Sex: The Myth and the Cult of the Virgin Mary* (New York: Alfred A. Knopf, 1976), 206–23.

The splash of ripples
As she bends to rinse tired feet
Paint her flesh an instant shine
Bright as tears. Or hope.[9]

Traditionally her reflection has been dark. A borderland figure who combines aspects of both the long-suffering *Virgen* and the rebellious *puta*, she is most often depicted as a "wicked woman" and a "monstrous image of depravity."[10] Like La Malinche, she "roams the streets . . . wailing for her children and revenging herself on men"; both women have been known to entice men from their paths after dark, "calling to them in the familiar voice of their wives and sweethearts." In some legends, La Llorona is explicitly identified with La Malinche, who murdered herself and her son by Cortés when he threatened to take the boy to Spain.[11] In "Malinchista, a Myth Revised," Alicia Gaspar de Alba locates La Llorona in the borderlands where nations cross and history is silent:

The woman shrieking along the littered bank of the Río Grande is not sorry. She is looking for revenge. Centuries she has been blamed for the murder of her child, the loss of her people, as if Tenochtitlan would not have fallen without her sin. History does not sing of the conquistador who prayed to a white god as he pulled two ripe hearts out of the land.[12]

Candelaria suggests that La Llorona survives because her "meanings are multiple" and culturally resonant. Her story appears in many forms; its origins remain subterranean and obscure. Many commentators believe that La Llorona substantially predates La Malinche and colonial history. Richard Dorson discovers La Llorona in "an Aztec goddess who sacrificed babies and disappeared shrieking into lakes or rivers." She appears sometimes as the goddesses Cihuapipíltin, who died in childbirth and then

9. Octavio Paz, "The Sons of *La Malinche*," in *Labyrinth of Solitude*, 75, 85; Candelaria, "Letting *La Llorona* Go," 113, 115.
10. See Anzaldúa, *Borderlands/La Frontera*, 30; Frances Toor, *A Treasury of Mexican Folkways* (New York: Crown Publishers, 1947), 532–33; and Ramón Saldívar, *Chicano Narrative: The Dialectics of Difference* (Madison: University of Wisconsin Press, 1990), 189.
11. See, for example, Candelaria, "Letting *La Llorona* Go," 113; John M. Ingham, *Mary, Michael, and Lucifer: Folk Catholicism in Central Mexico* (Austin: University of Texas Press, 1986), 110–12; and Edward Garcia Kraul and Judith Beatty, foreword to *The Weeping Woman: Encounters with La Llorona*, ed. Edward Garcia Kraul and Judith Beatty (Santa Fe: Word Process, 1988), xi.
12. Alicia Gaspar de Alba, "Malinchista, a Myth Revised," in *Three Times a Woman: Chicana Poetry*, Alicia Gaspar de Alba, María Herrera-Sobek, and Demetria Martínez (Tempe, Ariz.: Bilingual Review/Press, 1989), 17.

returned to haunt the living, more often as Cihuacóhuatl, who roamed the night "dressed in white with a cradle on her shoulders, wailing for her lost child."[13] In *Borderlands/La Frontera*, Anzaldúa resurrects "Cihuacoatl/La Llorona" as "Snake Woman . . . Daughter of the Night, traveling the dark terrains of the unknown searching for the lost parts of herself" (38).

In "My Black *Angelos*," Anzaldúa explores the lost terrains of her fore-mothers Cihuacoatl and La Llorona, taking on the power and darkness of the spirit who whimpers softly at her door, and whose "*grito* splinters the night." The poet's black Angel "turns upwind tracking" her, sensing "fear" and the "stink of carrion," their dark kinship. First "putting words" in the poet's head, then crawling into her very spine, "shining under my skin in the dark/whirling my bones twirling/till they're hollow reeds," the Muse crosses the threshold of her "door," erases the boundaries between self and other, and finally between the living and the dead: "We sweep through the streets/*con el viento corremos*/we roam with the souls of the dead" (*Borderlands/La Frontera*, 184–85).

Like Anzaldúa's speaker, Cisneros's Cleófilas also feels the urgent tug of personal connection with La Llorona, her sorrow and also her subversive power. She hears "La Llorona calling to her. She is sure of it" (51). The stream that is "only a muddy puddle in the summer" rushes now that it is spring—"because of the rains, a good-size alive thing, a thing with a voice all its own, all day and all night calling in its high, silver voice" (51). The "alive thing" does not call Cleófilas to death, however, but to a springlike renewal. As Cisneros renews La Llorona's story, and rewrites her fate, she releases La Llorona from her tears. She frees her to leave her unfaithful and abusive husband and to take her children away with her—to choose life instead of death, and to cross the river instead of remaining eternally trapped on its banks.

Cisneros's La Llorona cries for the lost women, mourning the victims and casualties of male violence, mourning Cleófilas. As the men laugh outside the kitchen window, Cleófilas washes dishes and thinks of Maxi-miliano from across the road, "who was said to have killed his wife in an ice-house brawl when she came at him with a mop" (51), and of the mute and nameless women whose stories flood the newspapers:

Was Cleófilas just exaggerating as her husband always said? It seemed the newspapers were full of such stories. This woman found on the side of the

---

13. Candelaria, "Letting *La Llorona* Go," 114; see Richard Dorson, foreword to *Folktales of Mexico*, ed. Américo Paredes (Chicago: University of Chicago Press, 1970), xvi, and Toor, *Treasury*, 534.

interstate. This one pushed from a moving car. This one's cadaver, this one unconscious, this one beaten blue. Her ex-husband, her husband, her lover, her father, her brother, her uncle, her friend, her co-worker. Always. The same grisly news in the pages of the dailies. She dunked a glass under the soapy water for a moment—shivered. (52)

If her husband "always" discredits Cleófilas's fears, nevertheless the "grisly news" is "always" the same. Her own bruises bear mute witness to the reality of "such stories" even if her husband dismisses her recital of the facts as "just exaggerating." Lorraine Code observes that women's stories, one of the "principal vehicles of self-understanding," are routinely subjected to a disempowering "double standard of credibility." Only certain "kinds of utterances" can be voiced and heard within male-dominated "rhetorical spaces." Cleófilas's voice is lost in the jeering silence of what Code calls "systematic incredulity," where stories of abuse and sexual assault are dismissed or contradicted, "undermin[ing] not just the 'truth' of the experiences, but [women's] sense of self, of credibility, of trustworthiness."[14]

Beneath the talk at home and in the icehouse a silent subtext struggles for expression. Cleófilas is mute in the face of her husband's violence; "speechless, motionless, numb," the first time and each time thereafter, "she could think of nothing to say, said nothing" (48). She is also voiceless with the men in the icehouse, where she "sits mute beside their conversation, . . . and finally becomes good at predicting where the talk will lead . . ." (48). Their talk will lead nowhere, for the discourse of the men is strangled as well, "never finds its way out" (48). Their long evenings will end in tears "if they are lucky." If they are not lucky, violence will be their only mode of expression, as their "fists try to speak" (48). In her own home Cleófilas suffers both modes of frustrated male utterance. After every beating, she silently "stroked the dark curls of the man who wept and would weep like a child, his tears of repentance and shame . . ." (48).

For Cleófilas, the quietly insistent voice of La Llorona in the creek counters the relentless "whispering" and "murmur of talk" in Seguín, where there is "no more privacy" than there was in the town of her birth (50). Communication among the women on both sides of the border revolves around the *telenovelas* and around men. Her Texan neighbors Soledad and Dolores might have known more about the etymology of "Woman Hollering Creek," Cleófilas guesses, but "they were too busy remembering the men who had left through either choice or circumstance

14. Lorraine Code, *Rhetorical Spaces: Essays on Gendered Locations* (New York: Routledge, 1995), 183, ix, 59–60.

and would never come back" (47). Gossip, in this town as in the other, is the provenance not just of women but of men as well. In Mexico she locates it in the town center and on the church steps, in Texas at the icehouse, a gathering place for the men (50). While some anthropologists suggest that gossip functions as "an important source of social power for women," others have concluded that "being under constant verbal surveillance restricts the behavior of women and helps keep them in their place."[15] Cleófilas fears her husband, but she also fears the "whispering" and "murmur of talk" in both towns, the social "disgrace" that would attend her return to her father's house. "What would the neighbors say?" (50).

If town gossip and her husband's strictures keep her in her place, Cleófilas mobilizes another discourse of power to break free from them: "Because the doctor has said so" (53). Deploying the American doctor's voice to counter her husband's voice, she secures permission to cross the *arroyo* and journey to San Antonio for the health of her unborn child and for her own safety (physical, and also emotional and spiritual): "Because she is going to make sure the baby is not turned around backward this time to split her down the center" (53). In return, she agrees to maintain silence, assuring her husband: "No, she won't mention it. She promises. If the doctor asks she can say she fell down the front steps or slipped when she was in the backyard, slipped out back, she could tell him that" (53). She keeps her promise, but La Llorona speaks through her: Cleófilas's torrent of tears and the "black-and-blue marks all over" her body tell the story she still has no voice for herself. "This lady doesn't even speak English," says Graciela to Felice on the phone as they plan Cleófilas's escape, "She hasn't been allowed to call home or write or nothing" (54).

Now crossing in reverse her husband's threshold, the bridge over Woman Hollering Creek, the U.S./Mexico border, and her father's threshold, Cleófilas has "slipped out back" in another sense, slipping out while her husband is still at work. Although she remains within the patriarchal economy of exchange in returning from husband to father, she has also encountered a woman in her border crossings "like no woman she'd ever met" (56). Independent, self-determined, self-possessed, Felice drives her to San Antonio in a pickup that is "hers," that "she herself had chosen," that "she herself was paying for" (55). Cleófilas wonders "what kind of talk" this is "coming from a woman," when Felice explains, "I used to have a Pontiac Sunbird. But those cars are for *viejas*. Pussy cars. Now this here is

---

15. See ibid., chap. 7; and Ruth Borker, "Anthropology: Social and Cultural Perspectives," in *Women and Language in Literature and Society*, ed. Sally McConnell-Ginet, Ruth Borker, and Nelly Furman (New York: Praeger, 1980), 34, 36.

a *real* car" (54). And she is even more amazed by the "yell as loud as any mariachi" that Felice lets rip as they cross Woman Hollering Creek (55). When Cleófilas had asked about La Gritona, "no one could say whether the woman had hollered from anger or pain" (46). Now through Felice this binary opposition is undone; Hélène Cixous might suggest that La Llorona/La Gritona begins to laugh.[16] "Who would've thought?" Cleófilas wonders back in Mexico. "Who would've? Pain or rage, perhaps, but not a hoot like the one Felice had just let go. Makes you want to holler like Tarzan, Felice had said" (56).

When the motherless Cleófilas returns, by way of two women—or *comadres*,[17] to her father and brothers, maternal bonds crisscross with paternal bonds. It is through maternity that she realizes the strength of the literal bond between parent and child, as opposed to the symbolic bond conferred by marriage. She remembers her father's words—"I am your father, I will never abandon you" (43)—only "as a mother," with her son beside her and her unborn child inside her: "Only now as a mother did she remember. Now, when she and Juan Pedrito sat by the creek's edge. How when a man and a woman love each other, sometimes that love sours. But a parent's love for a child, a child's for its parents, is another thing entirely" (43).

Felice and Graciela speculate that Cleófilas has been named after "one of those Mexican saints . . . a martyr or something" (54).[18] Her son Juan Pedrito has been named after his father. But she may pass on new knowledge and new names to her next child, for as Graciela and Felice joke, "When her kid's born she'll have to name her after us, right?" (55). Graciela's sonogram of the child *in utero* is on more than one level a sounding

16. Cisneros's revision of La Llorona suggests parallels to Hélène Cixous's revision of Medusa: women's history as a history of silences, a language written in mother's milk, and above all a liberation from false polarities within male discourse. "You only have to look at the Medusa straight on to see her. And she's not deadly. She's beautiful and she's laughing" (Cixous, "The Laugh of the Medusa," trans. Keith Cohen and Paula Cohen, in *New French Feminisms: An Anthology,* ed. Elaine Marks and Isabelle de Courtivron [New York: Schocken Books, 1981], 255).

17. The term *comadre,* or, literally translated, "co-mother," traditionally refers to the woman a mother has chosen as godmother for her child. Today it is also used simply as a term of respect and affection for a female friend. Graciela calls Felice *comadre* at the end of their phone call (55).

18. My research has not yielded a saint or martyr named Cleófilas, but St. Felicitas is famous as one of the relatively few saints and martyrs who was not a virgin; she faced martyrdom as an expectant mother. This cross of names and saints prefigures the crossing of Cleófilas and Felice in the last lines of the story. See Rev. Hugo H. Hoever, ed., *Saint Joseph Daily Missal* (New York: Catholic Book Publishing, 1957), 816.

of the invisible, a cloudy and fluid image of a form still forming, a picture of the future.[19] The nationality, language, appearance, and even the sex of the baby are indeterminate, as the doctor—or perhaps Cleófilas herself— refers to "he," and Graciela later—perhaps on the basis of the sonogram— refers to "her" (53, 55). Occupying what Julia Kristeva lyrically evokes as a realm before language, a realm without "borders, separations," the "formless unnameable embryo" curled within the body of the mother transcends boundaries and definitions: "FLASH—instant of time or of dream without time; inordinately swollen atoms of a bond, a vision, a shiver. . . . Photos of what is not yet visible and that language necessarily skims from afar, allusively."[20]

Cleófilas's new child embodies an emerging "hybrid" *mestiza* language and consciousness, as Graciela, Felice, Cleófilas, and the child yet-to-be-born, yet-to-be-named cross over in the polyglot interzone of the border-lands. When Cleófilas tells the story of Felice to her father and brothers, she enacts this crossing in a moment of laughter where she interchanges identities to become Felice, La Llorona, and the "silver voice" of the creek, thereby giving birth to her own felicity (Felice, *felicidad*), and grace (Graciela, *gracia*): "Then Felice began laughing again, but it wasn't Felice laughing. It was gurgling out of her own throat, a long ribbon of laughter, like water" (56).

The creek itself contains a linguistic crossing, known both as "Woman Hollering" and as "La Gritona." When Cleófilas wants to know more about the name, the natives can only speculate that the Indians might know: "*Pues, allá de los indios, quién sabe*—who knows . . ." (46). The languages mark shifting national boundaries: before the institution, in the 1840s, of the border that Cleófilas crosses twice, Texas was part of

19. Given the fluidity of the embryo's boundaries, and the fluid interchange between the women in the border zone, it is interesting to note that Limón identifies "fluid boundaries" as the central characteristic of the legends of La Llorona. Not only are the contours of the narrative fluid (the tale survives in countless variants) but the content as well: "For a female sensibility of *fluid* boundaries is precisely what is articulated in La Llorona's initial denial of her children through water; her fluid crying of tears for them and finally her implied hope of their restoration from the water-of-birth even as she herself becomes fluidity itself walking at the boundaries of the water in her flowing gown" (Limón, "La Llorona, the Third Legend," 418).

20. Julia Kristeva, "Stabat Mater," trans. Leon S. Roudiez, in *The Kristeva Reader*, ed. Toril Moi (New York: Columbia University Press, 1986), 176, 162. For a particularly suggestive treatment of language, pregnancy, and laughter, see also Kristeva's "Place Names," in *Desire in Language: A Semiotic Approach to Literature and Art*, ed. Leon S. Roudiez, trans. Thomas Gora, Alice Jardine, and Leon S. Roudiez (New York: Columbia University Press, 1980).

Mexico; before the Spanish conquest of Mexico, Mexico was Indian. Indeed Mexican independence from Spain was launched with a revolutionary "cry": Hidalgo y Castillo's *Grito de Dolores* in 1810. And this town north of the border, once south of the border, was named after a creek before 1838, when it was renamed Seguín in honor of the *tejano* Juan Seguín, who sided with the Americans over the annexation of his Mexican homeland Texas.[21] The "townspeople shrugged" at Cleófilas's questions, "because it was of no concern to their lives how this trickle of water received its curious name" (46). Yet it is through the hidden strata of meaning in the creek that Cleófilas recollects and claims her own life, history, identity, and voice.

In *Borderlands/La Frontera*, Anzaldúa insists on the importance to the *mestiza* of recuperating history and prehistory, of establishing a multi-tongued linguistic and ethnic identity, and of voicing what has been silenced: "I will have my voice: Indian, Spanish, white. I will have my serpent's tongue—my woman's voice, my sexual voice, my poet's voice. I will overcome the tradition of silence" (59). Cisneros invokes the centuries-old "tradition" of female silence, subservience, and suffering underwritten by Mexican culture and the Catholic Church in the names of Cleófilas's neighbors, both aspects of the Virgin celebrated widely in Mexico: La Virgen de la Soledad ("Virgin of the Lonely"), and Nuestra Señora de los Dolores ("Our Lady of Sorrows").[22] As Cleófilas and her driver hurtle over the bridge spanning Woman Hollering Creek, Felice laughs at the ubiquity of the Blessed Virgin, and the singularity of the mysterious La Gritona: "Did you ever notice, Felice continued, how nothing around here is named after a woman? Really. Unless she's the Virgin" (55).

In this androcentric culture of silently weeping women, where Soledad and Dolores devote themselves to the memories of their lost men, Cleófilas is bound to "this man, this father, this rival, this keeper, this master, this

21. Juan Seguín straddles the border in his divided loyalties and also in the mixed treatment he was accorded by Texan Anglo-Americans, who drove him out of San Antonio into Mexico, in 1842. He thereafter occupied an uneasy political position between the United States and Mexico, living in one and then the other country. He died in Mexico in 1890; in 1974 he was reburied in Seguín (formerly Walnut Creek), Texas. See Genaro M. Padilla, *My History, Not Yours: The Formation of Mexican American Autobiography* (Madison: University of Wisconsin Press, 1993), esp. 64–72.

22. See Toor, *Treasury*, 246; and Joseph L. Cassidy, *Mexico: Land of Mary's Wonders* (Paterson, N.J.: St. Anthony Guild Press, 1958), 92–102. In "Little Miracles, Kept Promises," Cisneros mentions Nuestra Señora de la Soledad, Nuestra Señora del Perpetuo Socorro, and also "Our Lady of Sorrows"; in "My Tocaya," a student at "Our Lady of Sorrows High School" disappears somewhere "in the vicinity of Dolorosa and Soledad" (*Woman Hollering Creek*, 128, 38).

husband till kingdom come" (49). The language reinscribes the "Our Father"—"Thy kingdom come: Thy will be done on earth as it is in heaven,"[23]—and the rigid ecclesiastical hierarchy used to subjugate women and sanction male dominance. "Wives, submit yourselves unto your own husbands, as unto the Lord," instructed St. Paul, "For the husband is the head of the wife, even as Christ is the head of the church. . . . Therefore as the church is subject unto Christ, so let the wives be to their own husbands in every thing" (Ephesians 5:22–24). On earth as defined by this heaven, it is the will of Cleófilas's husband, of Maximiliano from across the road, of the men in the icehouse and the newspapers, that will be done.

Cleófilas's spiritual transformation closely parallels the healing process for battered women that Susan Brooks Thistlewaite describes, a process of redefinition and reinterpretation. "Because the Bible is part of the fabric of the oppression of battered women," Thistlewaite argues, reinterpreting scripture from a feminist perspective is central to authorizing a voice and grounding a new sense of self.[24] Fleeing Juan Pedro, named for John and Peter, the two apostles associated with the patriarchal foundations of the Word and the Church,[25] Cleófilas returns to her father, Don Serafín, whose name derives both from "serpent" (associated with women in Christian as well as pre-Christian contexts) and "seraphim" (the choir of angels most ardently devoted to the divine).[26] When she married, "already did

23. Hoever, *Daily Missal,* 685.

24. Susan Brooks Thistlewaite, "Every Two Minutes: Battered Women and Feminist Interpretation," in *Weaving the Visions: New Patterns in Feminist Spirituality,* ed. Judith Plaskow and Carol P. Christ (New York: Harper and Row, 1989). Thistlewaite, who as a pastor counseled and organized Bible study groups for abused women, emphasizes the importance for battered women of taking control of Biblical texts—through feminist scriptural reinterpretation, through a liberation theology that stresses Jesus' protection of the powerless and his care for women, and through a recognition of the active role women played in discipleship, apostolic witness, and leadership in the early Church.

25. See John 1:1 ("In the beginning was the Word, and the Word was with God, and the Word was God") and Matthew 17:18 ("thou art Peter, and upon this rock I will build my church"). Much controversy surrounds the question of apostolic authority and the silencing of women in the early Christian community. See chap. 5, "Taming a Wild Tongue," in Anzaldúa's *Borderlands/La Frontera;* chaps. 10 and 11 in Margaret Brackenbury Crook, *Women and Religion* (Boston: Beacon Press, 1964); chap. 3 in Elaine Pagels, *The Gnostic Gospels* (New York: Random House, 1979; New York: Vintage, 1981); and chap. 8 in Rosemary Radford Ruether, *Readings toward a Feminist Theology* (Boston: Beacon Press, 1985).

26. See Jori Bas i Vidal, *Diccionario de los nombres de persona* (Barcelona: Editorial de Vecchi, S.A., 1988), 297.

he divine the morning his daughter would . . . dream of returning" (43). His parting words to Cleófilas, which she repeats with growing certainty, evoke a merciful God who will not abandon her in her distress. At first her memory of Don Serafín's promise is oddly tentative:

> He had said, after all, in the hubbub of parting: I am your father, I will never abandon you. He *had* said that, hadn't he, when he hugged and then let her go. But at the moment Cleófilas was busy looking for Chela, her maid of honor, to fulfill their bouquet conspiracy. She would not remember her father's parting words until later. *I am your father, I will never abandon you.* (43)

Cleófilas's initial uncertainty might suggest that the words are not her father's, but her gradual sense of conviction, the firmness of the italics, could also suggest her increasing confidence in her own scriptural interpretation, now that she is no longer distracted by the cultural "bouquet conspiracy."

Sensing what "drives a woman to the darkness under the trees" where La Llorona wails for her forsaken children (51), Cleófilas meditates on the bond between parent and child and the fate of her unborn infant. Her father's promise echoes lines from a Catholic hymn: "Could the Lord ever leave you? Could the Lord forget his love? Though a mother forsake her child, he will not abandon you."[27] Freeing herself from the scriptural interpretations that would designate Juan Pedro "this father . . . this husband till kingdom come," Cleófilas undergoes a spiritual metamorphosis from sorrow to grace, turning from the aptly named Soledad and Dolores to accept the help of Graciela and Felice.

Back home with her children, father, and brothers, Cleófilas overcomes the "tradition of silence," and claims her right to speak in tongues. Her gurgling laughter bears what Julia Kristeva terms "the imprint of an archaic moment." If place names function as "a *replacement* for what the speaker perceives as an archaic mother," then Cleófilas summons the mother tongue before or behind "Woman Hollering," "La Gritona," and the creek's hidden Indian name, a maternal semiotic *chora* preceding the paternal symbolic order. Felice spoke a "Spanish pocked with English" with her passenger, and Cleófilas "doesn't even speak English" (55, 54), but their crossing has released a lost mother tongue "like water," suggesting both the words from the Catholic Pentecost vigil—"He who believes in Me, from within him there shall flow rivers of living water," and also the ancient Aztec

27. See Dan Schutte, "Though the Mountains May Fall," *Seasonal Missalette* 8(8) (June 6, 1993): S8. This section of the hymn adapts Isaiah 49:15.

"goddess of running water, springs, and streams," Chalchiuhtlicue, who was invoked by her worshippers for the "protection of newborn children."[28]

Fluid and multiple, Cleófilas herself has become "woman hollering creek."[29]

Cleófilas's crossing through the borderland territory of the new *mestiza* is complex. As Anzaldúa writes, "Every increment of consciousness, every step forward is a *travesía*, a crossing. I am again an alien in new territory. And again, and again" (48). The shifting borders in "Woman Hollering Creek" are geographical, national, political, historical. They are also gendered, in the social divisions between men and women; biological, in the newborn's passage from its mother's body; psychological and spiritual, in Cleófilas's "step forward" into a new *mestiza* consciousness and voice. They are also linguistic, in the crossing of languages, the recovery of lost tongues, the discovery of new etymologies and definitions for the river and the legendary mother who haunts its banks: " . . . now in springtime, because of the rains, a good-size alive thing, a thing with a voice all its own, all day and all night calling in its high, silver voice. Is it La Llorona, the weeping woman?" (51).

Through successive dislocations, Cleófilas relocates herself and her posterity, leaving behind a dusty town "built so that you have to depend on husbands," reclaiming herself in the fluid liminal space of this "trickle of water" with its "curious name," this "muddy puddle" growing in strength to become a musical torrent (50–51, 46, 51). If she made her first passage across the Rio Grande in thrall to romantic dreams, she frees herself from this ethos of feminine submission in her passage back. The creek with its multiple names and meanings serves as a natural resource for Cleófilas's new self-expression and emerging identity. In her "long ribbon of laughter,

28. See Kristeva, "Place Names," esp. 283, 291, 276, 281; Hoever, *Daily Missal,* 426. The words are from John 7:37–39; Felix Guirand, ed., *New Larousse Encyclopedia of Mythology,* trans. Richard Aldington and Delano Ames (London: Hamlyn, 1959, 1968), 438. Cisneros includes Chalchiuhtlicue among the names and aspects of her revised Virgen de Guadalupe in "Little Miracles, Kept Promises," 128.

29. Margaret Homans argues that "the reproduction of mothering will also be the reproduction of a presymbolic communicativeness, a literal language," and that the "lost relation to the mother" might possibly be found in the "nonsymbolic figure" of a "new child." Positing childbirth itself as a "structure of literalization," Homans identifies moments of passage from the figurative to the literal in literary texts as embodying a specifically female linguistic practice "at the heart of gender difference in language." The conclusion of "Woman Hollering Creek" would seem to exemplify one such moment. See chap. 1 in Homans's *Bearing the Word: Language and Female Experience in Nineteenth-Century Women's Writing* (Chicago: University of Chicago Press, 1986), esp. 25, 26, 29–30.

like water," La Llorona's ghostly *llanto,* or tearful lament, becomes a *grito* or shout, a "Tarzan holler" of joyous strength and independence.[30]

30. In an interview Cisneros emphasizes the crossing of cultures in La Llorona's new "holler": "Yes, this other woman—the Chicana woman—could understand the myth in a new way. She could see it as a grito, not a llanto. And all of a sudden, that woman who came with all of her Mexican assumptions learned something. The Chicana woman showed her a new way of looking at a Mexican myth. And it took someone who was a little bit outside the culture to see the myth in a new way" (Reed Way Dasenbrock, "Sandra Cisneros," in *Interviews with Writers of the Post-Colonial World,* ed. Feroza Jussawalla and Reed Way Dasenbrock [Jackson: University Press of Mississippi, 1992], 294).

II

Immigrations

America, Romance, and the Fate of the Wandering Woman

The Case of *Charlotte Temple*

KAY FERGUSON RYALS

A strong case could be made that Susanna Rowson's *Charlotte Temple*, published in Philadelphia in 1794, was the first great American novel. Leslie Fiedler has called it "the first book by an American to move American readers," and indeed its popularity with the reading public was such that it remained the top seller of any American novel until the publication of *Uncle Tom's Cabin* over half-a-century later.[1] Such success might strike the modern reader as surprising, for Rowson's tale of virtue-under-threat seems entirely conventional, the stuff of sentimental melodrama. The novel recounts the migration of its eponymous heroine from England to America during the Revolutionary War, a migration that begins with the false promises of a seducer and ends tragically with Charlotte's death as an abandoned "fallen" woman. Still, the very popularity of the novel in the early years of the Republic suggests that the story of Charlotte's misadventure provided a model in terms of which readers, many of whom were women, could imagine the promises and perils of their own novel political and cultural adventure.

In this essay, I will examine the connections between *Charlotte Temple* and the political and cultural circumstances of its publication during the United States' own "post-colonial" moment. I will argue, first, that *Charlotte Temple* is best understood not as a sentimental novel, but rather as a kind of quest romance in which a female character attempts to occupy the position of the wandering, "errant" hero; second, that Charlotte's

---

1. Leslie A. Fiedler, *Love and Death in the American Novel* (Cleveland: Meridian, 1962), 68.

failure as a romance hero is linked to a certain gendered "inadequacy," and that the novel thus invites readers to consider the social and institutional constraints that contributed to that inadequacy; and, finally, that Rowson's subsequent career as an early feminist and educational reformer constituted a response to the conditions fictionalized in *Charlotte Temple*, conditions that—in reducing women to a state of dependency—threaten to corrupt both women's sexual virtue and the Republic's political virtue. The concepts of "virtue" and "corruption" are key here, for they are central not only to the didactic sexual language of women's fiction, but also to the political vocabulary of the founding era. Indeed, Rowson's novel can be read as a feminist intervention in the post-revolutionary debate about the extent to which the American polity should continue to be imagined in terms of the ideology of classical civic republicanism; the relationship between virtue, commerce, and corruption is the decisive point of contention in this debate. It is against the backdrop of such ideological struggle that we can begin to see what is at stake in Fiedler's observation that *Charlotte Temple* is, in effect, the novel in which many early American *readers* are able for the first time to recognize themselves as *American* readers. What sets *Charlotte Temple* apart from the more overtly politically minded novels of the period—and what makes it relevant to ongoing discussions about the role of "otherness" in the history of the American experience—is the fact that Rowson's project for imagining America is one in which the protagonist's dual status as a woman and a wanderer is absolutely crucial.

The Error of Her Ways

Charlotte Temple opens with a question posed by Montraville, the heroine's seducer, to his even more treacherous friend Belcour: "Are you for a walk?" The men's ensuing amble takes them on a side trip through the village of Chichester as they make their way to Portsmouth, which is at once their immediate destination and their point of departure on a military expedition bound for the rebellious American colonies. Significantly, this detour through Chichester—which results in Montraville's meeting of and ultimately in his seduction of Charlotte—both begins and prefigures the men's journey to America, a journey which, replete with ocean crossing and battles set at a moment of national founding, is in many ways an archetypal romance journey. But the walk through Chichester is also a *diversion* from the men's journey, a moment of wandering or "errancy" that postpones their more serious military mission. Montraville and Belcour head towards Chichester "knowing they [have] sufficient time to reach the place of destination before dark, yet allow them a walk." Hence within the framework of the men's own itinerary, this casual stroll is both a *part* of their journey and a departure *from* it, a wandering away from their goal that nevertheless moves them toward their destination. The genre of romance is characterized by precisely such a structural tension between the quester's progress towards his destination and moments of errancy that swerve away from that destination. Indeed, the ubiquity of such tension in romance narratives has led Patricia Parker to describe romance as "a form which both projects and postpones or wanders from a projected ending." Moreover, Parker has shown how, throughout the long tradition of Western romance, the term "error" itself has functioned as "a romance pun," for its own meaning has wandered to include not only geographical, mental, and moral deviation, but also the semantic wandering or slippage that emerges from the rhetorical and figurative dimension of language as such.[2]

But the traditional romance paradigm of progress-via-errancy is also marked by a persistent pattern of gendering. Describing romance as a genre that "necessitates the projection of an Other," Parker maintains that romance is typically structured around "the narrative topos of overcoming a female enchantress or obstacle en route to completion and ending."[3] In many a classic romance, an enclosed, feminine space of temptation—be it Circe's island, Dido's cave, or Acrasia's Bower of Bliss—serves as the male hero's testing ground, and the conquest of that feminine space constitutes his "education." In *Charlotte Temple*, Montraville's diversionary walk, made in order to "take a survey of the Chichester ladies as they returned from their devotions" (3), also functions in accordance with this gendered logic, for his detour into the cloistered feminine space of Chichester and thence into a distracting liaison with Charlotte is but a *temporary* deviation, a moment of moral errancy that he overcomes in the New World. There, as a determined male quester, Montraville achieves military honor, economic prosperity, and sanctioned marriage—with, of course, someone other than the pregnant and abandoned Charlotte. While Montraville's sexual wandering is represented as causing him some emotional anguish, his errancy does not ultimately interfere with either his military promotion or his social advancement; indeed, his affair with Charlotte even generates

---

2. Susanna Rowson, *Charlotte Temple*, in *Charlotte Temple and Lucy Temple*, ed. Ann Douglas (1791; reprint, New York: Penguin, 1991), 3, 3. Subsequent citations will appear parenthetically in the text. Patricia Parker, *Irresistible Romance: Studies in the Poetics of a Mode* (Princeton: Princeton University Press, 1979), 13, 20.

3. Parker, *Irresistible Romance*, 4; Patricia Parker, *Literary Fat Ladies: Rhetoric, Gender, Property* (London: Methuen, 1987), 11.

a certain moral profit by teaching him the "value" of Julia Franklin's chaste love.

In its traditional form, then, the romance plot unfolds according to a *speculative* pattern that is explicitly gendered: the male hero's errancy can be understood as a *strategic* loss—one that will be retroactively transformed into an "investment"—because the generic conventions of romance pre-ordain that the hero's swerving away from his goal in an encounter with a female "otherness" will eventually be recouped in a moment of triumphal return. Yet if, as Northrop Frye maintains, romance is in some sense "the structural core of all fiction," this is perhaps because the story of language has itself so often been told *as* a romance—one that exhibits this same gendered, speculative logic. Thus Margaret Homans has observed that "the dominant myth of Western languages has their operation structured as a quest romance, based on the boy's postoedipal renunciation of the mother and his quest for substituted objects of desire." In the "myth" of language put forward by Jacques Lacan, for example, signification entails—at least for men—an economy of sacrifice and gain that makes it a speculative venture with a logic akin to that of romance. For Lacan, the loss of a pre-oedipal state of imaginary wholeness is the "sacrifice" that is necessary for the subject's accession to the symbolic order of language; the signifier of this "self-sacrifice" is the phallus, "that pound of flesh which is mortgaged in [the male subject's] relationship to the signifier."[4] This "mortgage" is a sound investment, yielding precisely the ability to signify and to symbol-ize that makes possible successful action within those complex modern institutions in which all power is, to some extent, discursive power.

As feminist critics like Homans have noted, the Lacanian account of lan-guage, with its emphasis on the phallic quality of signification, represents the relationship of women to language as problematic, given woman's biological "lack": to already lack the penis, to be "literally" castrated, is to be identified with the literal. As Homans observes, this identification means that those social structures and institutions through which power is exercised are grounded in a form of symbolization from which women are by "nature" excluded: "The symbolic order, both the legal system and language, depends on the identification of the woman with the literal,

4. Northrop Frye, *The Secular Scripture: A Study of the Structure of Romance* (Cambridge: Harvard University Press, 1976), 15; Margaret Homans, *Bearing the Word: Language and Female Experience in Nineteenth-Century Women's Writing* (Chicago: University of Chicago Press, 1986), 40; Jacques Lacan, "Desire and the Interpretation of Desire in *Hamlet*," in *Literature and Psychoanalysis: The Question of Reading: Otherwise*, ed. Shoshana Felman (Baltimore: Johns Hopkins University Press, 1982), 28.

and then on the denial that the literal has any connection with masculine figurations."[5] Thus while the male Lacanian subject, like the romance hero, supposedly "has what it takes" to navigate the treacherous and deceptive shoals of the signifying chain, the alignment of women with the literal condemns them to a position of passivity and powerlessness outside the symbolic order.

Bearing in mind the gendering of romance, both in its strictly generic sense and in its broader alignment with Western narratives of language and identity, we can return to Rowson's novel. Immediately, however, we must address a difficulty: for obviously, although *Charlotte Temple* accords with the narrative logic of romance when we take Montraville as the questing hero, the book is named not after its male adventurer but after its "fallen" heroine. Yet, there are a number of ways in which the novel invites us to read its plot in terms of the generic conventions of romance, but of a romance filtered through the lens of a gender reversal in which a female character occupies—or attempts to occupy—the subject position of the quester. For example, Charlotte's journey to America begins on her birthday, an occasion that would, in the narrative of the traditional romance quester, mark a rite of passage signifying the hero's transition into independent adulthood. Thus it is not surprising that, at the start of Charlotte's "maiden voyage," Montraville promises the girl love, marriage, and motherhood—the New-World-as-family—so that her wandering appears to her to offer a route to personal fulfillment and the assumption of her proper social role. Moreover, throughout the novel Charlotte invokes the language of the romance quest to describe her own circumstances, as when she responds to Mrs. Beauchamp's query about whether she would return to her parents should they agree to take her back: "Would I! . . . would not the poor sailor, tost on a tempestuous ocean, threatened every moment with death, gladly return to the shore he had left to trust to its deceitful calmness? Oh, my dear Madam, I would return, though to do it I were obliged to walk barefoot over a burning desart [*sic*]" (82).

Yet the romance pattern of testing and return invoked by this last image is precisely what Charlotte will be denied, and this denial is evidence that—given the pattern of gendering so crucial to romance—Rowson's attempt to narrate a quest romance from a uniquely female perspective is bound to be extremely problematic. In fact, the shift from a male to a female protagonist within a fairly conventional romance plot structure and the jarring disruptions that result from that shift are central to Rowson's project in *Charlotte Temple*. The imagery of the novel often calls attention to the

5. Homans, *Bearing the Word*, 10.

consequences of this gender reversal. Hence while Charlotte is persistently depicted in accordance with the traditions of the romance quester, the cumulative effect of such imagery is ironic, for it makes clear that she is unable to become either an epic Columbus or a bourgeois Robinson Crusoe, whose shipwreck proved to be but the perfect opportunity for his heroic self-assertion and "progress." On the contrary, Charlotte finds that having "trusted [her] happiness on a tempestuous ocean," she is "wrecked and lost forever" (115) when her chastity is forfeited during passage from the Old World to the New.

Such imagery becomes even more poignant and ironic when we note that Charlotte is in part seduced away from her home shore by rhetoric in which Montraville portrays *himself* as the adventurous hero in danger of shipwreck. He urges her, for example, to "reflect, that when I leave my native land, perhaps a few short weeks may terminate my existence; the perils of the ocean—the dangers of war—" (37); Montraville's plea, which the overwrought Charlotte breaks off, is able to elicit Charlotte's sympathy precisely because it alludes to that realm of "generic" threats that confronts the romance hero. Similarly, when Montraville's father warns him against "a precipitate union with a girl of little or no fortune"—a warning that will cause Montraville to desert Charlotte—his advice employs imagery of peril that ultimately proves relevant not so much to Montraville as to Charlotte: "Your happiness will always be dear to me," Montraville's father tells him, "and I wish to warn you of a rock on which the peace of many an honest fellow has been wrecked" (40). That rock, of course, is Charlotte herself. From Montraville's perspective, the female wanderer is but, to recall Parker's formulation, an "enchantress or obstacle" to be overcome; the ambitious young man's entanglement with this girl of modest means poses a threat to his own quest for social advancement through prudent marriage.

Clearly, then, errancy has very different and far more dangerous connotations for Charlotte, the female quester, than it does for the male hero. Although Montraville successfully recoups his wayward dalliance with Charlotte, Charlotte's "error"—as Rowson insistently calls it—takes her away from the "path of rectitude" (35) to which she, unlike the errant male of romance, cannot return. This essential difference is especially evident in Charlotte's illegitimate pregnancy. Although Montraville's own moral errancy is in effect invisible, it nevertheless inscribes itself quite visibly on Charlotte's body in the form of her swollen womb. Yet Rowson is at pains to make clear what actually prevents Charlotte's "return," what makes her—in contrast to her seducer—unable to recoup her errancy: the culprit is society's sexual double standard, a form of institutionalized hypocrisy that insists on regarding the physical sign of a woman's temporary moral errancy as evidence of an irredeemable fallenness. A poignant scene near the end of the novel makes this double standard painfully clear: very pregnant and deathly ill, the forsaken Charlotte wanders in the cold in search of refuge, only to hear a soldier exclaim, "[M]ay God bless [Montraville], for a better officer never lived, he is so good to us all" (117). For Montraville, the male quester, a speculative gap exists between body and character that allows a space for self-fashioning and thus for the projection of a virtuous public reputation. By contrast, Charlotte's pregnant body represents a literalizing of symbolic moral errancy in which signifier and signified are collapsed; the moral character of this *female* quester is allowed no redemptive wandering from the site of her body, which is presumed to serve as an "inerrant," strictly determined material signifier of an errant inner state.

Unlike her male lover, then, Charlotte is already marked as fallen when she enters the "new Eden," and consequently she is forbidden access to whatever social and economic opportunity America might have offered to women immigrants. Charlotte's movement is, as we shall see, always circumscribed by the institutions of patriarchy, and yet—paradoxically— the way that patriarchy constrains and limits her mobility causes her wandering to be one from which there is no way home. Because she does *not* "have what it takes" to succeed as an autonomous agent within this patriarchal world, because she lacks the underwriting by phallic authority that could ensure the recuperation of error, adventure leads Charlotte not to triumphal return, but to an absolute and literal errancy. For this "dear wanderer" (97), this "poor forsaken wanderer" (116), errancy leads not to advancement-by-trial and accession to a privileged position in the symbolic order, but rather to madness, regression, and that ultimate form of errancy without return—death.

The Sting of Dependence

As chronicles of a hero's adventures, traditional romances tend to be episodic, recounting a series of seemingly random incidents and encounters that, despite their initially threatening nature, end up benefiting the hero. Northrop Frye sees the hero's conspicuously fortuitous relationship to chance as central to the romance genre: "The success of the hero," he writes, "derives from a current of energy which is partly from him and partly outside him. . . . The most basic term for this current of energy is luck." I would add that the "luck" that comes from "without" the hero is constituted by the generic conventions that govern romance as a literary form, conventions that function in a sense as the institutional supports that guarantee in advance the hero's success; those favorable gods who pull the strings behind the scenes in classical romances can perhaps be seen as personifications of these generic guarantees. Of course, luck is also important to romance at the more mundane level of character and story, but the luck that comes from "within" the hero—his uncanny ability to master whatever contingencies fortune throws his way—is of a specific kind. For the hero's success in overcoming obstacles depends in large part upon his epistemological sophistication—that is, his ability first to interpret or "read" correctly the circumstances in which he finds himself and then to act so as to turn those circumstances to his advantage. Above all, he must be able to distinguish truth from dissembling, and this requires in turn that he be able both to understand and to employ for his own ends the gap between signifiers and signifieds that marks the rhetorical errancy of language and of other symbolic systems. Just as, in the stories about language told by critics like Lacan and Jacques Derrida, symbolization is an effect of errancy, deriving from a space of difference and deferral that sunders any univocal and "necessary" relationship between signifier and signified, so too the romance hero's "luck"—his ability to manage his own physical and moral errancy—is an effect of his ability to manage the space of epistemological errancy that intervenes between surface appearance and actual reality.[6]

In *Charlotte Temple*, Montraville's career seems to follow this pattern of "luck," of chance turned to advantage. For example, Montraville's introduction to Julia Franklin, his wife-to-be, is occasioned by an "accident" (71). When a fire breaks out next to the Franklins' house, a stranger who is helping to save the house places in Montraville's hands for safekeeping a box containing "jewels to a large amount, about two hundred pounds in money, and a miniature picture set for a bracelet" (72); this picture is of Julia's deceased mother, whose painted likeness to her daughter conveniently leads Montraville to the box's owner. Julia's box is an emblem for her financial fortune and her intact sexual "virtue," both of which are delivered to Montraville through a stroke of good fortune so improbable as to seem almost destined from "outside him" (to use Frye's terminology). Yet Montraville's luck is also "partly from him," for he plans and

6. Frye, *Secular Scripture*, 67; for Derrida's account of linguistic "presence" as an effect of difference and deferral within the signifying chain, see Jacques Derrida, *Margins of Philosophy*, trans. Alan Bass (Chicago: University of Chicago Press, 1982), 1–27.

profits from this initial boon. Even before he has met Julia—and even as he continues to admit his responsibility towards Charlotte—Montraville schemes to increase Julia's "debt" to him for recovering her treasure; thus when he returns the box to Julia, he slyly removes the picture of her mother so that "by presenting it to her when she thinks it is lost," he will "enhance the value of the obligation" that Julia feels towards him (72). His strategy is, of course, successful, and the wily speculator embarks upon his own romance with Julia.

Montraville's relationship with Charlotte is also driven by a combination of luck from without and acuity from within. After he gets an initial glance at Charlotte and spends "three whole days in thinking on her and in endeavouring to form some plan for seeing her," Montraville determines once again "to set off for Chichester, and trust *to chance* either to favour or frustrate his designs" (4, my emphasis). Yet the language here is rather misleading, for "chance" is only imagined as helping or hindering a plan that has already been devised by Montraville. Thus when he does "chance" upon Charlotte on this trip, Montraville is prepared with "a letter he [has] *purposely* written" to her (5, my emphasis), a letter that effects her seduction. To ensure that happenstance has no further part in his meetings with Charlotte, he bribes her teacher, Mademoiselle La Rue, to continue to bring Charlotte "into the field" (5). Indeed, in a passage describing Montraville's interception of a letter written by Charlotte that would have summoned her parents to her aid and averted her departure for America, the novel mocks the very notion that chance has any role in determining Charlotte's future: "Montraville knew too well the consequences that must unavoidably ensue, should this letter reach Mr. Temple: he therefore wisely resolved to walk on the deck, tear it in pieces, and commit the fragments to the care of Neptune, who might or might not, as suited his convenience, convey them to shore" (58). Obviously, the future course of Charlotte's errant letter, and thus of Charlotte herself, is not actually subject to the realm of chance such that it "might or might not" reach its destination, depending on the heroine's "luck"; instead, the letter's "fate" is controlled from without by the scheming Montraville who, like the figure of Neptune, stands for the constraining external "reality" that in the end determines the female quester's destiny. This irony suggests that for Charlotte the possibility of a properly "speculative" subjectivity—one that can profit from errancy—is foreclosed from the outset, not by any essential deficiency of Charlotte's but rather by the institutional forces that Montraville-as-Neptune represents and that ensure that the female quester is never "lucky." Thus while chance in the traditional romance plot allows the male hero a certain space of indeterminacy in which to prove his mettle and plot his course, the female quester quite literally never *has a chance;* what appears to happen by accident to Charlotte is in fact the result of the ruthless machinations of the "plotting" men who surround her.

In subjecting romance conventions such as that of the errant letter to a heavy dose of dramatic irony, Rowson's novel invites readers to consider ways that women's "accidental" failures are often a consequence of invisible but pervasive institutional constraints, just as the "accidents" of a conventional romance plot are not really fortuitous at all but are in fact the determined effects of generic norms and authorial decisions, and just as— within the story—the "accidents" that befall Charlotte are really the designs of men. Indeed, to lay bare the gendering at work in romance is also, by analogy, to critique those patriarchal social and political institutions in the young Republic that, rather like the generic supports guaranteeing the male romance hero's success, ensure that only male citizens "have what it takes" to act as autonomous agents. Because such institutions—university, counting house, legislative assembly—at once impart to and demand of their initiates considerable discursive power and symbolic acuity, they share with the literary institution of romance a valorization of speculative subjectivity; whether as rhetorician, merchant adventurer, or revolutionary founding father, the successful male quester displays an epistemological sophistication that enables him to manage errancy in all its forms, and so to reap *symbolic* profit (signification, money, political power) from the threat of *literal* loss (castration, shipwreck, execution). Charlotte's attempt to play the role of quester demonstrates that women's exclusion from the symbolic order and its speculative errancy dooms the female romance plot to failure.

Moreover, set as it is during the United States' founding moment, *Charlotte Temple* is engaged in an analysis of the politics of gender. The story of Charlotte's fall demonstrates that if the adventuress cannot make her way in the world, it is largely because the kind of flexible subjectivity that makes possible effective agency in a world of contingency is itself an effect of epistemological power, a power that has been denied to all women insofar as they have been systematically excluded from the institutions that cultivate it. Lacking this power, women also lack the ability to act as autonomous subjects, and this in turn places them in a precarious condition of which Charlotte's own is exemplary. In contrast to men, whose success lies largely in their own hands, women face an enforced dependence on those with power, and this dependence makes their "virtue" vulnerable to attack and thus to corruption. As Montraville's father expounds the matter, Montraville's "success in life depends entirely on [himself]," for young men "may exert their talents, make themselves friends, and raise their fortunes on the basis of merit" (39). Montraville's sisters, however, must "have some [economic] provision made, to place them above the snares and temptations which vice ever holds out to the elegant, accomplished female, when oppressed by the frowns of poverty and the sting of dependance [*sic*]" (39).

Rowson's analysis of the institutional constraints that render women vulnerable to manipulation employs a vocabulary that would have had a powerful political resonance in the 1790s, for the notions of dependency, corruption, and virtue—so central to Rowson's novel—are also central to the vocabulary of civic republicanism, an ideology that historians have come to regard as a dominant conceptual force of the founding era. J. G. A. Pocock, in particular, has traced the genealogy of civic republicanism from eighteenth-century Britain and America back to its decisive articulation in the writings of Machiavelli. This mode of thought maintains that man is by nature a political being who can fulfill his *telos* only when he "acts as a citizen, that is as a conscious and autonomous participant in . . . the polis or republic." Arrayed against the ever-present threat of the polis's decay or "corruption"—symbolized by the female figure of Fortune—is the citizens' capacity for masculine *virtù*, that "active ruling quality . . . practiced in republics by citizens equal with one another and devoted to the public good." Republican virtue is presumed to be strictly incompatible with any kind of economic or social dependency on the part of the citizen, for only personal independence would enable the citizen, as Drew McCoy explains, "to pursue spontaneously the common or public good, rather than the narrow interest of the men . . . on whom he depended for his support." But republican virtue also entails a crucial cognitive dimension, which Pocock calls "the epistemology of the particular"; in order to enact the public good, the citizen must first be able to discern what constitutes the good under particular circumstances and act accordingly. Rather like the romance quester, then, the citizen must be—as Quentin Skinner puts it, glossing Machiavelli—"a man of 'flexible disposition': he must be capable of varying his conduct . . . 'as fortune and circumstances dictate.' "[7]

7. J. G. A. Pocock, *Politics, Language, and Time: Essays on Political Thought and History* (New York: Atheneum, 1971), 85; J. G. A. Pocock, *Virtue, Commerce, and History: Essays on Political Thought and History, Chiefly in the Eighteenth Century* (Cambridge: Cambridge University Press, 1985), 41; Drew McCoy, *The Elusive Republic: Political Economy in Jeffersonian America* (Chapel Hill: University of North Carolina Press, 1980), 68; J. G. A. Pocock, *The Machiavellian Moment: Florentine Political Thought and the Atlantic Republican Tradition* (Princeton: Princeton University Press, 1975), 117; Quentin Skinner, *The Foundations of Modern Political Thought*, vol. 1, *The Renaissance* (Cambridge: Cambridge University Press, 1978), 138.

Given the emphasis on epistemological power that we have seen in both romance and republicanism, then, it is hardly surprising that the heroine's "dependence" in *Charlotte Temple* is not simply economic, but also epistemological. The most obvious sign of this is her initial rhetorical ineptness, her inability to understand or to deploy words effectively. At the novel's beginning, it is clear that Charlotte's sheltered experience has left her with a naive, literalist understanding of language, making her an easy prey for the "sophistical arguments" (102) and skillful duplicity of Belcour and Montraville. The "eloquent harangue[s]" of Montraville's accomplice, La Rue, typically leave Charlotte "so confused, that she [knows] not what to say" (47), and La Rue's "advice and machinations" (51) are largely responsible for Charlotte's surrender to Montraville. Yet, in presenting Charlotte's epistemological dependence, Rowson is at pains to make clear its origins in the social and political realities of the day. Thus, as we have seen, once Charlotte begins to see through Montraville's promises of marriage, she does attempt both to shake off passivity and to employ language to effect her escape, only to be thwarted by Montraville. By calling attention to the way that Charlotte's epistemological dependence itself *depends upon* the constraining power of patriarchal institutions (as figured in the "machinations" and thefts by Montraville, Belcour, and their accomplices), the novel subverts republican assumptions about the *inherent* incapacity of women even as it acknowledges the *de facto* state of dependence in which women like Charlotte find themselves. Rowson's appropriation of such republican motifs as virtue and corruption is thus trenchantly critical. That the female quester's missives are never even "posted" is emblematic of her exclusion from the institutional networks through which symbolic power circulates, an exclusion that leaves her dependent.

One institution that quite clearly abets the relegation of Charlotte to silence and dependency is the legal system. Charlotte's sense both of her own lowly status before the law and of the tenuous nature of her legal claims on Montraville is evident in her failed attempts to hold the seducer to his promise of marriage, most notably in a plea that begins eloquently but that breaks off in mid-sentence: "But should you, forgetful of your promises, and repenting the engagement you here voluntarily enter into, forsake and leave me on a foreign shore—" (44). The absence of a main clause that marks Charlotte's retreat into silence here is indicative of the harsh truth that the fallen woman has no access to legal redress. But while Charlotte's seduction renders her particularly dependent upon the very men who seek her undoing, married women in the founding era were subject to a similar dependence. According to the common law policy of coverture, which continued after the revolution to regulate most marital contracts in the United States, the legal identity of the wife, the *feme covert*, was "covered," or "hidden," by that of her husband, who took legal possession of her property and whose rights and will were presumed to represent hers. The "protective interpretation" of coverture argued that the law was "protective rather than restrictive in nature" because, in jurist William Blackstone's words, "[e]ven the disabilities, which the wife lies under, are for the most part intended for her protection and benefit."[8]

Yet this "protective" system placed even married women in a position of vulnerability not unlike that of the fallen Charlotte. Indeed, to be "under the protection" of a man was at this time also a euphemistic expression for being a mistress, as when Belcour calculates that if Charlotte were rendered completely destitute, "she would more readily throw herself on his protection" (105); for him, this clearly means only that she would submit to sexual servitude. This link between the female body and "protection" as a form of economic exchange is presented as being so tenacious that it infects almost every male-female relationship in the novel. The distinction between marriage and prostitution thus emerges as a tenuous one, and the fundamental difference between them proves to lie in the degree of female dependency each entails, not in the fact of dependency. Rowson suggests as much in describing the genteel marriages of Mr. Temple's sisters—alliances made to "old, decrepit men" for the sake of wealth, security, and social status—as "legal prostitution" (6). Such unsettling similarities between wife and mistress suggest the degree to which women's multiple dependencies continually threaten female virtue and, by extension, the integrity and virtue of the Republic itself.

Throughout *Charlotte Temple*, then, the speculative systems of exchange governing language and money are shown to be related, and women's "inadequacy" in negotiating such systems is shown to lead to a corrupting dependency. The defining event of the novel—Montraville's seduction or "corruption" of Charlotte—is itself presented as a consequence of these two forms of symbolic power working together, for when, on their first meeting, Montraville places that "letter he [has] purposely written, into Charlotte's hand," he simultaneously "[slips] . . . five guineas into that of Mademoiselle [La Rue]" (5). Similarly, the letters that Charlotte writes to Montraville after he has been tricked into believing that Charlotte has

8. Linda Kerber, *Women of the Republic: Intellect and Ideology in Revolutionary America* (New York: W. W. Norton, 1980), 139; quoted in Kerber, *Women of the Republic,* 140; for an account of how "law in the new Republic did not protect the seduced (or raped) woman," see Cathy N. Davidson, *Revolution and the Word: The Rise of the Novel in America* (New York: Oxford University Press, 1986), 107.

become Belcour's mistress are intercepted by Belcour, who prevails upon Montraville's servant to steal them by means of "the powerful persuasion of a bribe" (92); as this phrase suggests, rhetorical "persuasion" and economic exchange work together in a powerful alliance to ensure that the dependent woman remains in a position of dependency. It is not surprising, then, that as Charlotte is driven to the conclusion of her plot—the plot of the thwarted female quester—she is rendered both penniless and increasingly silent. When the indignant farmer's wife throws her out of the house for which she can no longer pay rent, Charlotte "bow[s] her head in silence," for "the anguish of her heart was too great to permit her to articulate a single word" (114). In desperation, she wanders to the home of La Rue, now Mrs. Crayton, to seek shelter, where her appeal is made with "a voice rendered scarcely articulate" (118). When the hardened Mrs. Crayton refuses to respond to her last desperate missive, Charlotte is finally pushed into madness: after giving birth, "she lay for some hours in a kind of stupor; and if at any time she spoke, it was with a quickness and incoherence that plainly evinced the total deprivation of her reason" (120).

Denied every avenue of rational appeal, Charlotte is thus forced back upon a different kind of language, for in response to her powerlessness she succumbs to hysteria, the language of the so-called "wandering womb." This dangerous, literalizing language of the body is reflected in the text's increasingly melodramatic style. As the novel winds down, more and more episodes dissolve from narrative progress into static display, as Charlotte's emotional states are signified not only by reports of tears, shrieking, convulsions, delirium, and fainting, but also by the narrative retardation effected by these sentimental tableaux, a retardation that ultimately precludes the narrative closure of Charlotte's romance plot. Hence the very form of Rowson's novel becomes a kind of allegory of its theme, for these scenes of emotive display function as "feminine" obstacles that the forward thrust of the plot seems ever less able to overcome. In a sense, then, this devolution to the conventions of female *sentiment* registers the failure of a female *romance* fully to constitute itself as such.

Of course, the language of emotional display at work in *Charlotte Temple* is in one sense merely typical of the sentimental novel. As John Mullan has argued, this "language of feeling," or of "sensibility," arises from the typically eighteenth-century hope—shared by Shaftesbury, Hutcheson, Hume, and Adam Smith—of overcoming the centrifugal forces of modernity by creating a community founded upon bonds of sympathy. Mullan argues that this hope for community fails because the celebration of sensibility—with its valorization of the female body as a locus of sympathy—is marked by an inherent ambiguity, as a result of which the emotional intensity that is supposed to be the basis of sympathy and thus of community always threatens to "become excessive and self-destructive." Sentimental novels thus describe "a sociability whose fate is isolation."[9] Yet I have argued that the generic shift to sentimental melodrama near the conclusion of Rowson's text should be interpreted as a self-conscious sign of the novel's failure fully to become a female quest romance, and that this failure in turn points towards the social and political strictures that foreclose the possibility of female agency and citizenship in a civic republican polity. Thus, if *Charlotte Temple* does exemplify the paradox noted by Mullan— i.e., that sentiment leads away from the goal of community and towards individual isolation—it also offers an alternative analysis of that paradox. For Rowson's novel represents the isolation wrought by the dangerous literalness of sentiment's hysterical language as not simply a threat to an already existing community, but as itself a consequence of a *prior* failure of community: the exclusion of women from those social institutions that, by providing epistemological power, make possible autonomous agency and thus a truly "virtuous" community.

America, Commerce, and the Virtuous Adventuress

There is a certain irony in the fact that Susanna Rowson is best known for her account of an unfortunate American immigrant whose trip across the ocean proves disastrous: Rowson herself was an extraordinarily successful immigrant, and in her post–*Charlotte Temple* literary career, she not only showed a decided penchant for composing popular sea chanteys, but also created numerous female characters who *do* wander abroad and successfully survive "real" shipwrecks with "virtue" intact. She created so many such heroines that one commentator has characterized her as primarily "a vivid portrayer of the virtuous woman adventuress."[10] In a sense, then, *Charlotte Temple* is merely the pre-text for the rest of Rowson's corpus; that is, the novel delineates a problem that the balance of Rowson's literary career sets out to resolve. By looking to one of Rowson's best-known chanteys we can begin both to see how Rowson conceives of the virtuous

9. John Mullan, *Sentiment and Sociability: The Language of Feeling in the Eighteenth Century* (Oxford: Clarendon Press, 1988), 201, 235.
10. Arthur Hobson Quinn, *American Fiction: An Historical and Critical Survey* (New York: Appleton-Century-Crofts, 1936), 17; for critical biographies of Rowson, see Dorothy Weil, *In Defense of Women: Susanna Rowson (1762–1824)* (University Park: Pennsylvania State University Press, 1976); and Patricia L. Parker, *Susanna Rowson* (Boston: Twayne, 1986).

adventuress as a response to the aporias of female romance dramatized in *Charlotte Temple* and to understand more fully how that novel might be read as a commentary on the civic republican political context from which it emerged.

Rowson's song "America, Commerce, and Freedom" was written in 1794, the year of *Charlotte Temple*'s American publication. The song, which celebrates sea life, trade, and the hardy sailors who "earn [money] but to spend it," maintained its popularity throughout the decade. The first stanza and refrain are particularly relevant:

> How blessed the life a sailor leads
> From clime to clime still ranging
> For as the calm the storm succeeds
> The scene delights by changing.
> Tho' tempests howl along the main
> Some object will remind us,
> and cheer, with hope to meet again,
> the friends we left behind us.
>
> For under snug sail, we laugh at the gale;
> and tho' landsmen look pale, never heed 'em;
> But toss off the glass, to a favourite lass,
> To America, commerce, and freedom.[11]

Like the classic romance, these lines feature a sailor-quester seeking to "profit" from a world highly changeable and subject to storm and tempest, and like the romance hero, the sailor endures a dangerous adventure that finally ends in his return home. Yet what is significant about this song for the problematic put forward in *Charlotte Temple* is its reversal of the conventional opposition between domestic security and seafaring danger: here it is the "landsmen"—those who should be snugly secure on shore—who nevertheless "look pale" and are fearful of the storm, while the sailors, out in the midst of the turbulence, "laugh at the gale" from "under snug sail." According to this inverted image of vulnerability and safety, those dependent upon shelter are exposed to danger while those whose experiences have equipped them to adapt to and indeed to control the contingency of the storm are the more secure. A similar irony is evident in the phrase "still ranging," for the one constant of the "blessed life" the sailor leads is its "ranging" from "clime to clime"—its mobility and

---

11. Susanna Rowson, "America, Commerce, and Freedom," composed by A. Reinagle (Philadelphia: Carr's Musical Repository, 1794).

openness to variety and chance. Rowson's song thus implies that in a world in which contingency can be neither prevented nor evaded, it is far better to be prepared to maneuver in a gale than to seek the illusory safety of a harbor removed from fortune's tempests.

But the inversion of shelter and storm also recalls that irony—so central to *Charlotte Temple*—that results from the fact that attempts to preserve a woman's "virtue" by sheltering her and making her passively dependent upon a man's "protection" instead render her virtue highly vulnerable to the machinations of eloquent "adventurers." The circumscription of female mobility in *Charlotte Temple* results not in safety, but in a wandering without return. It is just here, however, that we can begin to see how Rowson's chantey points towards a solution, equally paradoxical, to the dilemma of female dependency. In the song, the sailors acquire the autonomy or "virtue" that enables them to combat the storms of fortune precisely from their continual exposure to varied circumstances and conditions, an exposure that is part and parcel of their pursuit of commerce. Hence commerce, broadly understood as a heightened mobility and *interdependence* of both people and things, emerges as an aid to the cultivation of virtue and *independence.*[12]

From a civic republican point of view, however, such talk must seem less a paradox than sheer nonsense, for republican purists understood commerce to lead to myriad dependencies and thus to the corruption of civic life. Only property in the form of land was seen to grant the personal independence and impartial zeal for the public good that the citizen needed if he was to avoid corruption; as Pocock explains, for eighteenth-century republicans "the function of property remained the assurance of virtue. It was hard to see how [the citizen] could become involved in exchange relationships . . . without becoming involved in dependence and corruption. The ideals of virtue and commerce could not therefore be reconciled." But Rowson has here moved beyond the republican paradigm, as is obvious from the way that her song links the term "commerce" in a trinity with "freedom" and "America." Indeed, the song's later stanzas suggest that civic life and sociability are themselves dependent upon the sailors' "speculative" adventure abroad, for their return gives rise to song, dance, and communal celebration, even as it brings the material goods on which the community depends. The material exchanges of commercial life and the social exchanges of civic life are seen to be intimately connected,

---

12. For the central text on the evolution of the term *commerce,* see Albert O. Hirschman, *The Passions and the Interests: Political Arguments for Capitalism before Its Triumph* (Princeton: Princeton University Press, 1977).

not diametrically opposed. Rowson's project must thus be assigned a place within that late eighteenth-century countercurrent to civic republicanism that eventually issued forth in liberalism, "an ideology and a perception of history which," as Pocock puts it, "depicted political society and social personality as founded upon commerce: upon the exchange of forms of mobile property and upon modes of consciousness suited to a world of moving objects."[13]

It was above all in the social philosophy of the Scottish Enlightenment that a historic transition from a paradigm of civic republicanism to one of commerce was explicitly theorized. Whereas republicanism had advocated a political society in which autonomous citizens relied on their virtue to ensure that they acted strictly for the public good rather than out of base self-interest or vassalage, thinkers like David Hume and Adam Smith began to argue that the refinement of manners brought about by the rise of commercial society itself entails the pursuit of "virtue" by other means. They maintained that propriety—acting in a manner appropriate to one's circumstances—also demands what Smith calls the "virtue of self-command," the sacrificing of self-interest for the sake of "civil" society. However, such decorum is possible only if society's members—like the romance quester and the republican citizen—are able accurately to "read" the particular social context in which we are to act. In the final edition of his influential *The Theory of Moral Sentiments* (which appeared in 1790, a year before the English publication of *Charlotte Temple*), Smith gave definitive form to his argument that "mannered" cognition requires first that we abstract from our self-interest in order to see our actions through the eyes of an ideal "Impartial Spectator," and second that we discipline our own feelings (or "sympathy") so as to accord with the Spectator's judgments. In effect, Smith's theory builds on the cognitive element already latent in Machiavellian *virtù* in order to transform virtue from an essentially political capacity for self-rule into an essentially epistemological capacity for a speculative self-distancing that allows us to make impartial judgments about complex social situations. Pocock neatly summarizes this drift in commercial ideology by saying that "[v]irtue was redefined . . . with the aid of a concept of 'manners'" and that commercial man lost his "antique virtue" but gained in its stead an "infinite enrichment of his personality."[14]

Indeed, what makes Smith's project especially relevant to Rowson's is the decisive role that Smith attributes to "commerce," in the broad

13. Pocock, *Virtue, Commerce, and History,* 48, 109.
14. Ibid., 48, 48, 49.

sense, in creating a mannered personality. He maintains that the sophisticated appreciation of one's surroundings necessary for mannered behavior is achieved not through isolation from social intercourse, but rather through immersion in it. Polite conversation offers one important form of "exchange" by providing an education in variety that helps to refine perception. Yet Smith holds that the highest virtues of character are forged from a more worldly and adventuresome kind of commerce: the "man of real constancy and firmness," writes Smith, "has been thoroughly bred in the great school of self-command, in the bustle and business of the world, exposed, perhaps, to the violence and injustice of faction, and to the hardships and hazards of war." In a paradox already familiar to us from "America, Commerce, and Freedom," it is precisely the exposure to tumult and contingency that teaches firmness and a mastery of fortune, for it provides what Smith calls "constant practice" in the exercise of mannered cognition.[15]

If, however, the logic that links "commerce" to the republican shibboleths of "America" and "freedom" in Rowson's song seems to emerge from that broad movement toward a liberal conception of society of which Smith's work is an exemplar, then the story of Charlotte Temple's failure in the "great school of self-command" nevertheless subjects Smith's commercial logic to a decidedly feminist twist. Indeed, a cursory reading of *Charlotte Temple* might lead us to conclude that the novel—as opposed to "America, Commerce, and Freedom"—shares republicanism's suspicion of commerce, since it is Charlotte's exposure to the hazards of romance that leads to disaster; immersion in "commerce" proves not the making of the heroine, but her undoing. And yet, unlike Smith's "man of real constancy," Charlotte has not been "thoroughly bred" in the bustle of worldly ways. On the contrary, her confinement to a sheltered domestic space and her restricted education have left her lacking in just those epistemological skills that might have enabled her to read the intentions of the men around her and thus to steer a "virtuous" course once she found herself afloat and exposed. Charlotte's predicament is, to borrow the language of Rowson's chantey, that of a "landsman" suddenly set adrift in a gale, with predictably unhappy results.

A scene early in the novel perfectly captures the way that confinement and isolation make women vulnerable to conquest. When Montraville goes in search of Charlotte at the secluded boarding school, he finds that "the wall which surrounded it was high" and fears that "perhaps the Argus's

15. Adam Smith, *The Theory of Moral Sentiments* (1790; reprint, Oxford: Oxford University Press, 1976), 146, 147.

who guarded the Hesperian fruit within, were more watchful than those famed of old" (4). The hyperbole in this allusion only calls ironic attention to the ease with which Montraville, who leans on a "broken gate" as he surveys the erstwhile barrier, will attack Charlotte's integrity. A similar irony is evident in the account of the Temples' preparations for Charlotte's birthday. Anticipating their daughter's return from school, Charlotte's parents have planned a party in a doubly protected area—the "little alcove at the bottom of the garden" that they will "deck . . . out in a fanciful manner" (31) and in which Charlotte will entertain her visitors. That this secluded, enclosed space goes unused because of Charlotte's elopement is itself evidence of the inadequacy of a purely defensive approach to the preservation of female virtue. The rural house where Montraville "keeps" Charlotte, and which becomes her prison in America, is yet another image of female confinement, but in this instance the incarcerating function of the supposedly protective domestic space is more clearly evident. When Charlotte is eventually forced out of this isolated house, she is unable to fend for herself because she "knew so little of the ways of the world": "Alas poor Charlotte," the narrator laments, "how confined was her knowledge of human nature" (112).

In a sense, then, the problem that *Charlotte Temple* reveals is the vulnerability of the passive, naive woman who does not know how to "read" the world around her, a world whose institutions do not work to protect women. Conversely, this very revelation suggests that if female confinement and passivity are simply an invitation to attack, a more reasonable strategy for preserving female virtue would seem to lie in providing women with adequate preparation for an active engagement with the world; the wandering woman must, in sum, be empowered to face the contingencies of experience. The notion that a structured introduction to the ways of the world rather than seclusion from the world offers the best defense against the lures of vice had, in fact, been put forward by John Locke's influential educational writings, in which he suggested that "[t]he only Fence against the World, is thorough Knowledge of it; into which a young Gentleman should be enter'd by degrees, as he can bear it; and the earlier the better, so he be in safe and skillful hands to guide him."[16] For Locke, however, such knowledge "enter'd by degrees" remained the exclusive provenance of men, and this fact points to the innovative nature of Rowson's project. Unlike the liberal texts of British philosophy, Rowson's literary texts of the

16. John Locke, *Some Thoughts Concerning Education*, in *The Educational Writings of John Locke*, ed. James Axtell (Cambridge: Cambridge University Press, 1968), 195.

1790s point toward the quite novel conclusion that women, too, must be taught to participate in the bustle and business of civic life.

At the same time, this suggestion that women should be prepared to lead active lives constitutes an important element of the novel's sustained critique of republican commonplaces. Indeed, Charlotte's fall serves to demonstrate an inherent shortcoming of republicanism's patriarchal logic: the social and economic dependency of all women, including sexually virtuous women, places them in a position of extreme vulnerability that almost inevitably invites attempts at seduction. In republican terms, the political "corruption" of women-as-dependents leads all too easily to their sexual corruption. But because republican thought did tend to allot women a significant role in the early education of male citizens, such endemic moral decay in the domestic heart of the body politic must—from a republican perspective—eventually exert a corrosive and corrupting influence on the life of the republic itself; *sexual* corruption, in short, has *political* consequences.[17] I would argue, then, that Rowson's program incorporates elements of both republican and liberal theory while rejecting the traditional sexual politics of each: For Rowson, the virtuous republic must not only rethink its rejection of commerce, but it must allow women to explore those mutual interdependencies that, as a school for epistemological virtue, laid a foundation for the kind of independence and autonomy on women's part that alone could equip them to maintain their sexual virtue.

Educating Charlotte

If Rowson's dramatization of the failures of republican community at once provides a worst-case scenario regarding women's status in America and gestures broadly towards the necessity of a more "liberal" and inclusive conception of women's roles, it also begins to articulate a practical strategy through which that conception might be realized. The author's preface to *Charlotte Temple* explicitly notes that the novel is intended as a cautionary tale for "the many daughters of misfortune" who are in danger of repeating Charlotte's tragedy because they are either "deprived of natural friends, or spoilt by a mistaken education" (xlix). These twin impediments—a failure of friendship and a failure of education—in turn suggest a twofold remedy

17. For a discussion of the ideology of the term *Republican Motherhood*, according to which women were seen as important to the Republic due to their role as mothers to the future male citizens, see Kerber, *Women of the Republic*.

to the threat of corruption posed to, and by, the isolated and dependent woman, a remedy that Rowson sought both to represent in her novel and to effect in her career as an educator.

On the one hand, the novel argues for the vital importance of friendship and community between women in light of the disadvantages that they faced in a nation built around a legal framework of patriarchal custom and an ideological framework of civic republicanism. Indeed, what Charlotte laments most often throughout her ordeal is not that she has left her parents, not even that Montraville has abandoned her, but that she has no female companionship: "Alas!" she sighs, "how can I be happy, deserted and forsaken as I am, without a friend of my own sex to whom I can unburthen my full heart" (104). The narrator characteristically intrudes into the tale to insist that "many an unfortunate female, who has once strayed into the thorny paths of vice, would gladly return to virtue, was any generous friend to endeavour to raise and re-assure her" (70), and the doctor's prescription for the distracted Charlotte is "the soothing balm of friendly consolation" (123). Such a consoling friend is figured within the novel by Mrs. Beauchamp, who is moved to help her "wandering sister" because she is "a witness to the solitary life Charlotte led" (77), and who claims to empathize with Charlotte because they "are both strangers in this country" (80). Both the respectable, married Mrs. Beauchamp and the single, stigmatized Charlotte are isolated within the domestic sphere, and thus they are "strangers" to the institutions that make self-determination possible. The book's portrayal of the women's friendship at once serves as a model for and calls into being what might be termed a "community of strangers" composed of like-minded readers who are alive to Charlotte's isolation and recognize it as representative of their own. Like Mrs. Beauchamp, the members of this community would be able, in spite of Charlotte's sexual vagrancy, to read correctly "the goodness of her heart" (66)—that is, to reinterpret female "virtue" as a symbolic rather than a literal, physical quality. By recognizing the possibility of a disjunction between apparent signifiers of female vice and the reality of inner virtue—and by thus opening up to women the kind of "flexible disposition" and creative agency that republican men already enjoyed— such a community would allow even the "fallen" woman to "become an useful and respectable member of society" (125); Mrs. Beauchamp holds out just this hope for Charlotte until it becomes clear that she is going to die. With its emphasis on an interdependent community of women, *Charlotte Temple* suggests as a solution to the problem of women's isolation, dependence, and corruption, a kind of female commerce between "natural friends."

On the other hand, Rowson's novel also works to redress the second great impediment women face, for by employing Charlotte's career as a negative exemplum, it seeks to correct the kind of "mistaken education" that Charlotte herself has received. By illustrating the dangers that sexual "errancy" posed for women in a society with a sexual double standard, the novel provides moral instruction, but by providing descriptions of worldly affairs it also serves in part as a substitute for the formal education provided for men at academic institutions. In this didactic role, *Charlotte Temple* is typical of the early American novel, which, as Cathy Davidson has observed, "regularly provided a kind of education that could even parallel—admittedly, in a minor key—that which was provided by the men's colleges." But *Charlotte Temple* does not represent the only "parallel" to male education extended by Rowson, for in her own eventual capacity as a founder of girls' schools and author of textbooks for girls, Rowson continued to push for the twin goals of female education and female community. Her commitment to education was evidenced above all in the establishment of her Young Ladies' Academies in the Boston area (established in 1797) and in her creation of textbooks dedicated specifically to "the arduous (though inexpressibly delightful) task of cultivating the minds and expanding the ideas of the female part of the rising generation." These textbooks were written, she claimed, because "it is observable that the generality of books intended for children are written for boys," and her project thus reflected the increasing interest in women's education that occurred at the end of the eighteenth century. At the same time, the founding of women's schools with a distinctive curriculum was an important impetus for the creation of a sense of female community and solidarity, a process that Nancy Cott has called the "construction of a sex-group identity." Cott argues that this development constituted a key step in the evolution towards the broader feminism of the nineteenth century, for this later movement was "predicated on the appearance of women as a discrete class and on the concomitant group-consciousness of sisterhood."[18]

In the early Republic, then, girls' academies such as Rowson's were essential in providing both the education and the friendship needed to constitute the community of strangers that Rowson suggests is vital to the preservation of female "virtue" in a republican polity. Even though Rowson's education agenda was, by modern standards, largely conserva-

18. Davidson, *Revolution and the Word*, 73; Susanna Rowson, *Reuben and Rachel; or Tales of Old Times* (Boston: Manning & Loring, 1798), iii, iii; Nancy F. Cott, *The Bonds of Womanhood* (New Haven: Yale University Press, 1977), 190, 194.

tive, her vision of "commerce" seems to demand that women's horizons be expanded beyond the narrow path that leads from girls' academy to republican homestead. For example, Rowson routinely complains of the limits placed on her own education. In the preface to *Mentoria*, she includes a preemptive apology for her stylistic shortcomings, citing the constraints imposed on her education by the conventions of the day that had denied her the kind of broad familiarity with the world so vital to a serious writer: "Then alas!" she complains, sounding more than a little like Charlotte Temple, "What may not be my fate? whose education, as a female, was necessarily *circumscribed*, whose little knowledge has been simply gleaned from pure nature?" Similarly, in the preface to her play *Slaves in Algiers*, Rowson asserts that if her work is not found to be equal to that of male dramatists, it is because she has suffered the disadvantages of a "*confined* education" rather than benefiting from the classical education granted the typical male writer due to his "sex or situation in life."[19]

The imagery of spatial constriction in these passages links the limits placed on female education with the notion that women's civic role should not exceed the bounds of the domestic, private sphere. Hence it is hardly a coincidence—especially given the fact that Charlotte's "fall" is figured by the ocean voyage during which it takes place—that an abiding concern with geography was central to Rowson's own attempts to redress the female's "circumscribed" education. In her textbook *An Abridgment of Universal Geography*, Rowson explains that geography was a subject that "I had myself ever found . . . an interesting and amusing study."[20] In fact, two of the six books that Rowson wrote for her female students were geography texts. These included descriptions not only of various countries' physical terrains but also of their cultural characteristics, which Rowson often evaluated according to the prescribed treatment of women.

Yet perhaps an even more telling sign of the concerns underlying Rowson's innovative approach to the female curriculum was her supplementation of these protofeminist geography lessons with instruction in the principles of nautical navigation—a subject on which her students were often required to deliver orations. This concern that women be able to reckon or "plot" their physical coordinates under even the extreme conditions

19. Susanna Rowson, *Mentoria; or The Young Girl's Friend* (Philadelphia: Robert Campbell, 1794), iii, my emphasis; Susanna Rowson, *Slaves in Algiers; or a Struggle for Freedom: A Play Interspersed with Songs* (Philadelphia: Wrigley and Berriman, 1794), my emphasis.

20. Susanna Rowson, *An Abridgment of Universal Geography, Together with Sketches of History. Designed for the Use of Schools and Academies in the United States* (Boston: John West, 1805), iii.

of oceanic voyage is simply a logical extension of Rowson's more general commitment to the epistemological empowerment of women. Indeed, we can see Rowson's broader project, both literary and pedagogical, as aimed at enabling all female "questers" to engage in what Fredric Jameson has termed "cognitive mapping." Such mapping permits "a situational representation on the part of the individual subject to that vaster and properly unrepresentable totality which is the ensemble of society's structures as a whole." Jameson maintains that this "situational representation" is effected through the construction of a kind of mental grid that allows the subject to "map and remap [her position] along the moments of mobile, alternative trajectories," and that thus entails "the practical reconquest of a sense of place." It is a tempting anachronism in this context to imagine Rowson's educational program—with its ethos of female mobility—in dialogue with two instances of quest imagery in nineteenth-century American letters: first as a prescient rejoinder to Melville's nautical tales, which exploit sailing as the most masculine of professions and the ship as a metaphor for the patriarchal state; and second as a model for Margaret Fuller's "radical" vision of what full equality of rights could someday mean for women: "But if you ask me what offices [women] may fill, I reply—any. I do not care what case you put; *let them be sea-captains, if you will*"![21] If, for Fuller, navigation was at the extreme margin of female possibility, for Rowson it was the central metaphor, and Rowson's personal quest, whether as fiction writer, social critic, or educational reformer, was to enable American women better to map their own experience and to plot their own destinies.

21. Fredric Jameson, *Postmodernism, or The Cultural Logic of Late Capitalism* (Durham: Duke University Press, 1991), 51; Margaret Fuller, *Woman in the Nineteenth Century* (1855; reprint, New York: W. W. Norton, 1971), 174, my emphasis.

Slum Angels

The White-Slave Narrative in Theodore Dreiser's
Jennie Gerhardt

KATHERINE JOSLIN

> There comes a time in nearly every girl's life when her cry is
> to go to the city.
>
> —Florence Mabel Dedrick,
> "Our Sister of the Street"

Emma, Mame, Sylvia, the shocking Dreiser sisters, alluring, voluptuous,
flashy, strutted through the streets of Terra Haute, Indiana, bored with
small-town America, immigrant customs, and working-class poverty. Arrayed in patent leather shoes and fancy clothes, they eyed the local dandies
as income, money that might pay their way to Chicago or New York. "I done
the best I could," their father lamented, "The girls they won't ever agree,
it seems." Emma spoke for them all when she explained, "I don't know
whether it was because we were poor or because Father was so insistent on
the Catholic faith, but I was wild for anything that represented the opposite
of what I had. Father was always talking about honorable marriage, but
I didn't want to get married." Florence Mabel Dedrick, a missionary at
the Moody Church in Chicago, understood the desire to escape the often
stultifying traditions of small-town and rural living: "many girls have an
ambition and aim in life, which they are seeking to attain, and the city
offers advantages for this development which the country does not, and
we should not seek to put obstacles in her way." Jane Addams, founder
of Chicago's Hull House, spotted such girls, immigrants or daughters of
immigrants, disenchanted with the life provided by their parents: "As these

overworked girls stream along the street, the rest of us see only the self-conscious walk, the giggling speech, the preposterous clothing. And yet through the huge hat, with its wilderness of bedraggled feathers, the girl announces to the world that she is here."[1] Every bit as much as Ishmael longed for the sea, the country girl longed for the city.

Telling the story of girls like the Dreiser sisters, however, in anything like the way life may have been for them was nearly impossible. Theodore Dreiser's second novel, *Jennie Gerhardt* (1911), struggled to portray the poor woman in Chicago as mobile, intelligent, experimental, pugnacious, imaginative—all traits of the Dreisers, both female and male—but failed because his manuscript could not get beyond the popular narrative of white slavery. He wrote for an audience obsessed with the issue of the untended "girl" from Europe or rural America imperiled by the seductions of urban life. In the popular imagination, poor women adrift in the city became unwitting victims of sexual slavery, a depiction that avoided a more powerful image of urban poor and working women forging neighborhood communities and organizing labor unions, claiming their place in the city and even reshaping the manners and mores of the middle class. Ostensibly investigations of the sex trade protected a young woman, but in reality they limited her movement into the city and curbed her activities, professional and educational as well as sexual, once she got there. Over the years the story of sexual slavery became an urban myth, used as a warning to adventurous young women who want to explore the city.

The Vice Commission of Chicago, in its report *The Social Evil in Chicago* (1911), typifies the official portrait of female sexual vulnerability: "Huddled away among coarse and vulgar male companions, lonely, underfed and hungry—hungry not only for food, but for a decent shelter, for a home, for friends, for a sympathetic touch or word; tired from a hard day's toil even to the point of recklessness—starving for honest pleasures and amusements—and with what does she meet?" Huddled, hungry, filthy, outside the shelter of a sympathetic sisterhood, tainted by the indecencies of male companionship, poor women were seen as easy prey for what was called "white slavery," a supposed international conspiracy to traffic in young women and girls. Although "white" explicitly distinguished the trade from black slavery, it tacitly supported the racism of American culture and focused attention on the sexual enslavement of European American

1. Richard Lingeman, *Theodore Dreiser: An American Journey,* abridged ed. (New York: John Wiley and Sons, 1993), 48, 15; Florence Mabel Dedrick, "Our Sister of the Street," in *Fighting the Traffic in Young Girls, or The War on the White Slave Trade,* ed. Ernest A. Bell (Chicago: G. S. Ball, 1910), 106; Jane Addams, *The Spirit of Youth and the City Streets* (1909; reprint, Chicago: University of Chicago Press, 1972), 8.

women even though traffic in women of color, especially Asian women sold in California, was more verifiable.[2] The issue generated vice commission reports, vigilance committee exposés, newspaper accounts, and magazine warnings, presenting versions of the "white-slave narrative," a sentimental genre akin to the nineteenth-century novel of seduction and rescue.

The white slave, in "actual" accounts and in fictive portrayals, was a young, beautiful, passive, inarticulate, usually white angel, albeit of the slums. The white-slave narrative offered a reductive and stylized version of female sexual experience in response to what Jeffrey Weeks terms a "moral panic" over the relocation of poor women to the city. In the first decade of the twentieth century, American society placed the poor and potentially promiscuous woman, perhaps its most threatening taboo, at the center of public attention. As Peter Stallybrass and Allon White theorize, the culturally "high" may seek to eliminate the "low" as a measure of prestige and status and yet ironically embrace the low as a "primary eroticized constituent of its own fantasy life." The dynamic results in a seeming paradox: "what is *socially* peripheral is so frequently *symbolically* central." The slum and prostitution represented the grotesque world of dissipation, disorder, debauchery, and sloth. Judith Walkowitz argues that the prostitute in England embodied "the corporeal smells and animal passions that the rational bourgeois male had repudiated and that the virtuous woman, the spiritualized 'angel in the house,' had suppressed."[3] To a nervous American middle class, the grotesque threatened the stability, order, and health of the family, especially in cities where the rapid influx of rural and immigrant people was in fact changing patterns of community and influencing middle-class manners.

2. The Vice Commission of Chicago, *The Social Evil in Chicago* (Chicago: Gunthorp-Warren Printing Company, 1911), 44. George Kneeland directed the investigation and Edwin W. Sim, the U.S. District Attorney in Chicago featured in the exposé *Fighting the Traffic in Young Girls,* served as secretary. Both books, one supposedly scientific and the other openly sentimental, demonstrate the attempts of socially prominent citizens of Chicago to regulate behavior in lower-class immigrant communities. Carol Green Wilson, *Chinatown Quest* (San Francisco: California Historical Society, 1974). Wilson reports the documentation by Donaldina Cameron of the traffic in Asian women in San Francisco at the turn of the century.

3. Jeffrey Weeks, *Sex, Politics, and Society: The Regulation of Sexuality since 1800* (London: Longman, 1981). Peter Stallybrass and Allon White, *The Politics and Poetics of Transgression* (Ithaca: Cornell University Press, 1986), 171–80; see especially the chapter "Bourgeois Hysteria and the Carnivalesque." Judith R. Walkowitz, *City of Dreadful Delight: Narratives of Sexual Danger in Late-Victorian London* (Chicago: University of Chicago Press, 1992), 21.

The socially marginal poor woman alone in the city, often an immigrant or a daughter of immigrants, came to symbolize the central issues surrounding women and social change in America. The movement of women out of the domestic sphere, female sexuality, divorce, birth control, venereal disease, female education, and even suffrage coalesced around her. Add to those issues nervousness over the rapid influx of immigrants to American cities, suspicion of differing racial and ethnic groups, fear of miscegenation and the taint of foreign blood, lamentation over the loss of rural agrarian culture, and anxiety over the strength of urban industrial capitalism.[4] The poor woman, pressed by economic necessity, reared outside genteel culture, often rebelling against immigrant customs, threatened middle-class society, who feared she might ignore their social codes, manners, and mores.

From 1880 to 1900 the Chicago population tripled, bringing poor women—European immigrants, rural Americans, and southern African Americans—into the city. Statistics about prostitution at the beginning of the century fluctuated wildly; anywhere from hundreds to thousands of women worked in the sex trade. Much of the confusion is semantic: a prostitute might be "actual," involving sex for direct payment, or "clandestine," including women who lived with men outside marriage or who, for whatever reason, coupled with a variety of men. Kathy Peiss has found from the few actual records of the time that urban working women often indulged in dancing, flirting, touching, kissing, and trading ribald jokes with working men as part of the manners and mores of their social class. Close quarters in tenement buildings brought people into the streets and into public places—dance halls, ice cream parlors, amusement parks, and nickelodeon theaters—where women and men intermingled with a familiarity unapproved of in middle-class society. What crime commissions and reformers labeled as prostitution included a considerable variety of behaviors. Peiss notes that many young women flirted and engaged in sex for "treats," things they could not afford to buy with the money they earned from factory work, domestic service, or sales and clerical jobs. As George Kneeland had found in his contemporary research into prostitution, often such women, known as "charity girls," refused direct payment for sexual favors, seeking instead presents, attention, and pleasure from their encounters with men.[5] Theodore Dreiser's sisters might be categorized as clandestine prostitutes or charity girls looking for treats.

4. Mark Connelly, *The Response to Prostitution in the Progressive Era* (Chapel Hill: University of North Carolina Press, 1980), 22.
5. Kathy Peiss, *Cheap Amusements: Working Women and Leisure in Turn-of-the-Century New York* (Philadelphia: Temple University Press, 1986). See also her

The "moral panic" came late to the United States. Sexual slavery, as an issue, had grown out of the movement against the regulation of prostitution in England. The antiregulation crusader Josephine Butler and muckraking journalist William Stead had led the fight against sexual slavery in Britain in the last decades of the nineteenth century.[6] In response to skepticism about the existence of a conspiracy to sexually enslave British girls, Butler had helped Stead arrange to "buy" thirteen-year-old Eliza Armstrong from her parents for five pounds (ironically Stead was prosecuted for his success). He used the situation to launch a series of sensational articles in the *Pall Mall Gazette*, entitled "The Maiden Tribute of Modern Babylon" (1885), inciting a demonstration of 250,000 people in Hyde Park who demanded passage of legislation that would raise the age of consent for girls from thirteen to sixteen years. International conferences on sexual slavery were held in Geneva in 1877, Genoa in 1880, and Paris in 1902, which issued an International Agreement for the Suppression of the White Slave Traffic, ratified by twelve nations in 1904. The United States responded with the Mann Act in 1910, prohibiting movement of women into the country or across state lines for purposes of sexual activity (over one thousand people were prosecuted under the act from 1910 to 1918). Kathleen Barry agrees with Walkowitz that public outrage over white slavery had the ironic effect of dislodging feminists from power in England, handing the problem of prostitution over to male professionals, conservative churchmen, and advocates of social purity, a campaign that led to vigilance committees, who attacked popular entertainments as well as art, burning and condemning the literature of Balzac, Zola, and Rabelais. The purity movement in the United States would threaten the publication of Theodore Dreiser's novels about his sisters.

Although contemporaries and later scholars have found evidence of schemes to sexually enslave women and girls, the "moral panic" was a gross exaggeration of the actual situation. Teresa Billington-Grieg, in "The Truth about Sexual Slavery" (1913), called into question sensational

essay, "'Charity Girls' and City Pleasures: Historical Notes on Working-Class Sexuality, 1880–1920," in *Passion and Power: Sexuality in History,* ed. Kathy Peiss and Christina Simmons (Philadelphia: Temple University Press, 1989), 57–69; George Kneeland, *Commercialized Prostitution in New York City* (New York: Century, 1913).

6. Kathleen Barry, *The Prostitution of Sexuality* (New York: New York University Press, 1995), 91–113. See also Judith R. Walkowitz, "Male Vice and Female Virtue: Feminism and the Politics of Prostitution in Nineteenth-Century Britain," in *Powers of Desire: The Politics of Sexuality,* ed. Ann Snitow, Christine Stansell, and Sharon Thompson (New York: Monthly Review Press, 1983), 420–33. For a contemporary account, see Josephine Butler, *Personal Reminiscences of a Great Crusader* (1911; reprint, Westport, Conn.: Hyperion, 1976), esp. 221.

accounts of the period by pointing out that there was no official proof that "organized trapping" was occurring. The next year in Massachusetts, a crime commission reported that stories of white slavery appeared to be based on hearsay and on fiction: "[s]everal of the stories were easily recognized versions of incidents in certain books or plays." For all the fear of the danger to and the danger from poor immigrant women, Ruth Rosen and Barbara Meil Hobson have found that prostitutes in Boston, New York, and Philadelphia tended to come from the upper lower class, American daughters of immigrant artisans and farmers, and that most held other jobs and many married.[7]

That is not to suggest that women were not coerced into sex for money. William Sanger, *The History of Prostitution* (1858), and James Buel, *Metropolitan Life Unveiled; or the Mysteries and Miseries of America's Great Cities* (1883), argued that three quarters of prostitutes were victims. Coercion, however, most often took the form of economic necessity as Emma Goldman metaphorically identified the beast in "The Traffic in Women" (1910): "Exploitation, of course; the merciless Moloch of capitalism that fattens on underpaid labor, thus driving thousands of women and girls into prostitution." Goldman voiced the radical view that the difference between marriage and prostitution was "merely a question of degree whether [a woman] sells herself to one man, in or out of marriage, or to many men." Economic conditions for single women prohibited earning a living on their own since factory workers or salesgirls might earn $8 to $10 per week in 1910, hardly enough money to pay for room and board, certainly not enough to pay for clothing or amusements or treats. A bar girl might earn $25 a week, a prostitute even more. Ruth Rosen argues prostitution was "a dangerous and degrading occupation that, given the limited and unattractive alternatives . . . enabled thousands of women to escape even worse danger and deprivation."[8] Much prostitution, in fact, involved young women who wandered in and out of the business during their early lives and who left the trade as raises in pay for other labor allowed. The novel *Susan Lenox: Her Fall and Rise* (1917) by David Graham Phillips comes closer than most narratives to the probable experiences of many turn-of-the-century prostitutes.

7. Teresa Billington-Grieg quoted in Barry, *Prostitution of Sexuality,* 117; Ruth Rosen, *The Lost Sisterhood: Prostitution in America, 1900–1918* (Baltimore: Johns Hopkins University Press, 1982); Barbara Meil Hobson, *Uneasy Virtue: The Politics of Prostitution and the American Reform Tradition* (New York: Basic Books, 1987).
8. Emma Goldman, "The Traffic in Women," in *Anarchism and Other Essays* (1910; reprint, Port Washington, N.Y.: Kennikat Press, 1969), 184; Rosen, *Lost Sisterhood,* xvi.

Regardless of the evidence that patterns of life for poor women new to the city, especially sexual experiences, varied considerably, the white-slave narratives read like nineteenth-century novels of seduction and rescue. The story of sexual slavery, so popular in America, romanticized the prostitute, cleansing her of the grotesque, dressing her in the ideal of middle-class femininity, and presenting her as a slum angel. After all, as Henry George warned in *Progress and Poverty* (1879), "Noisome cellars and squalid tenement houses" might rob "woman of the grace and beauty of perfect womanhood." Armchair tourists read about the dark, sinful details of sexual debauchery from the safety of their bourgeois homes, titillated by the rape of innocence. By telling the story of victimization, the narratives avoided the larger question of female sexuality, a subject no one wanted to discuss. Laura Hapke finds that only male novelists depicted the prostitute and, even then, they sanitized the story to deny the "reality of women's sexuality itself."[9] Dressed in the ideology of middle-class womanhood, the poor woman, symbol of so many changes in American society, appeared less threatening.

The sentimental novel of seduction and rescue, the type of story that his biographer Richard Lingeman tells us the young Theodore Dreiser avidly read in dime novels, depicts the diverse lives of poor and working women as a single story. Lured from her family or kidnapped by force, the working-class heroine, in novel after novel, saves herself by holding fast to her religious and moral training and, as reward, regains the safety of her home and family. In *Night Scenes in New York: In Darkness and by Gaslight* (1885), for example, the heroine proclaims, "I am but a poor shopgirl; my present life is a struggle for a scanty existence; my future a life of toil; but over my present life of suffering there extends a rainbow of hope."[10] Literary sister of the Horatio Alger hero, the sentimental domestic heroine succeeds by struggling upward morally. Instead of becoming a powerful financial and civic leader as the Alger hero does, she goes back home and gains her place in the family and community, upholding traditional demarcations between male and female spheres of activity.

The twentieth-century narratives of sexual slavery, like those in the exposé *Fighting the Traffic in Young Girls* and in Jane Addams's book on

9. Henry George, *Progress and Poverty: An Inquiry into the Cause of Industrial Depressions and of Increase of Want with Increase of Wealth: The Remedy* (1879; reprint, New York: Robert Schlakenbach Foundation, 1945), 549; Laura Hapke, *Girls Who Went Wrong: Prostitutes in American Fiction, 1885–1917* (Bowling Green, Ohio: Bowling Green University Popular Press, 1989), 20.

10. Lingeman, *Dreiser*, 24–25; Old Sleuth, *Night Scenes in New York: In Darkness and by Gaslight* (New York: G. Munro, 1885), quoted in Lingeman.

prostitution, *A New Conscience and an Ancient Evil* (1912), follow a similar pattern. The slum angel, always young and beautiful and usually white, leaves the country for the city or Europe for America, finds herself tricked by wily slave traders, dark, suspicious types, often Jews or Italians, who lie in wait at train stations, hotels, dance halls, ice cream parlors, or movie houses, or linger outside sweatshops or in department stores. The swarthy men promise marriage or offer help with lodging or they drug the heroine with chloroform or spiked drinks and haul her off to a brothel, where they force her to surrender her street clothes for filmy, lacy, flashy garments and lock her up. Her debasement and isolation heighten a plot meant to arouse the reader, who gets a peek at the life of sexual excess and vicariously experiences the rape of innocence. The denouement, however, provides for the rescue and restoration of the heroine to her family or, perhaps more comforting to the reader, provides for her death, an ending that avoids returning the tainted woman to the community. The narrative ultimately disarms the dangerous transgressor by moving her from the street or the brothel into middle-class domesticity or Christian salvation.

The supposedly factual narratives that Jane Addams reported were mirrored in the fiction of the period, and there is evidence to suggest that, as the Massachusetts crime commission reported in 1913, the narrative moved back and forth between literature and testimony. Certainly Theodore Dreiser, in the examples of his sisters, had material for a more realistic account of female activity in the city, yet his second novel fails to rise above the sentimentality of the white-slave narrative. Depictions of immigrant women and their daughters as powerless to control their sexual fate reinforced the American crusade for social purity, a movement that included the censorship of fiction.

Although he began *Jennie Gerhardt* in 1901, immediately after publication of *Sister Carrie*, Dreiser fretted over the story, abandoning it for years. When he finally finished it in 1911, he kept his eye on the Boston Watch and Ward Society and the New York Society for the Suppression of Vice (sister societies to the Chicago Vice Commission and the Illinois Vigilance Association), knowing that the threat of censorship would force deep editing of his manuscript and fearing that without successful publication of his second novel, his career as novelist—he was thirty-nine and the author, at the time, of one morally questionable novel—might well be over.

In *Sister Carrie* Dreiser had blended realism and naturalism with the novel of manners to write about his sister Emma's early life. Richard Lingeman explains that Emma had had an affair with "Grove" Hopkins, a married man who stole thirty-five hundred dollars from his employer to elope with her to Montreal and on to New York, where they made a living renting rooms to prostitutes. Although the two lived well from their brothel money, he went to seed and Theodore convinced his sister to abandon him. Emma, who had put up with Hopkins's philanderings over the years, tended her sister Sylvia when she was pregnant and her brother Paul as he was dying at age forty-eight. Emma married John Nelson, another ne'er-do-well, and reared two children, Gertrude and George. In writing the novel, Theodore grafted the story of his brother Paul, a successful showman and lyricist, onto elements of Emma's early life. Sister Carrie's stage career owed more to Paul's experience as a vaudeville performer and writer of popular songs than it did to the more prosaic events of Emma's mature years. Attaching a male success story to a female tale of sexual promiscuity, Dreiser was to discover, enraged editors, publishers, and readers, who wanted Carrie to suffer as transgressors always did in female narratives.

The story of the publication of Dreiser's second novel, based on the experiences of his sister Mame, is a study in the resistance of American publishers and readers to a realistic narrative about poor women and their sexual adventures in the city. Dreiser tried and failed to interest Macmillan, Century, A. S. Barnes, and McClure Phillips in publishing his novel; Ripley Hitchcock also initially put him off by insisting that the novel be "less drastic" than *Sister Carrie*.[11] He finally signed a contract with J. F. Taylor, who wanted the title to be *The Transgressor*, reflecting the "moral panic" over poor women and sexuality. Dreiser's first version, a handwritten manuscript, told the story of a daughter of immigrants and her life as a charity girl and clandestine prostitute. Each revision of the original story required him to move farther away from Mame's experiences and closer to those of the angel of the white-slave narrative. Rather than a novel of manners or a realistic social history or a naturalist portrait of women, poverty, and sexuality, Dreiser settled in the end for a sentimental tale of sexual slavery with a curiously modern rescue.

When she was quite young, sister Mame had had an affair with an older man, Colonel Silsby, and had become pregnant, perhaps by Silsby, although there had been other lovers. After the stillbirth of her baby, Mame took up with Austin Brennan, a casket salesman twenty years her senior, whose socially prominent family disapproved of his connection to the poor, sexually experienced Dreiser sister. Mame apparently married Brennan and settled in Chicago, moving later to Rochester, New York, where she cared for her religiously dogmatic father at the end of his life

11. James L. W. West III, "The Composition of *Jennie Gerhardt*," in Theodore Dreiser, *Jennie Gerhardt*, ed. Thomas P. Riggio, James L. W. West III, and Lee Ann Draud (Philadelphia: University of Pennsylvania Press, 1992), 421–60.

and, as her sister Emma had, helped care for other family members from time to time.

The unfinished manuscript re-created the early poverty of the Dreiser family, focusing on Mame's sexual barterings. The heroine Jennie Gerhardt, the daughter of German immigrants, is seduced, impregnated, and abandoned by Senator Brander, who takes a job as an ambassador, leaving Jennie to her fate. After the birth of her daughter, Vesta, she goes to work in a factory and then meets another rake, Lester Kane, on the street. She is a version of the charity girl looking for treats in the form of financial help for her family, and he is looking for a mistress or clandestine prostitute. The sexual exchange is obvious and crass, probably close to what Dreiser thought he saw Mame doing. Jennie, in this early version of the story, understands the nature of the exchange and is pleased by the luxury she earns. The novel stalled after ten chapters. Miss Gardinnier, who had typed the manuscript, reminded Dreiser of the "moral panic" over poor women and sexuality: "Unless Jennie reaps the proverbial whirlwind in the closing chapters I fear me that the issue of your book . . . will break up the type-writing profession, not to mention other employments."[12] Why settle for eight dollars a week as a typist when you might make twenty-five, fifty, or more as a prostitute?

Dreiser suffered a lengthy depression as he tried to negotiate a course through the terrain of contemporary publishing and popular literary taste. He had begun the novel still confident that *Sister Carrie* would succeed, and as criticism of that novel mounted, his health declined, taking the form of neurasthenia, requiring a stay in a sanitarium and a stint as a laborer to ready Dreiser to return to journalism, magazine editing, and finally to fiction. His first completed manuscript, finished in 1911, significantly alters the early story. Jennie willingly has sex with Brander, becomes pregnant, but loses him as a possible husband because he dies. Her harsh father casts her from the house after the birth of her illegitimate daughter, and she goes to work as a servant, meets Lester, and negotiates an affair with him, based on his willingness to help her family financially. Lester and Jennie move to Chicago where Dreiser allows her a happy ending through marriage, an ending that approximated Mame's experience. Lillian Rosenthal, a young woman who read the manuscript, echoed Gardinnier's concern: "Poignancy is a necessity in this story."[13] She suggested a sad ending, one that would link illicit sex to personal loss.

12. Lingeman, *Dreiser,* 191.
13. See West, "Composition," 426–28; Lingeman, *Dreiser,* 254; West, "Composition," 431.

Dreiser's decision to rewrite the denouement marks his capitulation to the moral imperatives of the white-slave narrative: his heroine would have to suffer "poignantly" for her sexual behavior. The revised manuscript that Dreiser sent to Harpers for consideration left the cast-off heroine to suffer alone through the deaths of Lester Kane and her daughter, Vesta. H. L. Mencken admired that version of the novel because he believed Dreiser had balanced the sordid sexual tale of Jennie Gerhardt with the philosophical struggle of Lester Kane who abandons Jennie for marriage to the socially prominent Letty Gerald.

James L. W. West reports in his discussion of the reconstruction of Dreiser's novel that the 1901–1902 holograph, what he calls the "ur-manuscript," along with its typescript copy, still exists, as does a 1911 "fair copy" manuscript of the completed version of the novel. The fair copy reveals Dreiser's technique of cobbling together pieces of the early manuscripts with new material. Although, West explains, the ribbon copy of this manuscript no longer survives, a carbon copy, complete with Dreiser's revisions and splicings-in of new chapters, does exist. This carbon copy text has formed the basis of West's 1992 edition of the novel, a version he claims approximates Dreiser's intention before the novel was edited and revised by Ripley Hitchcock at Harpers. Even this text marks Dreiser's movement away from realism and toward the stylized narratives of sexual slavery. In the version Dreiser hoped to sell to Harpers, West points out, "Jennie is more innocent, less calculating about her loss of virtue and less practical-minded about viewing sex as a commodity to be exchanged for food and shelter."[14]

The final evisceration of the novel, however, one would have to conclude after reading the 1992 edition against the Harpers 1911 text, came at the hands of Hitchcock, who changed or removed sixteen thousand words from the manuscript before he would publish it. West's reconstructed text of the novel Dreiser first submitted to Harpers allows us to look at the pattern of censorship by editors who wanted the novel to sell well to readers familiar with the usual stories of female sexual slavery.[15] Hitchcock and his editorial staff finally took on the publication of the

14. West, "Composition," 433.
15. Ibid., 441; Theodore Dreiser, *Jennie Gerhardt* (1911; reprint, Schocken, 1982); and *Jennie Gerhardt*, ed. Thomas P. Riggio, James L. W. West III, and Lee Ann Draud (Philadelphia: University of Pennsylvania Press, 1992). As the general editor Thomas P. Riggio explains in his preface, the Harpers edition "can now be read as a work of art that is a product of its time and of publishing conditions" (x). I am reading the two versions of the novel side by side. Pages cited in the text distinguish between the Harpers text of 1911 and the Pennsylvania reconstructed text of 1992.

novel but only with the understanding that they would have the authority to make significant changes; Dreiser was not in any position to argue. They bowdlerized the manuscript by removing many of Dreiser's attempts to depict the coarseness of city life, his descriptions of drinking, for example, and his use of slang and profanity. They pandered to the social purity crusaders, whose committees were poised to censor sexually explicit material, by excising a discussion of birth control, a description of Lester's "feral" sex drive, and any trace of Jennie's sexual desire or power. The edited version denied sexual adventure, desire, or pleasure to males as well as females.

Sister Jennie, in both the published 1911 edition and the reconstructed text of 1992, fits contemporary notions of the female as intuitive, sympathetic, self-sacrificing, nurturing, philosophically mystical, as well as beautiful, blue/gray eyed, sexually appealing and yielding and, of course, white. Senator Brander calls her "You Angel!" because he sees her in terms of popular narratives (1911: 73). Lester Kane reads her as well through literary convention as the "ideal woman" (1911: 124), soft, yielding, providing him with "love, tenderness, service" (1911: 136). Her father, a rigid German Lutheran, comes to understand by the end of his life that Jennie is, as the other men read her, "a good woman" (1911: 346).

Dreiser had intended to move beyond the conventions of popular literature to reveal, over the course of the novel, the maturing of her feminine intellect, bound together by the "mystic chords of sympathy and memory" (1911: 364), and thus to present his heroine as more than a slum angel. Hitchcock's editing, however, assured that the heroine would remain an angel without a strong, maturing intellect. The youthful Jennie is portrayed in both versions as naive, nubile, and angelic, yet in the uncensored version Dreiser suggested her sexual power. He described her effect on Brander, "The beauty of her moved him as did cut lilies, wet with dew" (1992: 71); Hitchcock's revision denies her agency, "The fresh beauty of her seemed to him like cut lilies wet with dew" (1911: 65). In the revised text, Jennie's beauty does not actively "move" Brander, rather his mind moves by making the judgment. Gone as well from the Harpers edition are lines about Jennie's desire for sexual knowledge, her sense of the "beauty and pleasure in this new thing" (1992: 74).

Dreiser had meant for her growth to be revealed by a series of epiphanies that mark changes in outlook, tone, and demeanor; in every case, Hitchcock altered these pivotal scenes. At her banishment from the family home because of her pregnancy, for example, Hitchcock edits out the line, "Rich pathos was in her soulful eyes, and a tenderness that was not for herself at all" (1992: 87). The effect is to flatten her character by erasing any sign of affect or spirituality. Dreiser presented the scene as a rite of passage, but Hitchcock denies her growth by excising the line, "she had already grown more womanly." He even makes the house itself the agent of her ouster by changing "she recovered herself, and on the instant began the new life" to "the door closed upon her as she went forth to a new life" (1911: 81). Hitchcock's Jennie is less aware and less confident of her journey into the world, more a victim of sexual slavery than an agent in her quest for economic power or sexual pleasure or intellectual experience.

Perhaps the most damaging editing of her epiphanies occurs at the scene of the European tour, where Lester is finishing Jennie's education. Dreiser meant the travel to mark her philosophic and aesthetic maturation as a woman and to set her femininity against Lester's masculinity. The scene opens with the line, "It is curious the effect of travel on a thinking mind" (1992: 307). Hitchcock replaces the line with, "Jennie, on the other hand, was transported by what she saw, and enjoyed the new life to the full" (1911: 264). His revision undercuts the philosophical insight of the paragraph, denies Jennie a "thinking mind," and makes Dreiser, the putative author, look like a fool, not to say a bad writer.

Dreiser originally sought to portray Jennie's situation in larger literary and social terms. He may have wanted the reader to think of Jennie as literary kin to Thomas Hardy's Tess by explaining that the heroine is "no unwilling but only a helpless victim" and to Nathaniel Hawthorne's Hester in the admonition that the fallen woman must "go hence a marked example of the result of evil-doing" (1992: 94). Hitchcock's deletion of those allusions to serious literary works has the effect of tying the novel more closely to popular sentimental fiction.

He further blunts the serious social and moral dimensions of the novel by removing a long passage on the culpability of American society, a "brutal . . . pompous and loud-mouthed" group of hypocrites (1992: 93). Dreiser adds, "She must contemn herself, contemn that which in the more approved limits of society is of all things the most sacred and holy." Hitchcock, unwilling to condemn his middle-class readers or even to make them uneasy, removes the lines about social hypocrisy. At another point Dreiser straightforwardly links social class to prostitution: "There are many men who looked upon women outside their own circle as creatures suited for the purpose of temporary companionship, as it were" (1992: 129). Hitchcock, in rewriting this statement, tampers with Dreiser's diction and tone: "These are the men, who, unwilling to risk the manifold contingencies of an authorized connection, are led to consider the advantages of a less-binding union, a temporary companionship" (1911: 119). The legalistic jargon—"manifold contingencies" and "authorized connection" and "less-binding union"—obscures Dreiser's point about social inequities by garbling his language and blunting his sarcasm.

What the publisher demanded and the middle-class reading public desired was the simplistic survival of "ideal womanhood" in the figure of a slum angel. Dreiser himself killed off Jennie's illegitimate daughter, Vesta, the remaining threat to that ideal: "Vesta was evidently going to be a woman of considerable ability—not irritably aggressive, but self-constructive" (1911: 313; 1992: 262–63), both versions tell the reader. Jennie's child, the granddaughter of immigrants, represents the self-possession, intellect, and capability of a new generation of women, self-constructed and "constructive." Named for chastity and the hearth, Vesta might indeed have signaled radical changes in domestic life. Hitchcock moves against her more sharply than Dreiser does by removing two years from the novel, years that the mother and daughter have to become friends after Lester's abandonment of Jennie. Hitchcock also removes the description of their companionship as a "strong bond of intelligent sympathy" (1992: 385) and censors their physical contact by removing the line, "she caressed Jennie fondly." The censored Jennie is not capable of strong affect nor of physical pleasure, even in relationship to her daughter. But the truth is that Dreiser wanted Vesta dead as much as Hitchcock did; the idea of female energy causing real social change apparently scared both men.

Dreiser's ending curiously twists the white-slave plot, not only by removing the feminist daughter but also by relocating the heroine to the sanitized safety of the suburbs where second-generation Americans were being absorbed into bland patterns of economic and political conformity. Elizabeth Ewen in her study *Immigrant Women in the Land of Dollars* discusses the movement of second- and third-generation Americans to the suburbs: "Successful adoption of the suburban consumer ideal meant hiding all traces of one's roots. All telltale signs of the old way were smothered."[16] Dreiser may have been comforted by such an ending: the tawdry stories of his sisters' sexual knowledge and pleasure smothered and his German immigrant roots thoroughly, if fictionally, Americanized.

In Sandwood, a community of lakeshore cottages north of Chicago, Jennie, her erotic energy exhausted, comes to embody all that urban, commercial, industrial Chicago had supposedly lost in the rise of industry and influx of immigrants: "The care of flowers, the care of children, the looking after and maintaining the order of a home were more in her

16. Elizabeth Ewen, *Immigrant Women in the Land of Dollars: Life and Culture on the Lower East Side, 1890–1925* (New York: Monthly Review Press, 1985), 268.

province" (1911: 397). With her two illicit lovers and her illegitimate feminist daughter dead, the heroine adopts two children, readies herself for a sexless middle age, and becomes the angel of the suburb, the new site of safety for the American middle class. All that the sexually active Jennie had symbolized—female mobility, the breakdown of the family, illicit sexuality, birth control, even the taint of foreign blood (the marriage, perish the thought, of a German to an Irishman)—loses its power to frighten the reader. The relocation of the Gerhardt family from Germany to America and Jennie's movement from the country to the city made her a dangerous woman, and only by moving her to the middle-class suburbs can Dreiser divest a woman like Jennie of her difference, her potential for disruption.

Through the fusing of opposites, the grotesque and the ideal, the white-slave narrative neutralizes the power of the poor urban immigrant woman. Rather than being a bold creator of new female community in the city, a woman of clear cultural difference, she becomes the conventional angel of the slums, a bourgeois American after all. Dreiser further transports Jennie Gerhardt out of the chaos of urban living, where the differences of custom, dress, manners, and values threaten his readers, into the supposed safety, cleanliness, and order of suburbia. The novel may indeed have calmed readers eager to deny the social changes that poor rural immigrant women like Mame, Emma, and Sylvia Dreiser brought with them to Chicago.

Constructing "Home" in Mary Paik Lee's *Quiet Odyssey: A Pioneer Korean Woman in America*

MONICA CHIU

Home, as a concept, often conjures up images of a safe and familiar place, a romanticized refuge, or what Gaston Bachelard calls an intimate, nurturing space bound up in the maternal. Yet such representations must be approached cautiously, for in their positivistic bent, they conveniently overlook other constructions of home: in abusive families, for example, home is couched in physical or emotional violence; for migrant workers, home evolves around available employment; and for many immigrants, home may be ephemeral. I would like to consider dislocated, transnational subjects by contextualizing *home* and the Asian immigrant experience in Mary Paik Lee's autobiography *Quiet Odyssey: A Pioneer Korean Woman in America*, edited by Sucheng Chan. I chose this particular text because it typifies, on the one hand, the constant relocation endemic to many Asian experiences abroad and the contradictions involved in being culturally displaced at the same time that Lee and other Asians are racially placed, or named, by the dominant communities in which they live from the turn of the century to the 1950s. On the other hand, Lee's ability to overcome challenges incurred by racism or by an unyielding landscape as a migrant worker endows the autobiography with a refreshing optimism that merits excavation. The text investigates notions of placelessness within public sectors and exterior spaces—that is, the manner in which racist laws circumscribe this immigrant's daily living. My reading teases out a personal, interior space that most profoundly emphasizes how Lee's private terrain and her early-twentieth-century public arena is less a split between two mutually exclusive territories than it is a seam, suturing co-existing *topos* and affecting the creation of home. As Rajini Srikanth reminds us, and as Lee so tellingly illustrates, home can be both "a physical space and a cultural construct" in that immigrants of the past and present never relocate to and from homogenous places, but rather negotiate their lives in contentious locations that invite constant change between "native" and newcomer.[1]

Immigrating as a child in 1905 from Korea, Mary Paik Lee (née Kuang Sun Paik) was forced to abandon her native home, along with her mother and father, to trek to and across foreign soil, joining the ranks of other *yumin*, or Korean drifters abroad. With optimism, Korean immigrants like the Lees sought better lives, or a refuge from their Japanese-occupied country, in Hawaii. However, the duress of sugar plantation work—in which most Asians to Hawaii were employed—sent many to the mainland while others returned to Korea. The Lee family moved at least twenty times, from Hawaii to numerous locations along the U.S. West Coast, mostly in and out of dilapidated structures. In 1960, Lee, as a widow, finally settled permanently in Los Angeles, terminating a migratory lifestyle spanning more than fifty years.[2]

In order to contextualize Lee's experiences, I must consider, in general, immigrants of the Asian diaspora from the mid–nineteenth century to the early twentieth and how their imagined constructions of this space called "home"—both those they left behind and those they pursued in America—conflicted with the realities of a country that welcomed Asian immigrants at the same time that it feared them; in a nation that hired Asian labor at the same time that it condemned Asian employees for appropriating jobs often held by white Americans. The Chinese, the first

---

1. Gaston Bachelard, *The Poetics of Space*, trans. Maria Jolas (Boston: Beacon, 1994, 1969), 37; Mary Paik Lee, *Quiet Odyssey: A Pioneer Korean Woman in America*, ed. Sucheng Chan (Seattle: University of Washington Press, 1990). Chan has contributed significantly to the field of Asian American studies through a text that not only unearths Lee's biography, but also raises questions concerning what kinds of stories the academic arena or the reading public demands from Asian Americans. If "Mrs. Lee's autobiography is compelling" because it is "a story of hardships," as Chan writes, would Asian American stories unmarked by labor and poverty be uninteresting and thus not useful (xiii)? Do narratives like Lee's position the speaking subject as the collective sign for the "thousands and thousands of Asian immigrants in early twentieth-century America" (introduction to *Quiet Odyssey*, xvi)? Lee's experiences cannot speak for all Asian immigrants, nor do I intend them to; Rajini Srikanth, "Gender and the Image of Home in the Asian American Diaspora: A Socio-Literary Reading of Some Asian American Works," *Critical Mass: A Journal of Asian American Criticism* 2, no. 1 (Winter 1994), 148.
   I thank David Brakke for patiently reading each new draft of this essay.

2. The term *yumin* is from Ronald Takaki, *Strangers from a Different Shore: A History of Asian Americans* (New York: Penguin, 1989), 277. Also see Takaki for more information about Japanese immigration to Hawaii (270). Throughout, I concentrate on Lee's childhood years rather than her later married years.

wave of predominantly male Asians to arrive, were eager to escape political and ecological problems in their own *home*land at the prospect of
striking it rich in gold mines of the West Coast and British Columbia.
Koreans, Japanese, and Filipinos, immigrants of the second wave, were
initially recruited by American representatives in their own countries to
work on Hawaiian sugar plantations. A third wave in this Asian diaspora
were employment-seeking Indians from the Punjab region who arrived in
smaller numbers and without significant recruitment.[3] While the Chinese
were often sojourners, intending to return to China as wealthy men, other
Asians immigrated on the hopeful premise that America would offer them
an economically solid home. However, once on American soil, Asian
immigrants confronted racist land laws and fierce job competition with
whites, sometimes with European immigrants, and often with Asians of
different nationalities.

Meanwhile, the numbers of immigrating Asian women were significantly fewer than those of immigrating men. In the case of the Koreans
and Japanese, their plantation owners feared that married employees
would create growing families with subsequent economic needs; thus
they frowned upon permitting wives, still in their homelands, to join
their husbands. "The sex ratio in the Korean community [in Hawaii]," says
Sucheta Mazumdar, "was ten men to one woman. . . . Of the 7,296 Korean
immigrants in Hawaii during this period, only 613 were women." A few
Asian women engaged in what Mazumdar calls "atypical employment"
for their sex: some Chinese and Japanese women mined in western states;
others joined fishing industries on California's Monterey Coast; and a few
Chinese women were employed in railroad construction. However, most
pre–World War II Chinese women's employment occurred in domestic
settings: washing laundry, putting up boarders, and sewing, or, in the case
of Japanese and Korean women, in farming. Mazumdar states, "By 1920,
14 percent of all Oahu plantation laborers were women, about 80 percent
of whom were of Japanese origin, the others Chinese, Korean, Portuguese,
and Norwegian descent."[4] The necessity dictating that women work to sup-
plement the family income influenced and interrupted individual desires
of establishing economically solid homes. Such obstacles delineated how

3. Sucheng Chan, *Asian Americans: An Interpretive History* (New York: Twayne,
1991), 3. For more detailed explanations of why Chinese, Japanese, Korean, and
Indian immigrants chose America as a site of immigration—or to what extent
political circumstances opened passages to America—see Chan's first chapter.

4. Sucheta Mazumdar, introduction to *Making Waves: An Anthology of Writings by
and about Asian American Women*, eds. Asian Women United of California (Boston:
Beacon Press, 1989), 6, 9.

pioneer Asian homes in America were contested arenas, inimical to the typical, nostalgic representations associated with the term.

They also emphasize that, by necessity, Asian immigrants adapted their understanding of *home* to a legal atmosphere prohibiting citizenship and denying Asian ownership of land. Lisa Lowe suggests that "the life conditions, choices, and expressions of Asian Americans have been significantly determined by the U.S. state through the apparatus of immigration laws and policies, through the enfranchisements denied or extended to immigrant individuals and communities, and through the processes of naturalization and citizenship." Furthermore, limited employment opportunities exemplified the contradictions inherent to Asians attempting to establish an American home, contradictions involving not only race, but gender and class as well. For instance, while culturally displaced Asians and Europeans alike, regardless of gender, filled labor positions in both public and private domains, and thus dismantled some gender barriers imported from their respective countries, they established hierarchies of ethnic laborers in their place. Sau-ling Wong finds that both immigrant groups experienced similarities of "dislocation, poverty, prejudice." "With European ethnics, however," Wong says, "there is enough cultural congruence with the Anglo mainstream . . . to validate the rhetoric of consensual nationbuilding." Europeans were eventually mainstreamed, while physically differentiated Asian immigrants often competed not only with white laborers over jobs, but also with other Asian workers.[5] It is through this subjection to a fluctuating immigrant status vis-à-vis employment, citizenship, land, and race restrictions that presented the greatest challenge to what the culturally displaced imagined as home and how they defined themselves in relation to it.

Yen Le Espiritu concludes that gendered relations and inequalities are not homogenous, but are "structured" in accordance with social definitions of race and class. If race "remains a fundamental organizing principle," as Howard Winant suggests, in that it is "a way of knowing and interpreting the social world," then those constituents who are "raced" by others are also organized, often under the rubric of biological determinism. Or, as Henry Louis Gates Jr. records of attitudes about race conceived

5. Lisa Lowe, *Immigrant Acts: On Asian American Cultural Politics* (Durham: Duke University Press, 1996), 7; Sau-ling Cynthia Wong, *Reading Asian American Literature: From Necessity to Extravagance* (Princeton: Princeton University Press, 1993), 43. Koreans, for example, were actively recruited between 1900 and 1905 as strikebreakers in disagreements between Japanese laborers and Hawaiian plantation owners, says Yen Le Espiritu in *Asian American Men and Women: Labor, Laws, and Love* (Thousand Oaks: Sage, 1997), 200, 3.

during the Enlightenment (even as early as the Renaissance), it was "an ineffaceable quantity," determining physiology as much as intellect.[6] In such a racial hierarchy, blacks and Asians were regarded as more biologically suited for hard labor than their white counterparts, justifying their exclusion from white-collar jobs or their marginalization outside dominant communities.

Eventual interaction with a dominant community, which occupies the same or contiguous spaces, demands that private conceptions of place be mediated with and against their public definitions. Language, for example, initially created a barrier for non-English-speaking immigrants. But when communication is essential to survival abroad, so are finding resolutions to such barriers, complicating the transplantation and acculturation of the so-called unassimilable Asian immigrant. This process of Asian inclusion and exclusion—whether through language, community structuring, or legal acts—produced what Lowe calls "the *agency* of Asian immigrants and Asian Americans" and contributes to what I consider other constructions of home, such as those illustrated in Lee's *Quiet Odyssey.* Typifying the constant removal of Asians seeking employment, Lee positions herself within each new community, most visibly through labor available to "Orientals" at the turn of the century, predominantly in migrant farming, mining, cooking, and cleaning. During such exigent relocation, invisible barriers defined by discriminating labor and land laws minimized contact between dominant and ethnic communities. Demanding entry into a homogenized workforce often proved futile; passively accepting such barriers, however, indicated an acquiescence to perceived Asian inferiority. Amid this twofold path, Lee chooses the "quiet odyssey," following, by necessity, established rules explicitly directed toward ethnics while simultaneously resisting them through telling actions and angry words. What I discover through Lee's text is that places are not essentialized, unmalleable entities.[7] Rather, they represent a crossroads, absorbing people and their ideas insofar as the imbrication of personal experience and regional history results in the inevitable renegotiation of what creates place, and ultimately, what constitutes home and for whom. Despite political, social, and economic regulations that attempt to define the Asian individual, Lee navigates

6. Espiritu, *Asian American Men and Women*, 3; Howard Winant, *Racial Conditions: Politics, Theory, Comparisons* (Minneapolis: University of Minnesota Press, 1994), 2; Henry Louis Gates Jr., ed., *Race, Writing, and Difference* (Chicago: University of Chicago Press, 1986), 3.

7. Lowe, *Immigrant Acts*, 9–10; Doreen Massey, "Double Articulation: A Place in the World," in *Displacements: Cultural Identities in Question*, ed. Angelika Bammer (Bloomington: Indiana University Press, 1994), 118.

among such obstacles, resisting cultural confinement in order to render America her *home*land.

Even so, that new space is neither pure nor homogeneous, for "all places are, and are already, articulations," and no immigrant (or migrant) moves from one "pure" place to another. Asian immigrants, likewise, did not desert intimate homes, the Bachelard-type of havens created in memory. Rather, Lee's Korean home at the time of her emigration was collapsing under Japanese invasion, prompting the family's move overseas. "For the diasporic individual," says Srikanth, "the home one leaves behind is both the idealized site and the fractured site." The home of the future, however, becomes laced with optimism. The Chinese called America *Gan Saam,* or gold mountain, after listening to exaggerated stories of U.S. wealth. The Japanese embarked for this country in hopes of finding metaphorical money trees. Korean immigrants headed for Western shores with the rally cry of *Kaeguk chinc wi,* or "the country is open, go forward."[8]

The Lees represent many nineteenth-century Asians who listened eagerly to such tales from relatives abroad or from ambitious recruiters, who created images of a vast and boundless America. Lee says, "My parents came to America with high hopes for a better way of life" (132). Political marketing strategies inextricably bound labor on the land to freedom and economic success. Japanese and Korean picture brides— those who chose their stateside spouses by photo because these men were financially unable to return home to wed and accompany their brides overseas—naively regarded America as an opportunity to escape gender restrictions in their own countries. Or, says Mazumdar, "sometimes the motivating factor was a straightforward desire for travel and excitement."[9] Thus, Asian immigrants proceeded with high expectations of economic progress and with hopes of liberation from conflicts in their respective countries.

Likewise, American frontier men and women had once conceived of the vast stretches of Western land as a symbol for spiritual, emotional, and psychological growth. Intranational movement was fueled by stories of adventure and expansion, luring prospectors and families who were willing to become future generations of an American-style empire, to create

8. Massey, "Double Articulation," 111; I thank Sau-ling Wong for pointing out the possibility of an Asian homelessness (private correspondence, March 1995); Srikanth, "Gender," 147; Takaki uses the term "money trees," one often associated with turn-of-the-century Japanese immigrant dreams of America, to name a chapter in his book *A Different Mirror: A History of Multicultural America* (Boston: Little, Brown, and Co., 1993); see p. 246; Takaki, *Strangers,* 270.
9. Mazumdar, introduction to *Making Waves,* 7.

a unified national mentality, and to bathe unclaimed regions in a positive light. Wong claims that "America is founded on myths of mobility." However, Asian immigrants and later Asian Americans were excluded from the liberating movement of their American counterparts. While white settlers penetrating the heartland acknowledged their contributions to settling the vast and unconquered West, Asians' and Asian Americans' "deeper penetration into the land mean[t] exclusions from . . . the nation's development." The endpoint of all Asian or Anglo mobility is immobility, says Wong, which is found in the "home-seeking or home-founding narrative."[10]

Furthermore, prejudiced Americans hoping to include Koreans in movements similar to that of the Chinese Exclusion Act helped create the Japanese and Korean Exclusion League. In 1907, President Theodore Roosevelt passed an executive order banning Japanese and Korean workers from migrating from Hawaii to the mainland. Additionally, because Koreans were prohibited from becoming citizens, the Alien Land Act of 1913 barred noncitizens "from owning land and limited leases in California." Those who had "U.S.-born children" (and these children were therefore citizens) bought land in their names or tenant farmed on their own land "which they registered in the name of an eligible white neighbor or friend."[11] The land, a direct representation of denied citizenship and nationality, excludes Lee from making a home as she is forbidden from taking root as a laborer and as a resident.

10. Henry Nash Smith, *Virgin Land: The American West as Symbol and Myth* (New York: Vintage, 1957), 46. Also see Richard Slotkin, *Regeneration through Violence: The Mythology of the American Frontier, 1600–1860* (Middleton, Conn.: Wesleyan University Press, 1973). Both Smith and Slotkin approach the political and literary constructions of America through its proliferation of myths; Wong, *Reading*, 118; Annette Kolodny illuminates such a conclusion in her investigation of women's writing and metaphors of home on the western frontier. Kolodny explains how conquering and expanding predicated motivations for male pioneers to forge west. The women accompanying them, however, were more concerned with cultivating gardens and personal spaces reflective of order and familiarity that established a new home or reminded them of an old one. Annette Kolodny, *The Land before Her: Fantasy and Experience of the American Frontiers, 1630–1860* (Chapel Hill: University of North Carolina Press, 1984). Also see Susan H. Armitage's "The Challenge of Women's History," in *Women in Pacific Northwest History: An Anthology*, ed. Karen J. Blair (Seattle: University of Washington Press, 1988). For a discussion of women and contemporary social spaces, see Gillian Rose's *Feminism and Geography: The Limits of Geographical Knowledge* (Minneapolis: University of Minnesota Press, 1993); Wong, *Reading*, 139, 141, 122.

11. Information on exclusionist policy and racist land acts is from Takaki, *Strangers* (272). See the same book for a discussion of racist land acts (203–8, 411–13) and discriminating immigration acts of 1917 (309), 1924 (209–10), 1965 (419–22); Mazumdar, introduction to *Making Waves*, 10.

However, Lee's "failure of home-founding" was not a failure after all, even though she was destined, through such laws and restrictions, to follow another's map. Lee creates a "psychological privacy," a term I borrow from Jeanne Wakatsuki Houston, a second-generation Japanese who was interned in a World War II Japanese relocation camp. Houston says of her own dislocation, "It was not until recently that I realized mobility and time do not mean freedom. The freedom is *within* me. I must *feel* free to be free."[12] The concept of "feeling free" is an emotional flexibility, expanding in converse proportion to limiting physical and societal restrictions, such as the crude housing Lee's family initially occupies in California. Despite their rough and unsanitary conditions, Lee relates them matter-of-factly, as if reducing emphasis on the physical structure in order to cultivate her own inner strength. Consider the following descriptions:

> My family was living in a long building with one long hallway in the middle and several small rooms on each side. There was no bathroom and no hot water tank. A toilet was attached to the house outside the back door. The building had one small kitchen with a gas stove and a small dining area with benches and small tables. There was electricity for lights. (52)

> It was an old building with no bathroom or bathtub. The toilet was built onto the house, outside, after the outhouses were removed. We didn't have a hot water tank, so we had to heat the bathwater in buckets on the gas stove and we used a large tin tub for baths. There were electric lights, however. The house had four small rooms, a kitchen, and a dining area. (67)

While exterior conditions, including legal restrictions, culminate in prohibitions from the mainstream, Lee focuses on the play of nature, its boundlessness and inability to confine her psychologically. For while the changing landscape symbolizes labor, it is also a catalyst for appreciating other non-labor-related external factors. Nothing can circumscribe the beauty of a night sky, for example, nor the opportunity to relish the first taste of an orange from nearby groves. In the introduction to *Quiet Odyssey*, Chan says of Lee, "Her obvious love of nature—which she now expresses

12. On following another's map, see Wong, *Reading*, 128–29. Jeanne Wakatsuki Houston, "Beyond Manzanar: A Personal View of Asian American Womanhood," prepared for the "Seminar on Asian Americans," Oklahoma State University, March 8–9, 1978, 18. Houston illustrates how her first-generation Japanese mother manages an interior, personal space amid an external one: "She never confused her tasks with who she was. This concept of the inner self . . . allowed her to form her own image, distinct from the one in the exterior world. This ability to create a psychological privacy, inherited from a people who for centuries have had to create their own internal 'space' . . . This was her way to survive . . . and to succeed."

through oil painting, a hobby she took up at age seventy-five—suffuses her narrative with a visual, almost tactile, quality that enables her readers to feel, hear, and see the world through her eyes" (xiv).

Passionate exclamations about nature punctuate *Quiet Odyssey* with mystery and excitement. At one point, inhabiting shacks in Riverside, California, her father hastens the children to the window to observe a brilliant constellation, which Lee describes as "a big star with a very long sparkling tail" (20). "It was a spectacular, awesome sight," she continues, and "we couldn't sleep the rest of the night." The scene evokes her un-fettered imagination—perhaps representing Lee's goals to temper hostile communities and to find a harmonious home/place. Her delight at what extends beyond her ken eradicates issues of legal landownership. For, in essence, can humans truly own land or are we only its temporary inhabi-tants, who, like Lee, can marvel over its spectacular sights with impunity?

This reach beyond material conditions occurs again when the family attempts potato farming on Roberts Island, situated on a river and offering the protein of fish to the family diet. On the farm, Lee marvels at the variety of animals, stating that she and her siblings "felt alive and eager to see everything" (27). Again, the father rouses the children out of bed in the middle of the night, this time to view masses of spawning shad, glutted like a silver carpet the width of the river (31). The family enjoys barrels of salted roe and dried fish the entire following year, perhaps each meal a reminder of that awesome sight on the riverbank. The silver fish are a sight of excess, spilling beyond an everyday drudgery and into an imagination that cannot be legally inhibited. Lee embraces nature with vigor and appreciation because it does not reject her, unlike many of her prejudiced neighbors and employers. She is grounded to the land on which she works even though ownership of tillable acreage is beyond her reach. Nonetheless, her home is part of that larger world. Much of her internal strength arises from the realization that while aspects of America are formidable, there is also joy. While crying from exhaustion as she toils in the fields, for example (97), she stops frequently to admire the large rainbow-colored carp that swim in her rice paddies (69); as a child, she collects pine branches and berries with which to adorn the schoolhouse (39); or she gathers flowers blooming in the surrounding hills (40).

Lee's keen observations of the natural realm often subdue a more sinister note, signifying her world in a microcosm. She notices that the helpless grunion on the beach, once "a blanket of sparkling, shimmering silver" (119), fall prey to those admirers who effortlessly scoop them into buckets for their evening meal. The carp residing in her rice fields, as well as the migrating ducks and geese who pillage the crops, become dinner for hungry field hands (71). On Roberts Island, a starving rat—too large for even the cats to tackle—engages in a midnight scuffle over the young Lee's nose (29). While Lee provides no interpretation of such events except to narrate their occurrence, nature signifies her present life of racial labor hierarchies: here, the dominant prey upon the weak, and human relations can represent a stinking mass of fighting bodies—akin to the ball of snakes she discovers one day in a deep pit, inextricably wound about each other (41)—in which individuality often supersedes the necessity to act together.

These survival-of-the-fittest dramas also echo the prevailing views of turn-of-the-century social scientists on the role of industrialization, modernization, and capitalism, especially in terms of place. Borrowing from the rhetoric of natural history and social Darwinism, geographers and scholars at that time predicted that society would evolve into a higher form of civilization. In such a theory, class and community arose briefly to dominate over place. Place, defined as a collection of local customs and folklore and thus the antithesis of progress and modernity, was eventually overcome by the sophistication of what was called society. The order of nature became the order of society, the rational, logical extension of place. In the same vein, Homi K. Bhabha addresses how social Darwinism circulated within colonial societies—and I would add diasporic societies internally colonized in America—at the turn of the century. Because the colonized, or the raced, individual is considered the opposite of the "white man [who is] universal, normative," mid-nineteenth-century inquiries into "the 'origin of races' provided modernity with an ontology of its present and a justification of cultural hierarchy within the West and in the East."[13]

Turn-of-the-century scholars steeped in social scientific inquiry investigated the organic nature of social, economic, and political growth and decay "analogous to those [theories] used to describe the competition between plants in biotic communities," says J. Nicholas Entrikin. Accordingly then, a balance of diverse-minded people who shared similar goals and values would establish a harmonious community in the manner of a balanced environment (37). Asian families, however, rapidly occupying West Coast areas, were prohibited from contributing to such harmony or from being included in any broader notion of community. Anglo communities that fed on Asian stereotypes—rumors of Asian drug rings, gang wars, and prostitution circles—justified ethnic exclusion across *all* Asian nationalities in the interests of a like-minded, white moral harmony. Safe havens, like Chinatowns or Little Tokyos, arose to accommodate displaced

13. Homi K. Bhabha, *The Location of Culture* (London: Routledge, 1994), 248, 246.

Asians; Korean populations, however, remained too small to support what Ronald Takaki calls their own "ethnic economy and community." Instead, they relied upon a strong sense of "ethnic solidarity," one fostered by the Japanese invasion of their home country. Or, in the case of the Lees and their Mexican neighbors, they were isolated at the borders of white communities. Lee, however, is guilty of committing similar disturbances to a moral harmony. She admits in one of Chan's appendices that she chose to avoid all contact with Japanese, even crossing to the other side of the street when she saw them approaching. When mistaken for a Japanese, Lee says that she became extremely angry, but later developed a cordial working environment with them (136). Given her own angry feelings about discrimination against Koreans, as well as Koreans' general contempt for the Japanese, Lee's words, couched in Chan's editorial notations, offer rich material for addressing hypocrisy and an absent moral harmony among Asian immigrants and nationalities themselves.[14]

Lee's ability to foster compatibility between an external environment of prejudice and an internal acknowledgment of the hypocrisy evident in her own nationality is inspired by her father, Sin Koo Paik. He sacrifices his health, through hard labor, for the benefit of his ten children (eight born on American soil) and serves as a role model of kindness, perseverance, and a broader understanding of race relations. When the family first arrives in San Francisco, a group of white men "waiting to see what kind of creatures were disembarking" from the boat, spit upon the Lees (12). Her father explains that such behavior is no different from Korean reactions to "white devils," what Koreans called American missionaries. He adds that Koreans now in America must prove their worth through good behavior and hard work.

Lee attests to modern speculations on the recovery of place. Her experiences converge on the border between place as a politically and socially constructed community and as a particular area infused with regional lore,

14. J. Nicholas Entrikin, "Place, Region, Modernity," in *The Power of Place: Bringing Together Geographical and Sociological Imaginations,* ed. John A. Agnew and James S. Duncan (Boston: Unwin Hyman, 1989), 37. Entrikin discusses three geographical sociologists, Robert Park, Howard Odum, and Carl Sauer, who offer varying views on the evolution from place to modernity through "ecological aspects of the social order" (37); "The derogatory Chink is 'generic,' " says Wong about the nation's tendency to view Asians collectively (*Reading,* 61); Takaki, *Strangers,* 270. It was ironic, then, that many whites often mistook them for Japanese, a designation against which the Koreans fought vigorously, as they also competed with whites for jobs. Takaki states, "On the mainland, the Korean immigrants found whites associating them with the Japanese" (*Strangers,* 271); Takaki, *Strangers,* 281.

the latter recuperating the traditional values that place was thought to have lost once it became society.[15] While work is a fact of her survival, the contributions she makes as an individual, or as a family member, impact the larger community. She influences "pure" place, for her Asian presence introduces ethnicity within the communities she circulates, forcing its members to think and react, tying itself into and out of social knots. However, unlike the stinking mass of snakes she once discovers, the sophistication of human relations is based upon solving such knots, as Lee attempts to do, through a capacity to reason and communicate.

When the Lee family's presence in more comfortable accommodations inside town is lawfully prohibited, they occupy a series of dilapidated shacks once owned by Chinese railroad workers, filling the social and political footsteps of their predecessors: "the shacks were constructed for the Chinese men who had built the Southern Pacific Railroad in the 1880s" (14). While the Chinese were initially regarded as a "yellow peril," a cancer infecting America's moral and economic health, the Japanese and the Koreans were subsequently demonized at the advent of World War II. In this same vein, the Vietnamese were regarded as enemy "gooks" during the Vietnam War, and now many Southeast Asian refugees have become the new victims of "yellow" discrimination.[16] In this first California "home"— "one-room shacks, with a few water pumps here and there and little sheds for outhouses"—Lee fills the physical place and socially constructed space of the Chinese, but escapes psychological confinement to these designations by fashioning an interior, psychological strength (14). "Side by side with her recollection of hard times are memories of kind gestures," says Lee's editor. "She is ever mindful of people's ability to rise above meanness and hate" (xiv).

The former Chinese presence, like the Lees' immediate presence, was tolerated strictly through marginalization. This attitude is reinforced when one woman for whom Lee works as a domestic servant forbids her to eat with the family, demanding that she hover at the edges of the familial circle, even refusing to give Lee dinner leftovers—duly deposited in the garbage—

15. John A. Agnew, "The Devaluation of Place in Social Science," in *The Power of Place: Bringing Together Geographical and Sociological Imaginations,* ed. John A. Agnew and James S. Duncan (Boston: Unwin Hyman, 1989), 10.

16. The Chinese were treated with contempt at the turn of the century, accused of being opium addicts and of oppressing their own people, while the Japanese were revered, especially for their interests in westernization. However, the Japanese were regarded favorably only until World War II, when the Chinese, as new U.S. allies, rose heroically in the eyes of American citizens. The Japanese, ravaging China and finally bombing Pearl Harbor, were regarded with increasing hostility, resulting in the internment of Japanese American citizens from 1941 until 1945.

with which to feed her hungry family. White domestics were equally denied places at the table and consistently commanded to eat in servants' quarters, despite daily tasks central to the culinary domestic sphere. Yet their employment options were usually more vast than those of Asians. For example, Evelyn Nakano Glenn investigates three generations of Japanese immigrants—*Issei* (first-generation Japanese), *Nisei* (second-generation), and war brides—who labored in predominantly domestic settings from the turn of the century until the 1940s. Glenn clarifies that first-generation European immigrants, as young live-in help, eventually married as a means to elevate their social status, this simple alliance preventing the necessity of returning to such demeaning work. Domestic labor was a "bridge," says Glenn, forcing them out of their familial setting and into a larger sphere to learn the middle-class skills and behavior that would ultimately improve their social status. Their second-generation daughters refused to degrade themselves in such labor, choosing clerical and sales work instead. Blacks, Glenn adds, "experienced neither individual nor intergenerational mobility." Rather, domestic work became a lifetime proposition as they struggled against institutional racism that kept them in "their place." Issei, Nisei, and the newly arriving Korean and Filipina immigrants continued to fill domestic employment vacated by white women. Matrimony hardly elevated them into more respected social or financial positions, given an environment where opportunities for Asian men were restricted to low-wage manual labor. Mazumdar documents that by 1940, "one-fourth of all employed issei women in San Francisco worked as domestic maids," and that this scenario is repeated at this century's close when "thousands of Filipino, Korean, and Chinese hotel room cleaners don uniforms in tourist spots across the country each day." Today, these female domestics forgo learning English in the face of necessary employment, prohibiting their advancement to more lucrative jobs.[17]

Koreans and other Asians were restricted from climbing the socioeconomic ladder. While white women at the turn of the century contended with the cult of true womanhood, Yen Le Espiritu suggests that minority women, and especially Asians, engaged in "subsistence labor." America

17. Evelyn Nakano Glenn, *Issei, Nisei, Warbride: Three Generations of Japanese American Women in Domestic Service* (Philadelphia: Temple University Press, 1986), 102–3; in *Quiet Odyssey*'s introduction, Chan says that Koreans "were simply lumped together with the other Asians" (xlix). See Kim Ronyoung's *Clay Walls*, where the main female character, a recent Korean immigrant, is hired to scrub toilets and dust the furniture of a wealthy and insensitive white woman (Seattle: University of Washington Press, 1987); see specifically part 1, "Haesu." Mazumdar, introduction to *Making Waves*, 8.

offered Asians a homeland only insofar as they remained segregated from the mainstream. Thus, both in response to racism and in a desire to fraternize among those of similar backgrounds, ethnic enclaves like Chinatowns arose. As well, the individual family became a matrix of changing ideals. By way of example, Asians were only employed in types of manual labor demanding much strength and stamina: gold mining, farming, laying railroad tracks, and sugar caning. The so-called masculine attributes necessary to complete these jobs, however, did little to prevent the eventual feminized depiction of Asian men who were later employed in what was considered women's work: waiting tables, doing laundry, running boarding houses. The juncture between the construction of the Asian man and his own self-representation provoked strife within the home. For those men whose families accompanied them, or whose wives arrived at a later date as picture brides, this forced emasculation encouraged Asian men to reestablish their masculinity vis-à-vis wives and daughters, sometimes through violent words and actions. Meanwhile, those women who had not engaged in much manual labor in their native countries found themselves working side by side with men and were, in a sense, masculinized. Once inside the home, they were required to adopt the feminine roles demanded of their own cultures. Espiritu notes how existing gender roles fluctuate when they intersect with race and class.[18]

These changes profoundly affected home as it had been intended to be transplanted, with its patriarchal dictates circumscribing female domesticity. Women, now as laborers and wage earners, gained "more authority to challenge men" while men, who suffered "social and economic loss," relinquished patriarchal privileges they once enjoyed. Whatever gains working women enjoyed within patriarchy, however, they lost in the marketplace, experiencing minority labor exploitation while continuing to perform domestic chores. And those who established family businesses hoping to circumvent racist hiring and racist wages could only profit through "the unpaid labor of the family members—women and children included."[19]

The immigrant home is never an unchanging condition of stability, as Sylvia Junko Yanagisako explores in her discussion of the Japanese American household or the *ie*, designating the hierarchical structure among current members. Yanagisako examines the changing relations among the Issei, Nisei, and the *Sansei* (third-generation Japanese), attempting to "conceptually organize and make meaningful changing patterns of solidarity

18. Espiritu, *Asian American Men and Women*, 10, 3. She states, "Through the process of migration and settlement, patriarchal relations undergo continual renegotiation as women and men rebuild their lives in the new country" (8).
19. Ibid., 37.

rather than unchanging ones" and arguing the insufficiency and naive simplicity of comparing so-called traditional Japanese structures against their perceived modern American counterparts.[20]

According to bell hooks, the black American "homeplace" is, predominantly, "a site of resistance," a "radical political dimension," where outside forces of racism are countered by inside (or home) constructions of black dignity, respect, and "humanization."[21] However, this construction of home presupposes that the existing home is occupied by those who can offer sustained emotional and psychological security. Lee discovers otherwise. She is alerted to her family's impoverished state when severe hunger brings her to the kitchen, hoping water will quell her cramps. She observes her parents in tears, suffering in the knowledge that their children are deprived of life's basic necessities. While the Lees continue to provide bare necessities, theirs is more readily a homeplace of sustenance than it is of resistance.

Performing domestic service in places she cannot call home, laboring on the land but denied its ownership, Lee recognizes the uncomfortable position of her cultural placement. Neither her dedication to work nor her integrity, but rather her Asian features, serve as place holders within society. Her so-called inherent, or biologically determined, inferiority prohibits mainstreaming. Thus, central to a community dependent on cheap Asian labor and yet always marginal to it, Lee manufactures a space from which to build home. Indeed, when the physical structure of the house as home (here a series of run-down shanties) and the ideological structure of a racially stratified—as well as a gender-stratified—society intersect with Lee's own internal, psychological space, they create a dynamic, syncretic "home-site."

Lee consciously eradicates obstacles to her reconceptualized home whenever the necessity arises. She leans on her father's advice about proving Korean worth and ability by working hard and remaining honest, as is exemplified in her reactions to Mrs. Bauer, in whose home she lives rent-free, in exchange for farming the land in the Bauers' absence. The contemptuous Mrs. Bauer claims aloud in Lee's presence that "dirty Japs," as she erroneously regards this Korean family, will ruin her home, despite the fact of her own slovenly housekeeping. But Lee proves her dead wrong, scrubbing the house from top to bottom, transforming the place into a veritable wonderland. Her actions speak towards disproving Mrs. Bauer

20. Sylvia Junko Yanagisako, *Transforming the Past: Traditions and Kinship among Japanese Americans* (Stanford: Stanford University Press, 1985), 16, 13.

21. bell hooks, "Homeplace: A Site of Resistance," in *Yearning: Race, Gender, and Cultural Politics* (Boston: South End, 1990), 41–42.

and not necessarily towards creating a home within the Bauer house, from which she is soon removed when the family returns. The Bauers become friendly with the Lees, "except for Mrs. Bauer, who didn't want to admit we were civilized people" (88).

When a history teacher discusses China and Japan as "the lands of 'stinking Chinks and dirty Japs,'" and Korea as a wild country civilized only through invasion (56), Lee calls upon her father's advice to "speak up when the occasion demanded and stand up for what is right" (44). She confronts the "smart aleck" instructor, reminding him that while the community prohibits "dirty" Koreans from residing inside the town, he *chooses* to frequent an unspecified "Chinese place" across from her house, as she has observed numerous times in the past (56). Asian history is never broached in the class again.

With spirit and determination, Lee approaches such instances in hopes of destroying barriers between whites and Asians. Her community is not impermeable; its so-called folk stories, based on prejudice, can change, exemplifying the manner in which Lee cultivates her own place within the landscape while simultaneously crossing into others. The walls barring her from full participation in owning land, voting, and attending certain schools and churches cannot contain her spirit. Lee's understanding of life, projected through years of hard work and constant motion, does not foster a resistance to relocation, but rather promotes an awareness of what the changing landscape offers a poor, displaced family in a foreign land. Her sense of foundation, more spiritual than physical, resonates in her autobiography through a harmony forged between exterior and interior environments. Surviving a life built on uneven ground, rife with the economic hardship and misunderstanding of the society around her, Lee manages to find friendship, rooting faith in herself and a place called America. For Lee, the idea of home can only be constructed from within, then projected outward. These interior constructions profoundly influence the exterior structure of a stratified society, breaking down naively established foundations and rebuilding those that rely on the bricks, wood, and mortar of revisioned ideals, which must be developed by Asians and Americans together. Literature by ethnic male and female pioneers indicates the "*un-doing* of home-founding narratives" in characters' constant dislocation as migrant laborers and female domestics, in enclaves and as part of the larger community.[22] *Quiet Odyssey* is Lee's narrative about the consistent fluctuation of "home" on a conflicted American and Asian American landscape.

22. Wong, *Reading*, 136, emphasis in text.

Always Becoming

Narratives of Nation and Self
in Bharati Mukherjee's *Jasmine*

D E E P I K A   B A H R I

In "The Other Question: Difference, Discrimination, and the Discourse of Colonialism," Homi Bhabha states that "Colonial power produces the colonized as a fixed reality which is at once an 'other' and yet entirely knowable and visible. It resembles a form of narrative in which the productivity and circulation of subjects and signs are bound in a reformed and recognizable totality."[1] Bharati Mukherjee's 1989 novel, *Jasmine,* about an immigrant woman might be read as an attempt to disrupt this totality through its challenge to static notions of Otherness. The journeys of the novel's eponymous heroine, a syncretic symbol of the global migrant now familiar in metropolitan postcolonial literature, detail possible escape routes from assigned subjectivities for the Third World woman.

Briefly, the novel tracks the itinerant career of its determined young protagonist as she strives to escape the confines of a restrictive Indian society and thereafter to take on the challenges of survival in an alien landscape, that of the United States of America. The story of Jasmine's movement from her village to an Indian city, followed by her tortuous journey and illegal entry into the United States after her husband's death in a terrorist attack, and continuing with her move from Florida to New York and New York to Iowa, ends with yet another journey, this time to California.

But Jasmine's quest for an autoarticulated self, it might be and has been argued, entails the crystallization and/or erection of various Others

---

1. Homi Bhabha, "The Other Question: Difference, Discrimination, and the Discourse of Colonialism," in *Out There: Marginalization and Contemporary Cultures,* ed. Russell Ferguson et al. (Cambridge: MIT Press, 1990), 76.

as well as the projection of difference and her own movement on America, the space that ostensibly permits both. The relocation of self thus becomes an inherently conflicted project. First, the dismantling of "Third World woman" as a homogenous, monolithic category through Jasmine's "liberation" from static typology relies on its more or less unproblematic retention in other typified figures both in India and in America. Second, the choice of America as a nation-space in the process of articulation might be seen as an implicit comment on the comparative "fixity" of Jasmine's original homeland, a very stereotypically Third World sort of India she must escape from in order to become individuated. The guiding principle of the disconcerting motion inherent in Jasmine's remakings, to rest is to rust and rot, is intended to menace colonial enunciation, a project always threatening to stabilize, fix, and encapsulate the figures and signs of its own hegemonic power. Even so, the transformative and regenerative method used by Jasmine to destabilize the notion of a passive and victimized Third World woman and escape typification, it would seem, paradoxically paralyzes the Other left behind at the origin of difference.

If one said no more, however, one would not have said enough. Despite the problems noted above, Mukherjee's novel is significant because it succeeds in identifying for us some particular dilemmas of the postcolonial enterprise: how to reconcile our aversion to the rampant individualism demonstrated by characters like Mukherjee's Jasmine and Mira Nair's Mina in the film *Mississippi Masala*,[2] while asserting individual difference and arguing against the fetishization of the static and collective Other; how best to deal with a *fictional* creature who represents the necessity principle rather than a moral imperative in the context of a field traditionally located on the moral high ground; how to read the postcolonial novel as social text without abdicating the right to also read it as a novel and a fictional exercise in probability; how to free ourselves from a critical discourse intent on competing for maximum victimization and a more Other than thou rhetoric; and how to resist demonization while acknowledging that any cultural collectivity, to the extent that it can be generalized at all, betrays, like any other, an unseemly underbelly. While these issues are pertinent to any discussion of *Jasmine*, in this essay I will focus neither on these nor on the novel's lapses into essentialized and Orientalist notions of the Third World and its women while attempting to dismantle them. Rather, given the focus of this collection, the ensuing discussion will dwell on Mukherjee's strategy of destabilizing the center/margin split as it operates

2. *Mississippi Masala*, directed by Mira Nair, with Denzel Washington, Sarita Choudhury, Michael Nozik, and Mira Nair, 1991.

in Anglo-American conflict politics through the liminal, evasive figure of its (anti)heroine and its challenge to the notion of "American" identity.

According to a review from the *Baltimore Sun* quoted on the jacket cover, *Jasmine* is "the story of the transformation of an Indian village girl, whose grandmother wants to marry her off at 11, into an American woman *who finally thinks for herself*" (emphasis mine). Another blurb from the jacket encapsulates the story thus: "A Hindu woman feels her family's poverty, and the Sikh terrorism that bloodies her village. . . . After a time in New York . . . she moves to a small town in Iowa" (*Los Angeles Times Book Review*). Both of these brief excerpts suggest the discursive dichotomies supposedly inherent in Jasmine's spatial movement from India to the United States—from object to subject, from victim to agent, from Third World abjection to First World individualism, from Indian to American. The novel's deft play of the borders between these polarities through the mapping of Jasmine's plural selves, I would however suggest, problematizes these dichotomies considerably. Jasmine's constant movement as a survivalist strategy would indicate that stable identity—Indian or American—is constantly deferred. Moreover, her persistent in-between status in that she never acquires an institutionalized "American" identity through citizenship or any other modicum of civic recognition has not been deemed particularly important in much of the criticism of the novel. Both factors, actually, are crucial to an understanding of her status.

Movement, signaling change of state or spurred by fear of detection by immigration and criminal investigators, constitutes a central metaphor for Jasmine's state of being throughout the novel. It suggests, moreover, the shifting and multiple identity of the migrant postcolonial subject *between* static polarities while rejecting the fixity that would be indicated in the acquisition of civic identity. Certainly, Mukherjee's occasional traffic in facile dichotomies when dealing with those from one part of the globe to develop strategies for another and her elision of questions of class compromise her project considerably at several points in the narrative. Jasmine's individuation at the cost of certain collectively and reductively clumped others—the passive Vimla who commits "Sati" in India, the Sikhs of Punjab unproblematically sketched in broad brushstrokes as fanatic terrorists, or the Indian immigrants in Flushing who might be read as ethnic caricatures—is, however, achieved through a strategy that is nevertheless worth examining for its own merits.[3] It is instructive to read

---

3. While stereotypical representations of minorities and underrepresented groups are obviously unproductive, as Ella Shohat and Robert Stam point out, obsession with the issue of representation carries its own dangers: "First, the

the novel as a lesson in the logical challenges posed by the immigrant's goal of differentiated and interventionist assimilation, particularly given Jasmine's attempts to survive by choosing a kinetic, liminal space to evade "detection." The novel has been roundly berated by postcolonial critics for its unholy trade in oppositional identity politics where American is clearly the privileged half of the equation; it has been lauded in the mainstream press for much the same reason. Readers on both sides of the issue seem to have too easily dismissed a vital strategic maneuver on Mukherjee's part. In the context of Anglo-American culture wars, I would argue that Mukherjee presents us with the option of reimagining questions of immigrant identity radically.

Jasmine, it has been assumed, is faced with a dilemma of identity that limits her choices: she can either remain the transfixed Other (Indian woman) or become the actualized, powerful self (American individual). Let me proffer the suggestion that Jasmine and the reader are confronted with not two, but *four* possibilities, in short with a tetralemma. Tetralemmic logic permits more than the two categories normally associated with Aristotelian logic. The latter, based on the dilemma, is also referred to as the law of contradiction or the law of the excluded middle or excluded third. The law is so called "since there are only two parts between which the respective whole is divided."[4] If we inserted the middle between the oppositionalities, we would recognize other possibilities. The tetralemma, seen in sixth-century Buddhist texts and developed extensively later in Buddhist logic, allows one to confront and explain the ambiguities inherent in language and concepts. Indeed, Buddhists would argue that existence is like a flow of eternal becoming since what we understand as reality is kinetic. A potent instantiation of such ambiguity is the characterization of Mukherjee's work itself. In an instance not devoid of irony, scholarship on Mukherjee's fiction continues to be placed in the *MLA Bibliography* under "Canadian Literature," dating from her residence in Canada before her

---

exclusive preoccupation with images, whether positive or negative, can lead to a kind of *essentialism*. . . . This essentialism generates in its wake a certain *ahistoricism;* the analysis tends to be static, not allowing for mutations, metamorphoses, changes of valence, altered function" ("Stereotype, Realism, and the Struggle over Representation," in *Unthinking Eurocentrism: Multiculturalism and the Media* [London: Routledge, 1994], 199).

4. Th. Stcherbatsky, *Buddhist Logic* (1932); reprint, The Hague: Mouton, 1958. This is not to suggest that America and its Third World Other are necessarily in opposition or could not share overlapping features but that they have been so constructed. While deconstruction would serve just as well to explode binarisms, I have used the Buddhist system of logic here since it is a much earlier instantiation of deconstructive thinking.

move to the United States, despite her enthusiastic and vocal adoption of a "United States" identity. Her Indian origins, in the meanwhile, continue to be referenced in interviews and criticism. So, which is she? The fuzziness of tetralemmic logic allows us to blur distinctions, to find space between the opposition of the two-sided dilemma, and to extend the possibilities of meaning fourfold. The multiple identities of the author illustrate clearly the ambiguous status of the new immigrant since she herself is and is not Canadian, American, or Indian. Rejecting rigid dichotomies, we might then posit that Jasmine is and is not a Third World woman. Moreover, she is also neither a Third World woman nor not one. Similarly, Jasmine is and is not American. Thus, if we are willing to engage this kind of logic, Jasmine would emerge as both Other and not Other, neither Other nor not Other, both American and not American and neither American nor not.

But if Jasmine insists on her *genetic* transformation into an American, as she does in the novel, can this logic hold? Only if we concede that what is American is itself as elusive as what is Indian, and that American is also an identity comprising Jasmine by virtue of her presence and agency, and thus also, in some part, its counterpart in this formation— Indian. Challenging our usual notions of both is not the least of the possibilities suggested in the novel; also inherent in this proliferation of possibilities is a conscious "unmarking" of identity to make it so elusive as to render it invulnerable to interested political constituencies.[5] Political identity marks a moment of stasis in the dynamics of being. Yet, Jasmine never becomes an American legally; in fact, she does not interact with "systemic" America at all. She remains undocumented, unmarked. The reality she engages with exists in the borders and limits of structured society as such. It is in this mobile, shifting space that Mukherjee writes her supplementary narrative for the immigrant woman. Kinesis and strategic *in*visibility mark Jasmine's identity throughout as she constantly changes her persona with every move. While a great deal of minority literature is geared toward making the marginal visible, Mukherjee manages to blur the center/marginal distinction by keeping Jasmine in a state of endless *das zwischen*—a condition of "always becoming" to escape "having become." This does not mean that the category of Third World Other has been exploded but that *Jasmine*, despite its limitations and pitfalls, obliges us to confront both it and our conception of what and who is American.

The espousal by mainstream America of assimilationist rhetoric and its rejection by those celebrating "difference" share and assume an essentialist

5. See Peggy Phelan's *Unmarked: The Politics of Performance* (London: Routledge, 1993).

definition of "American" that serves to enhance the former's superiority while forcing the latter to bear the burden of self-definition against it. To reject this essentialism is to launch us into the next progressive stage in cultural politics where we might rework the self/other as eternal dialectic while according both a greater measure of complexity than binarism allows us. Thus might we say that the minority is and is not part of America. Thus might we better explore the implication of immigrants in the cultural and economic systems of their country of domicile and their status as both victims and agents. "We can explode the assimilation argument," says Gayatri Chakravorty Spivak, "if we look at ourselves as also American, hyphenated. But American is hyphenated. In that sense, we then begin to see that, having thrown in our lot with a northern economy, an exploitative economy, in fact, whether we like it or not, we are in our everyday, agents of exploitation."[6] While Jasmine survives in the spaces between organized, documented, and socialized states of being, she nevertheless gestures at the immigrant's undeniable implication in the systemic economies of his or her adoptive country.

In an interview with Bill Moyers, Mukherjee has insisted on the necessity of Asians in America making a commitment to the country of their choice, becoming agents even if they have suffered discrimination. At the same time, she has called for a more complex understanding of the dynamics between the immigrant and the culture s/he enters. She refers to this as a "two-way traffic," explaining that if America has claimed Jasmine, "she has transformed America, too, in her ways." Jasmine's becoming American is thus axiomatically dependent on America's "becoming" Jasmine. The mainstream narrative of "America" is interrupted by this challenge to its fixity, making visible rather than the heterogeneity of the margin—which the novel largely fails at—the critical flux at the center.[7] Instead of the collective redemption of various Others, we are obliged to deal with the survivalist maneuvers of an individuated Other (both fabled and fabulist), a "special" case who eschews the status of marginal (read victim, powerless,

---

6. See my interview with Gayatri Chakravorty Spivak, "Transnationality and Multiculturalist Ideology," in *Between the Lines: Postcoloniality, Identity, and South Asians*, ed. Deepika Bahri and Mary Vasudeva (Philadelphia: Temple University Press, 1996), 84.

7. *Conquering America with Bharati Mukherjee*, prod. Bill Moyers, 58 min., Public Affairs Television, 1990, videocassette; Michael Connell, Jessie Grearson, and Tom Grimes, "An Interview with Bharati Mukherjee"; *The Iowa Review* 20, no. 3 (fall 1990): 20; as Lillian B. Rubin suggests, "There's no such thing as an American without a hyphen somewhere in the past" (*Families on the Faultline: America's Working Class Speaks about the Family, the Economy, Race, and Ethnicity* [New York: Harper Collins, 1994], 179).

morally superior) and explores agency, albeit of a morally compromised sort, disentangles herself from roots and traditions designed to keep the woman and native in place, and forces the while a recognition of the center itself in crisis.

In stressing the fabulist nature of this strategy, I am not dismissing the novel as only a story, although it is useful to remember that it is *also* a story. The realist framework invites tests of plausibility that readers have objected the novel does not pass. I have argued elsewhere for the need to place female praxis at the heart of feminist postcolonial politics *in whatever shape it presents itself.* Too, I have pointed out the dangers of making our "minority" writers meet a paralyzing and totalized code which obliges them to cast their characters and stories into a formula that maintains their moral high ground.[8] I am less interested in whether Jasmine is Other enough for comfort or in identifying the stories the novel obscures or does not tell than in reading it as a text of subversive possibilities and costs of female resistance and survival, and in doing so outside the framework of binaries that some accuse Mukherjee herself of having used. If the novel in its excision of the more probabilistic realities of discrimination, racism, and class-based barriers should ultimately seem no more than a fairy tale (albeit somewhat dark), it nevertheless remains useful in its projection of the possibilities of renegotiated immigrant and American identities.

Fundamentally, Mukherjee's project might be fruitfully read as an overhaul of epistemological exercises that have traditionally been geared to construct an enunciated product of its exertions. Sharing an ambivalent, shifting reality that prevents static enunciation are both Mukherjee's protagonist, Jasmine, and Mukherjee's alter protagonist, the nationalist construct, America. Jasmine (also known as Jyoti, Jazzy, Jase, and Jane in different phases of her eventful life), whom I will name and refer to as "J." to represent all her potential avatars, is always in the process of dodging the stasis demanded of her through her assigned subjectivity as Third World underclass woman/victim and migrant. At the same time, America is presented as a geographic and temporal state/space that is always in the process of becoming a new nation. The scening of America as the space of and for transformation is clearly in excess of the usual metropolitan postcolonial project that focuses on the transnational migrant who moves through a liminal corridor space without significantly changing the

8. See Deepika Bahri, "Disembodying the Corpus: Postcolonial Pathology in Tsitsi Dangarembga's *Nervous Conditions," Postmodern Culture: An Electronic Journal of Interdisciplinary Studies* 5, no. 1 (1994): 1–59; and Deepika Bahri, "Once More with Feeling: What Is Postcolonialism," *Ariel: Review of International Literature* 26, no. 1 (January 1995): 51–82.

traversed landscape. In Mukherjee's text, however, J. is becoming American even as America is becoming J. Each new immigrant who enters its space, legally or otherwise, shifts and transforms its boundaries. America is presented as a corporeal body undergoing constant change. Not only is the face of America shifting as new races and colors join the fray, but immigrants, like J., are capable of changing its palate and sensibilities. J., for instance, claims that she is "subverting the taste buds of Elsa County" when she takes *gobi aloo* to a Lutheran function or serves *matar panir* with pork.[9] Metaphorized as body (face, palate, pulsing organism) America is also simultaneously technological machine; it can perform the rest/movement of an escalator, which is an ingenious invention for J. Her question, "How can something be always moving and always still?" characterizes both her condition and that of the ever-evolving nation with which she chooses to identify (119). America may well be the desideratum, but marked thus by the desire of the Other, it is reproduced constantly and ectypically in the image of the Other. Using the grammatical shift from noun to verb, from being to becoming, from stilled, enunciated subjectivity to a dynamic, shifting identity, Mukherjee attempts to (dis)articulate Jasmine as Third World woman at the same time that she rediscovers the New World and makes America/American visible in the process of change.

Besides its foundation in an immigration past, its history of often violent appropriation, and a continuous remaking of its constituent peoples through ongoing immigration, the launching of America on its present orbit of change is a force also set in motion many miles away with the commencement of J.'s narrative. In the conspectus of contemporary history, it is only a matter of "connect time" before the fate of America is plugged into the cosmogonic event of J.'s birth in Hasnapur. The village is so named by Mukherjee after V. S. Naipaul's birthplace as a challenge to his "thesis of tragedy," the suggestion in his fiction that the individual born outside the metropolitan center is doomed to an "incomplete and worthless little life."[10] J.'s life may not ultimately be entirely complete or worthwhile, but Mukherjee does uproot her from the village and allows her agency, a good measure of ruthlessness, and a dogged determination to survive no matter what violence that entails to herself or what cost to others. The ambiguous

9. Bharati Mukherjee, *Jasmine* (New York: Fawcett Crest, 1989), 16. Subsequent citations will be made parenthetically in the text. The spicy Indian dishes mentioned are made with potatoes and cauliflower, and peas and homemade cheese, respectively.

10. In computer terminology, *connect time* is the elapsed time during which a user of a remote terminal is connected with a time-sharing system; Connell, Grearson, and Grimes, "An Interview," 26–27.

morality and remorseless ruthlessness of Mukherjee's protagonist alert us to a world that is perforce post-heroic. J. is not being touted as a heroine—for one thing, like an unrepentant Moll Flanders, she is in the service of no one but herself, of no goal but survival.

In challenging the predictability principle that condemns her to a foreseeably abject fate (the condition of the static undifferentiated Other even in benevolent Western feminist catalogs), J. unwittingly replots the borders of a country she will (un)settle in due course of time. This is not to suggest that J.'s is a single-handed career of geographical revision, but rather that she and "whole nations on the move" are forces turning the globe with their collective gypsy wanderings. In "Defining Genealogies," Chandra Talpade Mohanty observes that:

> worldwide migration is at an all-time high in the early 1990s. Folks are moving from rural to urban areas in all parts of the Third World, and from Asia, Africa, the Caribbean and Latin America to Europe, North America and selected countries in the Middle East. Apparently, two percent of the world's population no longer lives in the country in which they were born.

Noting that in the 1980s, 2.5 million immigrants came to America from Asia, and a third of a million in 1990 alone, Lillian B. Rubin comments in *Families on the Faultline*, an ethnographic account of the intersections between family, race, ethnicity, and the economy, "suddenly the nation's urban landscape has been colored in ways unknown before."[11] J. is only the simulacrum of the migrant subject, endlessly replicated in the scores of boat people, stowaways, and legal and illegal immigrants, the birth of any one of whom changes the aggregate fate of the world much in the way that Columbus or the arrival of the *Mayflower* changed that of the Americas and the imperialist machine changed that of three-quarters of the globe. No less a force, J.'s career demonstrates, is currently at work reconstructing the West.

The momentum of this force can only gain strength when the agent of change is herself dislodged from fixity. As a young Punjabi peasant girl, Jyoti would be all too "known" in benevolent hagiographies as the very type of Third World female stereotypically victim to native patriarchal and colonial malpractices, a function efficiently performed in the novel by her hapless young neighbor, Vimla. Vimla, to no one's surprise or particular

---

11. Chandra Talpade Mohanty, "Defining Genealogies: Feminist Reflections on Being South Asian in North America," in *Our Feet Walk the Sky: Writers of the South Asian Diaspora*, ed. The Women of South Asian Descent Collective (San Francisco: Aunt Lute, 1993), 351; Rubin, *Families on the Faultline*, 181.

dismay in the novel, sets herself on fire after being prematurely widowed at the age of twenty-two. It can be argued with reason that this presentation of Sati as matter of routine in contemporary India is a species of Orientalist misinformation. But one might also note that in many Indian societies the lot of a widow is far from desirable; besides, this plot device allows Mukherjee to disengage the hagiographic machinery that locates the Third World female as an unfortunate victim ennobled by passive suffering. She can then make the known abject/subject (dis)appear in all her stereotypical habits and re-invest her with the pluriform possibilities available outside assigned subjectivity; she can thus challenge the "crippling assumptions" that would cast a Third World woman as a passive victim.[12]When *her* husband is killed by terrorists, Jasmine, admittedly somewhat implausibly, goes to America intending to perform a Sati at the site where he was to have gone for higher education. But instead of consuming her own body, she consigns to fire the suitcase containing her benevolently patriarchal husband's belongings, and continues on a journey begun in India. When the scene shifts to the United States, the novel's potential for addressing questions of immigrant identity vis-à-vis American identity becomes apparent.

It is the quest for agency and an inherent resistance to victimization that sets J. in motion. J. substantiates her eligibility for a status other than the passive Other when she ruthlessly kills a rabid dog intent on savaging a group of women at their morning ablutions in her Punjab village. J.'s quest for emancipation and survival as an individual rather than a token victim is subsequently furthered by the assistance of a sequence of (mostly) male benefactors. She continues her transformation with her marriage to Prakash, a liberated if still conservative English-speaking Indian man who wants to immigrate to America. Named Jasmine by Prakash in honor of her liberation from traditional Indian duties, the erstwhile Jyoti's renaming suspends her "between worlds," the traditional one where feudalism is still operative and the one to which Prakash beckons her as he teaches her independence and self-reliance (69). One might observe that J. learns from Prakash the possibility of breaking from the past and the heady pleasure of shuttling "between identities," between becoming and being, between the unknown and the not yet forgotten (70). With the knowledge of this desire, J.'s trajectory becomes marked with the need to constantly become anew, to shift her borders and her identity at the very moment that they are in danger of crystallizing. This, of course, is the goal of the supplementarity implicit in the postcolonial enterprise. In this way,

12. Connell, Grearson, and Grimes, "An Interview," 12.

she is able "to antagonize the implicit power to generalize, to produce sociological solidity."[13]

Given that "women's oppression is most complexly tied to . . . [their] bodies, because patriarchal culture gives women's bodies such variable meanings and submits them to so many controls," the "sociological solidity" of the category of woman must be contested on the body itself. J.'s remaking is thus expressed on occasion in corporeal terms: On her way to America, J. experiences the euphoria of renewal when she clears the Hamburg Polizei on her fake visa stamps; as she weeps at the beauty of her forged papers, she feels like "the recipient of an organ transplant" (92). Others like her will experience this almost bodily transformation when they shed old skins (clothes) on their arrival in America to escape detection as illegal immigrants. "Some of us are forced," says Gloria Anzaldúa in her introduction to *Making Face, Making Soul*, "to acquire the ability, like a chameleon, to change color when the dangers are many and the options few. . . . [S]ome of us . . . have been forced to adopt a face that would pass."[14] Learning to dissolve her identity is for J. a matter not merely of convenience, but of survival. Later she will refer to this as her "genetic" transformation. The shedding of old theca is subsequently instantiated in the symbology of vesture.

Having arrived on American soil, J. wanders up the Florida highway in her high heels and sari, looking for a place to fling herself upon her husband's burning clothes. Instead, "Half-Face," the captain of the boat that illegally brought her over, picks her up on the highway and rapes her. After the rape, Jasmine slices her tongue; returning to Half-Face, she has become Kali, goddess of destruction.[15] Dripping blood on his face, she plunges her knife into him. As Kali, she leaves her status as a victimized, lost immigrant woman, tossing Prakash's suitcase into a garbage can and burning its contents, thus symbolically immolating Jasmine and a past that she will later learn she "was still fleeing" along with the vestments of (an)other life (30). Mukherjee's very deft use of an Indian stereotype, Kali, to consume a passive, suffering J. and re-create her into avenging agent indicates the power of a mythic past to atavistically surface and

---

13. Homi Bhabha, *Nation and Narration* (London: Routledge, 1990), 306.

14. Iris Marion Young, *Throwing Like a Girl and Other Essays in Feminist Philosophy and Social Theory* (Bloomington: Indiana University Press, 1990), 11; Gloria Anzaldúa, "Haciendo Caras, Una Entrada: An Introduction," in *Making Face, Making Soul: Haciendo Caras: Creative and Critical Perspectives by Women of Color*, ed. Gloria Anzaldúa (San Francisco: Aunt Lute, 1990), xv.

15. In the Hindu pantheon, Kali represents the female incarnation of dynamic energy.

offer new options for change. Already, J. has learned the technique of generating the self when necessary even if she has to use originary value and belief systems transported across the ocean. If J.'s act of agency can be read as "American" because it challenges passive suffering and celebrates individualistic enterprise, with the figure of an avenging Hindu goddess, it can also be read as stereotypically and inscrutably "un-American."

After being "rescued" by Lillian Gordon, who has made a career of rehabilitating illegal immigrants in Florida, Jasmine re-creates herself as Jazzy and sets out for New York wearing jeans and a T-shirt. The choice of clothing is as much a move toward seeming American as it is toward distancing herself from Other markings that might betray her illegal alien status. Following a brief interlude with an Indian family in Flushing where her burgeoning new identity is threatened, J. is ready to move on. In Dev and Nirmala Vadhera's Flushing flat, J. is in temporary danger of regressing to a new, if superficially improved, Hasnapur where she must live as Jyoti, a dependent recluse whose recently improving English appears to be deserting her as it is overwhelmed by the Hindi and Urdu videos that Nirmala brings home every night. J. is quick to sense that she is in renewed peril of being "fixed" into the type of a Third World woman whose widowed lot holds no prospect for change. Once J. decides that "I wanted to distance myself from everything Indian, everything Jyoti-like," the fates (or the laws of her powerful desire) facilitate her next metamorphosis (128). Having accidentally stumbled upon her patron Professor Dave Vadhera's "shame," that he is an importer of hair from India rather than a distinguished professor, J. is able to exchange her silence, and a promissory note pledging her future hair when it becomes twenty-four inches long, for fake papers and an exit into the maelstrom world of change that the Vadheras and their ilk choose to retreat from in favor of their cultural ghettoes.

J.'s response to her benefactors is one the reader encounters with some disapproval. One bemoans her lack of compassion for Dev Vadhera, a man with scholarly ambitions who has been reduced to splitting hair for precision instruments in a dark basement for his livelihood. One also marvels bemusedly at the ease with which J., a village girl with limited education and preparation, is allowed access and entry to mainstream America. Neither reservation should, however, prevent us from acknowledging that through this encounter, Mukherjee does suggest ways of challenging two equally paralyzing positions in contemporary race politics in America: the first is retreat from the politics of power in gestures of self-effacement and self-enclosure by immigrants of color; the other is the obdurate failure of the dominant majority to allow minorities a safe space outside the ghetto where a negotiated sense of American identity might be forged. Mukherjee, moreover, outlines clearly that minority individuals outside the "safety" of their ghettoes will suffer considerable assaults to their sense of self as they try to erode the solidified notion of American identity.

J.'s life outside the ghetto, while presented as a preferable option, is thus one characterized by renewed and continuous violence on the self that attempts to survive. Having chosen to reenter "America" again, J. contacts Lillian Gordon's daughter, Kate, who puts her in touch with Taylor, a New York professor, and his wife, Wylie, a book editor for a Park Avenue firm. In her new home as "care-giver" for Taylor and Wylie's daughter, Duff, Jazzy-almost-in-danger-of-returning-to-Jyoti becomes Jase, thus renamed by Taylor. Remaking the self invokes "two temporalities: that of oppression, memory, and enforced identity, and that of emergence after the 'break,' the counter memory, and heterogeneous difference."[16] J. comments on this continual process of change: "We murder who we are so that we can rebirth ourselves in the images of dreams" (25). The violence inflicted upon one self to generate another is a necessary condition for survival. J. internalizes the violence that surrounds her—the strife in Punjab, her own encounter with her rapist Half-Face, even the score-settling attack by a disgruntled loan applicant in small-town Iowa that leaves banker Bud paralyzed. The logic of violence applied to consume one identity to forge another is as much a coping strategy as it is a critique of the violence in the world J. finds herself in. J.'s pliant and largely unreflective acceptance of the names given her nevertheless reveal her sense that as a woman and an immigrant, her identity is constantly in negotiation.

Not surprisingly, then, Jase is by no means her final incarnation. The tides of change continue to transport her whenever she begins to "beach." In the legal economy, we should recall, she is a murderer, a forger, and a larcenist; as a criminal, she must keep moving before she is sighted. In the libidinal economy, where her exchange rate is high till the very end, J. always has the currency necessary to finance her travels. J. is unashamed and unapologetic about using her charms to gain the support and assistance of a series of men—Prakash, Taylor, Bud. But the same libidinal economy that gives her valence as an attractive gendered subject exposes her, as woman, to the danger of being silenced, fixed, and subjugated. J. is continually extricated by the author from situations where she is becoming fixed in suppliant positions—whether it is as compliant wife to Prakash,

16. R. Radhakrishnan, "Ethnic Identity and Post-Structuralist Difference," in *The Nature and Context of Minority Discourse,* ed. Abdul R. JanMohamed and David Lloyd (New York: Oxford University Press, 1990), 62.

glorified maid to Dev Vadhera and his family, nanny to Taylor's daughter, or caregiver to a handicapped Bud. Mukherjee is not particularly careful about distinguishing how these states are different or similar or why it is preferable for J. to be a nanny at Taylor and Wylie's rather than a de facto maid at the Vadheras'. What is clear is that even within these limited options, J. is allowed to exercise some choice and the freedom to chart a new course.

In the political economy, where she is the Other always in danger of being enunciated by a discursive system anxious to place her, J. learns early that her survival depends upon untiring movement, an impulse akin to what ornithologists call *zugunruhe,* a migratory instinct helping some birds to survive. This movement is J.'s dramatization of existence as eternal becoming. But it is not the only lesson she has learned. Her teachers, who range from Prakash to Half-Face, have schooled her well. Half-Face tells her, "Travel light, sweetheart, always travel light" (101), and Lillian Gordon, who "had a low tolerance for reminiscence, bitterness or nostalgia," tells her, "Let the past make you wary, by all means. But do not let it deform you" (117). Both injunctions impel her to abandon the baggage of her past and flee the condition of fixity in the present. Half-Face, her rapist, and Lillian Gordon, her savior, both teach her to use the past as a lesson for the future. As a new arrival, albeit illegal, J. soon realizes that "in America, nothing lasts" (160). To prolong the past in the face of a new future would be un-American, a condition as foreign to this illegal alien as it is dangerous because, as she candidly admits, "For me, experience must be forgotten, or else it will kill" (29).

But the past cannot so easily be dismissed. Her next move, this time to Iowa, is the consequence of having spotted Sukhwinder, the murderer of her husband, in Central Park. One might find this a somewhat contrived ploy on Mukherjee's part, but those intent on historical justification might consider that Mukherhee's extensive research on Sikhs and the Khalistan movement did unearth evidence of Khalistani cells operating in New York.[17] J.'s move to Elsa County, Iowa, to avoid being "sighted," propels her along the liminal, "fugitive's" space where she exists and survives by mutating constantly. In Iowa, J. re-creates herself as the common-law wife of banker Bud Ripplemeyer, who renames her Jane. She resists his offers of institutionalized status in marriage, persisting in her liminal, in-between state where she is both wife and not wife, both mother of their adopted son, Du, and not. Lest her transformation into "Jane," with its attendant stability in terms of family, lead us to consider it a final point for J., she reminds

17. Connell, Grearson, and Grimes, "An Interview," 27.

us that "Plain Jane is a role, like any other" (22). Bud's renaming reveals her as an adaptable chameleon, but one that always contains the potential for that transformation: "My grandmother," J. says, "may have named me Jyoti, Light, but in surviving I was already Jane, a fighter and adapter" (35). The transformation from Jyoti to Jane is presented as a continuum in a warped space outside the systematic identities of citizenship or marital and maternal status.

Predictably, J.'s days as Jane are also short-lived. Even when the reasons to move are no longer compelling, no further Sukhwinders having been spotted or INS officials found on the rampage in the area, J.'s trajectory hurtles her along like a comet whose path cannot be altered. "Every night the frontier creeps a little closer," she says (16). But it is not the frontier that is moving; J. herself is carrying the frontier with her. As if in the wake of her own incessant movement, Taylor and Duff, seeking a home in Berkeley, come through Baden, Iowa, and sweep J. away with them. J. chooses to go to California with Taylor, deserting, without so much as a good-bye, the crippled Bud, father of her child to come. Leaving Bud to be tended by his ex-wife, J. proceeds to who knows how many other identities and lives, responding to another atavistic call that beckons her West to the "promise of America" (214).[18] As the novel ends, she leaves "greedy with wants and reckless from hope," tossing a casual "watch me reposition the stars" over her shoulder (214).

J.'s need and willingness to change and transform herself are rooted in her desire to be always becoming in order to escape having become; she is determined not to allow her agency to succumb to the forces of fate. She remembers the stench from the water-bloated corpse of a dog in Punjab and avers, "I know what I don't want to become" (3). The bloated fixity of stasis and "that stench" that always stays with J. are the materials for her desire for endless change (3). Those who would insist that there is such a thing as knowable "Indianness" compel her to distance herself from what they believe to be Indian. J.'s relish in pork chops and Mary Webb's comment, "I though you'd be a vegetarian," effortlessly destabilize the latter's schema for Indianness (113). It is Bhabha, again, who clarifies in "DissemiNation" that the people are a complex rhetorical strategy and the claim to be representative would create a crisis in the process of signification. People must be seen as continuous process, as living principle. More importantly, "that cannot be knowledge that is stabilized in its enunciation."[19] While J.'s

18. At another point in the novel, J. asks, "How many more shapes are in me, how many more selves, how many more husbands?" (190).
19. Bhabha, *Nation and Narration*, 303.

dizzying metamorphoses destabilize what might be described as western knowledge about the Third World woman immigrant, when projected onto an American landscape, they also undermine any sense of a congealed and static American identity.

J.'s objective is a transnational hybridized identity that is consistent with her conception of America. Her project is to disrupt the natural chain of primogeniture and conceptualize a novel nation peopled with adoptive children like Duff and Du who will create new nongenetic families. Linking unlikely threads together, Mukherjee reminds us that with his proclivity and genius for wiring and rewiring electronic equipment, Du might seem to be J.'s own son by technically adept Prakash, even though he has been adopted by Bud and J. from Vietnam.

The unexpected alliance of white "father," Vietnamese "son" and Indian "wife" challenges the "straight lines and smooth planes of [a] history" Bud and those of his kind have so far been familiar with (190). It also places the essentialist notion of nationalist identity in jeopardy. In *Nations without Nationalism*, Julia Kristeva contends that "the United States suffers in its immigrations, which, from within, challenges not only the idea of a national 'organism' but also the very notion of confederacy."[20] Upon seeing people with vaguely Asian features on her first day in the country, J. had remarked, "I had been in America nearly a day and had yet to see an 'American' face" (115). Now she demonstrates through her own career that the essence of America is changing with the arrival of every new immigrant upon its promising shores. In this altered space that is almost a postnation, like the add-ons to Bud's low, squat house, "all of us Ripplemeyers," says J., "even the new ones, belong" (10).

While the immigrant (neo)identity is being produced in the currents of historic forces and transnational migration, the national body as organism seems to be breaking down, now replaced by abstract productions of a far more global sort. In "Patriotism and Its Futures," Arjun Appadurai suggests that "we are in the process of moving to a global order in which the nation-state has almost become obsolete and other formations for allegiance and identity have taken its place," calling into being a world that is postnational and diasporic. His focus on the question of allegiance is interesting with regard to the cases of J. and Du, since J. says, "My transformation has been genetic; Du's was hyphenated" (198). Appadurai contends that the "formula of hyphenation . . . is reaching the point of saturation, and the right-hand side of the hyphen [as in "Asian-American"] can barely contain

20. Julia Kristeva, *Nations without Nationalism*, trans. Leon S. Roudiez (New York: Columbia University Press, 1993), 11.

the unruliness of the left-hand side. . . . [T]he idea of the nation flourishes transnationally. Safe from the depredations of their home states, diasporic communities become doubly loyal to their nations of origin and thus ambivalent about their loyalty to America."[21] Incorporating the left-hand side of the hyphen with the right, and creating a new space for mutant identity, where neither is complete in itself and both have been melded, is the strategy we are presented with in the adventures of J.

Indeed, this is a strategy growing from J.'s sense of transnational interdependence: "Fates," J. muses, "are so intertwined in the modern world" because "it was no exaggeration to say the security of the free world, in some small way, depended on the hair of Indian village women," imported by Dev Vadhera and used in precision scientific instruments (12, 135). Rootlessness, metaphorized in the transportation of hair from a distant continent to America, reinforces her sense of a global melee of cultures perpetually on the move: "The hair from some peasant's head in Hasnapur could travel across oceans and save an American meteorologist's reputation. Nothing was rooted anymore. Everything was in motion" (135).

In "DissemiNation," Bhabha explains that colonials, postcolonials, migrants, and minorities, "wandering people who cannot be contained within the heim [place] of national culture," are "the marks of a shifting boundary that alienates the frontiers of the modern nation."[22] Entire nations are in the process of subverting national borders: "Whole peoples are on the move" (91). The role of the American transnation is central in this global order: "It is by now only a passing wave of nausea," admits J., "this response to the speed of transformation, the fluidity of American character and the American landscape. I feel at times like a stone hurtling through diaphonous mist, unable to grab hold, unable to slow down, yet unwilling to abandon the ride I'm on" (123). J.'s suggestion that this movement is both inevitable and irresistible reveals her identification with and consistent euphoria in responding to the global order that makes available liminal space for survival.

Euphoria, however, is not the response of those who would like to continue to envision America as static and invariable, who wish it to remain orderly and ordered, with all the spaces known and marked. J. is sensitive to the paranoia and fear that constitute resistance to this alteration of national borders by the influx of immigrants: "People were getting a little scared of immigrants and positively hostile to illegals" (122). Immigrants, who

---

21. Arjun Appadurai, "Patriotism and Its Futures," *Public Culture* 5, no. 3 (1993): 421, 423, 424.

22. Bhabha, *Nation and Narration,* 315.

carry liminal "difference" and the capacity to transform static nations, are intimidating precisely because they threaten the straight lines and smooth planes of history made comfortable through familiarity. They conjure up a nation-space in the *"process* of the articulation of elements: where meanings may be partial because they are *in media res;* and history may be half-made because it is in the process of being made; and the image of cultural authority may be ambivalent because it is caught, uncertainly, in the act of 'composing' its powerful image." Liminal identity, reliant on unheimlich maneuvers, is plural and transitional. Dotbusters in New Jersey recognize that their own identity is being made provisional as immigrants shift the definition of "American."[23] That violence should mark this shift should not be surprising since "there are no harmless, compassionate ways to remake oneself" (Mukherjee 25). This "becoming" is not always becoming by the rubric of a transcendent morality; it is merely inevitable.

J., eternal escapee from the exchange systems of legal, political, and societal economies, is the (dis)appearing Other who is attempting "subtle realignments of identities, priorities and commitments" to remake the self/other endlessly.[24] The propulsion of identity into a condition of always becoming is a powerful call to reimagine it as a site for negotiation, both for the immigrant self and for the country she is becoming a part of. J.'s "always becoming" is posited on coming "home" to America and signaling from its shores that this new nation, too, is "always becoming."

23. Ibid., 3; "dotbusters" are racist and violent gangs that target Indians, particularly women who wear the traditional dot (bindi) on their foreheads. New Jersey is home to a large immigrant Indian population and has been the site of several such attacks.

24. Marilyn Frye, *Politics of Reality: Essays in Feminist Theory* (Trumansburg, N.Y.: The Crossing Press, 1983), 97.

III

Dislocations

Comic Displacement

Caroline M. Kirkland's Satire of Frontier Democracy in *A New Home, Who'll Follow?*

CAROLINE GEBHARD

In her groundbreaking work on diaries of frontier women, Lillian Schlissel argued for the need to read "the obscured patterns" in such women's writing, yet ironically only recently have critics begun to value the complex literary form of Caroline M. Kirkland's work about settling the West. Most have been content to label her a "pioneer realist" (Langley C. Keyes was the first to recognize her as a "pioneer in American Realism," but Kirkland's importance as an early contributor to this major American development in literature was largely obscured until feminist critics such as Annette Kolodny and Judith Fetterley rediscovered her). However, critics, both then and now, have assumed that her first book, *A New Home, Who'll Follow? or, Glimpses of Western Life* (1839), is simply autobiographical. Even its title, however, suggests a puzzle: is this a manual by an insider for prospective settlers, as Annette Kolodny has argued, or is it a travel diary by a "cultivated outsider" on "the natives of a strange land," as Henry Nash Smith first asserted?[1]

---

1. Lillian Schlissel, "Diaries of Frontier Women: On Learning to Read the Obscured Patterns," in *Woman's Being, Woman's Place: Female Identity and Vocation in American History,* ed. Mary Kelley (Boston: Hall, 1979), 53–66; Langley C. Keyes, "Caroline Matilda Kirkland: A Pioneer in American Realism" (Ph.D. diss., Harvard University, 1935); Annette Kolodny, *The Land before Her: Fantasy and Experience of the American Frontiers, 1630–1860* (Chapel Hill: University of North Carolina Press, 1984), 134; Judith Fetterley, "Caroline M. Kirkland (1801–1864)," in her *Provisions: A Reader from Nineteenth-Century American Women* (Bloomington: Indiana University Press, 1987), 117–58; and Henry Nash Smith, *Virgin Land: The American West as Symbol and Myth* (1950; reprint, Cambridge: Harvard University Press, 1970), 226.

The author's signature, "By Mrs. Mary Clavers, an Actual Settler," is equally enigmatic. Signing both as "Mrs." and as an "actual settler," suggests contrary authorial desires: she wanted to retain, as she once put it, "the usual mark of respect claimed by married ladies,"[2] and yet to give "an unvarnished transcript" of reality.[3] The desire to tell the unladylike truth about the raw society she saw taking shape on the western frontier, even if written "under the assured belief that the author would never be discovered," created a dilemma for Kirkland.[4] The solution that would allow her to remain a private and proper married woman, and yet allow her ample scope for social critique, was comic self-invention. By means of the pseudo-autobiographical persona of "Mrs. Mary Clavers," she could write a travel book about the West from the perspective of one who lived there. At the same time, she created not a practical guide, but a tongue-in-cheek "how-to" book on settling the West not only for those who might come, but also for those back home; in short, she could write a satire on pioneering life that would still do justice to the beauty, the difficulty, and the promise of life in the Michigan backwoods.

This essay will pay close attention to the complexities of Kirkland's first book in order to understand why, in a work often celebrated for its distinctively female perspective on frontier life, the author avoids discussing her own marriage and motherhood. The essay seeks to show why, instead of what we might expect in this supposed fount of "pioneer realism," there is so much comedy. By tackling the question of how autobiographical the work in fact is, and then by understanding how its comic form relates both

---

For recent work on Kirkland, see Sandra A. Zagarell, introduction to *A New Home, Who'll Follow?* (New Brunswick: Rutgers University Press, 1990), xi–xlvi; and Brigitte Georgi-Findlay, *The Frontiers of Women's Writing: Women's Narratives and the Rhetoric of Westward Expansion* (Tuscon: University of Arizona Press, 1996), 21–37. Robert Bray, "The Art of Caroline Kirkland: The Structure of *A New Home: Who'll Follow?*" *Midwestern Miscellany* 3 (1975): 11–17, was one of the first critics to appreciate the unusual complexity of her narrative form.

2. Letter from C. M. Kirkland to Mssrs. Sartain & Co., December 30, 1850, in the Cornell University Library; see also Audrey J. Roberts, "The Letters of Caroline M. Kirkland," 2 vols. (Ph.D. diss., University of Wisconsin–Madison, 1976), 2:275; hereafter cited as "Letters."

3. Caroline M. Kirkland, *A New Home, Who'll Follow? or, Glimpses of Western Life*, ed. Sandra A. Zagarell (New Brunswick: Rutgers University Press, 1990), 3. This edition, set from the first edition published in 1839 in New York by C. S. Francis, is the first complete and annotated modern edition available to the common reader; hereafter cited as *A New Home*.

4. Letter from Caroline Kirkland to Rufus Griswold, January 21, 1843, in the Alderman Library of the University of Virginia. See also Roberts, "Letters," 1:49–52.

to the author's own life and to the book's "realism" of social type, it will be possible to appraise the gendered, multilayered, literary performance of a remarkable woman writer coming to terms with her move to the American frontier more than a hundred and fifty years ago.

The Question of Autobiography

Like her first western readers, critics have read *A New Home, Who'll Follow?* as an autobiographical account of her experiences on the frontier. In 1835 the Kirklands, with family help, acquired some thirteen hundred acres when the vast tracts opened up for white settlement by the land cessions of the Chippewas, Ottawas, Potawatomis, and other Indians finally became accessible. Although the 1807 Treaty of Detroit had granted the United States a significant land cession in southeastern Michigan where the Kirklands settled, the Ottawas and neighboring tribes proved adept at resisting removal; however, the Erie Canal's opening in 1825 insured that the slow settlement of the Michigan Territory would accelerate rapidly. The Kirklands, part of the great emigration from New York State to Michigan made possible by the canal, founded Pinckney in 1837, not far from present-day Ann Arbor, living in a log cabin until their house, along with a mill, a tavern, and a store, could be built.[5]

When her book about "my adventurous journeyings and tarryings beyond the confines of civilization" (*A New Home*, 1) came out, it "wrought an undoubted sensation." The thirty-eight-year-old schoolteacher and mother of four found herself famous. Praising her style as "full of variety, faultlessly pure, and yet bold," Edgar Allan Poe joined many who recognized Kirkland as a remarkable new writer on the American scene: "Unquestionably, she is one of our best writers." He concluded that to her

---

5. My account of Kirkland's life is based on Jane Clark, "Life of Caroline Matilda Kirkland" (copy of unpublished monograph [1934], Alderman Library, University of Virginia); Fetterley, "Caroline M. Kirkland"; Roberts, "Letters"; William S. Osborne, *Caroline M. Kirkland* (New York: Twayne Publishers, 1972), and Zagarell, introduction to *A New Home*, xi–xlvi. William E. Unrau and H. Craig Miner, *Tribal Dispossession and the Ottawa Indian University Fraud* (Norman: University of Oklahoma Press, 1985), 24–30; and introduction to *The Making of Michigan, 1820–1860: A Pioneer Anthology*, ed. Justin L. Kestenbaum (Detroit: Wayne State University Press, 1990), 10. White displacement of Indians in Michigan has not been given the same attention as Indian removal from the Southeast, as Susan E. Gray points out in *The Yankee West: Community Life on the Michigan Frontier* (Chapel Hill: University of North Carolina Press, 1996), 205 n. 16.

alone was the nation "indebted for our acquaintance with the home and home-life of the backwoodsman."[6]

With its gritty pictures of "tumble-down log-houses" with their "perfumes of milk-emptins, bread, and fried onions"[7] and its eloquent descriptions of Michigan mud holes and backwoods personalities, her first book has led many to the assumption that the text is closely based on Kirkland's own life; the work has been labeled "pioneer realism." However, the autobiographical quality of this work is a much more complicated issue than is often admitted. Large gaps exist in what we know of Kirkland's actual life, in part because the great Chicago fire of 1873, which destroyed the house of her son, Joseph Kirkland, also a notable writer, destroyed many family papers as well. Fragmentary records and the long neglect of American women writers noted by Fetterley has meant that even something so basic as how many children Kirkland bore differs in the various sources. Audrey J. Roberts's dissertation includes the most carefully researched account of Kirkland's life; William S. Osborne's biography, the only one ever published, contains valuable information but is marred by his condescension. Only a few surviving letters provide a private record of Kirkland's life in Michigan; otherwise we must extrapolate from her works. According to Roberts, the only letters that report on her frontier life are the less than a dozen written to her daughter Elizabeth away at school, and none of these was written during the first three years of the Kirklands' pioneering experiment ("Letters," 1:xxviii).

The six or so extant letters she wrote from Pinckney to friends in New York City, including Nathaniel P. Willis, Rufus W. Griswold, and C. S. Francis, her eventual publisher, instead show her intense desire to be in contact with the literary world she has lost. To Willis, she complained of his long silence, telling him, "I write again to remind you of my being yet alive"; she wished news of him and how his play was received ("Letters," 1:16–17). In another letter, she urged Griswold to write a longer letter for "the letters of literary gentlemen have an especial value during a

---

6. Edgar Allan Poe, "The Literati of New York City," *Godey's Lady's Book* 33 (August 1846): 75–76. *A New Home* was widely praised; see, for example, the *New York Mirror* 17 (October 12, 1839): 127; *Godey's Lady's Book* 20 (January 1840): 45; and the *North American Review* 50 (January 1840): 206–23.

7. Caroline M. Kirkland, *Forest Life*, 2 vols. (New York: C. S. Francis, 1842), 1:23, hereafter cited in the essay. This is Kirkland's own description of her "literary" material in her second book. As in her first book, she tried to obscure the author's true identity. *Forest Life* simply proclaims, "By the Author of 'A New Home.' " For Kirkland's desire for anonymity, see also Audrey Roberts, "Caroline M. Kirkland: Additions to the Canon," *Bulletin of Research in the Humanities* 86, no. 3 (1983–1985): 338–46.

country winter, and my spirits require all sorts of aid in these dull times" ("Letters," 1:53).[8]

What we do know of Kirkland's own life suggests that *A New Home* leaves out far more than it tells. She and her husband, William, had come to the Michigan Territory with their three small children, Elizabeth, Joseph, and Sarah (a fourth, Lydia, had died in infancy) from Geneva, New York, to take charge of the Detroit Female Seminary. In Detroit, she gave birth to another daughter, Cordelia, but shortly before moving to the backwoods, three-year-old Sarah fell to her death from a third-story window of the school.[9] During the six years that they lived in their frontier village, she gave birth to her last two children, William and Charles; Charles lived only a few months. She expressed her grief in a letter she wrote to Griswold on the death of his young son: "We have buried three of our precious ones, and can feel for all who mourn" ("Letters," 1:53).

We also know that her move to the backwoods, probably in the late spring or early summer of 1837, coincided with heavy personal loss. She set up housekeeping in a cabin after losing both her baby daughter and her mother earlier that year. Judith Fetterley notes that Kirkland's mother had been a writer; her correspondence reveals a close, affectionate relationship.[10] Only two years earlier, during the year they went West, Kirkland's only sister, Cordelia, died at age twenty-five.[11] Yet in *A New Home*, none of these losses appears directly. It is other women who face grievous separation from mothers and sisters, other women who must cope with the horror of losing children to accident and to illness. Early in the book, the narrator hears of a woman whose son had been bitten by a rattlesnake and "was not expected to live" (16). It turns out that the boy's chances were better than reported: "the pale and weary mother had begun to hope" (17). Later, the narrator hears what Cora's wilderness elopement costs: "The wretched mother cast one look at its [the baby's]

8. Willis (1806–1867) was a popular writer and the influential editor of the *Home Journal;* Griswold (1815–1857) edited *Graham's Magazine* briefly, but is now primarily remembered as Poe's hostile biographer.

9. Roberts suggests this tragic accident may have spurred the Kirklands' move to the wilderness, "Letters," 1:xxxiv.

10. Fetterley, "Caroline M. Kirkland," 117. One gathers a deep and comfortable intimacy from Kirkland's newsy, affectionate letter to her mother: "Yes Mother it is very true, I feel much better than when I left home or even when I left *you*" (Kirkland to Elizabeth Stansbury, November 20, 1829, from Geneva, New York, "Letters," 1:15).

11. Cordelia's poor health, even at nineteen, was already cause for concern; to her mother, Kirkland writes of having "great hopes from the Panacea which has performed so many wonderful cures" ("Letters," 1:14).

altered countenance, and with a wild cry sunk senseless on the floor" (167). Happily, these mothers—unlike Kirkland in real life—have their children restored to them.

Yet in the allegedly autobiographical A New Home, Kirkland never directly alludes to her personal griefs, and even her family is sketched only in passing. Her husband is sparingly mentioned, never by his first name. David Leverenz complains that Kirkland goes so far as to suppress her identity as a mother:

> Not until the tenth chapter do we learn that she has her children with her (65), though she has introduced her prized greyhound, D'Orsay, long before (54–55). It takes Kirkland another five chapters to mention her three children's names [not their real names]. Either her servants handled almost all the child care, or, what seems more likely, Kirkland's astonishing censorship of her day-to-day domestic realities reflects her deliberate choice to write as a lady, not as a mother.[12]

For a book that many feminist critics have argued is particularly directed at women readers, it is odd that women's particular needs tend to be treated comically, or else pushed into the corners of the narrative. For example, enduring pregnancy and childbirth in the backwoods are rarely alluded to; the only reference she makes to caring for a newborn (again, another woman's) is her humorous mention of a certain "glass-tube" of hers and her knowledge of breast-feeding ("as I pass for an oracle in the matter of paps and possets" [71]). But even this allusion serves comic purposes, the narrator coyly leaving the reader to guess what a breast pump is called in Michigan.

Although the book is clearly based on the author's real experiences, and although Fetterley is surely right to stress that "at the heart of her enterprise is the education of her readers to the significance of the American frontier," the "realism" of this extraordinary text does not lie in the revelation of a personal self (autobiography), nor in the strict reporting of day-to-day events (travel diary). Its unique form has led some to conclude Kirkland did not quite know what she was writing; Smith reads her work as a bungled attempt to graft experiments in fiction onto an essentially "simple" travel narrative in the tradition of Charles Fenno Hoffman's A Winter in the West (1835) and James Hall's Letters from the West (1828). Kolodny goes so far as to claim, "it was not fiction she aimed at"; the

12. David Leverenz, Manhood and the American Renaissance (Ithaca: Cornell University Press, 1989), 156.

fiction, she argues, is only there to sweeten the all-too-sober advice the book contains.[13]

Sandra A. Zagarell, noting *A New Home*'s deliberate critique of popular literary genres such as western travel literature and sentimental fiction, is close to the mark when she contends the book's "original cultural commentary" bears a kinship to ethnographic accounts, and that the real subject of the work is "the slow process of community and culture formation." However, Zagarell reads Kirkland's persona, Mary Clavers, as "more culturally representative than individual."[14] I will suggest instead that she is much more than this: like Fielding's narrator in *Tom Jones*, she is a witty authorial persona, a narrative self-invention that enables the painful experience of moving to a distant place with few amenities and often uncongenial neighbors to be transformed into social comedy. Mrs. Mary Clavers, both as literary device and psychological projection, becomes the means by which Kirkland can give literary expression, albeit indirectly, to the very real traumas she experienced. Her text, densely allusive, mixing genres and styles boldly, suggests that social and psychic dislocation are finally only representable in a form that allows for anger and grief to be transmuted into laughter.

Comedy and the Realism of Social Type

Critics since Poe, who was taken with the "pure fun" of *A New Home*, have all remarked on the book's humor, but how the comic form of the work connects to its much-praised realism or to its autobiographical content has not been fully addressed. This form is loosely based on the letter from the margins of what was then the United States to those "back home" in the civilized East. The book's form does bear the marks of this origin, an intimate correspondence, as Kirkland phrases it, "for our private delectation" (3). The complications of who the "our" is here, and whose pleasure is gained at whose expense, I will take up later; the point here is that this book is more than the sum of its parts: Assimilating travel writing, sentimental fiction, and literary and social criticism into what Zagarell has

13. Fetterley, "Caroline M. Kirkland," 120; Hoffman, *A Winter in the West*, 2 vols. (1835; reprint, St. Clair Shores, Mich.: Scholarly Press, 1970); Hall, *Letters from the West; Containing Sketches of Scenery, Manners, and Customs and Anecdotes Connected with the First Settlements of the Western United States* (1828; reprint, Gainesville, Fla.: Scholars' Facsimiles and Reprints, 1967); Smith, *Virgin Land*, 226–27; Kolodny, *Land before Her*, 134.
14. Zagarell, introduction to *A New Home*, xxix.

aptly called "free-wheeling satire," the book enables an American woman devoted both to democratic principles and to literary art to become a writer who boldly—and not without a price—claimed the right to satirize democratic nation-building.[15]

Modern critics, with the notable exception of Zagarell, have paid too little attention to the satiric method at work in *A New Home*. More than a pseudonym, Mrs. Mary Clavers is a self-consciously constructed literary persona that enables the satire to cohere. Many critics have too readily assumed that Mrs. Mary Clavers and Caroline Kirkland are identical. *Clavers*, which means "to talk idly, to gossip, palaver, prate," ought to caution us that however close to Kirkland this imaginative "I" might have been, *A New Home* is not autobiography, but fiction. Moreover, the very things that twentieth-century readers sometimes find obtrusive or distracting from the "pioneer realism" of the work delighted nineteenth-century readers: the wit and charm of the narrator. However, as critics have since, her first western readers assumed that *A New Home* was modeled upon actual persons she met in Michigan. "It is a well-known fact that certain sketches of Western life have been appropriated by more than a dozen communities, each declaring them personal; while their sole personality lay in the attempt to adhere closely to the *general*, to the entire exclusion of the particular," she later vainly protested.[16]

Kirkland's "realism," I will suggest, is closer to the realism of Henry Fielding, Maria Edgeworth, and Charles Dickens: her characters are com-

15. Ibid, xii. Zagarell argues that "its comprehensiveness and outspoken satire make *A New Home* virtually unique among published works by antebellum American women." She also notes that Kirkland "apparently modulated her public voice" in response to her neighbors' angry reception of her first book (xii). For an extended discussion of the crisis of authorial self-confidence Kirkland suffered and its negative effects on her later career, see my doctoral thesis, "The Invention of Female Authorship in Nineteenth-Century America" (Ph.D. diss., University of Virginia, 1991), 55–118.

16. Of course, the line between fiction and autobiography is not so easily drawn; as Paul John Eakin has argued, "the self that is the center of all autobiographical narrative is necessarily a fictive structure" (*Fictions in Autobiography: Studies in the Art of Self-Invention* [Princeton: Princeton University Press, 1985], 3). However, autobiography is not usually understood to include works authored in the name of a persona. Moreover, as I argue, *A New Home* is not designed to tell the story of the writer's life—indeed it goes out of its way to avoid this—but instead to narrate a typical experience of moving to and becoming part of a frontier settlement. For a useful discussion of the debates over the status of autobiography, see Laura Marcus, *Auto/biographical Discourses: Theory, Criticism, Practice* (Manchester: Manchester University Press, 1994), esp. chap. 6, "The Law of Genre." Caroline Kirkland, *Western Clearings* (1845; reprint, New York: Garrett Press, 1969), viii, hereafter cited by page number in the text.

posites or "types" such as the western "lady" who smokes and spits and the illiterate backwoods politician who styles himself "Justas of Piece." Not mimetic according to the canons of the realism that triumphed at the end of the nineteenth century, these exaggerated types are designed to reveal the foibles and failings of a whole society, not to depict specific individuals. For example, Mrs. Mary Clavers shows up the type of the legendary backwoodsman in many particulars—his inclination to a touchy pride and his disdain for women and books as well as for anything that did not turn an immediate profit. She does not spare the reader the alcoholism and brutality of some of these men. "I can never forget the countenance of that desolate woman, sitting trembling and with white, compressed lips in the midst of her children," she writes of a backwoods wife, living in terror "owing to the horrible drunkenness of the master of the house" (7). But most of her portrayals of backwoodsmen strike a comic note, as she appraises the curious combination of masculine pride, shrewdness, and nose for political power typical of many enterprising frontiersmen. Her portrait of Simeon Jenkins exemplifies all three.[17]

When she first makes his acquaintance, he is offended that she does not permit smoking in her home and surprised her "old man" doesn't mind: " 'I tell you what, I'm *boss* at home; and if my old woman was to stick up that fashion, I'd keep the house so blue she could n't see to snuff the candle' " (56). She mocks his male posturing as he exits grandly, cigar butt in hand, by comparing him to Lord Burleigh, a character in Sheridan's play who only has to nod once to say everything. Yet she also appreciates his practical skills: "Is one of your guests dependent upon a barber? Mr. Jenkins can shave. Does your husband get *too* shaggy? Mr. Jenkins cuts hair. Does he demolish his boot upon a *grub*? Mr. Jenkins is great at a *rifacciamento*. Does Billy lose his cap in the pond? Mr. Jenkins makes caps *comme il y en a peu*" (80). What intrigues the author of *A New Home* most about this figure, however, is his emerging political clout in Jacksonian America. Kirkland satirizes the political ambitions of this barely literate but determined group. From a humble salesman of eggs, he graduates to hawking pies, almanacs, and whiskey on Election Day, and after mastering gambling, gin, and profanity, he's ready to become a candidate for office (170–71). She gives us a specimen of his political stump speech: " 'Hurra for patriotism! them 's my sentiments' " (171). When he finds himself in

17. Kelli A. Larson argues that Kirkland satirizes the myth of the American Adam celebrated by James Fenimore Cooper and others in "Kirkland's Myth of the American Eve: Re-visioning the Frontier Experience," *Midwestern Miscellany* 20 (1992): 9–13. I draw attention here to the political ramifications of this satire.

the awkward position of being a member of the losing party, he finds a way out of his dilemma:

> If I hunt over the history of the universal world from the creation of man to the present day, I see that men has always had difficulties; and that some has took one way to get shut of 'em, and some another. My candid and unrefragable opinion is, that rather than remain useless, buckled down to the shop, and indulging in selfishness, it is my solemn dooty to change my ticket. (172)

Long before Twain, she used her ear for dialect to parody the self-promotion and self-aggrandizement, as well as the fraud and corruption, that the West seemed to spawn. Her satire exposes what she saw as the greatest threats to democratic culture in the West—a profound anti-intellectualism coupled with the crudest utilitarianism, and a white, male, lower-class demand for "equality" at the expense of women and blacks. Perhaps, not coincidentally, these perceived threats to establishing a civil society on the frontier were also extremely threatening to her personally, as an intellectual, middle-class woman. Recently, Brigitte Georgi-Findlay has argued with a good deal of justice that "in Mrs. Clavers, Kirkland has constructed the subject of a newly emerging middle-class in the 'woods,' " whose privilege by class but marginalization by gender nevertheless results in what Mary Louise Pratt has identified as only "another branch of the civilizing mission . . . 'a form of female imperial intervention in the contact zone.' "[18] Despite Georgi-Findlay's recognition that women writers like Kirkland "are simultaneously part of an expansionist enterprise and members 'of that group itself most thoroughly colonized by patriarchal civilization,' " like Leverenz, she reads Kirkland's text as an "instrument for imposing cultural and social control and order upon the disorderly classes of the West."[19] This assessment, in my view, underrates her critical insights into the new social order in the making on the ragged edge of America

18. Georgi-Findlay, *Frontiers of Women's Writing,* 32–33, 298 n. 26, citing Mary Louise Pratt, *Imperial Eyes: Travel Writing and Transculturation* (London: Routledge, 1992), 160–61.

19. Georgi-Findlay, *Frontiers of Women's Writing,* 26, 297 n. 10, 30; she cites Susan Hardy Aiken's description of the woman writer's ambiguous "colonized" position, *Isak Dinessen and the Engendering of Narrative* (Chicago: University of Chicago Press, 1990). In Leverenz's decidedly hostile reading *(Manhood),* Kirkland's writing is primarily motivated by class snobbery and gender "resentment." He discounts her progressive politics as well as her honesty in confronting her class bias. Kirkland worked all her life to better the lot of others; see, for example, her *Helping Hand, Comprising an Account of the Home for Discharged Female Convicts and an Appeal in Behalf of That Institution* (New York: Charles Scribner, 1853).

and misses much of the trenchant self-critique in Kirkland's funny and thought-provoking comedy about nation-building on America's western frontier.

Satire is often the weapon of choice for those far from power. In *A New Home* and later writings, Kirkland wielded it to expose the political influence of backwoodsmen to ridicule, and no doubt its edge is all the sharper for her being a woman denied even the right to speak publicly on political affairs. Later, she would passionately argue for women's participation in the public sphere: "She is said to be represented even now, and so is the slave; yet this assertion depends on the fallacy that the identity of one accountable human creature can be merged in that of another."[20]

In her second book on the West, *Forest Life*, her commentary on patriarchal privilege is far more blunt than in her first book; the backwoodsman demands absolute subservience from women, she observes, and "would as soon give up his right hand as relinquish this supremacy" (1:123). *Forest Life* also makes explicit what is implicit in *A New Home*, how the ideology of America as a classless society often masks racism and promotes the interests of white men: a backwoodsman smugly extols the equal opportunities for all available in this country to an English visitor, " 'Give every man a fair chance. . . . Outside a'n't nothing,' " but then is "aghast" when the visitor suggests that he must therefore agree a man should not be denied equality because " 'God has given him a black skin.' " He tells the Englishman angrily, " 'What upon airth *are* you talking about? . . . Do you suppose I look upon a nigger as I do upon a white man?' " (1:205–6). In *A New Home*, however, Simeon Jenkins is not such an intractable backwoods bigot, but more a loveable buffoon whom the narrator believes amenable to reform.

Kirkland's "realism" of social type in *A New Home* is rooted in the eighteenth century; besides the celebrated portraiture of complex, individual character practiced by Samuel Richardson and Jane Austen, the eighteenth century also produced a realism grounded in the type as representative of distinctive groups or classes within society. Modern critics have usually preferred the former, but Kirkland favored the latter mode because it conformed better to the social ideals that she had also inherited from the previous century: the necessity for personal privacy and social decorum.[21]

20. Caroline Kirkland, introduction to *Woman; Her Education and Influence*, by Marian Reid (New York: n.p. [1847]), 9–29, 18.
21. Throughout her career, Kirkland manifested what seems—even in an age that insisted upon ladylike reticence—an almost morbid desire to shield herself from public view. In answer to John S. Hart's request for biographical details, she furnished him only the barest account, insisting, "there is absolutely nothing to

Kirkland, like Fielding in *Tom Jones* (1749), brings us into a "charmed circle" created by the "genial raconteur" who introduces us not only to comic types and satiric adventures, but also to the author's own favorite poets and moralists; as Wayne Booth once pointed out, the only truly developed "character" in *Tom Jones* is Fielding himself in the role of the author-narrator, and the same holds true for Kirkland in *A New Home*.[22] But unlike him, she had to defend herself for being a woman who dared to satirize her society.

Western readers especially objected; refusing to see themselves as types, they concluded she had libeled them individually. A visitor to Pinckney was told by the "ladies of the log cabin" where he stopped that "Mrs. Kirkland intended to point out real characters in her neighborhood, and slander them most scandalously"; he was also informed that she was writing another book that winter and had hired a girl to wash her dishes. They disapproved: "She should be more usefully employed."[23]

Comic Displacement

Displacement suggests literally being out of one's place, displaced from one's home, one's social milieu, one's country, as well as the complex psychic act of "displacement"—of projecting disturbing material onto another form or casting it into another shape. A highly educated woman, an intellectual and a writer, Kirkland was a "displaced person" on the frontier. Widely read in English literature—she eventually wrote a book on Spenser—she studied French, German, and Latin literature as well. She was, according to Roberts, "educated far beyond most American women of that period" ("Letters," 1:xxxi). Her comments to her daughter about a certain cultured couple that had come from the East to live in Michigan suggest what difficulties she herself must have faced: "We should be delighted with this acquisition to our society if it were not that we pity them too much—Such people attempting to live in this country is madness— 'Solitary confinement at hard labor' is only a step beyond it" ("Letters,"

---

say about me that the world should know" (Kirkland to Hart, January 18, 1851, from New York, "Letters," 2:277).

22. I borrow here from Ian Watt's description of Fielding's narrative presence in *Tom Jones, The Rise of the Novel: Studies in Defoe, Richardson, and Fielding* (Berkeley and Los Angeles: University of California Press, 1957) 285; see also 268–73. Booth was the first to elaborate on the significance of Fielding's "character," inscribed as both author and narrator of *Tom Jones* (*The Rhetoric of Fiction* [Chicago: University of Chicago Press, 1961], 215–18).

23. Osborne, *Caroline M. Kirkland*, 44–45.

1:43–44). To be a literary woman in America, let alone in Michigan, was bound to be isolating; she asks in a late essay, "How many literary women has any one person ever seen? How many has the world seen?" The answer: "literary ladies are hardly more abundant than dodos."[24] Characteristically, she has displaced the anxiety of belonging to an endangered species by wit. It is not hard, then, to imagine what her alienation from her frontier surroundings must have been. Yet as an urbane easterner, a teacher, and her husband's partner in founding a new settlement, she found herself at once isolated and at the center of the task of shaping a new society, a new home.

Her address to the reader in *A New Home* shows an acute awareness of how contradictory the author's own position is. Her race, class, education, and relative wealth grant her a measure of power, yet her comic alterego finds not only that her sex lowers her status on the frontier, but also that the very sources of her power—elite learning, refined manners, and material goods—are paradoxically often experienced as liabilities in the backwoods. In the book, Mrs. Clavers fears that, like the "delicate nest of japanned tables" she brings with her, only "gimcracks" to her new neighbors, all that is most precious to her, her learning and her books, her manners and her social ideals, will be seen as worthless, mere "superfluities" (42–43). She can see that common sense is on her neighbor's side as far as the tables go, but she, and no doubt her creator as well, clearly resists the idea that her notions of civilization have no place on the frontier.

Relocating to a place where people must depend upon their poorest neighbors and know each other's households down to the last detail has forced the author of *A New Home* to rethink both her democratic principles and her beliefs about social class, and the difficulty of this rethinking leaves its imprint on her satire. "The spirit in which was conceived the motto of the French revolution, 'La fraternité ou la mort,' exists in full force among us," Mrs. Clavers concludes, wryly adding, "though modified as to results" (184). But Kirkland's irony here does not disguise the very real costs of neighbors taking offense at any perceived sense of superiority: "there are in the country so many ways of being made uncomfortable by one's most insignificant enemy, that . . . warfare is even more costly than submission" (185). The rules of the Old World no longer apply and new ones must be devised, both in life and letters. Although Kirkland assumes a

---

24. Caroline Kirkland, "Literary Women," *Sartain's Union Magazine of Literature and Art* 6 (February 1850): 150–54 (150–51). This essay is reprinted in Zagarell's edition of *A New Home*.

genteel audience, comfortable with quotations from Shakespeare, Bacon, and Rochefoucauld, to name a few of her favorites, and although she writes with a certainty that this audience will share her amusements at backwoods brusqueries, at many points the text begins to question, even undermine, these class assumptions. The village "sketch" of Mary Russell Mitford, a contemporary well-known English writer that Kirkland presumes will no doubt be taken as the model for her "rude attempt," cannot really serve her purposes. Forms and manners, especially to do with class, are hopelessly out of place in the American backwoods.

Kirkland evokes Mitford only to measure the gulf between England and Michigan—and even the East and Michigan. Mrs. Clavers recounts the difficulties of trying to employ servants in a country where no one wants to be considered a servant. She disapproves of young women who spend an inordinate amount of time in curling papers and "slicking up" but who are unwilling to work as domestics except in the short term to buy clothes or to help their families, but never "as a regular calling, or with an acknowledgment of inferior station" (39). Mrs. Clavers apparently wants to believe that no good can come of ignoring such social distinctions. Amelia Newland, a girl from a poor, ne'er-do-well family and former hired help, is a case in point. Mrs. Clavers cannot understand why the Newlands grow poorer everyday, until one night when she accidentally stumbles upon a riotous party in progress when she stops by to inquire after the sick father. The most striking feature of the scene is Amelia herself. Her party dress "of rich silk, made in the extreme mode, and set off by elegant jewelry" and hair "drest with scarlet berries" (109), sharply contrast with the wretched log house and show the danger of living above one's station; the very luxury of Amelia's tasteful dress signals wantonness and impropriety in a girl who works as a servant. Her demise proves a sermon on lower-class extravagance and vice, when she dies from an abortion gone wrong.

Yet the narrator cannot so easily dismiss another young female servant "who was highly offended, because room was not made for her at table with guests from the city" (39). This figure, unnerving in a way that Amelia Newland is not, challenges the author's own ideas about social class and proper manners. This nameless young woman, angered by not being treated as an equal, provokes Mrs. Clavers to exasperation: "And this latter high-born damsel sent in from the kitchen a circumstantial account *in writing*, of the instances wherein she considered herself aggrieved; well written it was too, and expressed with much *naiveté*, and abundant respect" (39). Nevertheless the narrator cannot help but respect her for being able to state her case from the kitchen *in writing*—an act that Kirkland emphasizes and admires. Moreover, the ability to express oneself well in writing also suggests that one has some right to higher class status. Writing therefore blurs social class in troubling ways because if class is only a matter of owning more, it demystifies gentility by exposing gentility itself as crass—as based on money. This young American woman, though she is not "high born" and must earn her wages, evinces an unshakable belief in her own status as an equal, whatever she may lack in material goods. "It was not long before this fiery spirit was aroused again," Mrs. Clavers recounts, and thus she is "forced to part with her country belle" (39). Whether the young woman was fired, or whether she left of her own accord is not clear; what is clear is that the "republican" attitude she represents arouses strong and contradictory feelings in the author.

Such a scene, a female servant writing "a declaration of independence" from the kitchen to a mistress in the parlor, is unimaginable in Mitford's sketches of English village life. Social hierarchy appears as the natural order in Mitford's village, which is represented as a place where everyone instinctively knows his or her place. Fielding, of course, had made great comic capital of the idea of a female servant even being capable of an epistolary style in *Shamela* (1741). Indeed, the plot of *Tom Jones* turns upon the social order's being construed as necessarily fixed by birth; the hierarchy is affirmed as natural and true when Tom is revealed as the legitimate heir.[25]

By contrast, the social order Kirkland represents on the American frontier is fluid and volatile, though far from a classless society. Kirkland depicts the western backwoods as a place where the collective needs of survival have begun to break down ranks and distinctions. Still, she clings to a belief in the necessity for social hierarchy, but one based on talent and education rather than birth. But even this certainty no longer seems quite so certain. The contradictions in her own position raise the worrisome suspicion that her own claim to genteel status is no better than "rather a silly sort of pride" (39–40). As the wife of the founder of Montacute, the author's place in the social order should be as assured as Mitford's in *Our Village*. But it is not. Kirkland's "village" has no past, no landed gentry, no peasantry, no carefully graduated ranks in the middle—it barely has a stable population at all, as settlers keep pulling up stakes to move farther west or return to the East.

25. In *Shamela,* Fielding was satirizing Richardson's *Pamela* (1740), an epistolary novel that features a servant who is remarkably capable of expressing herself in writing; however, even Pamela, that paragon of propriety, could never have written to Mr. B—as Kirkland's young woman does—protesting her exclusion from the tea table as an equal.

The "fact" that Kirkland's fiction cannot avoid is bound up with America's own mobile and makeshift "made-up" origins; her American village is invented in a barroom. The actual violence that lies behind even these charming origins is largely suppressed in Kirkland's first book about the West. There are numerous examples of the way violence on the frontier and the displacement of its original peoples are alluded to, then passed over, but one may serve here. One night, when Mrs. Clavers and her friend Mrs. Rivers are returning from aiding a sick neighbor, they hear disturbing sounds—"shouts and howling," "Indian yells," and "the braying of tin horns" (118). They come upon a mob, ready to do violence to a ventriloquist. To prevent any harm, the two women raise a cry for help, providing a diversion, during which the hapless performer—whose offense turns out to be daring to ask "twenty-five cents a-head for the admission of the sovereign people" (120)—makes his escape. The scene is played for comedy, though Mrs. Clavers notes that the man was in fact armed "so even a woman's shrieks, hated of gods and men, may sometimes be of service" (119). She hastens to add, "Montacute is far above mobbing now" (119). The example is instructive. Mob violence and other specters of lawless behavior such as land fraud, theft, and vandalism are invoked only to be laughed at and quickly dismissed. Yet Mrs. Clavers cannot help adding after asserting that the settlement is "above mobbing now," that "it is not pleasant to find a dead pig in one's well, or a favourite dog hung up at the gate-post" (119). The threat of violence, especially from below, cannot be entirely repressed. This incident is also one of the few places in *A New Home* where Indians are mentioned, though the "Indian yells" are not those of Michigan's native inhabitants, but the settlers themselves.

As Lori Merish observes, the "narrative's (partial) erasure of Indians on the frontier metaphorically registers the violence of Jacksonian policies of Indian 'removal' and dispossession." She goes on to argue that Kirkland's later call for "humane 'treatment' of Native Americans while simultaneously characterizing them as a doomed race" mirrors the dominant culture's "logic of appropriation and erasure" of the indigenous people of the Americas. Her description of the way Indians appear only as "a shadowy, marginalized presence" in *A New Home* is just, but Kirkland is more cognizant of the contradictions and more concerned about the evils of American attitudes towards Indians than Merish credits her for. In her preface to Mary Eastman's *Dahcotah; or Life and Legends of the Sioux*, Kirkland acknowledges the greed and land hunger of her own kind, admitting that "we have driven [the Indians] before us just as fast as we have required or desired their lands"; she notes with pointed irony that it would have been "inconvenient" to "look upon the Indian with much regard, even in the light of literary material." In her last book about the West, *Western Clearings* (1845), Kirkland writes directly about the violent conquest of the frontier and its tragic legacy in the novella that concludes the collection, "Bitter Fruits from Chance-Sown Seeds." She paints a chilling portrait of a Richard Brand, now an old man, one of the region's first settlers, who delights in telling about how many Indians he killed: "Why, when I come first into the Michig*an,* they [the Indians] were as thick as huckleberries. We didn't mind shooting 'em any more than if they'd had four legs. That's a foolish law that won't let a man kill an Indian!" (211). Kirkland notes the "insane hatred of the very name of Indian" among "a portion of the original settlers," adding, "we may look in vain among the horrors of savage warfare for any act more atrocious, than some of those by which the white man has shown his red brother how the Christian can hate" (214). From this history of greed, cruelty, and disregard for human life springs a granddaughter who eventually burns down her foster family's home.[26]

Yet Merish is right to argue that, in *A New Home,* the "structuring opposition of savagery and civilization is displaced largely from its racial referents and is mapped onto gender and class relations."[27] But, as we have seen, the text operates on many levels and kinds of displacements. The traumatic loss of babies and of kin, the loss of familiar surroundings, of books and of a world where they mattered, all these losses Kirkland displaces by writing a comic fiction. In *Displacements: Cultural Identities in Question,* Angelika Bammer explains that for Freud, "displacement—*Vershiebung* (literally, 'pushing aside')—was central to the operation of dream-work, the process by which uncomfortable thoughts and feelings . . . are transferred to the safe remove of representational symbols."[28] J. LaPlanche and J. B. Pontalis explain that in Freud's thought, displacement is a primary process with a "clearly defensive function." Displacement may be understood, as Mark

26. Lori Merish, " 'The Hand of Refined Taste' in the Frontier Landscape: Caroline Kirkland's *A New Home, Who'll Follow?* and the Feminization of American Consumerism," *American Quarterly* 45, no. 4 (December 1993): 485–523, 494. Caroline M. Kirkland, preface to *Dahcotah; or Life and Legends of the Sioux around Fort Snelling* by Mary Eastman (New York: John Wiley, 1849), v–xi, viii. See also Dawn E. Keetley, "Unsettling the Frontier: Gender and Racial Identity in Caroline Kirkland's *A New Home, Who'll Follow?* and *Forest Life,*" *Legacy* 12, no. 1 (1995): 17–37.

27. Merish, " 'Hand of Refined Taste,' " 494. Although I agree with some of Merish's analysis, I reject her thesis that *A New Home* "sacralizes" the home and its domestic artifacts, thus creating a "domestic realism" that underwrites women's participation in a new consumer ethos. She misses the larger significance of Kirkland's self-conscious satire with its profoundly antimaterialist thrust.

28. Angelika Bammer, introduction to *Displacements: Cultural Identities in Question* (Bloomington: Indiana University Press, 1994), xiii.

Krupnick notes, through Freud's own example: instead of dreaming of his own professional anxieties, Freud dreams of a botanical monograph.[29] Kirkland's own description of her creative process is similar to Freud's concept of displacement.

Writing itself provided her "a new home," a means to work through "uncomfortable thoughts and feelings" in the safer realm of literary representation. Raw realities, she once insisted, required a "saving veil" of fiction (*Forest Life,* 2:232): despite professing "to relish most those fictions which are like transcripts of very life, we in reality covet a certain exaggeration, and an artful veiling of the more vulgar truths."[30] It is easy to see why writing became for her, as she put it, a "safety-valve," "a magic mirror," "a newly-explored world of inexhaustible enjoyment . . . undisturbed by a world of turmoil and care" (*Forest Life,* 1:32, 12–13). The "saving veil" of fiction for Kirkland was comedy, for in this realm, fraud, hostile neighbors, malaria, fires, floods, and mobs could all be turned into an occasion for laughter. Her de-emphasis on her own marriage and motherhood (and her wit at men's—including her husband's—expense) should not be primarily read, as Leverenz does, as animated by snobbery or female ire against men. Instead, it should be seen as part of a larger strategy of the displacement of grief over these losses, a defense against despair and a reaching toward the hoped-for happy ending.

A New Home closes on a note of humble, though hopeful, progress, as Mrs. Clavers remarks upon the many new buildings and signs of improvements in her frontier village. For Kirkland, too, a happy ending meant not only material, but also social progress. Although her writings show that the West was not the paradise it had often been made out to be, at the same time, her satire of western manners is intended to correct and improve the democratic society she was trying to help construct. Ultimately, however, she did not find a lasting place for herself or for her vision on the American frontier. The severe economic depression that followed the Michigan land boom caused Kirkland, only a few years after the publication of *A New Home,* to write her daughter during the hard winter of 1843, "this weight of poverty is too severely felt throughout the country to allow of much enjoyment of my kind" ("Letters," 1:44). "Scratchfor't," Kirkland's playful name for Pinckney, had doubtless become too close to the truth ("Letters,"

29. J. La Planche and J. B. Pontalis, *The Language of Psycho-Analysis* (1967; trans. Donald Nicholson-Smith, New York: W. W. Norton, 1973); Mark Krupnick, introduction to *Displacement: Derrida and After* (Bloomington: Indiana University Press, 1983), 7.

30. Caroline M. Kirkland, "Reading for Amusement," *Sartain's Union Magazine of Literature and Art* 6 (March 1850): 192–96, 193.

1:38). The same year, the Kirklands returned to New York City for good. And yet, despite all the hardships her first book leaves out, *A New Home* still bears witness to the great human costs of America's nation-building. Furthermore, her insight into the new type of man coming to power in Jacksonian America provides an early critique of the ideology of a "classless" America and the way enterprising lower- and lower-middle-class white men may deploy it to their advantage while disenfranchising women, Indians, and blacks. At the same time, her deep commitment to a democratic society forces her to turn her mockery against herself and her own pretensions. What is most extraordinary, however, is that she refuses to romanticize, to gloss over grubby realities, to resort to self-pity, or to boast of western wonders. Instead, she chooses laughter, a mode that allows for self-criticism as well as social critique. Although her comedy is often haunted by grief and anger, ultimately, her writings are a testament to the belief that laughter is the beginning of a cure, both for herself and for the democratic nation she loved.[31]

31. Roberts ("Letters") notes the irony of the name and that her sketch of "Scratchfor't" is part of the collection of descendent Louisa Sanborn Hill, 41 n. 1. Almost nothing has been written exploring the connection between the work of mourning and comic form. However, I can direct readers to Deborah-Maria Hatheway's recent dissertation on mourning in American women's writing, "The Last Remove: Women, Mourning, and the American West" (Ph.D. diss., University of California, Riverside, 1994).

"My Country Is Kentucky"

Leaving Appalachia in Harriette Arnow's *The Dollmaker*

RACHEL LEE RUBIN

Finding Appalachia

> Standin' on the mountain, standin' on the mountain,
> Standin' on the mountain, don't you want to go?
> O the last old train's a-leavin', the last old train's a-leavin',
> The last old train's a-leavin', don't you want to go?
> —Jean Ritchie, "Last Old Train's A-Leavin' "

In the important work of developing Appalachian culture studies as an academic discipline, much attention has been paid to the political, historical, and psychological consequence of place as a crucial factor in the creation of regional self-identity. Since the 1960s, able and compassionate scholars such as Helen Lewis, Allen Tullos, Harry Caudill, and others have challenged theories of inherent deficiency in Appalachian culture on the one hand, and theories of noble primitivism on the other, attempting to generate in their stead narratives that emphasize a groundedness to the experiences and communities of mountain dwellers. Such accounts have sought useful ways to conceptualize Appalachia as a region; this impulse resulted in numerous "insider" anthologies, oral histories, and area studies. There is a much-needed redemptive sense to these revisionist accounts; as Scott Devaux has pointed out in regard to jazz criticism, there are problems with seeking to disturb a narrative so recently established—and one that has served such important pedagogical purposes.

However, in order to contextualize the identity formation of twentieth-century Appalachians, it is necessary to expand this conception of place—

and the word "place" itself—to include *displacement* as a shaping force. Repeated coerced immigrations of mountain people, especially following both world wars, has amounted to a continuing national trauma of profound psychological significance for Americans whose ancestors had lived for generations in the mountains of the Appalachian range. Indeed, William Boelhower's characterization of turn-of-the-century immigration to the United States from Europe as a "catastrophic act of topological dislocation" seems to provide an apt description for the experience of internal immigrants from Appalachia as well. In the face of this transformative movement, the category *Appalachian* (and its derogatory pop-culture counterpart *hillbilly*) no longer carries strictly, or even chiefly, regional implications.[1]

Harriette Simpson Arnow's 1954 novel *The Dollmaker* demonstrates how the meaning of "Appalachia" or "the Kentucky mountains" for one family changes from a regional description, with meaning fixed in the present ("home"), to be understood as a designation of ethnicity, signifying both the historical past and the family's point of cultural origin. The force responsible for this change is the family's dislocation and its chief result: the newfound relevance of their status as "hillbilly" or "Appalachian" as different from, and equivalent to, the neighbors' identities as Irish, Polish, Japanese, and so forth. The novel chronicles the relocation of the Nevels family from a Kentucky farm to Detroit during the 1940s so that the father, Clovis, may contribute to the tail end of the war effort by working in a Flint factory. The period of the 1940s, with the increasing automation of the coal industry and the lure of relatively high pay at the wartime mass-production industries, marks the beginning of great migrations from Appalachia as well as internal migrations within the region. The Nevels's Kentucky community is designed to be self-supporting rather than cash-producing. But World War II, with its demands upon the settlement's inhabitants, changes that situation:

> "It's like the farmers," the officer went on. . . . "They can't exempt every little one-horse farmer who has little to sell. A man has to produce a lot of what the country needs."

1. William Boelhower, "Ethnic Trilogies: A Genealogical and Generational Poetics," in *The Invention of Ethnicity*, ed. Werner Sollors (New York: Oxford University Press, 1989), 158. This is not to say that *Appalachian* has not always been an ambiguous term: while the Appalachian Mountains extend from Maine along the eastern seaboard, the word as an appellation for the residents of the mountains, and their cultural productions, has tended to refer only to those living in the southern portion of the mountain range.

... "They warn't a farmer in our settlement big enough," she said, and her voice was low and sullen.[2]

Once the Nevels leave Kentucky they never return: *The Dollmaker* does not supply a portrait of the altered Appalachia.[3] Rather Arnow concerns herself with the family's painful and inevitable "adjustment" to endless facets of industrial living—flush toilets, strikes, buying on time, overpriced produce. With their move to Detroit, the Nevels have fallen into a new kind of history, one controlled by the marketplace and written by men. Their identity will never be the same. Indeed, the taxi driver who meets them at the train station in Detroit immediately acknowledges that hereafter, displacement is the key quality in the makeup of their ethnic identity:

> "When I went through that second reader forty years ago down in Alabama, they didn't teach us how to live in Detroit like they do little Kentuckians now."
> Clytie giggled. "How'd you know where we was frum?"
> "I've met youse atta station through two world wars. I oughta know." His mocking eyes searched the mirror in front of him for Gertie's face. "An I bet youses gonna go back pretty soon with money enough saved futu buy a farm, one a dem big bluegrass farms. Huh?" (165)

Sense of place (except to denote loss) has already become a humorously ingenuous fancy. By the time the children's art teacher asks Gertie where she is from, her identification as a Kentuckian marks distance and rupture from place rather than any geographical or historical continuity:

> "Mrs. Nevels," the man said, putting his hand on the basket, "pardon, please, this interruption, but we wanted to ask about this beautiful basket. We have never seen one like it. . . . Is it Polish?"

2. Harriette Arnow, *The Dollmaker* (New York: Avon Books, 1972), 22. All further references to *The Dollmaker* are to this edition.
3. Arnow did observe later: "When I went out to teach in 1926 there were hundreds of roadless creek valleys all through the Southern Appalachians, and almost no roads at all in Eastern Kentucky. . . .
"The hills are still there—that is most of them—though strip mining and super highways have taken their toll. Yet the life of the twenties and thirties that revolved about the communities in the shut away valleys is gone. One can walk for miles and miles through the upper reaches of the creek valleys and find only tumble-down houses, often the chimney alone, a rusted post office sign wind-lodged in a young pine tree, or a leaf-choked spring, around it scattered blocks of stone to remind the passerby that once a spring-house stood there. . . ." (in Guy Carawan and Candie Carawan, eds., *Voices from the Mountains* [New York: Knopf, 1976], 12).

Gertie shook her head. "It come frum back home. Ole Josiah Coffey made it, one a th last afore he died."

"Back home?" he asked, head tilted as he considered the fat sides of the basket.

"My country is Kentucky." (206)

As this exchange demonstrates, Gertie's sense that being from Kentucky is a national identity comparable to being Polish is a direct result of her displacement rather than her previous attachment to a place: she knows that this information will adequately answer the teacher's questions. Further pressed, though, she seems inarticulate about details closer to home—which part of the state (north or south) she came from, or whether her home was in the mountains or not.

Regional Economics and Artistic Colonization

Cupid came last Saturday night
Took him to my parlor,
Every time he'd hug my neck,
He'd say now don't you holler.
—Roba Stanley, "Single Life"

The violent accommodation of Appalachia to an industrial economy, carried out in *The Dollmaker* through coerced migration, is both paralleled and prefigured by the ravishment of Gertie as a woman colliding with the larger male institutions of society. After all, the plot pivots upon the tragedy that occurs when a woman has to submit to male will; in *The Dollmaker*, gender relations, even relatively successful marriages, are chillingly emblematic of larger control-submission schema of industrial capitalism.

Gertie Nevels has never had any intention of leaving Kentucky. Exhausted by years of sharecropping, she still abhors the idea of leaving for the city, as her sister has done. Rather, she has painstakingly saved to buy her own piece of land, going without and secreting money for years on end in the hopes that her family can "have us a little piece of heaven right here on earth" (77). As an additional benefit, Gertie anticipated that she would no longer be financially dependent upon her husband, Clovis, who is not much of a farmer either by inclination or ability. Gertie must save her money furtively because she knows full well that if she tells Clovis she has it, he will want to spend it on a new truck. Through this difference of ambition between a wife and her husband, Arnow early on genders the impulse to leave (represented by the truck) as male and the need to stay (represented by the multigenerational home) as female.[4]

But when Gertie has finally saved the money, and even negotiated the sale, she is thwarted in her purchase of the old Tipton place because her mother believes that a woman's place is at her husband's side:

> Her mother turned away, weeping now into the saddle blanket, talking both to the gray mule and to God. "Oh, Lord, oh, Lord, she's turned her own children against their father. She's never taught them th Bible where it says, 'Leave all else an cleave to thy husband.' She's never read to them th words writ by Paul, 'Wives, be in subjection unto your husbands, as unto th Lord.'" (141)[5]

Gertie's mother uses texts of patriarchy not only to silence Gertie, who (to the shock and dismay of her son Reuben) stands wordless in the face of her mother's verbal torrent, but also to pressure the family friend who had been himself delighted to sell her the property, managing to convince him that by helping Gertie he is "let[ting] a piece a land come atween a woman an her man an her people" (145). In this manner, Gertie's longtime dream is destroyed by male supremacist ideology, and she ends up in Detroit with her husband, where she lacks the fulfillment she had always found in farming, where her standard of living deteriorates, where one of her children is killed and another runs away because he is unable to adjust to city life. She enters a community of women whose aspirations and talents have been similarly destroyed or stupefied by the dominance of their men: Sophronie, who drinks in order to sleep through her memories of working on a revolving assembly line called the "merry-go-round"; Mrs. Anderson, who smiles frighteningly while uttering biting sarcasm about her husband's "modern" theories of child-rearing and his obsequiousness toward his boss; and Max, whose husband never understands why she finally leaves him to go home to the ocean.

Inequitable male-female relationships provide a taxonomy for other forms of oppression in *The Dollmaker*. The overall correspondence is to

---

4. For more on the particular pain of moving for women, see Audrey T. McCollum, *The Trauma of Moving: Psychological Issues for Women* (Newbury Park, Calif.: Sage Productions, 1990).
5. It is worth noting that "words writ by Paul"—"Servants, obey your masters"— were a favorite of slave owners attempting to use biblical texts to justify the institution of slavery.

the interplay of forces responsible for the ravaging of rural life. At the outset, the female protagonist is linked psychically to the land:

> She thought she was going to cry. She stood a long time bent over a potato hill, unable to see the spading fork, the undug potatoes forgotten. It couldn't be true. So many times she'd thought of that other woman, and now she was that woman: "She considereth a field and buyeth it; with the fruit of her own hands she planteth a vineyard." A whole vineyard she didn't need, only six vines maybe. So much to plant her own vines, set her own trees, and know that come thirty years from now she'd gather fruit from the trees and grapes from the vines. (112)

Working her own land is not only Gertie's lifelong dream, it is the center of a belief system that situates her in time according to her relation to the natural world.

Not surprisingly, male exploitation of women corresponds with the destruction of the land, and of land-linked tradition, for profit. Gertie must rip up her country roots in order to follow her husband. Migration means leaving her sphere of competence behind and adapting to the capitalist system that is forced upon her. Earlier she grew what her family needed to eat, outside of or peripheral to the market system:

> Gertie, sitting at the foot of the table with a lard bucket of sweet milk on one side of her, buttermilk on the other, a great platter of hot smoking cornbread in front, and other bowls and platters within easy reach, was kept busy filling glasses with milk, buttering bread, and dishing out the new hominy fried in lard and seasoned with sweet milk and black pepper. It was good with the shuck beans, baked sweet potatoes, cucumber pickles, and green tomato ketchup. Gertie served it up with pride, for everything, even the meal in the bread, was a product of her farming. (91)

Even the cash Gertie hoards in Kentucky for the purchase of her land has meaning for her only in terms of goods she herself produced, whose worth she directly understands. Counting the bills, she reinjects the reality of her own labor back into the symbolic value of the paper:

> Sometimes after a moment of puzzlement she whispered, "That was eggs at Samuel's two years ago last July," and to a five, "That was th walnut-kernel money winter before last," and to another one, "That was th big dominecker that wouldn't lay atall; she'd bring close to two dollars now." Of one so old and thin it seemed ready to fall apart at the creases, she was doubtful, and she held it to the light until she saw the pinhole through Lincoln's eye. (41)

Once in Detroit, however, Gertie, out of her own element, finds it difficult to adapt to the market system of food:

> "They're allus a makin a fast buck on you, Mom. Recollect them pork chops, two, three days ago. They all briled away into grease, like that hamburger and th sausage."
>
> "Grease at sixty cents a pound," Clovis said. . . . "Yer mom ain't used to buying. She's got to learn." (349)

As Gertie's homegrown meals demonstrate, women and the land are united by their ability to nourish. Capitalism, on the other hand, which interferes with Gertie's womanly ability to nourish, is associated with the male. Gertie's new refrigerator—an unwelcome present from husband to wife—cleverly represents this dynamic. Evocative of the soullessness of the war economy in its name Icy Heart, it has the power to ruin the nourishment that the land and the woman offer: " 'Don't let it freeze the eggs an frostbite th lettuce,' Max said with a shiver. 'They're powerful things, them Icy Hearts' " (283).

The most poignant manifestation of the defeminization enacted by industrial capitalism is its effect upon Gertie's "whittlin' foolishness." As the novel's title indicates, carving is an important part of Gertie's sense of self. Gertie generally carves dolls and other toys (in her twin roles of artist and mother); she also carves wooden baskets, ax handles, and other objects with understood use value in her Kentucky community. In addition, she has been engaged in a larger project: a cherry wood sculpture that will become either Christ or Judas, as soon as Gertie "finds a face" for the figure. Gertie's carving has psychological value for her as well: it is a comforting, almost ritualistic activity that strengthens her through times of extreme stress—she whittles at her ailing son Amos's bedside, for instance, and during the miserable train ride to Detroit. In Detroit "whittlin' foolishness" comes to represent, furthermore, Gertie's tie to Kentucky.

Clovis, on the other hand, has accepted the values of capitalism, including his own rightful dominance over the family economy. He and Gertie clash over the amount of time she spends working on a wooden crucifix commissioned by the Catholic next door. In fact, Clovis wants Gertie to mass-produce her toys so that she can make them cheaply and sell many of them:

> "You know what you need," he said, pulling off his jacket, looking at her as she sat, lax-handed, head drooping above the Christ he had flung in her lap, "you oughta have a jig saw. With one a them things a body can cut out

anything—Christ, er pieces for a jumpen-jack doll—it's all the same to a jig saw." (362–63)

Gertie fears that exactly this kind of homogenization will claim her children in Detroit. In a conference with her son Reuben's schoolteacher, she is told that the children need to become like all the others in order to fit in. Gertie responds that children cannot be stamped out identically like biscuit dough, at once affirming the homespun source of her wisdom and the repulsion she feels for the debased mechanical reproduction that surrounds her. Significantly, the schoolteacher is named Mrs. Whittle, indicating that Gertie's artistic integrity is already outside of her control, located here in the denatured, pseudorational advocate of "adjustment." Indeed, upon leaving the school building after bringing the children there for the first time, Gertie hears a sound issue from it that resembles the hum from a factory. Embodied sonically, mass production for profit motive becomes indistinguishable as a threat to the mother and a threat to the artist. This association is brought all the way home in Clovis's later "joke" that once Gertie has learned to use her new jigsaw, they could hang a sign over the door of their cramped home, "Nevels Woodworking Plant No. 1."

Generally speaking, then, Arnow casts women as the bearers of a rural tradition that is being defiled by men or male commercial institutions. This notion of the female as the bearer of tradition is not uncommon, informing, for instance, Zora Neale Hurston's *Their Eyes Were Watching God* or Meridel LeSueur's *The Girl*, among others. It must be noted that an internal contradiction lies within this notion of woman as the transmitter of tradition. After all, it originates in the male supremacist relegation of woman to the house. It is this same limitation of women that allows the ravaging of their traditions through their relative powerlessness or marginalization. As I have already suggested, Arnow uses the male-female relationship to figure various forms of regional, economic, and artistic colonization; the same paradoxical dynamic that problematizes Gertie's role as female "folk" is at work in her negotiations of her move from old to new environs. Renato Rosaldo has usefully termed this contradiction "imperialist nostalgia." In his study of the subjectivity of anthropology, Rosaldo explains that the language of yearning draws attention away from fundamental inequalities in social relations:

> Imperialist nostalgia revolves around a paradox: A person kills somebody, and then mourns the victim. In more attenuated form, someone deliberately alters a form of life, and then regrets that things have not remained as they were prior to the intervention. At one more remove, people destroy their

environment, and then they worship nature. In any of its versions, imperialist nostalgia uses a pose of "innocent yearning" both to capture people's imaginations and to conceal its complicity with often brutal domination."[6]

In this regard, it is extremely significant that Arnow, while demonstrating the acuteness of "homeplace" and "memory" for Gertie and her children, is *not* especially reverent or sentimental. Arnow is careful to establish, for instance, that Gertie's disempowerment begins long before she has ever moved from Kentucky. And Gertie's final, harrowing shattering of her statue-in-progress indicates that while she will use the materials, the raw stuff, of her former self in Detroit, she knows that the form, the reception, and the purpose will be irrevocably altered.

Linguistic Trauma

> The mountain people spoke a different language, and they were practically forced to leave their homes and go to industrial centers for the war effort.
> —Harriette Arnow, 1984

In addition to Gertie's whittling, a penchant she seems to inherit from her father and seeks to pass on to her son Reuben, the rural Kentucky "tradition" that Gertie is asked to relinquish during her dislocation is most figured through speech. As Sally Kitch points out, "[i]n the context of the city, Gertie's Kentucky dialect becomes a metaphor for the values of Gertie's female identity"; assimilation, by contrast, is revealed by a diminished accent.[7]

6. Renato Rosaldo, *Culture and Truth: The Remaking of Social Analysis* (Boston: Beacon Press, 1989), 69–70. Rosaldo also notes that "even in its origins, the term [nostalgia] seems to have been associated with domination," tracing its usage to the late seventeenth century, when a Swiss physician is supposed to have coined the term to refer to "pathological conditions of homesickness among his nation's mercenaries who were fighting far from their homeland" (71).

7. Sally L. Kitch, "Gender and Language: Dialect, Silence, and the Disruption of Discourse," *Women's Studies* 14, no. 1 (1978): 74. Sandra M. Gilbert and Susan Gubar refer to the assimilated language as "fallen," thereby drawing a parallel between linguistic dislocation and Gertie's expulsion from "the Edenic fields of Kentucky" (*No Man's Land: The Place of the Woman Writer in the Twentieth Century*, vol. 3, *Letters from the Front* [New Haven: Yale University Press], 257).

Appalachian speech patterns continue to function as one of the most prevalent markers of the "hillbilly" in popular culture.[8] They have frequently been cited as evidence of the static quality of Appalachian culture, which in this vision has remained for decades untouched (or untainted) by outside influences. Beginning around the turn of the century, northern culture workers at various settlement schools in the region emphasized the wonderfully atavistic language patterns supposedly surviving among those they tended to see as "our living ancestors."[9] "Over and over again," David Whisnant tells us, "the word went forth from the settlement schools that mountain culture was 'Elizabethan'; a picture was painted of mountain children speaking the language of Shakespeare and gravitating naturally toward his plays as preferred reading matter."[10]

Actually, linguistic trauma and alienation characterize hillbilly speech in relation to the United States as a whole and register graphically the displacement Arnow's characters suffer. In an interview given not too long before her death, Arnow addressed the notion of old speech in the mountains:

> They used words that were correct but not ordinarily used, like the word "carry." They spoke of "carrying their mules to town" because "carry" means to go with or convey. And they used the word "ill" the same way we use "ill wind." "Ill" can mean ugly, bad or evil. An "ill-favored" woman is just an ugly woman, because "favor" means feature or appearance. Too often, teachers in the northern cities couldn't understand the children and didn't bother to look in their dictionaries.[11]

Arnow is making the particularities of mountain speech do three kinds of work for her. She sets up speech as a category of difference for displaced Appalachians. Immediately, she reverses the usual hierarchy of "rightness" and "wrongness" by making the vernacular somehow more correct than the "standard" language of that most genteel figure of all, the northern

---

8. For instance, several aged comic strips that posit the ridiculousness of mountain speech are still syndicated nationally (*Snuffy Smith, L'il Abner*).

9. David Whisnant used this evocative term in his paper "Appalachia in Global Context," delivered at the 1994 American Studies Association meeting in Nashville.

10. David Whisnant, *All That Is Native and Fine* (Chapel Hill: University of North Carolina Press, 1983), 57. See this section for a more detailed investigation of popular descriptions of "Shakespeare's speech" in the mountains during the first part of the twentieth century.

11. J. W. Williamson and Edwin T. Arnold, eds., *Interviewing Appalachia* (Knoxville: University of Tennessee Press, 1994), 72.

schoolteacher. Finally, by displaying the pain caused by this linguistic alienation, Arnow disallows an envisioned idyll in the mountains where quaint anachronisms flourish. That comforting construction has been smashed as surely as the unfinished statue of Jesus that Gertie shatters at the novel's brutal, heartbreaking close.

Speech, therefore, is more than a marker denoting the degraded category of hillbilly in the city; it is emblematic of myriad resultant dichotomies: rural and urban, folk and modern, homemade and mass-produced, rich and poor. This web of concerns linking language, power, and history confronts Gertie on every turn once she is in Detroit: "All the new Detroit words—adjustment, down payment, and now Whit's eviction and communism—would get into her head and swim round for days until she got them fastened down just right so that they lay there, handy to her thinking; like the stars when she looked at them . . ." (245). Language is an easy marker of difference—Gertie reflects that she has never heard language like that the tough, urban Daly family uses: she and her children tend to be drawn to strangers who "kinda talk like us" (183). But even more, language is a significant indicator of the forced transmutation of the Nevels in Detroit. On parent-teacher night, Gertie's way of talking earns the disapproval of her unhappy son Reuben's schoolteacher:

" . . . My boy's name is Reuben. Maybe you don't recollect him, but—"
"I don't what?" And she frowned as she might have at a child giving the wrong answer.
" 'Recollect,' I said," Gertie answered.
"Does that mean 'remember'?" (333)

Obviously, Reuben's teacher is one of those Arnow tagged as not wanting to bother to look up the word "recollect" in her dictionary. On the other hand, Arnow also warns against the offensiveness of a curatorial attitude toward Appalachian speech (which traces back to the missionary philosophy of the settlement schools mentioned above). Arnow invokes the discourse of colonization through the academic Homer Anderson's voyeuristic relationship to the factory community. Like his more lofty namesake, Homer wishes to construct a narrative about the journeys of others. He has moved to the cramped development for the purpose of taking notes for his sociological dissertation, a fact that earns him and his wife derision as well as suspicion among their neighbors. Indeed, Arnow casts Homer's project as a kind of linguistic colonization, because while he is making his smug notations about the way Detroit's new workers speak, he is also cozying up to their exploitative boss at the Flint factory.

Arnow encloses Gertie's vernacular within a standard-English narration, signaling among other things a separation of consciousness between the novel's characters and the narrative or authorial voice. This distancing is important; speech habits serve in *The Dollmaker* to illustrate and highlight the alienation of big city life. Gertie first becomes aware of her otherness by listening to Detroiters talk as she gets off the train from Kentucky: "Once again she heard, in the sharp, broken-into-pieces language, the word 'hillbilly' " (162). The destruction of organic community is enacted daily in a language that is "broken into pieces," fragmented again in exactly the same way that Gertie's family will be, exactly the way that her sculpture of Jesus will be.

By writing a formally conventional novel, Arnow has chosen an arguably "mainstream" form. However, her inclusion of oral or vernacular forms within the text undermines the institutional authority of official literary language by virtue of their contradistinct presence.[12] These vernaculars (Arnow depicts linguistically not only Kentuckians but also Poles, Greeks, Irish Americans, and so forth) summon up a whole host of social, historical, class, or professional associations. Bakhtin notes the connection between multiple languages and ideologies in his discussion of "verbal-ideological systems," wherein the oral vernacular voice indicates a second point of view and system of morality corresponding to discrepancies of place within society.[13] Difference in language is resonant of the clash of lifestyles and the internal battles fought by the Nevels as they struggle to survive and adapt without utterly betraying their senses of self.

Arnow uses language, then, not only as a medium for describing change, but also as a concrete index of the measurable effect of social forces upon individuals. The Nevels and their heterogeneous group of neighbors face the necessity of changing their way of speaking to avoid not just ridicule but outcasting. When Gertie refers to a child as a "youngen," a neighbor shrieks: " 'Huh? Youngen? whatcha mean, youngen? In Detroit youse gotta learn to speak English, yu big nigger-loven communist hillbilly. Yu gotta behave . . .' " (313). Gradually, the Nevels's language is smoothed down by outside forces like the rocks Gertie "recollects" in the streambed back home. Two of Gertie's uprooted children are lost to the process of "adjustment": one becomes bitter and runs away, and one is killed by a train (perhaps even the same line that brought the child to Detroit in

12. Kitch, "Gender and Language," considers the dialect in Arnow's text to represent "the eruption . . . of the nonphallic" (68).
13. M. Bakhtin, *Problems of Dostoevsky's Poetics* (1929; trans. Caryl Emerson, Minneapolis: University of Minnesota Press, 1981).

the first place) after being deprived of her imaginary playmate from back home. But the remaining ones, by the end of the novel, are able to laugh at a picture of a woman with a mule, having copied from their fellows the fitting scorn for hillbillies: " 'Liar, liar, liar, hillbilly. Yu mom never had no shoes till yu come to Detroit. Yu mudder's a hillbilly son uv a bitch. Youse hillbillies come to Detroit un Detroit wenttu hell. Waitansee, waitansee, hillbilly bigmouth whitehead, brother sucker . . .' " (246). The woman in the cartoon is, of course, Gertie herself, first presented in the novel astride a mule, large and plain and determined. And the Nevels children's ability to laugh shows nothing less than the fall of Gertie's house, first described in loving detail—attic, stairs, windows, doors, porch—as the old Tipton place she had hoped to buy:

> She smiled on the shake-covered roof of the old log house. . . . Now in the yellow sun the moss shone more gold than green, and all over the roof there was from the quickly melting frost a faint steam rising, so that the dark curled shakes, the spots of moss, the great stone chimney, all seemed bathed in a golden halo and Cassie called that the house had golden windows. (53)

The dislocation of the Nevels as a fall is foreshadowed and elevated to mythical proportion through the names of Gertie's daughters, which invoke the fall of the house of Agamemnon: Clytie (recalling Clytemnestra), who adjusts, and the poor dead Cassie (recalling Cassandra), whose constitutional inability to adjust is ignored or called crazy until too late.

The Old Home Place?

> What have they done to the old home place?
> Why did they tear it down?
> And why did I leave the plow in the field
> And look for a job in the town?
> —D. Webb and M. Jayne, "Old Home Place"

The makers of the 1980 movie version of *The Dollmaker*, which starred Jane Fonda, changed the story's ending, intending, in all likelihood, to make it more commercially palatable. The movie resolves itself with a triumphant and joyous return to the Kentucky farm. This shallowly comforting, saccharine twist betrays Arnow's attempt to portray the miserable ending of a "rich and dignified" way of life.[14]

Arnow's illustration of what happens when a people is severed from its history is telling. Although Arnow elevates folk culture in contrast with the stiffness and tawdriness of the commercial world, her book is not an attempt to create an Appalachian Renaissance by using folk forms for "high" art. It is rather a eulogy for a dying culture; the role of language as the bearer of Appalachian tradition is encapsulated within the reification and eventual destruction of that tradition. The need to incorporate the southern Appalachian region into the consumer system necessitates the sacrifice of individuality for profiteering, the substituting of the "brought-on" for the beloved. The cartoon of the woman on the mule that Gertie's children must learn to laugh at is interesting because it so efficiently illustrates several intersecting processes of hegemonization: cultural vilification, appropriation through commercialization, severing from historical particulars, and displacement, for it is the woman's position on the mule—in transit—that marks her as an object of ridicule. For Gertie's family the resolution is tragic. What's gone stays gone; landscape and homespun wisdom, as Arnow lamented, "cannot be excavated or re-created."[15]

14. Carawan and Carawan, *Voices from the Mountains*, 12.
15. Ibid.

"This Ain't Real Estate"

Land and Culture in Louise Erdrich's Chippewa Tetralogy

T O M   B E R N I N G H A U S E N

> "How firm we stand and plant our feet upon the land deter-
> mines the strength of our children's heartbeat."
> —Louise Erdrich, "Who Owns the Land"

The sense of place, the ways by which individuals and groups relate to particular landscapes as sacred, is a distinctive feature of Native American literature and culture. While it is a commonplace to note the relative mobility of European American culture as compared to the rootedness of various Native American cultures in particular landscapes, that commonplace remains a profound and productive aporia for Native American writers. Louise Erdrich begins her essay "Where I Ought to Be: A Writer's Sense of Place" by remarking this contrast:

> In a tribal view of the world, where one place has been inhabited for generations, the landscape becomes enlivened by a sense of group and family history. Unlike most contemporary writers, a traditional storyteller fixes listeners in an unchanging landscape combined of myth and reality. People and place are inseparable.[1]

The ideal of the traditional storyteller forms an important context for understanding Erdrich's fiction, and specifically her sense of place, though she is quite conscious that in her own novels she is not a traditional

---

1. Louise Erdrich, "Where I Ought to Be: A Writer's Sense of Place," *New York Times Book Review,* July 28, 1985, 1.

storyteller. Her works are published, not oral, performances, and her audience encounters her stories as new experiences, not as the frequently repeated myths of their culture. On the other hand, though Erdrich's work is strongly marked by the tradition of the American novel—she has, for instance, frequently cited the influence of Faulkner—it stands apart from this context as well. As with many contemporary Native American writers, Erdrich has created a hybrid of the traditional story and the novel.

Louis Owens describes this process of hybridization in *Other Destinies: Understanding the American Indian Novel:*

> The Native American novelist works in a medium for which no close Indian prototype exists. The novelist must therefore rely upon story and myth but graft the thematic and structural principles found therein upon the "foreign" (though infinitely flexible) and intensely egocentric genre of the written prose narrative, or novel.

This mix of forms is closely connected to Owens's sense that mixed-bloodedness, literal and figural, is a fundamental characteristic of the contemporary Native American novel: "For the contemporary Indian novelist—in every case a mixedblood who must come to terms in one form of another with peripherality as well as both European and Indian ethnicity—identity is the central issue and theme. . . ."[2] Erdrich's poetry and fiction are clearly marked by her mixed-blood heritage in her representations of German American and Chippewa culture, but a more figurative use of the term *mixed-blood* also applies to her fiction. Erdrich writes what we might call "mixed-blood narrative" in that, like mixed-blood culture, her texts occupy, in terms of subject matter and formal qualities, the margin between purely traditional Native American modes of representation and those modes common in European American culture.

As a writer of mixed-blood narratives, Erdrich assumes a different responsibility from that of the traditional storyteller whose task is to enact culture. Erdrich has argued that the responsibility of contemporary Native American writers is to represent their culture, to represent it especially in context of the destruction of traditional culture. Erdrich has noted that "many Native American cultures were annihilated more thoroughly than even a nuclear disaster might destroy ours, and others live on with the fallout of that destruction, effects as persistent as radiation—poverty, fetal alcohol syndrome, chronic despair." These facts lead her to conclude

2. Louis Owens, *Other Destinies: Understanding the American Indian Novel* (Norman: University of Oklahoma Press, 1992), 10, 5.

that "in the light of this enormous loss, [contemporary Native American writers] must tell the stories of contemporary survivors while protecting and celebrating the cores of cultures left in the wake of the catastrophe."[3] This surely describes Erdrich's own mixed-blood narratives in that they celebrate a cast of "contemporary survivors" and the core that remains of their traditional Chippewa culture, especially their connection with particular landscapes. At the heart of Erdrich's tetralogy, composed of *Tracks, Love Medicine, The Beet Queen,* and *The Bingo Palace,* is the deep tie between her Chippewa characters, their culture, and the land that is their home. In Erdrich's fiction, as in the performance of the traditional storyteller, "people and place are inseparable."

Leslie Fiedler argues in *Love and Death in the American Novel* that classic American fiction, especially male-authored classic American fiction, consistently treats the subject of moving on. Huck's decision at the end of *Huckleberry Finn* to "light out for the Territory ahead of the rest"[4] exemplifies the pattern. Other novels that are less enthusiastic about leaving home, such as Melville's *Israel Potter* and Thomas Wolfe's *You Can't Go Home Again,* end up telling much the same story.

The impulse to move on, to wester, in European American culture meets its opposite in contemporary Native American novels. As William Bevis notes in his essay "Native American Novels: Homing In," Crevecoeur's classic essay from *Letters from an American Farmer* defines the European American by all that he is able to leave behind. By contrast, in Native American novels "the hero comes home": "In Native American novels, coming home, staying put, contracting, even what we call 'regressing' to a place, a past where one has been before, is not only the primary story, it is a primary mode of knowledge and a primary good." Bevis argues that in the works of D'Arcy McNickle, N. Scott Momaday, Leslie Silko, and James Welch the homing plot predominates and that "Indian 'homing' is presented as the opposite of competitive individualism, which is white success." Moreover, as the characters in these novels seek to establish their identities through their acts of homing, Bevis shows that in these fictions " 'identity,' for a Native American is not a matter of finding 'one's self,' but of finding a 'self' that is transpersonal and includes a society, a past, and a

3. Erdrich, "Where I Ought to Be," 23.
4. Mark Twain, *Adventures of Huckleberry Finn* (Berkeley and Los Angeles: University of California Press, 1986), 362; Leslie A. Fiedler, *Love and Death in the American Novel* (New York: Anchor Books, 1992).

place." That is, these writers emphasize "a tribal rather than an individual definition of 'being.'"[5]

This model of a quest for a transpersonal identity rooted in a sense of society, history, and place speaks directly to the dynamics of dispossession, displacement, and repossession of the land in Erdrich's tetralogy. The deracination, the loss of identity that is evident in many of her characters, involves dispossession and displacement in all three senses—loss of social context, disconnection from the past, and loss of the land. The attempt to repossess what has been lost involves reconstruction of all three aspects of a tribal transpersonal sense of identity—coming home in a social sense, being at home in the tribe's history, and returning to the particular landscape that is home.[6]

In the context of women's narratives of displacement and relocation it is noteworthy that the burden of reconstruction falls disproportionately on women in Erdrich's tetralogy. For all of the important male characters in the series—one thinks of Nanapush, Moses Pillager, Eli and Nector Kashpaw, Russell James, Gerry Nanapush, Lyman Lamartine, and Lipsha Morrissey—it is, nonetheless, Erdrich's female characters who most effectively preserve what remains of their culture and work toward cultural rebirth. The chief figure of preservation and reconstruction is doubtless Fleur Pillager, the alpha and omega of the series.

Erdrich's centering of female characters reflects a fundamental distinction between European American culture as an essentially patriarchal culture and the less patriarchal Native American cultures. Paula Gunn Allen offers an extreme statement of this difference in *The Sacred Hoop: Recovering*

5. William Bevis, "Native American Novels: Homing In," in *Recovering the Word: Essays on Native American Literature*, ed. Brian Swann and Arnold Krupat (Berkeley and Los Angeles: University of California Press, 1987), 581, 582, 585.

6. Bevis, "Native American Novels," notes one caveat in his generalization about place in contemporary Native American fiction—"all six novels [analyzed] are from inland West reservations and all six come from tribes not drastically displaced from their original territories or ecosystems" (592). In some senses this applies to the Chippewa as well, though it is important to note that the Chippewa have been in continuous contact with European Americans since at least the late eighteenth century. Although they have not been displaced from their original range, their culture has been more drastically transformed by contact with European Americans than have the Native American cultures of the inland West. While Bevis's six novels focus on male homing, Robert Silberman addresses the "homing plot" as specifically female in "Opening the Text: *Love Medicine* and the Return of the Native American Woman," in *Narrative Chance: Postmodern Discourse on Native American Literatures*, ed. Gerald Vizenor (Albuquerque: University of New Mexico Press, 1989), 101–20.

the Feminine in American Indian Traditions, concluding that "traditional tribal lifestyles are more often gynocratic than not, and they are never patriarchal." Though Allen may overstate the case, the term "gynocratic" fits as a description of Erdrich's world. Judith A. Antell adds a layer to Allen's argument by historicizing Allen's description of the timeless gender roles of traditional culture. Antell argues that nineteenth- and twentieth-century attempts by dominant culture to assimilate Native Americans focused on Native American men and resulted in a particular sense of alienation for them:

> The suppression of Indian people and the past they represent is clearly the cultural legacy of white America. In the view of dominant, white America, Indian men represent the more powerful and therefore the more threatening of the two sexes. The psychological, if not physical, impairment of Indian men is seen as critical to the colonial scenario. Indian women are more easily discounted regardless of the state of their mental health.[7]

The largely gynocratic world of Erdrich's fiction is surely a product of the relatively antipatriarchal character of traditional Native American cultures in combination with the effects of assimilationist policies and programs that targeted Native American men, placing greatest emphasis on undermining traditional roles for Native American males.

The four volumes of Louise Erdrich's recently completed tetralogy constitute a self-consciously historical series, treating the interconnected lives of various characters on and around a fictional North Dakota Chippewa reservation from 1912 to the present. *Tracks* covers the period of 1912 to 1924, while *Love Medicine* and *The Beet Queen* overlap one another, both treating roughly the period from the middle 1930s to the early 1980s. *The Bingo Palace*, though it doesn't attach specific dates to individual chapters as in the previous three volumes, is clearly a sequel to *Love Medicine*, tracing the main characters of that work through a series of events loosely situated between 1984 and the present.[8]

7. Paula Gunn Allen, *The Sacred Hoop: Recovering the Feminine in American Indian Tradition* (Boston: Beacon, 1986), 2; Judith A. Antell, "Momaday, Welch, and Silko: Expressing the Feminine Principle through Male Alienation," *American Indian Quarterly* 12, no. 3 (Summer 1988): 214.

8. The chapters added to the new edition of *Love Medicine* contribute to the sense of linear sequence in the series by providing connecting narratives, further linking *Love Medicine* to its prequel, *Tracks*, and its sequel, *The Bingo Palace*. The novels of Louise Erdrich cited in this text are: *Love Medicine* (1984; New York: Harper,

That Erdrich's work presents itself to the reader as historical seems beyond dispute, but the nature of the claim to significance as history is not as simple as it may at first seem. Erdrich's representations invite complex questions about authenticity, both in terms of the relation between her fictional history and historical events, and in terms of the presumed ethnicity of her texts. Though Erdrich is most frequently discussed as a Native American author, the question of whose history is being represented in the tetralogy remains open. Erdrich is enrolled in the Turtle Mountain band of the Chippewa and her grandfather, Pat Gourneau, was tribal chair of the band. The reservation life she depicts invites comparison with life on the Turtle Mountain Reservation in north-central North Dakota and the White Earth Reservation of Minnesota. Since Erdrich's novels are expressly fictional, offering fictional characters and settings, and yet are clearly linked to historical circumstances, they open the question of how Erdrich's imaginative world interfaces with historical reality.[9]

At another level, the subject of Erdrich's narrative "history" is complicated by her mixed-bloodedness. Some of her work honors her German American ancestors as much as her Chippewa ancestors. This is especially evident in the poems of *Jacklight* and in *The Beet Queen*. Erdrich's work is not then exclusively concerned with Native American experience, nor could it be, given the longstanding mixing of Chippewa with European Americans, especially French Canadians, which renders the category of purely Chippewa experience itself an idealization.

Leslie Silko's savage review of *The Beet Queen,* "Here's an Odd Artifact for the Fairy-Tale Shelf," opens up both of these issues in the extreme. Silko defines Erdrich as a postmodern writer who indulges in "self-referential writing." This sort of writing, according to Silko, is capable of "an ethereal clarity and shimmering beauty because no history or politics intrudes to muddy the well of pure necessity contained within language itself." In the place of history and politics, Erdrich is said to offer her readers a whitewashed fairy-tale version of reality:

> Good fiction need not be factual, but it doesn't obscure basic truth. In Erdrich's hands, the rural North Dakota of Indian-hating, queer-baiting white farmers, of the Depression, becomes magically transformed. . . . Hers

---

1993); *The Beet Queen* (New York: Bantam, 1987); *Tracks* (New York: Harper and Row, 1988); and *The Bingo Palace* (New York: Harper Collins, 1994). Citations will appear parenthetically in the text.

9. James D. Stripes poses precisely this question in his essay, "The Problem(s) of (Anishinaabe) History in the Fiction of Louise Erdrich: Voices and Contexts," *Wicazo Sa Review* 7, no. 2 (1991): 26–33.

is a rarified place in which the individual's own psyche, not racism or poverty, accounts for all conflict and tension.

Silko's attack is wrongheaded on a number of counts and several critics have mounted able defenses of Erdrich's connection to history.[10]

Erdrich is not a postmodern, self-referential writer in the vein of Robert Coover, nor is she a historian in the academic sense. She is a writer of mixed-blood narratives, a subgenre of the modern novel, and her work should be judged in the context of that genre. Silko is correct in noting that Erdrich places greater emphasis on the psychology of her characters than on historical or political explanations of their circumstances. Moreover, Erdrich's chosen mode of narration, employing multiple first-person narrators and no omniscient voice—with the possible exception of one voice in *The Bingo Palace*—inevitably gives readers access to the psychology of the characters who narrate the text and only gives readers access to historical and political contexts when particular narrators happen to think historically or politically.

Two narrators, Nanapush in *Tracks* and Wallace Pfef in *The Beet Queen*, do give readers some direct sense of political and historical context in their narrations, but most of Erdrich's narrators are not given to thinking much in these terms. This is especially true for the Native American characters of the middle volumes, *Love Medicine* and *The Beet Queen*. It is understandable that they are not especially politically or historically oriented given the fact that their culture, the necessary context for political and historical thought, has been rendered largely moribund by the catastrophic events described in *Tracks*. Most of the Native American characters in *The Beet Queen* and *Love Medicine* suffer from deracination, as is revealed in the relative emptiness of their lives, but they don't, and can't, bewail that loss in the terms called for by Silko because they are, given the nature of their circumstances, not fully conscious of what they have lost.

Still, the tetralogy is profoundly historical in that the various characters' lives are clearly shaped by historical forces of which they are only partially aware. The history of the Chippewa people is etched in even the most unreflective of Erdrich's characters. The challenge of reading Erdrich's work

10. Leslie Marmon Silko, "Here's an Odd Artifact for the Fairy-Tale Shelf," *Studies in American Indian Literatures* 10, no. 4 (1988): 179, 180; for readings of Erdrich's work in the historical context in addition to works cited here, see Susan Perez Castillo, "Postmodernism, Native American Literature and the Real: The Silko-Erdrich Controversy," *The Massachusetts Review* 32, no. 2 (Summer 1991): 285–94; Nancy J. Peterson, "History, Postmodernism, and Louise Erdrich's *Tracks*," *PMLA* 109, no. 5 (October 1994): 982–94.

comes with the realization that the burden of history has been placed on the reader. These books make a subtle moral gesture in their approach to the reader, one that is easily overlooked, in that to read them well is to take an interest in their historical context, indeed, even to take a degree of responsibility for that context.[11]

The Chippewa, or Anishinaabe, part of the larger nation of the Ojibwa, have a distinctive history. The Chippewa-Ojibwa were originally "part of the greater Algonquin nation that occupied much of what is now south-central Canada and the Great Lakes region." By the early seventeenth century, and possibly somewhat earlier, this tribe had moved westward to the Lake Superior region. By 1780, they were occupying the range that is now northern Wisconsin and northern Minnesota and pushing even further west. By 1800, some Chippewa were hunting buffalo with their Cree kinsmen on the plains of Saskatchewan. The Northwest Company of Montreal established a trading post in Pembina, the northeasternmost point of modern North Dakota in 1797, and from that time forward the Chippewa-Ojibwa were in constant contact with European Americans.[12]

Though the Chippewa were pushed westward by the pressure of European settlement, they reached their current range with their traditional culture fully intact. In that, they are like some western tribes that have had continuous tenancy on traditional tribal lands. Ironically, when the federal government sought to remove the Turtle Mountain band from the Turtle Mountains in the 1880s and 1890s, the plan was to move them east to the Minnesota reservation of the White Earth Chippewa. This projected move might have been interpreted as returning the band to its traditional range,

11. Stripes asks, "Do [Erdrich's] works stimulate research on the part of scholars in literature who teach her works into the problems of Indian and tribal histories?" ("The Problem(s) of (Anishanaabe) History," 26). But the burden of reading Erdrich historically can't be shifted to the teacher/scholar. Rather, Erdrich makes establishment of the historical context the reader's task. Assimilation, understanding events from an Indian point of view, becomes the reader's problem. Erdrich has also been criticized for being too accommodating to non-Indian readers. Louis Owens comments, "In *Love Medicine*, readers are allowed into an Indian world sans guilt, a wonderfully textured, brilliantly rendered fiction where the non-Indian reader is not forced to feel his 'outsidedness' " ("Acts of Recovery: The American Indian Novel in the '80s," *Western American Literature* 22, no. 1 [1987]: 54). Owens misses the epistemic question. Erdrich does not adopt the voice of dominant culture, nor does she bother to gloss terms for the non-Indian reader. Her work speaks the discourse of the "other" and implicitly "others" the non-Indian reader in the process. It doesn't provide guideposts, and it doesn't assign guilt; rather it speaks a voice that cuts out the outsider altogether.

12. Stanley N. Murray, "The Turtle Mountain Chippewa, 1882–1905," *North Dakota History* 51, no. 1 (1984): 15.

but as Gregory S. Camp notes, "what the Washington bureaucrats failed to recognize was the fact that the Turtle Mountains had long since become home to the band."[13] In the century since that plan for removal, the Turtle Mountain band and the White Earth Chippewa have fought to retain their tribal lands rather than sell or exchange them for land elsewhere.

But if the Chippewa have managed in some measure to maintain their traditional lands, they have nonetheless been transformed in significant ways by their two centuries of contact with European Americans. This is evident first and foremost by the percentage of mixed-bloods among the Chippewa. Erdrich has commented about the ethnicity of her characters in *Love Medicine*: "Well, everybody has a lot of French, but in particular the French and the Indian had been so blended by that time, it's a new culture." That new mixed-blood culture is already evident in *Tracks*, a representation that is consistent with the 1910 census of the Turtle Mountain band in which mixed-bloods outnumbered full bloods by more than ten to one.[14]

Yet another sign of the transformation of culture is change in the language of the Chippewa. Their native language, Cree, largely gave way to a mixed Cree and French language, Michif, which itself is giving way to English in the period of Erdrich's tetralogy. While there are still a few Cree speakers in *Love Medicine*, the younger traditionalists are, somewhat ironically, trying to maintain Michif.[15] Not surprisingly, the transformations of blood and language are part and parcel with other shifts in culture.

At the beginning of the tetralogy, Erdrich's Chippewas have an almost paradoxically mixed sense of identity. In many respects they have maintained their traditional culture, especially through their continuous connection with sacred tribal lands, and yet they have been transformed significantly by over a century of extensive contact with French American culture. In that sense, it is already not the purely traditional culture that some romantics might wish for, and yet it has an integrity, an identity that Erdrich celebrates in her novels. This new culture, however, is particularly vulnerable because it has always been in transformation and is therefore relatively difficult to define, and thus is difficult to protect. For instance, since the Chippewa lived on both sides of the U.S./Canada border, many

13. Gregory S. Camp, "Working Out Their Own Salvation: The Allotment of Land in Severalty and the Turtle Mountain Chippewa Band, 1870–1920," *American Indian Culture and Research Journal* 14, no. 2 (1990): 24.

14. Laura Cotelli, *Winged Words: American Indian Writers Speak* (Lincoln: University of Nebraska Press, 1990), 45; Camp, "Working Out Their Own Salvation," 30.

15. Julie Maristuen-Rodakowski, "The Turtle Mountain Reservation in North Dakota: Its History as Depicted in Louise Erdrich's *Love Medicine* and *The Beet Queen*," *American Indian Culture and Research Journal* 12, no. 3 (1988): 42–43.

were assumed to be of Canadian origin and were therefore dropped from tribal rolls. Moreover, due to the high percentage of mixed-bloods, it was relatively easy for federal officials to undercount the Chippewa by only counting full bloods. This partially accounts for the federal government's decision in 1884 to reduce the Turtle Mountain reservation, established just two years earlier, by 90 percent, from twenty townships to two townships.[16] Thus this "new culture" was by various measures defined as marginal by the dominant culture. Although these forms of marginality were either irrelevant to the Chippewa—such as the international border— or easily accommodated by the new culture's transforming identity—such as the high percentage of mixed-bloods—they were used effectively against the Chippewa.

The specific measures taken in the campaign to drive the Chippewa to assimilate form an important context for an appreciation of Erdrich's series as historical fiction. Erdrich's tetralogy opens in the winter of 1912, but the political and historical context for the catastrophe there described derives from a series of federal acts and policies established in the period between 1880 and 1910. Beginning in 1871, the Turtle Mountain band made known its claim to ten million acres in what is now north-central North Dakota. Even before the creation of the Turtle Mountain reservation in 1882, policies were being developed for the assimilation of the Chippewa, policies that inevitably included the eventual elimination of communally held tribal land. It was well understood that communal tribal land was essential to Native American identity in general and Chippewa identity in particular. Yet instilling the ethic of competitive individualism, essential for assimilation into the dominant culture, seemed to require individual private landownership. This attempt to assimilate the Chippewa to competitive individualism inevitably sought to root out basic features of Native American life, especially the concept of a transpersonal self defined in terms of one's relation to "a society, a past, and a place."[17] Altering the relationship between people and the land was essential to the success of the federal policy, transforming "home" into "real estate," commodifying the sacred so that it becomes property.

The first important codification of this policy, the General Allotment Act or Dawes Act of 1887, privatized reservation land by allotting it to individuals. Early versions of allotment policy partially protected reservations by giving new owners trust patents to their property. With trust patents the government acted as a trustee who, in theory, helped prevent

16. Camp, "Working Out Their Own Salvation," 26, 21–24.
17. Bevis, "Native American Novels," 585.

exploitation of the new landowners. The trust period was generally set at twenty-five years, at which point owners would be issued patents-in-fee simple, making them fully independent landowners. They could then be forced off their land if they defaulted on loans, mortgages, or taxes. In the forty-five years following passage of the Dawes Act, Native Americans lost ninety million acres of what had previously been reservation land.[18]

In 1906 Congress passed the Burke Act, which accelerated allotment by allowing the Commissioner of Indian Affairs to shorten the trust period. As late as 1911, only a few members of the Turtle Mountain band had received their trust allotments, but the new superintendent of the reservation, Stephen Janus, pushed hard in his reports between 1912 and 1924 to bypass the trust period and issue patents-in-fee simple to eligible tribal members. Janus believed that the "Indian Problem" had a simple solution: "There is in a large measure a certain cure, and that is to issue every ablebodied man and woman of the tribe his patent-in-fee and let him work out his own salvation."[19] The combination of hard work and individual landownership—cornerstones of American manhood—were clearly understood as keys to assimilation and therefore to "salvation." The use of the term "salvation" suggests that allotment was conceived of as a not altogether secularized version of missionary work, the federal government's companion plan to the Catholic Church's attempt to convert the Chippewa.

Though the Turtle Mountain Chippewa were not given allotments as early as many other Native Americans, their mixed blood led many officials to see them as "competent" to own land. Implicitly, if not explicitly, their mixed blood suggested to some bureaucrats that they were more like European Americans than full bloods and therefore more competent to own land, thus justifying an acceleration of their progress to full ownership. Indeed, some mixed-bloods were forced to "receive ownership of their land without consent and sometimes without knowledge." Predictably, the vast majority of the Chippewa—approximately 90 percent—quickly lost their allotments either through defaulting on taxes or mortgages, or through direct sale. Gregory S. Camp concludes that the policy that was supposed to lead the Chippewa to prosperity and enlightenment ended up "[stripping] them of their best economic asset," their land.[20]

The Dawes and Burke Acts were indeed economically devastating for the Chippewa, but it is also crucial to note that the loss of their lands brought

18. Owens, *Other Destinies*, 30.
19. Quoted in Camp, "Working Out Their Own Salvation," 32.
20. Ibid., 34, 36.

spiritual devastation as well. Erdrich recalls the loss of the land in her first volume of her tetralogy, *Tracks*, the middle volumes, *Love Medicine* and *The Beet Queen*, record the deadening effect of that loss, while *The Bingo Palace* seeks a restoration of tribal land and of the culture that is based in dwelling on that land.

For all the popularity of *Love Medicine* with general readers and critics alike, *Tracks* is the pivotal work of Erdrich's series in that it establishes the context in which the other works become readable as cultural history. The arc or shape of Erdrich's cultural history of her Chippewa band is established in the first lines of *Tracks*—"We started dying before the snow, and like the snow, we continued to fall. It was surprising there were so many of us left to die" (1). Having suffered through a smallpox epidemic and being driven west from Minnesota to a North Dakota reservation, Erdrich's Chippewas now face tuberculosis and finally a "storm of government papers" (1) that threatens their reservation land and their very existence as a culture. The catastrophe wrought by the federal policy of privatization, both in its undermining of tribal culture and in the subsequent loss of most of the land allotted to Native Americans, is the historical context of the entire tetralogy. The central question of the tetralogy is, will Chippewa culture survive, and if so in what form? The crucial issue of preserving sacred land is inseparable from this larger question of cultural survival.

Tracks is a story of cultural near-death; it is a holocaust tale. Traditional culture, represented by the Pillager clan, barely survives the widespread tuberculosis of the winter of 1912. The Pillagers are the keepers of knowledge of traditional medicine and are the conduit for the tribe to the manitou, the lake god/monster, Misshepeshu. Fleur Pillager, then seventeen, and her cousin Moses are the only remaining Pillagers, and though they retain the power of their clan, they do not have a full grasp of its lore. Nanapush, the narrator of half of *Tracks*, says of Fleur after he rescues her, "She was too young and had no stories or depth of life to rely upon. All she had was raw power, and the names of the dead that filled her" (7). Moses is similarly dislocated: "He had survived but, as they said of Fleur, he didn't know where he was anymore . . ." (7–8).

Where disease has cut the heart out of the tribe by sweeping away the Pillager elders, another even more deadly visitation descends upon the tribe with the spring thaw. The arrival of a new kind of outsider, the surveyor, heralds an unexpected catastrophe: " . . . that spring outsiders went in as before, and some of us too. The purpose was to measure the lake. Only now they walked upon the fresh graves of Pillagers, crossed death roads to plot out the deepest water where the lake monster, Misshepeshu, hid himself and waited" (8). Nanapush notes that "every year there are more who come looking for profit, who draw lines across the land with their strings and yellow flags" (9), but their encroachment takes on a new meaning when they desecrate Pillager graves. The imperialism implicit in surveying tribal land is at first barely visible. But the act of measuring the lake, so foreign to Erdrich's Chippewa characters, is a calling card of the European Americans who wish to exploit the reservation's resources. Moreover, the goals and cultural presumptions of those "who come looking for profit" render them indifferent, if not wholly oblivious, to what they destroy.

There are two main plotlines in *Tracks,* and both threaten the tribe. Fleur Pillager is the main force standing for tradition and opposing both forms of encroachment. She is, indeed, as will be said of her in *The Bingo Palace,* the center of the tetralogy, "the one who started it all in motion" (125).

One plotline of *Tracks,* treated mostly by the second narrator, Pauline, involves the Catholic Church's missionary work among the Chippewa. In *Tracks* Pauline denies her Chippewa blood in order to become a nun, and then subsequently reappears in *Love Medicine* as Sister Leopolda. Fleur, as a keeper of traditional medicine and as the "priestess" to the manitou, becomes the symbol of the heresy of traditional religion that Pauline hopes to stamp out. Pauline's various attempts to vanquish faith in traditional religion reach their climax in the penultimate chapter of *Tracks.* Pauline recounts in that chapter what she interprets as a final showdown between Fleur's lake god, Misshepeshu, and her god, Christ. Pauline forces this confrontation by venturing out onto the lake in a leaking boat, believing that either she will become Misshepeshu's latest victim or that her champion will come to her aid and defeat the lake god. In Pauline's interpretation of events, Christ is victorious:

> I believe that the monster was tamed that night, sent to the bottom of the lake and chained there by my deed. For it is said that a surveyor's crew arrived at the turnoff to Matchimanito in a rattling truck, and set to measuring. Surely that was the work of Christ's hand. (204)

Pauline's assertion of Christ's victory makes a provocative link between the encroachment of Catholicism and that of the timber interests. The dominant plotline of *Tracks,* enunciated primarily by the first narrator, Nanapush, has to do with control of the land. The surveyors prove to be the advance guard of a lumber company that hopes to log tribal lands, including the sacred Pillager land on Matchimanito Lake. Nanapush, whose character reflects his namesake, "the [traditional Chippewa or]

Anishinaabe trickster, *nanapush* or *nanibozhu*,"[21] joins forces with Fleur to fight the lumber company. At first the company approaches Nanapush in hopes of buying the land:

> The Captain and then the lumber president, the Agent and at last many of our own, spoke long and hard about a cash agreement. But nothing changed my mind. I've seen too much go by—unturned grass below my feet, and overhead, the great white cranes flying south forever. I know this. Land is the only thing that lasts life to life. Money burns like tinder, flows off like water. And as for government promises, the wind is steadier. I am a holdout, like the Pillagers, although I told the Captain and the Agent what I thought of their papers in good English. (33)

Two prominent features of the allotment policy are carefully depicted in Erdrich's novel. First of all, the land has become property, at least in the eyes of the law. Second, transpersonal identity, the essence of tribal culture, has been broken down through the allotment of land to individuals, provoking the divisive tensions between individual and tribal interests. This antitribal policy, employing the lure of cash, seeks to split off individuals from the tribe. And as Nanapush's remarks reveal, the policy is effective: "at last *many of our own*, spoke long and hard about a cash agreement." The encroachment of the lumber company made possible by allotment not only takes the land, but also destroys the tribe by setting its various members against one another.

Ultimately, the lumber company defeats Nanapush and Fleur, first by dividing the tribe, instilling a sense of competitive individualism in which characters seek self-interest to the detriment of others, and finally by manipulating the tax rolls to force defaults that open the way for subsequent land grabs. By the novel's end, Fleur is forced off Pillager land by the lumber company, and the sacred land is defiled by the invaders. As Fleur loses contact with the manitou of the lake, Misshepeshu, the last strand of traditional religion is apparently severed. Nanapush comments that when the Pillagers "were driven from the east, Misshepeshu had appeared because of the Old Man's connection. But the water thing was not a dog to follow at our heels" (175).

The culture cannot be simply transplanted, though Fleur tries desperately. At the end of *Tracks*, Fleur leaves Pillager land dragging a cart that contains the remnants of her culture. Nanapush, not quite comprehending her act, looks into the cart:

21. Owens, *Other Destinies*, 212.

> I looked inside the box of the cart expecting Fleur's possessions but saw only weed-wrapped stones from the lakebottom, bundles of roots, a coil of rags, and the umbrella that had shaded her baby. The grave markers I had scratched, four crosshatched bears and a marten, were fastened on the side of the cart. We left quickly. (224)

For all of Fleur's attempt to take her culture with her, with the loss of the land and of contact with the lake god at the end of *Tracks*, traditional Chippewa culture is rendered virtually moribund.

Tracks, then, as the opening volume of the quartet, focuses on an epic moment in Chippewa history, displacement from the land and the concomitant loss of traditional culture. The next two volumes of the tetralogy—*Love Medicine* and *The Beet Queen*—reflect the deracination and alienation felt by Erdrich's Indian characters in the wake of this catastrophe. Describing *Love Medicine*, Louis Owens notes, "the fragmentation of Indian community in this novel, the rootlessness that results in an accumulation of little, mundane tragedies amongst the assorted characters in the interrelated stories, suggests the enormity of what has been lost to the Chippewas Erdrich writes about." Louise Flavin amplifies Owens's point, noting that in *Love Medicine* Erdrich "depicts a cultural milieu where sacred ceremonies, tribal rituals, and Indian cultural identity have disappeared."[22]

Since Fleur Pillager is not only a character, but also an emblem for Erdrich of the core of culture "left in the wake of the catastrophe," it is altogether appropriate that she is largely absent from the deracinated world of *Love Medicine* and *The Beet Queen*. Fleur makes only two brief appearances in *The Beet Queen*. Early in the book Fleur rescues one of the central characters, Karl Adare, after he has jumped from a train and broken several bones. Eight years after her exodus in *Tracks* she is still wandering, dragging her cart full of stones from Matchimanito Lake. Fleur, a seemingly mad, spectral witch, places Karl in her cart and nurses him until, in her wandering, she finds a church where she can deposit him. After this appearance (43–49), she leaves the novel, only to reappear briefly (179–82) as a marginal character in a scene set on the reservation.

Even more tellingly, Fleur, the major character of the tetralogy, is completely absent from the series's best-known volume, *Love Medicine*. She is at best a poignant absence in the world of *Love Medicine*, a displaced wanderer that we only know by implication, an emblem of a lost culture.

22. Owens, "Acts of Recovery," 54; Louise Flavin, "Louise Erdrich's *Love Medicine*: Loving over Time and Distance," *Critique* 31, no. 1 (Fall 1989): 64.

In Fleur's place, the deracinated world of *Love Medicine* offers us lesser characters, characters who are so lost they hardly know that they have been displaced.

June Kashpaw's act of "homing," with which *Love Medicine* begins, makes her a prime example of this deracination. Her decision to walk home to the reservation, "to Uncle Eli's warm, man-smelling kitchen" (6), from Williston, North Dakota, in a driving snowstorm is at once self-destructive and oddly self-affirming. June's suicide on Easter Sunday marks the hope of return, the return home that Fleur's pilgrimage also seeks. Even June, reduced to random drunken sexual encounters with oil riggers in seedy bars and pickup trucks, retains a deep sense of home. June's son, Lipsha Morrissey, gives *Love Medicine* a more hopeful cast in his quest to complete June's fitful journey, his attempt to discover who he is and at the same time to bring his mother home. At the novel's end, Lipsha makes progress in these personal projects that suggest a larger cultural renewal. He discovers that Gerry Nanapush, another incarnation of the Chippewa trickster, is his father, and, with the car bought with June's life insurance, he takes another step in his quest. The last lines of *Love Medicine* pick up the action of its first chapter. Lipsha, thinking of his mother, June, says: "The morning was clear. A good road led on. So there was nothing to do but cross the water, and bring her home" (367). *Tracks*, as the overture to Erdrich's tetralogy, reaches its climax with Fleur being cast into exile, but the concept of home and the possibility of cultural renewal remain alive, though they are buried beneath a decidedly washed-out culture throughout most of the middle two volumes.

The Bingo Palace, with its many signs of cultural resurgence, is in some respects the double and opposite of *Tracks*. In that sense, Erdrich's history of Chippewa culture has a relatively simple shape and one that is common to the history of many Native American cultures in the twentieth century—it begins in catastrophe, passes through a long period of near-death quiescence, and finally begins to recover in the century's final decades.

Signs of cultural rebirth abound in *The Bingo Palace*, not the least of which is the continuation of Lipsha Morrissey's quest for identity that began at the end of Love Medicine. Like *Love Medicine*, *The Bingo Palace* begins with homecoming. As the novel opens, Lipsha's grandmother, Lulu Lamartine—who is also Fleur's daughter—calls Lipsha home from his wandering in Fargo, North Dakota. Lipsha seems to have lost track of the purpose that sent him homeward at the end of *Love Medicine*, and indeed the tribe has largely lost faith in him. In the first chapter the communal narrative voice says of Lipsha: "We give up on that Morrissey boy Marie Kashpaw rescued from the slough. Spirits pulled his fingers when he was a baby, yet he doesn't appreciate his powers" (7). In the course of the novel, Lipsha is given a second chance to "appreciate [and develop] his powers."

But the most striking figure of cultural resurgence in *The Bingo Palace* is none other than Fleur Pillager. The narrator recalls that after a lengthy exile, Fleur had finally returned to the reservation for "the fourth and last time" (139) many years before the action of *The Bingo Palace* begins. The reader learns that upon her return, Fleur, using a large white Pierce-Arrow for bait, managed to draw the Indian agent who had cheated her of her land in *Tracks* into a game of poker, winning back the Pillager land on Matchimanito Lake.

The Bingo Palace opens with a chapter focusing on Lulu Lamartine, Fleur's estranged daughter. Though Lulu is quite different from her mother, she mirrors Fleur's power in that she clearly has a special role in the life of the tribe, acting as its central maternal figure (1–5). The narrator comments in regard to Lulu that "The red rope between the mother and her baby is the hope of our nation" (6). Lulu embodies what Judith A. Antell calls the "feminine principle" in her role as the general mother figure for the tribe.[23] On the other hand, Fleur, though largely forgotten by tribal members, is the most profound embodiment of the "feminine principle" in the tetralogy because of her long struggle to preserve the sacred lands of her people. For in the longer term, the figural tie between the tribe and Mother Earth is as essential for the survival of the nation as the literal "red rope between the mother and her baby." Indeed, from the point of view of tradition, the two umbilical links are so interconnected as metaphors for each other that they may be virtually indistinguishable. In that context, Fleur is clearly the great, if only partially recognized, mother figure of Erdrich's series.

Fleur, now nearly one hundred years old, hangs onto life "waiting for a young one, a successor, someone to carry on her knowledge" (7). Although Lipsha seems never in the course of the novel to fully realize it, Fleur has been waiting for him, seeking to put him in her place. Though she is feared in the community because each time death has called for her she has put someone else in her place, at the novel's end she rescues Lipsha from death, going on the death road in his place (272). We learn no more of Lipsha's fate after the rescue, but it is strongly implied that in the exchange he will take up Fleur's place as the keeper of traditional knowledge. Even so, it is

---

23. Antell, "Momaday, Welch, and Silko," 213.

far from clear at the novel's end if he has sufficient will or power to act successfully as Fleur's successor.[24]

One further sign of a resurgent culture in *The Bingo Palace* is the use in several chapters of a first-person plural narrative voice. *The Bingo Palace* breaks with the earlier volumes, which employed multiple first-person narrators, by having only one first-person singular narrator, Lipsha Morrissey, who narrates about half of the novel. Most of the remaining chapters are presented through a third-person omniscient voice, but three crucial chapters, including the first and last, are in first-person plural voice. Where the multiplication of first-person singular narrators in *Tracks, The Beet Queen,* and *Love Medicine* suggests fragmentation of the community, the voices of *The Bingo Palace* tend much more toward an assertion of tribal identity. Though Lipsha's voice is that of an individual, and his conscious goals are more personal than communal, his path is, though unrecognized as such by him, toward cultural regeneration. His story represents the slow coming to consciousness of traditional ways and values for Chippewas in the late twentieth century. To the extent that Lipsha speaks as an inchoate shaman, tradition and tribe outweigh personal ambitions. Moreover, the first-person plural narrator of *The Bingo Palace* acts as a voice of the tribe.[25] For the first time in the tetralogy, Erdrich's Chippewas speak through a communal voice, reaffirming the sense of transpersonal selfhood essential to tribal culture. In narrating events in the first chapter, the choral voice remarks, "We don't know how it will all work out, come to pass, which is why we watch so hard, all of us alike, one arguing voice" (6). It is worth noting that Erdrich employs a virtual oxymoron as she seeks to describe the special character of this communal tribal voice, a voice that is at once multiple and unified, "one *arguing* voice." The very existence of a voice

24. My analysis of *The Bingo Palace* focuses on Lipsha Morrissey and Lyman Lamartine as each relates to Fleur Pillager's struggle to reclaim the vestiges of traditional culture. But a third character not directly linked to Fleur by Erdrich seems to be a more promising heir to Fleur's spirit than either Lipsha or Lyman, Shawnee Ray Toose. One might wish that Erdrich had developed her further since she alone seems to have the power to be a focal point of regenerative energies for the tribe, a role that Erdrich has generally reserved for female characters. Lipsha says of Shawnee Ray: " 'You can see [her] deep in the past, running down a buffalo on a little paint war-horse, or maybe on her own limber legs. . . . Shawnee Ray is the best of our past, our present, and our hope of a future' " (12–13). Others in the tribe share his sense that she is rooted in the past and is indeed "the hope of the nation" (6).

25. The voice is described by Lawrence Thorten in his *New York Times* review as a "chorus" of the "inhabitants of the Chippewa Reservation," in *The New York Times Book Review,* January 16, 1994, 7.

of the community in *The Bingo Palace* suggests that the tribe has a more palpable existence than it has had since the passage of the Dawes Act more than a hundred years earlier.

Still, for all of these signs of resurgence, *The Bingo Palace* is not a simple celebration of the return of tradition. Indeed, the arc of Erdrich's cultural history becomes uncertain at the novel's close. It fails to offer an inversion of the plot of *Tracks* in that it is more a book of hope than of hopes fulfilled. The main threat to cultural resurgence in *The Bingo Palace* is ironically represented by one of the tribe's favorite sons, Lyman Lamartine, owner of many successful businesses including the cash cow of the novel's title, a high-stakes bingo palace. Lyman's vision for the future of the tribe is to build an enormous casino on the shore of Matchimanito Lake.[26]

Lipsha, always in competition with Lyman, seeks his own vision by going on a vision quest at Matchimanito Lake. The quest is, on the face of it, a comic, even slapstick fiasco. Lipsha's hunger initially leads him to comic visions of Big Macs, and, when he is finally visited by a spirit animal, it is a skunk, "the mother of all skunks" (200), who inevitably sprays him, thus making him the laughing stock of the rest of the participants in the ritual.

Still, the skunk does speak to Lipsha before she sprays him, uttering the admonition, *"This ain't real estate"* (200). Lipsha's vision is not surprisingly connected to the great mother figure of Erdrich's tetralogy, Fleur Pillager— the skunk's message is her message. Though Lipsha seems to get the message, concluding that "what the skunk said [was] right. Our reservation is not real estate" (221), he is slow to connect his vision with Lyman's plans to build his casino on Pillager land and takes no action to stop the development.

The last chapter of *The Bingo Palace*, titled "Pillager Bones," circles back to *Tracks* in an uncanny repetition. The first lines, describing Lyman's eviction of Fleur in order to break ground for his casino, recall the confiscation of the sacred Pillager land by the Turcot lumber company:

> In the dead cold of winter, Fleur Pillager went out. It was said by those who came to call on her, who came to take her house away with signed papers, that to move at all the old woman had to oil her joints with a thin grease she kept by her door. (271)

---

26. *The Bingo Palace* mirrors *Tracks* in many respects. If the timber interests are the prime external threat in *Tracks*, the gambling interests, coming largely from within the tribe, are the greatest current threat to the tribe. Even Lyman Lamartine, the promoter of tribal gambling, recognizes that institutionalized gambling is a dubious enterprise.

The "storm of government papers" from *Tracks* is doubled by Lyman's "signed papers" with which he evicts Fleur from the sacred land that holds "Pillager bones," land that he further defiles by building his casino. Once again, the Chippewa's culture, based in a traditional relation to sacred lands, is at risk.

The final chapter is narrated in the choral voice of the Chippewa community, now operating a casino on Matchimanito Lake, and it is a voice full of trepidation, a voice unsure of its future. Lyman's vision has won out, at least for the moment, and the community feels Fleur's disapproving eyes upon them:

> We believe she follows our hands with her underwater eyes as we deal the cards on green baize, as *we drown our past* in love of chance, as our money collects, as *we set fires and make personal wars* over what to do with its weight, as we go forward into our own unsteady hopes. (273–74, emphasis mine)

The novel ends with the community questioning itself, knowing that the vision sent to Lipsha has been turned aside and that greed and opportunism have defiled the sacred ground upon which their traditions rest. The existence of the communal voice suggests that Erdrich's Chippewas have reconstructed tribal life in the social sense, but the other two dimensions, connection to the past and to the land, seem attenuated at best and "personal wars" threaten to divide the tribe and undermine the communal voice. *The Bingo Palace* ultimately circles back to the destruction of traditional life in *Tracks*, though ironically here it is the tribe that has turned on itself. The communal voice offers the novel's final line, recalling Fleur's passage to the spirit world:

> For that day we heard the voices, the trills and resounding cries that greeted the old woman when she arrived on that pine-dark island, and all night our lesser hearts beat to the sound of the spirit's drum, through those anxious hours when we call our lives to question. (274)

The tetralogy thus ends on a somber note. For all its figures of hope, *The Bingo Palace* finally waivers in its projection of a future. The tribal lands have been reclaimed and the tribe survives, but its survival is anxious, tenuous, as it calls itself, calls its will to preserve traditional culture, to question.

IV

Geographies of the Self

"With the Wind Rocking the Wagon"

Women's Narratives of the Way West

S U S A N   R O B E R S O N

Have a good view of Laramie Peak in the Black Hills (south side of the river) it, and some other hills are very snowy. . . . Passed 8 graves. Good grass. Camped in the Black Hills. You may call this a poor—but I write on my lap with the wind rocking the wagon. If we did not have so much rain everything would be pleasant. All well.

—Algeline Ashley

Typical of the journals written by women making the overland trek to the West, Algeline Ashley's entry for May 31, 1852, demonstrates the correlation between traveling and writing, the effect that movement, literally and figuratively, has on the text. Ashley readily recognizes the difficulty in producing a legible text for whomever her reader might be, the "you" to whom she alludes, as she tries to balance her diary in her lap while the wind buffets the wagon in which she is sitting. She probably also recognizes that the content of the diary is travel-based, determined by the road, the terrain, and the climate; in fact, like other overland journals Ashley's is written to record a journey perceived to be of historical value and interest. Moreover, for Ashley and other diarists of the way west, the autobiographical content of the diary is contingent upon and contiguous with the terrain and their movement across it. In this way topography, writing about the terrain, and autobiography, writing about the self, merge, demonstrating the "flexible positionality"[1] and fluid identity of the writer. More than determining the

1. Edward Said, quoted in Frances Bartkowski, *Travelers, Immigrants, Inmates: Essays in Estrangement* (Minneapolis: University of Minnesota Press, 1995), 19.

content and conditions for writing, as in Ashley's note, the journey has an effect on the writer, displacing her from the familiar, asking her daily to re-locate herself, and in the process effecting some degree of self-concept change that is enacted and inscribed by and on the road and on the ledger of the road. Thus, the ledger of place and journeying becomes a ledger of self as well.[2]

Indeed, the narratives of the women who went west during the last half of the nineteenth century, the journals, letters, and memoirs they wrote, demonstrate the tension that movement places on women, their texts, and their efforts to negotiate their way in a new environment. Travel has characteristically called into question and transformed the identity of the traveler, suggesting that the traveler's subjectivity is inseparable from her body and the physical condition of movement. As Eric Leed notes, "Travel is the paradigmatic 'experience,' the model of a direct and genuine experience, which transforms the person having it."[3] And travel literature has traditionally provided a space in which the writer can chart and nego-tiate the cartographic and personal displacements of journeying; likewise, westering women used their journals, letters, and memoirs to locate and write themselves as they described the journey west, its trails and trials.

But for women going west, the flexible positionality associated with travel was compounded by the more or less permanent dislocation asso-ciated with moving to and relocating in a new place. Though writing may lead the "displaced autobiographer . . . back to a new home," the westering woman had also to construct a new home and self in the new environment. Because "place identity is an integral part of the self,"[4] the woman who relocated to the West had both the task and the opportunity of reinventing herself to fit the new environment in which she now found herself. At the same time that she was extending spatial, territorial boundaries, going

2. I want to thank the Newberry Library for allowing me access to the travel diaries, memoirs, and letters of the women who went west, and the National Endowment for the Humanities for including me in the 1992 Summer Seminar that convened at the Newberry Library. Mason Lowance Jr., who directed the seminar, deserves special thanks for his encouragement and interest in this project.

3. Eric Leed, *The Mind of the Traveler: From Gilgamesh to Global Tourism* (New York: Basic Books, 1991), 71–72. According to Merleau-Ponty, subjectivity is located in the body and not the mind: "It is the body in its orientation toward and action upon and within its surroundings that constitutes the initial meaning-giving act," quoted in Iris Marion Young, *Throwing Like a Girl and Other Essays in Feminist Philosophy and Social Theory* (Bloomington: Indiana University Press, 1990), 147; Eric Leed corroborates this point in *Mind of the Traveler*, 5.

4. Bartkowski, *Travelers, Immigrants, Inmates*, 101; Theodore Sarbin, "Place Iden-tity as a Component of Self: An Addendum," *Journal of Environmental Psychology* 3, no. 4 (December 1983): 337.

from "the states" to the territories, the pioneer woman was opening up social and psychological spaces, new knowledges, powers, and discourses. Even so, the task of going beyond and of pushing boundaries was fraught with tensions as she attempted to negotiate the future against the claims of the past, to retain attachments to the home place and the familiar self and yet shape a new home and a new self out of the materials and demands of the new environment. These negotiations, compelled by a situation of contingency and in-betweenness, between familiar and new, between self and place, are enacted and translated in documents, themselves hybrid narratives, that become cognitive maps of the self.

Modeled in part after guidebooks written by male explorers and scouts to chart the way across the continent, the overland journals or diaries provided their authors a way of locating themselves and their readers on the terrain. Like the traditional diary or journal, there is an immediacy between author and event that is often unmediated by commentary or interpretation. And like the private diaries of nonliterary women, they are "so terse they seem coded" and "march along chronologically" without much foreshadowing, retrospection, or self-reflexivity, rooted as they are in the concrete and particular of everyday life.[5] Often written for readers back home as a way of sharing the adventure or as a guide for friends and family who may follow in their tracks, the journals attempt to provide objective descriptions of the landscape, weather, and road conditions, saying very little about the writer's other tasks, relationships, illnesses, or reproductive events. But unlike journals written under other circumstances, the overland journal, and hence the life inscribed in it, is completely framed by the trek across the landscape, beginning at the jumping-off point in Missouri or Iowa and ending with their arrival in the new territory. To sum up her experience on the road, Sarah Wisner ends her journal, "A Trip across the Plains in 1866," with this comment: "We have been on the road 110 days and have made an average of 17.38 miles per day." This kind of journal is much like a verbal map, describing the road and locating the traveling self at some point on that road without extending the text beyond the line the journey creates. Having given up home and its familiar patterns for a life on the road, the journeying writer finds a home in the "line that can be drawn on the map," in the pattern of life imposed by the road

5. Lynn Z. Bloom, " 'I Write for Myself and Strangers': Private Diaries as Public Documents," in *Inscribing the Daily: Critical Essays on Women's Diaries*, ed. Suzanne L. Bunkers and Cynthia A. Huff (Amherst: University of Massachusetts Press, 1996), 25–26; Elizabeth Hampsten finds that working women's diaries too were accountlike and rooted in the concrete and particular of the everyday in *Read This Only to Yourself: The Private Writings of Midwestern Women, 1880–1910* (Bloomington: Indiana University Press, 1982), 26.

and transcribed in a journal that regularly marks location and movement through space and time.[6]

A journal like Mrs. Wisner's demonstrates the influence of the road and of guidebooks written for travelers of the overland road on the private life account. Much like Hosea Horn's *Overland Guide from the U.S.* (1852), which charted the distances and conditions of the journey for travelers who followed their route to the West, Mrs. Wisner records the number of miles she has traveled and the condition of the camps. A sample page from Horn's *Guide* demonstrates the control by place and movement on this kind of writing. It also demonstrates the control the author has over his topic with its objective and distanced gaze at a landscape and journey devoid of personal meaning:

Watch Creek: —10 feet wide. The road here turns to the river, and runs close to it to a point opposite the	4	376
Lone Tree: —which stands about 350 yards south of the road	4	380
Ash Hollow, south of river: —Deriving its name from a grove of ash trees growing in it; it occupies near 20 acres, and is surrounded by high bluffs	3	383

A sample page from Wisner's journal illustrates the similarity between the two texts and suggests that a convention of overland writing may have existed:

May	1				Drove 8 miles and camped to wait for company. Company came up and we drove 20 miles more. The country is beautiful but not all settled. Presume it will be some day. Camped on a creek.
		3 4	42	28	(probably Wolf Creek.) Wednesday.
"	2				Drove 20 miles over beautiful country, nearly
		5	62	20	level. Thursday.
"	3				Drove 22 miles to-day. Three troops of
			84	22	cavalry passed us to-day. Friday.[7]

6. Sarah Wisner, "A Trip across the Plains in 1866" (original in private ownership; TS, Chicago, 1930), 29; quoted in Bartkowski, *Travelers, Immigrants, Inmates,* 18.

7.Wisner, "Trip across the Plains," 29; Hosea B. Horn, *Horn's Overland Guide from the U.S. Sub-Agency, Council Bluffs, on the Missouri River to the City of Sacramento, in California* (New York: J. H. Colton, 1852), 14; Wisner, "Trip across the Plains," 19.

Like Hosea Horn, Mrs. Wisner carefully records the mileage between places and the total accrued mileage. She, too, quickly notes conditions of the terrain and of the going forth, neglecting to say anything about herself or her companions. Like Horn's, Mrs. Wisner's account is a verbal map of the country; it is place- and movement-centered. But unlike Horn's map, which is meant only to help the reader find his or her way to the West, Mrs. Wisner's serves the additional purpose of locating herself in time and place. As Eric Leed observes of travel, " . . . the flows of passage not only provide information about the world; they provide information about the self of the passenger."[8] By charting the miles she has traveled and noting the landmarks along the way, by finding herself in relation to place and movement, she is also charting, in very indirect ways, a map of herself, a cognitive map by which she can discover not only *where* she is but *who* she is.

H. M. Proshansky, Theodore Sarbin, Stefan Hormuth, and others have demonstrated in psychological studies that "place identity is an integral part of the self." Place-identity, according to Proshansky, "is a sub-structure of the self-identity of the person consisting of broadly conceived, cognitions about the physical world in which the individual lives. These cognitions represent memories, ideas, feelings, attitudes, values, preferences, meanings, and conceptions of behavior and experience which relate to the variety and complexity of physical settings that define the day-to-day existence of every human being." Thus one way of knowing or identifying the self is to "locat[e] oneself in the geographical ecology." In essence, this is what Mrs. Wisner and other overland journalists are doing, discovering the self by locating the self on the geography and in the maplike journals that they write. Although the writers of movement narratives may claim that they give careful attention to the terrain and conditions of geography and weather for the benefit of others who may follow in their tracks, they are also at the task of constructing a map by which they can find and identify themselves. Both a cartographic map of the terrain and a linguistic map of the self, the overland journal joins "the activities of self-knowledge and the knowledge of the world." Like the more abstract cognitive map we all make within our minds, the journal as cognitive map assists the author in solving spatial problems of navigation and of organizing "personal experience along the twin dimensions of space and time."[9] Thus, the journal, like Mrs. Wisner's, constitutes a series of marks,

8. Leed, *Mind of the Traveler,* 72.

9. Sarbin, "Place Identity," 337; Harold Proshansky et al., "Place-Identity: Physical World Socialization of the Self," *Journal of Environmental Psychology* 3, no. 1 (March 1983): 59; Sarbin, "Place Identity," 338; Helen M. Buss, *Mapping Our Selves: Canadian Women's Autobiography in English* (Montreal: McGill–Queens University

a ticking off of daily "where I ams" in order to find the self and the self-in-location, both of which must be daily redrafted, for they were remarkably fluid, mobile, and destabilized.

Mrs. Wisner's account may be the most extreme example of journal as lexical map, but it is by no means uncharacteristic. The landscape and the progress of the journey, its physical linearity and spatial/chronological sequencing, structure the form and content of the narrative that the author sets out to write about her life's adventure. Stories of beauty and tragedy and of human life are rendered as emplotments of place and movement, constituting a metonymic chain of events that represents a wider range of meaning lying behind the text. Even as the journal attempts an objective description of the landscape and the journey, it voices the emotional response of the individual author to events of time and place, re-placing the author as subjective observer and subject within an experience and a discourse that would otherwise render her as object. Algeline Ashley, for instance, writes:

> June 2. Thunder shower in the afternoon. Very steep hills to cross—some heavy sand. A flowering bunch bean grows on the hills; it looks exactly like a gilliflower at a little distance. Child has the measles. Breedlove is quite unwell. Passed 11 graves. Two wagons left because they were dissatisfied.
>
> June 3. Pleasant till noon, rain in the afternoon. Sandy road and near the river. Passed no graves. Camped 8 miles from the upper ford of Platte. Excellent grass. . . . Found a bright green moss, flower like the bunch pink—very fragrant. John is better.
>
> June 5. Pleasant and very hot, two severe hail storms, ground white with hail. Camped near the ferry to fill the kegs with water for tomorrow. Passed 5 graves. Child and young man much better of the measles. John better.
>
> June 8. . . . 6 graves. No fuel but sage—abundance of that—it grows very stout along here and has a different leaf from that which grows further back. Camp on Sweet Water—excellent grass. The hills are very high and rocky, soil barren. Passed trading post. All well.[10]

Press, 1993), 9; Roger M. Downes and David Stea, *Maps in Minds: Reflections on Cognitive Mapping* (New York: Harper and Row, 1977), 27.

10. Hayden White notes the use in historical chronicles of "semantic metonymies that would transform [a] list of events into a discourse," in *The Content of the Form: Narrative Discourse and Historical Representation* (Baltimore: Johns Hopkins, 1987), 16; Algeline Ashley, "Diary of Mrs. Algeline Jackson Ashley, 'Crossing the Plains in 1852,' " TS from a copy in the San Diego Public Library, Newberry Library, Chicago.

Like other women who recorded their trip west, Ashley pays close attention to the terrain, the condition of camps, the weather, and the number of graves passed each day. The movement of the journey and the various landmarks along the way constitute most of what Ashley writes. At first glance hers looks like every other overland journal, a fairly objective description of place and movement. But if we listen closely, we hear the curve of emotion that makes this a personal account, an autobiographical account of Mrs. Ashley rendered through a geographic code. We notice that her close attention to flowers, their leaf shapes, color, and smell, forms a counterpoint against her withdrawal from tragedy and hardship. In fact, her description of the flowers, rendered through comparison—"like the gilliflower"—provides a reassuring sign of the familiar in the midst of this strange environment. Against her attention to the landscape, her accounts of illness are cryptic, suggesting her uneasiness with the human hardship that this journey also meant. While she names the various samples of flora, she condenses people to "wagons" and transforms markers of human mortality into landmarks of the road, to be counted as one counts the miles. It may be that this new kind of closeness to illness and death is too disturbing for Mrs. Ashley and that by fixing her gaze on the terrain and by plotting her story by the progression of the trip, she can avoid and repress emotions too unsettling to relate directly. In this way, the topography becomes a shorthand or metaphor for the self, a self not consciously or explicitly revealed or constructed in the narrative, but one, nonetheless, that exists behind the text, shaped and identified by movement and environment. Place here appears to be the significant signifier of self, subsuming person and the personal as landmarks of the self.

Indeed, in the hands of most of the diarists, the topography becomes the medium through which the author finds herself and by which the author writes herself symbolically through images of the landscape. Reluctant or unable because of real and cultural constraints on her writing to reveal herself, to explore her innermost feelings, even in a personal document, an author like Agnes Stewart dreams or thinks herself through geographic representations, projecting her own conflicts, tensions, and fears outward onto the physical world. Making the journey in 1853, Stewart writes:

> Mon 6 went up to the bluffs I could see nothing on the other side but valleys and bluffs I saw some rare specimens of wild flowers some of them more beautiful than I have seen cultivated in gardens. . . . I went down this morning into the pretty little valley to see it for the last time and saw a large rattlesnake lying by a bush we left it quicker than we intended thinking to myself . . . lies concealed beside us when all is fair to look at we stopped at

noon there grave dug up by the wolves saw a rib lying in the place lizzy and
I carried stones and filled up the hole again . . .

There is certainly a nightmarish quality about this scene: the beauty of
nature, its wide prospects and beautiful flowers, disrupted by the threat of
death and even threats against death. At the same time that Stewart writes
of viewing the panoramic horizon, suggestive of exploration, promise, and
the future, of her participation in journeying forward, she also writes of
another boundary crossed and extended. But this other boundary is the
grave that has been desecrated, the rib projecting out of its place. Her
impetus to explore new worlds, played out in representations of both
grand and delicate vistas, is threatened by the rattlesnake, lies, and death,
and the grotesque inversion of the ordered and familiar that they represent.
Stewart's representation of the landscape, the dream and the nightmare she
relates, suggests not only her anxiety and conflict about making the journey
to the West, but anxiety about herself, her situation and her sense of self,
about the psychic boundaries that she has attempted to "govern" but that
may also be transgressed.[11] By locating herself thus on the topography,
Stewart unconsciously mediates anxieties about herself, finding out to
some degree who she is.

Unsettled by where she finds herself, at one point Agnes Stewart looks
at a map to locate herself. But the map she ponders indicates not where
she is or where she is going, for as we have seen she is anxious about
both. Rather, she looks at a map that locates where she comes from—
home: "I am sitting now under pine tree on black hill and is it possible
that we are on the black hills away so far from home the place I have so
often looked at on the map but here we are and I often think can it be
possible." One reason that it became so imperative for travelers like Stewart
to continually locate themselves, to map out their journey and transcribe
themselves on the landscape, is that by leaving home, they left behind
the family and friends, the past and memories that constitute a part of
the self. By moving away from the familiar environment, they created "an
imbalance in the ecology of the self," destabilizing to some degree the sense
of self with which they were familiar, renaming themselves "strangers"

11. For a discussion of psychogeography, see Howard F. Stein, "The Influence
of Psychogeography upon the Conduct of International Relations: Clinical and
Metapsychological Considerations," in *Maps from the Mind: Readings in Psychogeography,* ed. Howard F. Stein and William G. Niederland (Norman: University
of Oklahoma Press, 1989), esp. 181–83; Agnes Stewart Warner, *The Diary of Agnes
Stewart, 1853* (Eugene: Lane County Pioneer–Historical Society, 1966), 10, 4.

and "wanderers in this wide, wide world." Moreover, with each day and with each mile, these women faced constant psychic anxiety and were compelled to re-find and reassess themselves daily. They were cast into a fairly constant "dialectic of change and stability" whereby accommodation and adaptation to the environment contested with strategies to maintain connections to the familiar self and place.[12]

For women engaged in a journey that could last seven months, the ledger of place and movement became as well the site for enacting and recording negotiations between the familiar self and a new self emerging with the passing miles. Helen Carpenter writes about "our growing indifference [to evidences of death], and can but think that what we are obliged to endure each day is robbing us of all sentiment—it is to be hoped we will not be *permanently changed*."[13] Carpenter certainly recognizes the change that she and her fellow travelers are undergoing; she also sees that change as threatening. Indeed, while the reinvention of the self can be exhilarating and expansive, the common reaction to this new experience is to see it as loss, as loss of the familiar self associated with the home, family, and friends left behind in "the states." Though boundary crossing may have some positive benefits in terms of breaking down the borders that confine us, it also means an unsettling deterritorialization of place and self.

In fact, the initial reaction to relocation is to grieve for the lost home and all that is associated with it—family, friends, security, comfort, and the familiar self. The degree of grief a particular individual experiences may be influenced by factors such as the person's involvement in the decision to move and the distance of the move. In the case of the women going out west, decisions to move were generally initiated by men; even when women think they are involved in movement decisions, "there are obstacles [related to feminine psychology] against making wise and responsible choices." Moreover, the degree of grief westering women experienced was compounded by a distance that was daunting; visits back home were virtually impossible before the transcontinental railroad later in the century. Many, like Elizabeth Goltra, who began her journal grieving for the loss of connection and belongingness, knew that they would never see their loved ones again:

12. Stewart Warner, *Diary*, 15; Stefan E. Hormuth, *The Ecology of the Self: Relocation and Self-Concept Change* (Cambridge: Cambridge University Press, 1990), 3; Harriet Ward, *Prairie Schooner Lady: The Journal of Harriet Sherril Ward, 1853* (Los Angeles: Westernlore Press, 1959), 151; Hormuth, *Ecology of the Self*, 163.

13. Helen M. Carpenter, "Diary" (1857; TS, Newberry Library, Chicago, 1911), 38.

> Kansas [City], Missouri, April 29th, 1853. Today we started across the dreary plains. Sad are the thoughts that steal over the reflecting mind; I am leaving my home, my early friends and associates, perhaps never to see them again, exchanging the disinterested solicitude of fond friends, for the cold and unsympathizing friendship of strangers. Shall we all reach the "Eldorado" of our hopes, or shall one of our number be left, and our graves be in the dreary wilderness, our bodies uncoffined, and unknown remain there in solitude. Hard indeed must that heart be that does not drop a tear as these thoughts roll across the mind.

Mrs. Goltra's entry, marked with negativity, resonates with sadness and depression, elements of grief, as she extends her sense of loss into the future, anticipating an eternity of separation and solitude. She feels that by leaving her friends and associates she is detaching herself from people who know and care for her, that something of her identity is lost by placing herself among unsympathizing strangers. As she envisions a land forlorn and destabilized, where bodies lie "uncoffined," she no doubt feels herself to be forlorn and destabilized, the boundaries of the self with its attendant kinship attachments, like the spatial boundaries she will cross, transgressed. The grief attendant with moving was based on a sense of final loss, and women mourned as if a loved one had died as Mary Ackley relates about her last visit to her grandmother: "The house was full of people, many in tears. Grandmother was prostrated. I went to her room to bid her good-bye and she said, 'Child, I will see you no more,' and they all said, 'We will never meet again.' (Which was true, for we never met again)." The separation in most cases, like death, was permanent. Although some wished to return home, to visit or to relocate, none of the women in this study ever did. Elizabeth Gunn wrote from California, "We should all like to go home, and I hope we shall one of these days." But she never did nor did any of her family back home visit her. Although many expressed the hope that they will meet loved ones in heaven, that did little to console their loss. Indeed, the idea of death as a medium of reunion was called into question when reassuring symbols of a life after death were desecrated by the constant evidence that those who die on the plains remain alone, often in unmarked graves or in graves dug up and ravaged by Indians and wolves. Saddened not only by their own situation, they imaginatively shared in the mourning of those who lost loved ones along the way, the "wife and two little children to mourn [their father's] loss here on the dreary plains."[14] The constant reminders of danger and

14. John Mack Faragher makes the point that women "played almost no role in the decision to emigrate" in *Women and Men on the Overland Trail* (New Haven:

death as they journeyed, the graves they passed almost daily, the dead oxen left in the deserts, must have accentuated the association between moving and loss for many women.

That sense of loss was not confined to people, but extended as well to things, mementos of home that homesteaders were often compelled to leave behind in the first place or discard along the way. Psychologist Audrey McCollum says that "leaving behind whatever embodies special memories and experiences—can feel like an amputation. It is the loss of a segment of family continuity, of personal history, the loss of a fragment of self." Mary Alice Shutes understood the symbolic value of things when she wrote, "We are findeing [sic] it a little rough to have to give away a lot of things you have owned since you can remember, things valuable to your self only, mostly sentimental value only." And many journals record the items unloaded onto the plains or desert in a desperate attempt to lighten the load their oxen had to bear. In making the journal entry, the author lingers over the things she is compelled to do without, demonstrating the symbolic as well as utilitarian loss associated with material goods. Esther Lyman pauses to write, "The most of my things were left about half of them among the rest a feather bed a pair of Pillows and Joseph's tools." And seventy years later, Phoebe Judson still remembered leaving her "little rocking chair" on the trail.[15]

Though the women mourned and recorded their losses, their grieving could not be sustained; they had somehow to reestablish psychic equilibrium, to balance the newness of their lives with the familiar. Though moving, especially to the frontier and across wide, open spaces, can provide

Yale University Press, 1979), 75, and Annette Kolodny, following Margaret Fuller's observation in *Summer on the Lakes* (1844), makes the point that women follow their men " 'for affection's sake' " in *The Land before Her: Fantasy and Experience of the American Frontiers, 1630–1860* (Chapel Hill: University of North Carolina Press, 1984), 121; Audrey T. McCollum, *The Trauma of Moving: Psychological Issues for Women* (Newbury Park, Calif.: Sage Publications, 1990), 21; Elizabeth Julia Goltra, *Journal Kept by Mrs. W. J. Goltra of Her Travels in the Year 1853* (Eugene, Oreg.: Lane Historical Society, 1970), 1; see McCollum, *Trauma of Moving*, chap. 2 for more on grief and loss; Mary C. Ackley, *Crossing the Plain and Early Days in California's Golden Age* (San Francisco: n.p., 1928), 19; Lewis Carstairs Gunn, *Records of a California Family: Journals and Letters of Lewis C. Gunn and Elizabeth LeBreton Gunn*, ed. Anna Lee Marston (San Diego: n.p., 1928), 156; Goltra, *Journal*, 21.

15. McCollum, *Trauma of Moving*, 71; Mary Alice Shutes, *Diary—Eight Hundred Miles Thirty Six Days Covered Wagon—1862*, ed. LeRoy L. Shutes (Bloomington, Ill.: L. L. Shutes, 1967) 2; Esther Lyman, *Esther Brakeman Lyman Diary* (Eugene: Lane County Pioneer–Historical Society, 1966), 6; Phoebe Judson, *A Pioneer's Search for an Ideal Home* (Bellingham: Union Printing, Binding, and Stationary Co., 1925; reprint, Lincoln: University of Nebraska Press, 1984), 59.

the freedom to reinvent the self, to try new modes of life to fit a new environment, radical changes of behavior or self-concept are unlikely. Instead, change is often subtle, and so the clues to self-concept change and to efforts to maintain the familiar in the face of the new are also often subtle, especially in texts centered on place and movement rather than self. These texts tell in slantwise fashion how the women making the long journey across the continent negotiated the dynamics of change and stability and the conscious and unconscious strategies they adopted to meet the physical destabilization of their lives. Because at this juncture of their lives they could not follow Mary Jane Long's advice, "if you own a home and are comfortably fixed stay with it and let the other fellow do the traveling," they had to find ways of meeting their situation.[16]

The act of writing provided one way of negotiating an acceptable narrative of the self amid the strains of destabilization and an often intense longing for home and the past. Certainly women had other means of negotiating their destabilization—through the work they did, their interpersonal relationships, private conversations with husbands in the hush of night—but all that remains for us at this distance in time are their letters, journals, memoirs, themselves become palpable sites of negotiation and exploration. Although memoirist Mary Jane Hayden claims that "Pioneer women were quite too busy in *making* history to write it," many women did write and by writing controlled to some extent the "history" they were living. Paul Rosenblatt observes about autobiography: "As one writes about what has happened and how one feels, one is defining the situation and one's reactions. The act of defining may be seen as an act of controlling, delineating, and shaping." Similarly, even though they are closer to events than are more conventional autobiographers, letter writers and diarists control, delineate, and shape the story they tell about both the historical moment and themselves. Like other authors, they exercise interpretive control over the events they recite. Sarah Raymond's journal is a case in point; her narrative, her version of the history she lived, is very much directed by her good spirit and faith in God's special Providence. Declaring the overland journey to be "an all Summer picnic," she focuses her tale on the adventures of riding her pony about the prairie, on the wholesomeness of camping outdoors, and her own self-sufficiency. Agnes Stewart, as we have seen, shapes and intones her rendition of the journey with depression and grief, focusing her attention on rattlesnakes, the "lies

16. Hormuth, *Ecology of the Self,* makes this point about the "basic stability of the self-concept" on page 197; Mary Jane Long, *A True Story: Crossing the Plains in the Year of 1852 with Ox Teams* (McMinnville, Oreg.: n.p., 1915), 17.

concealed beside us when all is fair," and graves plundered by wolves.[17] The author, moreover, controls the tale and thus the experience through her choices of what to tell and what not to tell. Though much of the story is plotted by the journey itself, the details belong to the author—the names of flowers, the condition of a camp. Most often, however, the details are ones of omission and silence, especially when they pertain explicitly to the private life of the author. Characteristically, women did not say anything about their pregnancies until, as if by magic, a baby appears who needs a name, often a name associated with place. While some of the omissions may be dictated or managed by the prevailing sense of feminine decorum, thus meliorating women's control over their own stories, the choice, finally, of what to tell about the 110 days on the trail or of life on the frontier is the individual's and renders the writer as interpreter and maker of her history, her story. The text about location becomes itself a location, a space in which the author discovers and maps herself, in which she negotiates the contingencies of her daily life. At the same time, the journal as ledger creates white spaces on the page that are filled with the unsaid and the unsayable, mapping invisibly the hidden terrain of the inner self, a terrain kept private and pristine because of its undecipherability.

Even so, the journal and the letter, more immediate forms of writing than the memoir, provided a cathartic outlet for their authors. As Robert Fothergill notes, "The function of the diary is to provide a compensatory outlet for that valuation of [herself] which circumstances conspire to thwart." Unsure perhaps about the wisdom of dis-assembling their lives and their families in pursuit of the dream of prosperity on the frontier, women could voice to their journals their misgivings or anxieties in ways they may not have been able to articulate, for one reason or another, to their husbands or fathers, or even to themselves. As the journals of Algeline Ashley and Agnes Stewart have demonstrated, the tension may be expressed symbolically through images of the terrain. Or anxiety may be expressed more directly, declaring as does Sarah Raymond, "I believe I am homesick this evening. It is so dreary to go into a strange place and meet so many people, and not one familiar face. But I must not complain, for we are all here."[18] Whatever the case, women were able to vent some

17. Mary Jane Hayden, *Pioneer Days* (San Jose: Murgotten's Press, 1918), preface; Rosenblatt quoted by Judy Nolte Lensink in *"A Secret to Be Buried": The Diary and Life of Emily Hawley Gillespie, 1858–1888* (Iowa City: University of Iowa Press, 1989), 382; *Overland Days to Montana in 1865: The Diary of Sarah Raymond and Journal of Dr. Waid Howard*, ed. Raymond W. Settle and Mary Lund Settle (Glendale, Calif.: A. H. Clark, Co., 1971), 44; Stewart Warner, *Diary*, 10.

18. Fothergill quoted in Lensink, *"Secret to Be Buried,"* 392; *Overland Days*, 176.

steam through their writing, talking out in writing different, difficult, and threatening experiences, emotions, and self-cognitions. In this way they were able to stabilize to some extent the psychic imbalance created by movement.

Writing also provided women a means of maintaining contact with home by establishing a dialogue with family and with the self that family represents. If, as Nancy Chodorow argues, "feminine personality comes to define itself in relation and connection to other people," then leaving family and friends must have been particularly difficult for the women going west. Indeed, it seems that connection is "central to women's experiences of self-esteem, particularly at points of life transition [like moving], when valued affiliations are sometimes threatened." For women in the nineteenth century, who, according to Carroll Smith-Rosenberg, "routinely formed emotional ties with other women," letter writing provided a means for retaining those ties even when the women were separated by distance. Their letters, "filled with discussions of marriages and births, illness and death, descriptions of growing children, and reminiscences of times and people past provided an important sense of continuity. . . ." Spanning two decades, Elizabeth Gunn's letters relate the daily events of her life in California, keeping up the conversation between herself and her female relatives that must have been an almost daily occurrence back in Philadelphia. Comparing her style of writing to that of her husband, Mrs. Gunn writes, "I'll bet his letters were all 'generals'; mine will be 'particulars' of course, for I am 'a woman and a sister,' and am writing to women and sisters." What Gunn suggests is that by sharing the particulars of life, she speaks a language that women can understand and a language that maintains the ties between women whose daily lives seem so often consumed in the particular. Moreover, by sharing the details of everyday life, Gunn can construct a bridge between herself and her kinfolk, allowing them to imaginatively construct life in Sonora at the same time that she re-members life in Philadelphia. She writes in November 1851:

> I have been thinking and the children talking about it. They say we must keep "Mamma Wrights Thanksgiving." At all events, I am to have a few of Douglas' eggs and some milk and to make a pudding. There are no turkeys here, and as chickens are three dollars apiece, we are not likely to have any of them: . . . I will keep your Thanksgiving, and I think it will be on the same day.

At the same time that she shares the particulars of her projected dinner, down to the price of chickens, Gunn imagines herself back in Philadelphia enjoying a traditional family Thanksgiving, "your" Thanksgiving. She also reaffirms her attachment for her Philadelphia home and family, ending the paragraph rather wistfully: "I only hope and pray we shall all be permitted to see each other again—and then we'll have a Thanksgiving all our own."[19]

Letter writing thus allows Gunn a means of sustaining long-standing ideas about herself formed at home and in connection with her mother and sisters that are threatened by the rowdiness of the Sonoran mining camp. But by presenting herself to her readers as the same person they know her to be, she is also attempting to deny to them and to herself that she has changed despite her change in situation. Retaining attachments and the familiar has the complementary effect of denying distance, change, and dissonance. When Mrs. Gunn attempts to sustain the idea of herself as a woman interested in fashion, for instance, she is also denying the reality of life in a dirty and rough mining town. Her inquiry about dress patterns retains her contact with the East at the same time that it underscores her dissatisfaction with her present situation: "I see by *Graham's Magazine* that 'mutton' leg is to be the fashion. Maybe you can send me a little pattern or draw one in your next letter, and do send me some number six needles, too."[20]

At the same time, then, that Gunn attempts to retain contact with home and the familiar idea of herself, she resists the new environment and the new self-in-place associated with it, employing denial as a defense mechanism by which to cope with the threat against her self-esteem and self-concept that accompanies her relocation. By constantly comparing life in California with that in Philadelphia, she articulates the tension between attachment and denial. Everything to her seems to be better or cheaper or cleaner in Philadelphia: "We have good dried apples and peaches but have not had very good flour. Lizzie asked me if 'Philadelphia' flour was better and I told her 'yes, and everything else in Philadelphia.' So we concluded that we would one day 'go home.' I don't intend to call California 'home.' " Similarly Mary Jane Hayden writes, "The reason I did not enthuse more over my Vancouver home was that I had not given up the idea of going back home." And Mary Ackley writes that in going to California, "The intention

---

19. Nancy J. Chodorow, *Feminism and Psychoanalytic Theory* (New Haven: Yale University Press, 1989), 45; Christine Bitonti, "The Self-Esteem of Women: A Cognitive-Phenomenological Study," *Smith College Studies in Social Work* 63, no. 1 (November 1992): 306; Carroll Smith-Rosenberg, "The Female World of Love and Ritual: Relations between Women in Nineteenth-Century America," in *The American Family in Social-Historical Perspectives*, 2d ed., ed. Michael Gordon (New York: St. Martin's Press, 1978), 334, 340; Gunn, *Records of a California Family*, 144–45, 159.

20. Gunn, *Records of a California Family*, 197–98.

was to go out to the new country, make money, regain health for Mrs. Medley, and then return to the beautiful farm and home on the Walkendaw River" in Missouri.[21] Unable to commit themselves psychologically to the place they had committed themselves to physically, many women tried to deny their association with the new place, reserving in their minds the possibility of returning home and resuscitating their former lives.

If they could not actually return to the old home place, they brought "home" with them, demonstrating once more the pioneers' uneasiness or unwillingness to plunge themselves into the new environment/self. Not only did they bring the artifacts of their previous home with them (Phoebe Judson writes that she could not "conceive of a home without a Bible"), but they brought their values, traditions, and ideologies with them. Indeed, many were careful to assert their ideological and actual difference from the native inhabitants, construing in their narratives a reality of dissimilarity. Using the rhetoric of bipolar negativity, Sarah Raymond describes the Native Americans she passed on her journey. The Indian dwellings, she writes, "are desolate-looking homes; no sleeping places, no tables, chairs nor any furniture, just some rolls of blankets and buffalo robes, some camp-kettles, and that was all." Her strategy here, while it shapes the native into an object of disgust, asserts for Raymond her own superiority and place at a time when both were threatened by movement and by the very people she attempts to disempower in her narrative. Even when women write more favorably of the native, they write from the position of the privileged other, patronizing and colonizing a people both curious and deadly. Francis Sawyer relates how she and her husband went out to look at an Indian who had been killed in a skirmish, as if he were a tourist site, albeit a "bloody and ghastly" one. In less grisly fashion, Phoebe Judson marks her difference from the native by rejoicing in the arrival of a Mrs. Holler so she "could enjoy the privilege of once more conversing with a woman of my kind."[22] Threatened by living in the midst of the wilderness with the prospect of becoming like the child of the wilderness, women shaped a narrative of difference by which they could retain their familiar definition of self as civilized, cultivated, and white.

Thus women often transferred to their new environment the traditions and interpretations of self they had learned at home, attempting to re-

21. Ibid., 163; Hayden, *Pioneer Days*, 38; Ackley, *Crossing the Plain*, introduction.

22. Judson, *Search for an Ideal Home*, 95; *Overland Days*, 108; Francis H. Sawyer, *Overland to California: Notes from a Journal kept by Mrs. Francis H. Sawyer, in a Journey across the Plains. May 9 to August 17, 1852* (Newberry Library, Chicago, Ill.), 4; Judson, *Search for an Ideal Home*, 217.

fashion the new environment into a familiar shape. Used to conceiving of themselves as domestic women whose "sphere" consisted of house and garden, some women, for instance, transformed the campsite and wagon into a "gypsy" kind of home, which, like the home back east, was cozy, sociable, and comforting; "Here I am," writes Harriet Ward,

> sitting on the front seat of the wagon, writing, Willie asleep beside me, Frank seated upon the bed playing her guitar and singing "I've Something Sweet to Tell You"; and just a few rods from us, seated around a blazing fire, are the gentlemen of our company, conversing as pleasantly as if they were in the parlour at home.[23]

In this representation of life on the trail, Ward both erases the real and creates a new reality more meaningful to her because it is infused with the images of home and domesticity she brings to her narrative. Similarly, many of the women represent themselves, despite what actually may have been the case, as doing only what was traditionally regarded as "women's work"—cooking, sewing, washing, and child rearing. Elinore Pruitt Stewart, who brags in *Letters of a Woman Homesteader* (1914) about the game she shoots and her outings in the Wyoming wilds, may be an exception to this generalization and may represent the attitude of the generation that came west after the first wave of pioneers. While we occasionally see women on the Oregon Trail driving the wagons, never do we read about women driving or managing the livestock, killing game, or later doing the heavy labor of farmwork. In fact, many of the journals suggest that women did little other than ride about and admire the landscape, casting themselves in the role of genteel tourists of exotic lands instead of hardworking emigrants. Moreover, the women seem to insist on their femininity, telling stories on themselves that demonstrate their inability to use weapons or find their way along a marked trail to a neighbor's farm. All of these portrayals, underwritten with denial, work to preserve an image of themselves that is consistent with previous cognitions and cultural definitions of womanly behavior.

Women attempted to make the new environment as much like home as possible. They brought with them their values, definitions of self, and institutions, and they worked to maintain traditional standards of behavior, even in the face of conditions that tried their best intentions. They felt it imperative "to put their personal stamp" on the landscape,

23. Ward, *Prairie Schooner Lady*, 27.

to master the wildness or unfamiliarity of the new place, to reshape the environment to their own demands and values.[24] They did this not only by transferring their values and ideologies but by physically effecting a change in the environment, most notably through the activities of homemaking—sweeping, hanging curtains, and gardening—making and marking their own spaces within and without the house and using the spaces of the narrative to write in the familiar territory. The broom, enemy of all that is unclean and hence foreign, seems to be the instrument most associated with and used by women in the task of marking their territory, of transforming the raw frontier into the tamed and familiar just as the pen, another instrument of civilization, transforms the blank space of the page into meaning coherent to its author.

But try as they did to resist change and to reshape the environment, it is inevitable that the new place would put its stamp on women pioneers, transforming to some extent the way they did things and the way they thought of themselves. Even though pioneer women immigrated to territory claimed or soon to be claimed by the United States, they entered what Mary Louise Pratt calls a "contact zone," a social space "where disparate cultures meet, clash, and grapple with each other." The effect on these women of entering a contact zone inhabited by Mexicans and/or Native Americans as well as the subclass of European Americans, the miner, was evidenced in their language, clothing, and habits. Though the pioneers soon gained political and economic dominance in the areas they acquired, making the original inhabitants feel their influence and power, pioneers also felt the impact of this meeting ground. Besides learning new western words like *bit* and a smattering of Spanish or Indian words, settlers found themselves adopting new modes of behavior to accommodate the exigencies of life in the West. Elizabeth Gunn had to learn to live economically and do her own wash; Phoebe Judson learned to use a gun; and Nancy Hunt found that for the first time in her life she had to work outside the home to support her children. Mary Alice Shutes was quite pleased with her new "western" appearance and writes in her journal, "I am dressed like Charles and straddle of my horse, I am to ride straddle like Cow Girls are supposed too [*sic*], out west in the Indian Country, besides it is the only safe way, no one wants to fall off their horse and be hurt." But more than learning new skills, many women learned new ways of considering themselves.

24. Kolodny, *Land before Her*, 48; see also the introduction to *The Land before Her* where Kolodny makes the point that "the landscape is the most immediate medium through which we attempt to convert culturally shared dreams into palpable reality," xii.

Miss Raymond too rode her pony, but her narrative suggests that with the journey she began to assert a new identity derived from a new sense of self-sufficiency: " . . . we girls proceed to saddle our ponies; some of the boys usually come and offer assistance, which is politely declined, as we are going to wait upon ourselves on this trip."[25]

With a widening of boundaries geographical and behavioral, some women experienced a widening of their sense of self. Deriving a sense of freedom just in the going, some women felt liberated from the confines of conventionality and inherited definitions of self. For some, going to the frontier meant progressive development, the opportunity to refashion themselves and not just the environment. To the extent that the frontier represents "the space beyond the last settlement," it also represents spaciousness and freedom. "Spaciousness," geographer Yi-Fu Tuan asserts, "is closely associated with the sense of being free. Freedom implies space; it means having the power and enough room in which to act." Fundamental to being free is "the elementary power to move," a power that was realized cartographically, psychologically, and politically for some of the women who went west. Although space, its untamed and unmarked solitude, can be intimidating, it also "invites the future and invites action."[26] For those who dared to go physically beyond the boundaries of place, the freedom of the frontier encouraged them to test other boundaries.

Thus, some of the narratives, especially the memoirs, evidence an emerging feminism, born in part from relocation, that asserts women's strength, ability, and self-reliance. Although some women reverted back into a cult of domesticity once the hardships of the overland journey and the first years of homesteading subsided, other women refused (at least without comment) to give up the political and social ground they had gained during the early years of western settlement. Phoebe Judson is an interesting example, for her memoir (written in 1925 when she was ninety-five years old) demonstrates a tension between the traditional definitions of women's sphere and femininity and her learned discontent with them:

> For four years, from 1883 to 1887, the territory of Washington enjoyed impartial suffrage [sic]. I took my turn on petit and grand jury, served on election boards, walked in perfect harmony to the polls by the side of my

25. Mary Louise Pratt, *Imperial Eyes: Travel Writing and Transculturation* (London: Routledge, 1992), 4; Shutes, *Diary*, 4; *Overland Days*, 51.

26. Lillian Schlissel, Byrd Gibbens, and Elizabeth Hampsten, eds. *Far from Home: Families of the Westward Journey* (New York: Schocken Books, 1989), 233; Yi-Fu Tuan, *Space and Place: The Perspective of Experience* (Minneapolis: University of Minnesota Press, 1977), 52, 54.

staunch Democratic husband, and voted the Republican ticket—not feeling any more out of my sphere than when assisting my husband to develop the resources of our country.

When relating women's loss of rights after the four-year experiment, Mrs. Judson demonstrates bitter discontent with the male political hegemony:

> Oh,—yes, Uncle Sam was very liberal in allowing us equal rights with the sterner sex in taking up land, paying taxes and sharing in their perils and labors; but when it comes to covering this fair land (which we have so dearly purchased and helped to make blossom like the rose) with licensed saloons, we have no voice in the matter. He would have us bear the disgrace, poverty and heartrending sorrow in silent tears, without protest.[27]

Clearly, this is the voice of a self whose political consciousness and sense of self has been shaped by her experiences in the new land; just as clearly, Mrs. Judson sounds the rhetoric and anger of what we have come to identify as feminism. It seems to me that her voice of anger and assertiveness is the result of her lifelong experience and not something she brought with her in 1853. Time and space played a role in these new definitions of self, for the memoirs written in the early decades of the twentieth century seem more self-assertive than the journals written in the mid–nineteenth century.

While it may be that women all over America were beginning to resist the ideological power of the cult of domesticity and to clamor for more rights, it seems also that women who moved to the far west felt they had earned the right to a political voice and some independence from the constrictions of "femininity." A sentimental novel, *From the West to the West* (1905), written by Abigail Scott Duniway, herself an emigrant of the Overland Trail and leader of the woman's suffrage movement in the Northwest, demonstrates the stir for equal rights and the rhetoric of feminism that may have been learned both by the times and by the author's own experience of homesteading. Certainly, the "rights of the pioneer women of Oregon" and the "heroines on this journey" inform the politics of the novel, itself a mix of sentimental fiction, overland journal, and political diatribe. Duniway has her leading character, Jean Ranger, a girl

---

27. For more about women's urge to "restore the domestic sphere" in the frontier, see Lillian Schlissel, *Women's Diaries of the Westward Journey* (New York: Schocken Books, 1982), 85; and chap. 4 of Julie Roy Jeffrey, *Frontier Women: The Trans-Mississippi West, 1840–1880* (New York: Hill and Wang, 1979); Judson, *Search for an Ideal Home*, 276.

of sixteen, advocate for new property and divorce laws and denounce the male hegemony that makes women captives and fugitives even of the most just men. Although this novel argues for women's rights, it nonetheless ends the way of most sentimental novels, with multiple marriages at the end, demonstrating the tension of redefining the self, women's roles, and women's voice evident in many of these narratives.[28]

Unlike diarists of midcentury who depict themselves in traditionally feminine ways, Sarah Olds, who did not go west until 1897, represents herself as a strong, assertive woman capable of providing for her family, almost on her own, on a desert ranch in Nevada. Minutes after her marriage to A. J. Olds, a miner who would soon contract miner's consumption, her new husband proposed that they weigh themselves and so determine who will wear the pants in the family: "He stepped on the scales and tipped them to 165 pounds. I tipped them at 168! I've been the boss ever since, but I don't think A. J. ever knew it." She did indeed wear the pants, insisting on moving to the desert ranch and manipulating her husband's "surrender" to her scheme. Undaunted by the conditions of desert living, five children, and a semi-invalid husband, Mom Olds actually thrived on hard work and gloried in her strength: "Apparently," she writes, "I thrived on hard work. I think there was never a woman blessed with better health than I. I seemed to have strength enough for both of us." As with the Judson memoir and the Duniway novel, Sarah Olds's story demonstrates the expansion of women's roles and self-definition possible in or shaped by this new land and time, for she is both mother and rancher, a woman who is exultant in her physical capability and her ability to provide for her family. Likewise, Elinore Pruitt Stewart brags, "Of course I *am* extra strong, but those who try know that strength and knowledge come with doing. I just love to experiment, to work, and to prove out things, so that ranch life and 'roughing it' just suite me."[29] Faced with a new environment and

28. Abigail Scott Duniway, *From the West to the West: Across the Plains to Oregon* (Chicago: A. C. McClurg, 1905), 234–35, 147; for more on Duniway, see Julie Silber and Pat Ferrero, eds., *Hearts and Hands: The Influence of Women and Quilts on American Society* (San Francisco: The Quilt Digest, 1987), 93–96; and Ruth Barnes Moynihan, *Rebel for Rights: Abigail Scott Duniway* (New Haven: Yale University Press, 1983). Susan K. Harris, *Nineteenth-Century American Women's Novels: Interpretive Strategies* (Cambridge: Cambridge University Press, 1990), makes the observation that oftentimes the middle section of nineteenth-century women's novels, which "establish an area of female independence, competence, emotional complexity, and intellectual acumen," belie the sentimental, conventional ending, 21.

29. Sarah E. Olds, *Twenty Miles from a Match: Homesteading in Western Nevada* (Reno: University of Nevada Press, 1978), 14; 21; Elinore Pruitt Stewart, *Letters of a Woman Homesteader* (1914; reprint, Houghton Mifflin, 1988), 282.

a new set of circumstances, women like Judson, Olds, and Stewart, who found they could do things beyond the restrictions of domesticity, were empowered by both the reality of having to test their strength and by their conscious recognition of themselves as strong, capable, and independent.

Mom Olds's narrative demonstrates a kind of reciprocity between the environment and herself; as she transformed the desert into a home, the desert participated in shaping her sense of identity. Because her narrative is a memoir, written after the fact of relocation, the self that she presents is to some extent already shaped by that experience. While we cannot say that movement itself determined Mom's character, for there are many variables in making and shaping personality, it is a factor in self-identity and self-concept, one that forces people on the move to make adjustments and accommodations in immediate and real ways. Even as women attempted to retain the familiar and to resist conscious accommodation to the new environment, the very acts of adopting strategies for coping with or of transforming the wilderness into a garden are themselves mechanisms of accommodation, of a shift in self-concept to meet the new circumstances of place.

Not every woman's story of relocation is as exultant as Mom Olds's. But all of them demonstrate that relocation involves more than just transporting family and goods to a new home. The women discovered that with geographic change terms of identity and social and political placings are also called into question, are blurred, crossed, extended, transgressed. As Peter Stallybrass and Allon White contend and these narratives show us, "transgressing the rules of hierarchy and order in any one of the domains [of the human body, psychic forms, geographical space and social formation] may have major consequences in the others."[30]

30. Peter Stallybrass and Allon White, *The Politics and Poetics of Transgression* (London: Metheun, 1986), 3.

On the Gatepost

Literal and Metaphorical Journeys in Zora Neale Hurston's *Dust Tracks on a Road*

BARBARA RODRÍGUEZ

Zora Neale Hurston begins her autobiography, *Dust Tracks on a Road*, by describing the founding of her hometown, Eatonville, Florida. Likewise, critical examinations of the autobiography also often implicitly ground themselves—at least in part—in considerations of the hometown; Robert Hemenway, Hurston's biographer, and other critics of the life story imply that the author's journey from rural Eatonville, Florida, to the Harlem Renaissance and unprecedented success for an African American woman as both an anthropologist and novelist, needs explaining. Hemenway writes:

> Zora Neale Hurston did not remain in Eatonville, and as she admits, after her mother's death, "I was on my way from the village never to return to it as a real town." She became an educated author, building a successful career for herself because she triumphed over obstacles placed in front of black women who happen to be Americans. From the publisher's point of view this success validated her autobiography; it served as a warrant to the reader that her life story had inherent interest. Yet Zora had spent a good part of her career proving that there were equally powerful talents, on Joe Clarke's store porch. . . . *Dust Tracks* eventually exposes Hurston's uneasiness over how to move beyond the Eatonville voice and, by implication, how to explain her fame and her townspeople's obscurity.[1]

1. Robert E. Hemenway, *Zora Neale Hurston: A Literary Biography* (Chicago: University of Illinois Press, 1977), 279. Subsequent references are cited in the text as *ZNH*.

That Hurston thwarts expectations for an African American woman, rising from rural anonymity and then homelessness to national success, seems to necessitate the fulfillment of structural expectations associated with the genre of autobiography, Hemenway implies. He explains Hurston's failure to meet those expectations as a mark of her inability to fuse Eatonville and New York into a unified "interpretive voice for her autobiography—a major reason the book should not be taken as the definitive statement of her character" (*ZNH*, 280). His defense of the author also explains that she does not write in a direct and honest voice because she writes for white publishers; Robert Hemenway supports his reading of Hurston's experiences by pointing to both the manuscript version of *Dust Tracks*, a document that appears more direct and candid than the final version, and to recorded editorial suggestions that Hurston simply omit some of the more controversial sections of her text.

Yet, at the time of its publication, the narrative enjoyed commercial success and won the *Saturday Review*'s Ainsfield-Wolf Prize in 1942 for its "contributions to the field of Race Relations." The publication of the text marks a new period in Hurston's life; Hemenway explains, "More than at any other point in her life Zora became a recognized black spokesperson, whose opinions were sought by the white reading public" (*ZNH*, 288). Less sympathetic than Hemenway, critics like Nathan Huggins and Darwin Turner read the text as a different sort of landmark, asserting that Hurston's "folksiness eventually became both style and substance" (*ZNH*, 277). Most critics implicitly agree, and read the gaps, silences, and inconsistencies involving both content and form in the sometimes puzzling, seemingly disjointed text as evidence of Hurston's decision to accommodate her audience's expectations at any expense; repeatedly, the author's lies about her birth date, her marriages, and her refusal both to structure her autobiography according to convention and to address the race issue directly all seem to foreground and shape most of the critical treatments of the text.

Seeming also to dismiss the solicited text as at least unfortunate, Hemenway indirectly addresses the intersecting issues of place and voice central to the life story with his assertion that Hurston displays "uneasiness over how to move beyond the Eatonville voice and, by implication, how to explain her fame and her townspeople's obscurity." Only hinting at these issues herself, Hurston provides an explanation for her popularity without discussing the circumstances surrounding the writing and publication of *Dust Tracks*. In the autobiography, the author explains that even an early audience welcomed her into its fold because she had "the map of Dixie on her tongue";[2] works like *Mules and Men,* a collection of African American folklore and the celebrated novel *Their Eyes Were Watching God* gained Hurston acclaim for her skillful representations of folk dialect and seemed to anticipate her later audience's intense interest in her opinions regarding the African American experience.

With her own gesture towards Eatonville and the American South, then, Hurston introduces the relationship between geography, self, and speech central to the life story. The text explicitly examines the conditions for speech and silence experienced by the author. After Hurston suffers a loss of voice with the death of her mother, the narrative's setting both literally and figuratively expands; images of Eatonville with its lively conversations on Joe Clarke's store porch darken with the discovery of other places, internalized geographies as Hurston enters a period she describes as one of "lone solitude . . . earless silences," and homelessness, a period against which the author orients the narrative of her life (115). Hurston's admission that she would never return to Eatonville as a "real town" after her mother's death thus seems not to reflect an inability to "fuse" Eatonville with New York, as Hemenway argues, but instead to intimate Hurston's own strategies for bridging worlds. *Dust Tracks* documents the constructions of a self that asserts its subjectivity by bridging both public and private, realistic and imaginary spaces, and by surviving physical and psychic dislocation and relocation through the processes of narration.

Documenting a cohesion that results from narration, Hurston's autobiography confirms the author's ability to speak both in worlds that expect her to speak (even as a representative figure) and in others that initially leave her speechless. The defining image of Hurston's childhood, the young girl on the gatepost who "speak[s] pieces," retains its significance, just as the Eatonville voice continues to express itself—and the new experiences it registers—throughout the narrative. The "threshold figure which mediates between the all-black town of Eatonville, Florida, and the big road traveled by passing whites" comments on the inside/outside structure of identity:

> The front porch might seem a daring place for the rest of the town, but it was a gallery seat for me. My favorite place was atop the gate-post. Proscenium box for a born first-nighter. Not only did I enjoy the show, but I didn't mind the actors knowing that I liked it. I usually spoke to them in passing. . . . They liked to hear me "speak pieces" . . . and gave me generously of their

2. Zora Neale Hurston, *Dust Tracks on a Road: An Autobiography* (Chicago: University of Illinois Press, 1984), 135. Subsequent references are cited in the text as *DT.*

small silver for doing these things. . . . The colored people gave no dimes. They deplored any tendencies in me, but I was their Zora nevertheless.[3]

This image, described in Hurston's essay, "How It Feels to Be Colored Me," also proves central to the life story. Throughout the autobiography, the author identifies herself in some respects as "everybody's Zora." That Hurston employs free indirect discourse and direct discourse to give voice to the communities that surround her in Eatonville and beyond, underlies the characterization. "Everybody's Zora" in fact speaks for everybody. Even so, the self-effacement expected in this process appears suspended with the passing of time; the text chronicles the development of a private Zora who answers her audience's expectations with expressions of her own determination, narrating what she must, the "things clawing inside [that] must be said" (*DT,* 256) and keeping to herself what she chooses for her own knowledge and interpretation.

American Context, Content, and Form

Attention to Hurston's descriptions of the town clarifies the author's focus on place. Seeming to counter the questions regarding her childhood and then her rise to success that readers like Hemenway formulate, Hurston describes Eatonville as a place surrounded by and incorporated into at least two different worlds and defying standard definition: it is the first town founded, incorporated, and administrated by African Americans in the history of the United States. Further, the town paradoxically symbolizes both wilderness and civilization. As with other American autobiographies, *Dust Tracks* demonstrates the relation between context—place and the communal voice associated with place—and the self that emerges in the text. In a discussion of this trend, Lawrence Buell analyzes two related lines of development of the genre during the American Renaissance:

> One is a commitment in keeping with traditional autobiographical practice, of objectifying the self either through its effacement in favor of a narrative of events (usually itself somewhat stereotyped, as in slave or frontier narrative), or through the subordination of the I's uniqueness to shared communal

3. Barbara Johnson, "Thresholds of Difference: Structures of Address in Zora Neale Hurston," *Critical Inquiry* 12, no. 1 (1985), 178; Zora Neale Hurston, "How It Feels to Be Colored Me," in *I Love Myself When I Am Laughing and Then Again When I Am Looking Mean and Impressive: A Zora Neale Hurston Reader,* ed. Alice Walker (New York: Old Westbury, 1979), 155.

models of the self: the convert, the slave, the famous self-made man, the successful domestic/professional woman, the frontiersman. The other— opposite yet symbiotic, indeed called into being by the pressure of the first as it exerts itself within an "I"-centered transatlantic culture accentuated by America's exceptionally centered civil religion—is the development of the more individuated "I" at the level of either protagonist or persona but especially the latter, an "I" that explicitly or implicitly proclaims its boundlessness in relation to social and literary norms, its impatience with preexisting narrative frames, its inability to be typed and formulated even by itself.[4]

The characterizations discussed here can easily be applied both to Hurston's autobiography and to the author's descriptions of her hometown. After the Civil War, men of her father's generation "set out to find new frontiers" only to return to the wilderness of the southern United States (4). Although Eatonville was unique in the American landscape at the time of its settlement, Hurston's description of the town depends on established contexts and characterizations. Eatonville becomes the new American frontier as the settlers formulaically clear and "tame" the lands to give the new population in the town equal opportunities in the administration of the settlement.

However, in the same descriptive passages, Hurston redefines and expands the conventional folklore of the "American Frontier" with the specific history of the town. She writes:

> I was born in a Negro town. I do not mean by that the black back-side of an average town. Eatonville is, and was at the time of my birth a pure Negro town—charter, mayor, council, town marshal, and all. It was not the first Negro Community in America, but it was the first to be incorporated, the first attempt at organized self-government on the part of Negroes in America. (3)

The author presents a new definition for "Negro town," noting that the town redefines the relationship between blacks and whites: "Now, the Negro population . . . settled simultaneously with the white. They had been needed, and found profitable employment. The best of relations existed between employer and employee" (8). Hurston's text demonstrates these new definitions as active constructions replace passive ones and a new set of terms come into play. The Negro population of former slaves and the

4. Lawrence Buell, "Autobiography in the American Renaissance," in *American Autobiography: Retrospect and Prospect*, ed. Paul John Eakin (Madison: University of Wisconsin Press, 1991), 64.

first African Americans born into freedom, *finds* profitable employment, benefiting from the fact that they are called upon by the white population. The author's characterization further defines the division within the population as one between employer and employed, using terms that appear neutral and do not seem to belie racial distinctions.

Buell's observations regarding the autobiographical "I's" "inability to be typed or formulated even by itself" apply even more effectively to Hurston's description of the town's environs, the surrounding wilderness. When Zora Neale Hurston describes the founding of Eatonville and neighboring Maitland, she concludes:

> The shores of Lake Maitland were beautiful, probably one reason they decided to settle there. . . . There was the continuous roar of the crashing of ancient giants of the lush woods, of axes, saws and hammers. . . . These wealthy homes, glittering carriages behind blooded horses and occupied by well-dressed folk, presented a curious spectacle in the swampy forests so dense that they are dark at high noon. It was necessary to carry a lantern when one walked out at night, to avoid stumbling over these immense reptiles in the streets of Maitland. (6–7)

The reptiles walk in streets that, the author writes, "look as if [they] had been laid out by a playful snake" (7). The wilderness, thus, seemingly both interacts with and contradicts civilization and its definitions of the town. In this passage, Hurston's use of the present tense both inserts her into the scene she describes and implies that civilization does not change the fundamental characteristics of the swamp, even at the time during which she writes, a time that had witnessed the passing of the horse and carriage.

That the author begins *Dust Tracks on a Road* with the narrative of the settling of Eatonville effectively locates both the origin of the life story and her reader's initial reference point within the arena of local folklore or story as well as place. Doing so, Hurston calls into question conventions of place, story, and self. This strategy, however, illustrates a recurring problem for the reader of autobiography. In a discussion of Hemingway's *A Moveable Feast* and Stein's *Autobiography of Alice B. Toklas* and *Everybody's Autobiography*, Albert E. Stone explains:

> Two perennial problems in interpreting any autobiographical act are here highlighted. One is the overdetermined nature of all assertions in autobiographical texts and the problem of their "truth" value to others as compared to the author. . . . In ways subtly different from other literary or historical narratives, autobiography conventionally presupposes a "pact" or "contract" by which creator and consumer tacitly agree on each others' co-creating roles,

duties and liberties. For many readers in the past, this understanding was explicitly historical: the autobiographer was expected to subordinate imagination to the attempt to communicate trustworthy, verifiable, subjective messages.

Hurston's text, like Hemingway's and Stein's, illustrates the modern breakdown of this convention. The narrative does not announce any claim to truthfulness or even to subjectivity. Rather, affecting a revision of the expected autobiographical pact, Hurston opens her life story by describing the reader's role. "Like the dead-seeming, cold rock, I have memories within that came out of the material that went to make me. Time and place have had their say. So you will have to know something about the time and place where I came from, in order that you may interpret the incidents and directions of my life" (3). Hurston replaces the usual claims to veracity made earlier in the African American tradition, the words "written by herself," and a sponsor's authenticating gesture, with a conscious identification of her reader and the reader's role as a kind of "listener" and therefore interpreter of an unfolding story that incorporates the kinds of form and content usually associated with orally communicated narratives. The reconstruction of the proverb "Time and place will have their say," as Claudine Raynaud notes, illustrates Hurston's manipulation of established forms to fit her own personal circumstances, as well as her validation of the collective knowledge represented by the form.[5] Further, the proverb depends on metaphors of speech to attribute significant power of creation to context—to time, place, and story.

Hurston also positions herself as an interpreter of her own story. Describing the autobiography as an "orphan text," Françoise Lionnet examines the author's attempt to reconstruct and interpret her own genealogy.[6] Lionnet's consideration of the role of folklore in the autobiography prompts a closer look at Hurston's chapter "I Get Born." The author writes, "This is all hear-say. Maybe some of the details of my birth as told me might be a little inaccurate, but it is pretty well established that I really did get born. The saying goes like this" (28). By characterizing this piece of personal history as a "saying," Zora Neale Hurston redefines the origin of

---

5. Albert E. Stone, "Modern American Autobiography: Texts and Transactions," in *American Autobiography: Retrospect and Prospect,* ed. Paul John Eakin (Madison: University of Wisconsin Press, 1991), 100; Claudine Raynaud, "Autobiography as 'Lying' Session: Zora Neale Hurston's *Dust Tracks on a Road,*" in *Black Feminist Criticism and Critical Theory,* ed. Joe Weixlmann and Houston A. Baker Jr. (Greenwood, Fla.: Penkeville, 1988), 111.

6. Françoise Lionnet, *Autobiographical Voices: Race, Gender, Self-Portraiture* (Ithaca: Cornell University Press, 1989), 101.

personal history; the strategy symbolizes a significant change in the representation of personal history in the African American literary tradition. Unlike the slave autobiographer's search for frequently undocumented information about personal history, Hurston identifies a new resource for the verification of this kind of information; however inexact or diluted, this body of folklore and local legend or story serves to document historical facts. The author thus affirms collective memory at the same time that she identifies herself as listener or interpreter of orally communicated African American folklore.

Zora Neale Hurston's adopted dual role as listener and storyteller operates even in earlier sections of the text. When she describes the founding of Eatonville, she acknowledges the transaction that underlies her own account; employing the language of storytelling, Hurston writes, "It all started with three white men . . . [who] set out to find new frontiers" (4). The construction seems to replace the preface associated with the fairy tale, "Once upon a time," as it makes no mention of the actual dates of the founding and does not immediately identify the frontier-seekers. Later, her account of another inherited story also acknowledges the tools of storytelling. "Into this burly boiling, hard-hitting, rugged-individualistic setting," she writes, "walked one day a tall, heavy-muscled mulatto who resolved to put down roots" (12). This passage identifies the author's father as a type, a representation of an African American folk-hero and makes explicit reference to the narrative component of setting.

Both narrative framing devices do not call attention to the author's distance from the events and seem to support Walter Benjamin's analysis of the process of storytelling. "[Storytelling] does not aim to convey the pure essence of the thing," he proposes, "like information or a report." Rather the form of communication identified as storytelling

> . . . sinks the thing [the material of the story] into the life of the storyteller, in order to bring it out of him again. Thus traces of the storyteller cling to the story the way the handprints of the potter cling to the clay vessel. Storytellers tend to begin their story with a presentation of the circumstances in which they themselves have learned what is to follow, unless they simply pass it off as their own experience.

Hurston relates events historically outside of her own experience without discussing the "circumstances" under which she first learned of those events. The retelling of communal and generational folktale and story as a way of telling her own story illustrates her immersion into the events described. The author thus incorporates the material of her parents' childhoods and courtship, like that of the founding of Eatonville, into her own life story. That the process of self-definition would involve representing parents as role models does not seem an unusual strategy. However, the author's method of incorporating the stories of her parents, and even those of others in her community, is both novel and provocative; Hurston uses free indirect discourse to represent dialogue attributed to other figures in the narration of her own life story. The method, which, according to Henry Louis Gates Jr., first finds its way into the African American literary tradition in works by Hurston, brings innovation to the genre of autobiography, expanding its boundaries and giving it structural and formal fluidity.[7]

Collapsing any narrative distance between her voice and the voices of many figures in the narrative—her mother, father, the voices of the store porch "liars" or storytellers among others—Hurston "reaffirms the link that binds her to communal lore." Significantly, the author also employs the narrative strategy to present dialogue without what Norman Page calls the "abdication of . . . [her] role as story-teller." In a passage important to the entire text, Hurston represents dialogue between her mother and father. The exchange centers itself on a discussion of the will and is prefaced with Mrs. Hurston's assessment of the values she imparts to her own children:

> Once or twice a year we might get permission to go and play at some other house. But that was most unusual. Mama contended that we had plenty of space to play in; plenty of things to play with; and furthermore, plenty of us to keep each other's company. If she had her way, she meant to raise her children to stay at home. She said that there was no need for us to live like no-count Negroes and poor-white trash—too poor to sit in the house—had to come outdoors for any pleasure, or hang around somebody else's house. Any of her children who had any tendencies like that must have got it from the Hurston side. . . . Mama exhorted her children at every opportunity to "jump at de sun." We might not land on the sun, but at least we would get off the ground. (20–21)

The passage presents a complex example of Hurston's adoption of free indirect discourse and direct discourse framed by the first person narration of her own story.[8] Here the narrator's voice merges with her mother's; the diction and tone characteristic of the narrator's voice is seamlessly replaced

---

7. Walter Benjamin, *Illuminations: Essays and Reflections* (New York: Schocken Books, 1968), 92–93; Henry Louis Gates Jr., *The Signifying Monkey: A Theory of African-American Literary Criticism* (New York: Oxford University Press, 1988), 181.

8. Raynaud, "Autobiography as 'Lying' Session," 119; Norman Page, *Speech in the English Novel* (London: Longman, 1973), 38; for an analysis of this passage with close attention to the shifting narrative voice, see Raynaud, 117–18.

with Lucy Hurston's firsthand maternal admonitions; no quotation marks call attention to the shifting of voices. Rather, Hurston effectively speaks in her mother's voice.

Visions, Blank Spaces, and Subjectivity

The identification that Hurston makes with her mother has extreme consequences during the author's seventh year. An abrupt announcement prefaces the author's account of the events surrounding her mother's death. She writes, "I do not know when the visions began. Certainly I was not more than seven years old, but I remember the first coming very distinctly" (56). The visions appear after Hurston instinctively escapes her mother's reach after committing childish pranks. Exiling herself to the home of an absent neighbor, Hurston writes, "I had not thought of stopping there when I set out, but I saw a big raisin lying on the porch and stopped to eat it. There was some cool shade on the porch, so I sat down, and soon I was asleep in a strange way" (57). Hurston becomes a kind of Alice in Wonderland figure after she consumes the seemingly magical raisin. The young girl begins to dream, seeing herself in a series of visions. While Hurston seems to chronicle a kind of subjectivity born of the specific historical context and place that surround her, she also documents a difficult obstacle to her self-definition:

> Like clearcut stereopticon slides, I saw twelve scenes flash before me, each one held until I had seen it well in every detail, and then be replaced by another. There was no continuity as in an average dream. Just disconnected scene after scene with blank spaces in between. I knew that they were all true, a preview of things to come, and my soul writhed in agony and shrunk away. (57)

Relating her "cold and friendless" wandering, the visions come to pass at different points in her life, Hurston says. The young girl witnesses a vision that depicts her as "an orphan and homeless." Another shows her standing beside a "dark pool of water and seeing a huge fish move slowly away at a time when [she] would be somehow in the depth of despair" (57). The last vision, one of a large house in which two women wait, would, the author knows, bring the experience of peace and love. Except for these brief descriptions and except to note that her experience isolates her as a child, the author does not explain the visions. And although she seems to intend to structure her text with them, the visions effectively disappear from the text before the author describes half of them. The first half of the text, Hurston's relation of her childhood years, ends with her moving account of her mother's death, marking the passing of the author's first vision that showed her leaving her childhood home forever. Two additional visions serve as endings for two later chapters. Except for the eighth vision, which represents her relationship with her white benefactor, Mrs. Charlotte Osgood Mason, little mention of the remaining visions is made. Nevertheless, Zora Neale Hurston organizes the second half of the text as a series of seemingly disconnected thematic chapters, a strategy that effectively calls to mind the stereopticon visions of her childhood; Hurston witnesses not only visual representation but blank spaces.

A significant key to the narrative, the visions and blank spaces clarify and illustrate the concerns of the autobiography. Hurston, it seems, must react to this experience with the construction of narrative. Instead of calling attention to reliance on memory in that construction, the visions call into question Hurston's own position as subject of her text and serve as metaphors for a fragmented self and for the self as sign and interpreter; in fact, the visions effectively literalize the fragmentation of the self that they both foretell and document. Hurston's mute reaction to the experience—she tells no one about the visions even as they come true—illustrates this fragmentation. Having been betrayed by her own eyes, the young girl also does not speak about the visions; the body, represented here by the senses, and the self, represented by the power to understand and to speak, become fragmented and to some degree lost from one another with the event.[9]

The episode further accentuates the tensions between the worlds described in the text, evoking Freud's discussion of the uncanny. Freud's examination of the word *heimlich* explains the word's evolution into its opposite, *unheimlich*, or "uncanny" and literally "unhomely."[10] He theorizes that the "unhomely" or uncanny appeals to the remnants of the primitive or childlike in us. Distinguishing experiences of the uncanny among children and adults, Freud creates several categories of uncanny experiences. Most notably, he discusses the child's willingness to accept the animation of the inanimate. Hurston's text takes up this immersion into the imaginary world and witnesses the transformation of the familiar into the uncanny; the home created by her mother is replaced with the world

9. This formulation was brought to my attention by Ashwini Sukthankar, a student.

10. See Freud's "The Uncanny," vol. 17 in *The Standard Edition of the Complete Psychological Works of Sigmund Freud*, trans. James Strachey (London: Hogarth Press, 1953–1974), 218–55.

of the visions. Left orphaned, without the familiarity of home, Hurston seeks to regain wholeness through subjectivity, "family love," and a "resting place" (124).

By relating the visions, then, the author depicts her position as object or sign and her lack of control over the narrative of her life; until she witnesses the realization of the visions she has little understanding of the importance and meaning of each. As a child, Zora Neale Hurston understands the visions as an experience that isolates her from others.

> I consider that my real childhood ended with the coming of the pronouncements. True, I played, fought, and studied with other children, but always stood apart within. Often I was in some lonesome wilderness, suffering strange things and agonies while other children in the same yard played without a care. I asked myself why me? Why? Why? A cosmic loneliness was my shadow. Nothing and nobody around me really touched me. It is one of the blessings of this world that few people see visions and dream dreams. (60)

Hurston's retrospective assessment of the experience involves unusual terms. Characterizing the visions as pronouncements, Hurston invites interpretation of the connection between place, truth, subjectivity, and speech. The writer's relation of the feeling of difference that the visions bring involves an assessment of the difference as real. Unlike Hurston's interpretation of racial difference as no difference—both in "How It Feels to Be Colored Me" and later in *Dust Tracks*—this feeling is one that she acknowledges as real and wants to hide from others. Her mute reception of the experience, like the label "pronouncement," illustrates her lack of subjectivity and even her speechlessness. Describing the fragmented self that results from the experience, Hurston refers to the separation of her outside from her inside: she stands "apart within" even though she plays and interacts with her peers. The author internalizes the wilderness around her and writes that her shadow, a natural component to the body, consists of cosmic loneliness.

Hurston, however, does not follow her account of the visions with a relation of the events that explain or support their place in the autobiography most effectively; the death of her mother and the subsequent dissolution of her family are not addressed until the author first discusses the "figure and fancy" that she cultivates as a child.[11] As a child, the author communicates with and exists within the worlds of family and community in ways that

---

11. Gates, *The Signifying Monkey*, examines the negation of plot that operates both at structural and thematic levels (184–86). This strategy evokes the negation

escape her in the analogous world of dreams, the world that sustains her experience of the visions. The contrast is sustained even further. Unlike the world of Eatonville, the world at once civilized and wild, where Hurston is "everybody's Zora," the world of visions leaves Hurston alone.

In retrospect, Hurston describes her pre-vision childhood as characterized by the belief that "death, destruction, and other agonies were never meant to touch [her]." She explains, "Things like that happened to other people and no wonder. They were not like me and mine. Naturally, the world and the firmaments careened to one side a little so as not to inconvenience me. In fact, the universe went further than that—it was happy to break a few rules just to show me preferences" (34). Hurston includes her family in the privileged group, emphasizing the similarities she shares with them. Even the event of Hurston's birth seems to prove this preference. The newborn is delivered by an unlikely midwife; a neighbor, a white man delivers Zora Neale Hurston after finding Lucy Hurston in labor and alone during hog-butchering season. Later, even the animal world participates in the young child's advancement when a sow teaches her to walk by pursuing the child's cornbread.

Reflecting her perception of her alignment with the natural world and even with the universe, Hurston incorporates into the autobiography an imaginary world of fantasy and the narrative forms of the fairy tale and the tall tale. Upon listening to lying sessions held on the town porch Hurston writes,

> It did not surprise me at all to hear that the animals talked. I had suspected it all along. Or let us say, that I wanted to suspect it. Life took on a bigger perimeter by expanding on these things. I picked up glints and gleams out of what I heard and stored it away to turn it to my own uses. The winds would sough through the tops of tall, long-leaf pines and say things to me. I put

---

of plot effected in Hurston's *Their Eyes Were Watching God*. Gates explains her early reference to death in a novel about affirmation:

> By introducing this evidence of [Janie's] return from burying the dead, Hurston negates the text's themes of discovery, rebirth, and renewal, only to devote the remainder of her text to realizing these same themes. Hurston also draws upon negation to reveal, first, the series of self-images that Janie does not wish to be and second, to define the matrix of obstacles that frustrate her desire to know herself. The realization of the full text of *Their Eyes* represents the fulfillment of the novel's positive potentialities, by which I mean Janie's discovery of self-knowledge.

Operating thematically also in the autobiography, this strategy juxtaposes description of her "cosmic loneliness" with her own description of the natural and imaginary worlds.

in the words that the sounds put into me. Like "Woo woo, you woo!" The tree was talking to me, even when I did not catch the meaning. . . . I named it "the loving pine." Finally all of my playmates called it that too. (69–70)

Here the author incorporates the communal folktale in her understanding of her own alignment with the natural world. Defining the world as dependent on verbal expression, Hurston relates that she talks to the tree and that it responds, speaking through her. She names it and shares the name with others. However, Hurston's structural juxtaposition of the tale with those elements of fantasy related in the discussion of her visions, which exist in a world that excludes verbal expression, calls attention to the author's changing point of view. The material of fairy tales and folktales betrays her when she consumes the magical raisin and sees mysterious images of her impending orphanhood and homelessness.

Resolution: Finding Home and Keeping Something for Herself

In her narration of her mother's dying, the author describes the promises she makes to her mother; the child takes responsibility for relating to the surrounding community that watches over the sick woman her mother's instructions for changes in the deathbed rituals. "Her mouth was slightly open, but her breathing took up so much of her strength that she could not talk. But she looked at me, or so I felt, to speak for her. She depended on me for a voice" (87). Here Hurston no longer depends on direct discourse or on free indirect discourse to narrate her mother's feelings. Instead, the narrative strategy reflects the episode on hand as Hurston must speak for her now silent mother. Communicating without speaking, the child gains understanding by looking into her mother's eyes. Yet the visual exchange proves ineffectual and untranslatable as Hurston's pleas that her mother's pillow be once again placed under the dying woman's head go unheard and unanswered. In this scene, the gap between visual and verbal representation first encountered during the experience of the visions returns; the eyes function as a conduit for understanding but do not serve to communicate understanding to others, beyond mother and daughter. Two years after her visions first appear to her, Hurston finds herself powerless and silenced; the event pits her loyalty to her mother against the power of communal ritual. She loses both her mother and her alignment with her community, her participation in ritual.

The death marks not only the end of Hurston's childhood, but effectively the end of the section of the text that critics find most successful. According to Robert Hemenway, "*Dust Tracks* fails as autobiography because it is a text deliberately less than its author's talents, a text diminished by her refusal to provide a second or third dimension to the flat surfaces of her adult image" (*DT*, xxxix). Hemenway assesses the second half of the narrative construct as an incomplete and unexpressed two- or three-dimensional work, and thus borrows Hurston's own metaphor for the self. Writing about childhood curiosity and the construction of the self-image, Hurston explains:

> Grown people know that they do not always know the why of things, and even if they think they know, they do not know where and how they got the proof. . . . It is upsetting because until the elders are pushed for an answer, they have never looked to see if it was so, nor how they came by what passes for proof to their acceptances of certain things as true. . . . (33)

She continues, "I did not know then, as I know now, that people are prone to build a statue of the kind of person that it pleases them to be. And few people want to be forced to ask themselves, 'What if there is no me like my statue?' " (33–34). The statue effectively substitutes for the self-image. Hurston, like Hemenway, thus calls attention to the design imposed by the author upon the life story. Both also support Françoise Lionnet's assertion that Hurston's text should not be read as "straight" autobiography but as self-portraiture.[12] In light of the author's indirection or license with the facts of her life story, the critics imply, alternative ways of reading and interpreting the life story are necessary.

An episode that marks the divergent views that Lionnet and Hemenway each describe involves another autobiographical act. Lionnet reads the larger narrative against its incorporated myth of Persephone and later against Hurston's account (also in *Dust Tracks*) of the last living African to have been brought to America on a slave ship. Kossola/Cudjo Lewis tells the story of the destruction of his village and his separation from his family. Lionnet sets the story against the author's own experience, citing Hurston: "After 75 years, he still had a sense of loss. That yearning for blood and cultural ties. That sense of mutilation." The critic asserts that Hurston tells her own story by telling Kossola's; the comparison of individual loss to the African Diaspora also evokes the production of collective experience from private experience. Lionnet largely ignores what Hemenway calls attention to, Hurston's fraudulent representation of Cudjo's story; she plagiarizes most of her "interview" with the old African. Instead, Lionnet asserts that the "collective functions as a silverless mirror," which both absorbs

12. Lionnet, *Autobiographical Voices*, 98.

and reflects the "images and metaphors [Hurston draws on] to portray a figural self."[13]

Although the material of the Greek myth and the account of the Diaspora illuminate Hurston's story, the second half of the narrative seems determined by private experience. In a discussion of plot in narrative, Robert Scholes and Robert Kellogg describe the problem of closure inherent in the form of autobiography. The critics write:

> The resolution of an autobiographical form cannot come from the protagonist's death. This easiest of equilibria to achieve in narrative art is barred to the writer of autobiography. He must find another kind of stasis on which to rest his narrative or leave it hanging unresolved, "to be continued." This means that some other order of resolution needs to be found for an autobiographical narrative to conclude its plot line with an esthetically satisfying end. . . . But to the extent that the autobiography is a story of the author's inward life, its natural concluding point is not his death but the point at which the author comes to terms with himself, realizes his nature, assumes his vocation.[14]

The author comes to terms with herself and her nature through the experience of her mother's death, which brings the knowledge of the "end of things." "Mama died at sundown and changed a world. That is the world which she had built out of her body and her heart. Even the physical aspects fell apart with a suddenness that was startling" (89).

The fragmentation of the self that results from the experience of the visions escalates after her mother's death. She writes:

> I wanted what they could not conceive of. I could not reveal myself for lack of expression, and then for lack of hope of understanding, even if I could have found the words. I was not comfortable to have around. Strange things must have looked out of my eyes like Lazarus after his resurrection. (117)

Implicitly claiming firsthand experience of death, Zora Neale Hurston aligns herself with her mother and with the biblical figure; before she describes her own resurrection, she describes the experience further: "So I was forever shifting. I walked by my corpse. I smelt it and felt it" (117). Literalizing the objectification described earlier, here Hurston describes the physical aspects of the corpse, the image of the self as dead.

---

13. Lionnet, *Autobiographical Voices,* 112; Hemenway examines the event in *Zora Neale Hurston,* 96–99; Lionnet, 115.

14. Robert Scholes and Robert Kellogg, *The Nature of Narrative* (New York: Oxford University Press, 1966), 214–15.

Like her own subjectivity and the "physical aspects" of her mother's person, Hurston's complicity with the natural world, so clearly in evidence in her descriptions of her childhood, dissolves. Fantastic tales of the loving pine and of a quiet neighbor's nighttime transformations into an alligator as well as realistic descriptions of the wild settlement of Eatonville are replaced; she writes, "I was deprived of the loving pine, the lakes, the wild violets in the woods and the animals I used to know. . . . Just a jagged hole where my home used to be" (95). When Hurston's second vision is realized as she leaves her childhood home after her mother's death, the author continues:

> I had seen myself homeless and uncared for. There was a chill about that picture which used to wake me up shivering. I had always thought I would be in some lone, arctic wasteland with no one under the sound of my voice. I found the cold, the desolate solitude and earless silences, but I discovered that all that geography was within me. It only needed time to reveal it. (115)

The metaphors of internalization extend to the author's own descriptions of her pilgrimage. Her journey, a search for subjectivity and voice, begins from a void within the author herself created by her real loss and homelessness.

Juxtaposed to the internal geography she must traverse, the world beyond Eatonville does not at first contain many allies:

> Jacksonville made me know that I was a little colored girl. Things were all about the town to point this out to me. Streetcars and stores and then talk I heard around the school. I was no longer among the white people whose homes I could barge into with a sure sense of welcome. (94)

This passage demonstrates the autobiographical moment described by Paul de Man as "an alignment between the two subjects involved in the process of reading in which they determine each other by mutual reflexive substitution."[15] In Hurston's story that moment involves self and place; at this juncture the town of Jacksonville defines Hurston as a "little colored girl." Similarly, the author identifies the defining elements as "things," making explicit their status as objects. These "naming objects" Hurston identifies specifically as streetcars and stores and then "talk" she hears and does not attribute to a speaker. The personification of the streetcars and stores and later the "talk" constitute a type of prosopopoeia. Implying

15. Paul de Man, *Rhetoric of Romanticism* (New York: Columbia University Press, 1984), 81.

that the little black girl can claim neither subjectivity nor welcome from the town's "white folks," the author illustrates the process described by de Man; the animation of the inanimate effects her own objectification, supporting her descriptions of her own corpse.

That Zora Neale Hurston explicitly acknowledges her reader as interpreter at the beginning of *Dust Tracks on a Road* seems especially relevant as she provides interpretations that counter those imposed by surrounding society. The text relates her position as object on two levels; Hurston is read first by the society that surrounds her within the text and then by that without, her readers. Hurston's awareness of herself as text seemingly originates in Jacksonville, where she learns of the identity imposed upon her. Her time in Jacksonville also marks the beginning of her adult life. The condition of homelessness, which the author identifies when her mother dies, is made explicit after she accompanies her older sister to boarding school. After a year passes, that condition is reinforced when her father attempts to give his daughter away: "Papa said that the school could adopt me" (109).

Even so, the author's alignment with Lazarus becomes less complete as she becomes largely responsible for her own resurrection. In her description of the years after her mother's death, she writes:

> There is something about poverty that smells like death. Dead dreams dropping off the heart like leaves in a dry season and rotting around the feet; impulses smothered too long in the fetid air of underground caves. The soul lives in a sickly air. People can be slave-ships in shoes.
>
> This wordless feeling went with me from the time I was ten years old until I achieved a sort of competence around twenty. Naturally, the first five years were the worst. Things and circumstances gave life a most depressing odor. (116)

Employing metaphors of the senses, Hurston extends her experience of death by suggesting that "poverty smells like death" and that the heart is a thing akin to a dying tree. Likewise, dreams, important earlier to the child, here hold no promises of continuity and creation. Poverty, loss, and wordlessness become defining characteristics of her youth. She continues:

> The five years following my leaving the school at Jacksonville were haunted. I was shifted from house to house of relatives and friends and found comfort no-where. I was without books to read most of the time, except where I could get hold of them by mere chance. That left no room for selection.

The passage implies a connection between "comfort" and reading. A selection of books, Hurston seems to imply, can ease the wordless and homeless feeling precipitated by poverty. Later Hurston explains her journey as one defined by her desire for "family love and peace and a resting place. I wanted books and school" (124).

When Hurston receives word that her brother wants her to live with him and his family, she believes she has found a home for herself. Instead, she's expected to delay her return to school in order to help with housekeeping. The "way of life inside [her]" that she desires with a "want that [twisted her]" finally finds its way out when an "unexpected friend," a poor white woman, helps Hurston find a job with the traveling light opera company (*DT*, 130–31). The author describes her instant popularity with the group. "In the first place I was a Southerner and had the map of Dixie on my tongue" (135). Throughout the narrative, Hurston refers to this identifying characteristic as frequently as she identifies herself as "Mama's daughter."

Then, except for extensive acknowledgments of her friends and benefactors, glimpses of the author's private journey to self-realization become few as the text progresses. However, in her chapter, "Love," Hurston discusses her relationship with the man, identified only as A. W. P., who lays her "by her heels" (252). After she briefly reveals a bit of information about her first, unsuccessful, and apparently loveless marriage, and without acknowledging her second marriage, she writes:

> I did not just fall in love. I made a parachute jump. . . . His intellect got me first for I am the kind of a woman that likes to move on mentally from point to point, and I like my man to be there way ahead of me. . . .
>
> His great desire was to do for me. *Please* let him be a man! . . .
>
> That very manliness, sweet as it was, made us both suffer. My career balked the completeness of his ideal. I really wanted to conform, but it was impossible. To me there was no conflict. My work was one thing, and he was all the rest. But I could not make him see that. Nothing must be in my life but himself. . . .
>
> He begged me to give up my career, marry him and live outside of New York City. I really wanted to do anything he wanted me to do, but that one thing I could not do. . . . I had things inside of me that must be said. . . .
>
> In the midst of this I received my Guggenheim Fellowship. This was my chance to release him, fight myself free from my obsession. He would get over me in a few months and go on to be a very big man. So I sailed off to Jamaica [and] pitched in to work hard on my research to smother my feelings. But the thing would not down. The plot was far from the circumstances, but I tried to embalm all the tenderness of my passion for him in *Their Eyes Were Watching God*. (252–60)

In her analysis of this passage, Barbara Johnson asserts, "The plot is indeed far from the circumstances, and, what is even more striking, it is lived by what seems to be a completely different woman."[16] Johnson emphasizes the contrast between Hurston's protagonist Janie, who repeatedly strains to "attain equal respect in relation to men," and the author herself, who in Johnson's view, "readily submits to the pleasures of submission yet struggles to establish the legitimacy of a professional life outside the love relation." Read against the loss of voice that the author suffers during her childhood and young adulthood, however, the disparity between the experiences depicted in the life story and the novel should not surprise. After explaining that her lover wants her to give up her career, marry him, and leave New York, Hurston relates that she is happy do whatever he wants, "except that one thing." While she refers to his request that she stop writing, Hurston essentially does not distinguish between that request and the others mentioned in the same sentence; voice, place (specifically home), and identity all seem at risk.

That marriage has historically constituted a loss of identity for women has been addressed in studies of women's literature. The institution has proven antithetical to the act of self-definition and subject creation at the center of the autobiographical act. Examining marriage and other historical conditions that determine the circumstances surrounding women writers in the late 1800s, Deborah Nord writes: "The limitations of time and energy and the pressures of social convention made work and marriage—or work and love—appear to be mutually excluding alternatives." Among others, Nord cites Florence Nightingale, who after rejecting several marriage proposals, writes that for some women the institution results in the "sacrifice of all other life" and, Nord paraphrases, "an annihilation of self behind the destinies of men."[17]

The resolution of the opposing forces, the need for independence and for love, Nord asserts, does not find its way into autobiographical texts of the Victorian period but instead is represented in the fictions of the same period. The costs for the expression of both needs, Nord writes, is often so great that the autobiographer chooses self-effacement, focusing either on her personal or public life. Thus, that Hurston would choose to imagine resolution however qualified in the novel appears grounded in

16. Barbara Johnson, *A World of Difference* (Baltimore: Johns Hopkins University Press, 1987), 170.

17. Deborah Epstein Nord, *The Apprenticeship of Beatrice Webb* (Amherst: University of Massachusetts Press, 1985), 68. Nord's paraphrase of Nightingale appears in her own text, page 69. She cites Nightingale directly from "Cassandra," reprinted in Ray Strachey, *Struggle* (New York: Duffield, 1930), 407.

tradition. Beyond trends in women's writing, however, the author reacts to the loss of voice that shapes much of her life story. Marriage to A. W. P. would necessitate the repression of those things "clawing" inside of her and would endanger the author on a fundamental level. Hurston would also lose her home in New York. The conditions that accompany the marriage ceremony mirror those that follow the mother's death. Indeed, her father's gesture of giving her away to the school anticipates the marriage ceremony. Thus when forced to choose between the relationship and the expression of the material within her, Hurston cannot stop working, claiming her own subjectivity and leaving the resolution of her life as whole and consummated to the realm of fiction.

Hurston's refusal to compromise her self-determination with marriage also evokes her treatment of race issues in the text. The question that begins the chapter on love, "What do I really know about love?" echoes the question, "Who knows?" that appears at the end of her essay, "How It Feels to Be Colored Me." Likewise, the same assessment of racial difference as no difference, described in the essay, also characterizes the chapter, "My People! My People!" In her conclusion, she writes, "I maintain that I have been a Negro three times—a Negro baby, a Negro girl and a Negro woman. Still, if you have received no clear cut impression of what the Negro in America is like, then you are in the same place with me. There is no The Negro here" (237). The passage clearly communicates with the author's earlier description of herself in Jacksonville, where she becomes aware of her identity as a little colored girl. Here, however, the author elides any identification of the self as different. As Nellie McKay notes, "If one of her desires for her book was to present a more balanced view of the effects of racism on black life, it was not because Hurston was unaware of the seriousness of racial politics. She simply refused to accept the oppression of blacks as a definition of her life."[18] Instead, Hurston writes from a position of subjectivity in which race is not a function of identity and in which identity in turn cannot be generalized.

The fairy-tale structures that represent vast possibilities available to the child return in her discussion of her adulthood, reflecting further the changes in Hurston's perspective. Operating paradoxically in a realistic realm, fantasy appears to be imposed externally. As an adult, Hurston becomes indebted to a white benefactor who insists that the author address her as "Godmother" (175), and her classmates at Barnard introduce her

---

18. Nellie Y. McKay, "Race, Gender, and Cultural Context in Zora Neale Hurston's *Dust Tracks on a Road*," in *Life/Lines: Theorizing Women's Autobiography,* ed. Bella Brodzki and Celeste Schenck (Ithaca: Cornell University Press, 1988), 188.

as "Princess Zora" in order to gain entrance into exclusive establishments. Although she was widely criticized by contemporaries for her position within white society, Hurston seems repeatedly to reject this kind of reading, refusing to comment on the problematic nature of these imposed characterizations. Instead, she seems to point only to the ineffective qualities contained in these fairy-tale constructions, explaining, "It would be dramatic in a Cinderella way if I were to say that the well-dressed students at school snubbed me and shoved me around, but that I studied hard and triumphed over them" (149). Hurston finally provides her readers with rational and credible explanations for her journey from Eatonville to mainstream success, chronicling the friendship, hard work, and good fortune that would take her to the heights of great success.

Finally, reminding the reader of Hurston's sense of journey and of ongoing discovery of both place and identity, the title of the autobiography, *Dust Tracks on a Road*, also figures in the concluding paragraph of the autobiography, as Hurston identifies herself as one who "walk[s] in the dust" (286). The line evokes Lionnet's conclusion regarding the literal and figurative journeys recorded in Hurston's life story. She asserts:

> These allegories of death and rebirth, change and permanence, temporality and eternity, retroactively map the territory of the autobiographical text and the life it attempts to represent. . . . Her journey, like that of the storytellers who never leave [Joe Clark's] porch, is an itinerary through language, "a journeying by way of narrating," as Alexander Gelley puts it. That is why it is impossible to make, on a theoretical level, "any clear-cut division between theme and form, between journey as geography and journey as narrative."[19]

The autobiography reflects the life described; in the first half of the text, the incorporation of form and content usually associated with the fairy tale, folktale, and frontier narrative metaphorically represent the worlds open to Hurston during her childhood. And the limits of history, audience, and interpretation become manifest both in Hurston's reworking of the genre, especially evident in the second half of the narrative; disjointed, without chronological structure, and frustrating to readers, it documents the author's construction of a professional and public identity, an identity that nevertheless seems determined by the private experiences that shape the first half of the text.

19. Lionnet, *Autobiographical Voices*, 114. The author cites Alexander Gelley, *Narrative Crossings: Theory and Pragmatics of Prose Fiction* (Baltimore: Johns Hopkins University Press, 1987), 31.

Dust Tracks on a Road thus chronicles the talents possessed by Hurston as she records her journey in a narrative that effectively represents a new form for the life story; Zora Neale Hurston leaves questions asked by the genre and by her audience unanswered without any loss of subjectivity. Instead, the expression of this subjectivity is one the author decides and designs. And as she contemplates the end of that journey, the Eatonville voice continues, "Life poses questions and that two-headed spirit that rules the beginning and end of things called death had all the answers." From a position of subjectivity, Hurston relates her response to this: "What will be the end? That is not for me to know. . . . And even if I did know all, I am supposed to have some private business to myself. Whatever I do know, I have no intention of putting but so much in the public ears" (260).

"By Being Outside of America"

Gertrude Stein's "Geographical History" of Gender, Self, and Writing

HUGH ENGLISH

Gertrude Stein's response to an Associated Press reporter's question, upon her return to Paris in 1935 from her American tour, suggests how deeply Stein's idea of America intersects with her concerns about gender and sexuality.

> Yes I am married I mean I am married to America, it is so beautiful. I am going back to America sometime, someday not too long. I am already homesick for America. I never knew it was so beautiful. It was like a bachelor who goes along fine for twenty-five years and then decides to get married. That is the way I feel, I mean about America.

Stein's evasive response, suggesting the extent to which she avoided explicit reference to her lesbian "marriage" with Alice B. Toklas,[1] points toward the deep figurative associations between Stein's relation to both the place and the idea of America and her often less explicit focus on her gender and sexuality. Here, gender-crossing bachelorhood and marriage figure a development in her relation to America. We might also claim, however, that Stein's *America* (dis)places the ways in which her self-representations in the 1930s could consider gender and sexuality; with her trope *America*, Stein

---

1. W. G. Rogers, *When This You See Remember Me: Gertrude Stein in Person* (New York: Rinehart, 1948), 152. See Catharine Stimpson's "'Gertrude/Altrude': Stein, Toklas, and the Paradox of the Happy Marriage," for a discussion of how Stein (and Toklas) conceived of their relationship as a marriage in ways that reinvented, rather than merely reproduced, the form of the sanctioned heterosexual union, in *Mothering the Mind: Twelve Studies of Writers and Their Silent Partners*, ed. Ruth Perry et al. (New York: Holmes and Meier, 1984).

can locate her otherwise, and perhaps for her unrepresentable, eccentric subject position, as a woman and as a lesbian, in the center of the literary production of the twentieth century. *America,* as a figure and concept, offers Stein ways of figuring her subjectivity.

In *The Geographical History of America or The Relation of Human Nature to the Human Mind,* Gertrude Stein writes her "self" as an example of the self-making rhetorical activity of the "human mind." *The Geographical History of America* is both a theoretical rhetoric of the human mind (it offers a theory of writing and of grammar) and a rhetorical play (a dramatization) of the human mind. Like her lectures, her literary autobiographies, and her experiments with biography, also undertaken in the 1930s, *The Geographical History of America* plays through multiple articulations of an autobiographical, rhetorical, American, and gendered self.[2] In this extended meditation on identity and grammar, the idea and the figure *America* enable Stein's new compositions of the grammar of subjectivity and gender.

For Stein, thinking of her (and the) self as a subjective process, and not as identity, enables and requires her choice of genre: geographical history. Moreover, her "geographical history" lays claim to the conceptual and imaginative "space" that she finds in the "United States," and that she articulates as the defining characteristic of "America":

> Now the relation of human nature to the human mind is this.
> Human nature cannot know this.
> But the human mind can. It can know this.
> In the United States there is more space where nobody is than where anybody is.
> This is what makes America what it is. (53–54)

Stein's initial "this," above, refers to the necessity of mortality or "death," as a characteristic of "human nature," in order to ensure that "there be room enough" (53) for those who come after. Knowledge of death, which is not available to "human nature," constitutes *the* crucial difference between

---

2. See especially *Four in America* (Freeport, N.Y.: Books for Libraries Press, 1947); *Lectures in America* (1935; reprint, Boston: Beacon, 1985); and *Everybody's Autobiography* (1937; reprint, New York: Random House, 1973). *The Geographical History of America or The Relation of Human Nature to the Human Mind* (1936; reprint, New York: Vintage, 1973). Subsequent citations from *Geographical History* will appear parenthetically in the text.

Richard Bridgman's "Key to the *Yale Catalogue,* Part 4" suggests the following dates of composition: *Four in America,* 1933; *Lectures in America,* 1934; *The Geographical History of America or The Relation of Human Nature to the Human Mind,* 1935; and *Everybody's Biography,* 1936 (Richard Bridgman, *Gertrude Stein in Pieces,* New York: Oxford University Press, 1970).

human nature and the human mind. Only available to the human mind, this knowledge explicitly linked here with the "more space" available in the United States, becomes "what makes America what it is." Through her connecting sentence, "It can know this," with its strategic indefinite pronouns, Stein manages to imply her analogy; "this" can point back toward the knowledge of death or forward toward "more space," and "it" refers us back explicitly to the human mind and turns us implicitly toward the "it" in the last sentence: "This is what makes America what it is." We are meant to understand this linking of "the human mind," "more space," and "America" as the primary argument of Stein's "geographical history," an argument that can only emerge as we do our work as readers, exploring the meditative, syntactical, rhetorical, and grammatical spaces of *The Geographical History of America*.

William Gass describes *The Geographical History of America* as "the stylized presentation of the process of meditation itself, with many critical asides."[3] Gass's implicit spatial metaphor, "many critical asides," seems illuminating—Stein's text spreads out, expands, and repeats, rather than moving forward toward conclusions. In this "stylized presentation of the process," however, much is discovered and mapped. Stein took seriously her conviction that American space—the lay of the land and the geographical history of its inhabitants—would lead to discovery, to new understandings of what constitutes "masterpieces." Significantly, Stein is concerned less with argument than with demonstration. She asserts and demonstrates that the human mind is (that is, it exists in its own present moment) and that the human mind makes writing that is; in this text, then, she works to represent how the human subject participates in *the* human mind, and how this subjective process that is not identity but *genius* takes place in locations that we can define simultaneously as both geography and rhetoric. These locations are best mapped in representations of the spatial and temporal experience of writing and reading and perception.

In *Everybody's Autobiography*, Stein describes how, during their tour of the United States of America in 1934, she and Toklas first flew in an airplane. This experience of being above America becomes, in *The Geographical History of America*, an opportunity to represent how subjective perception can be changed with new geographical relations, with new spatial relations to "the country":

3. William Gass, "Gertrude Stein, Geographer: I," *The New York Review of Books* 20, no. 8 (May 17, 1973): 8. See also Gass's "Gertrude Stein, Geographer: II," *The New York Review of Books* 20, no. 9 (May 31, 1973): 25–29.

Why does the human mind not concern itself with age.

Because the human mind knows what it knows and knowing what it knows it has nothing to do with seeing what it remembers, remember how the country looked as we passed over it, it made designs big designs like human nature draws them because it knows them without ever having seen them from above.

Why in an aeroplane is one not afraid of being high.

Because human nature has nothing to do with it.

Nothing.

I repeat yes and no nothing.

When you climb on the land high human nature knows because by remembering it has been a dangerous thing to go higher and higher on the land which is where human nature was but now in an aeroplane human nature is nothing remembering is nothing. . . . (63–64)

The contemporary experience, "now in an aeroplane," which accompanies and makes possible a rejection of the past ("age" and "remembering"), provides a new purchase on the lay of the land, which for Stein is another way of saying a new purchase on the order of things, or what *is*. Stein's revisionary work with what she embraced as the peculiarly American genre of geographical history articulates a transcendent possibility that is not away from the actual world, but literally "above" it. Stein's historical concerns are geographical precisely because they are in and of the immediate world, immanent; history becomes geography when one actually can see "designs big designs," the way the land arranges itself for the perception that can get above it, and consequently above the mere remembering that human nature can achieve. What Harold Bloom calls "possibilities of transcendence,"[4] in his discussion of *The Geographical History of America*, are for Stein always relations between the immanent, immediate world of experience and her subjective abstractions.

Stein's geographical locations for the subjective and cognitive acts that characterize the human mind are necessarily everywhere: the human mind is, in the widest geographies and the most local (autobio)graphies, in the "big design" of the land and the page before her. She inserts a little autobiographical reading advice, both as a suggestion for reading her text and as an analogy to "being one":

I found that any kind of a book if you read with glasses and somebody is cutting your hair and so you cannot keep the glasses on and you use your

4. Harold Bloom, *Gertrude Stein: Modern Critical Views* (New York: Chelsea, 1986), 1.

> glasses as a magnifying glass and so read word by word reading word by
> word makes the writing that is not anything be something.
> Very regrettable but very true.
> So that shows to you that a whole thing is not interesting because as a
> whole well as a whole there has to be remembering and forgetting, but one
> at a time, oh one at a time is something oh yes definitely something. (151)

"Being one" is not bound to time; it *is*, without remembering and forget-
ting. Subjective experience and anecdotal representation of "one" word
as "something" shifts to a larger abstract distinction between "a whole
thing" and "one at a time." Here, the human mind is seen in its most
representative activities—reading, writing, and composing "not anything"
into "something," through subjective and abstract revision. Stein blurs
the boundaries between "one" word, "one" generalized "thing," and the
human subject who, through singular revision, becomes an I (an eye)
capable of abstracting what had been a mere part into a "one." The analogy
between "being one"—as thing and subject—and reading one word at a
time shows how profoundly material Stein is in her meditations. Moreover,
the analogy makes clear how radical is her rejection of identity; "being one"
is not about being "whole"; rather, "being one," "one" human subject or
"one word," means being one in a series, one and one and one.

In the social context where "somebody is cutting your hair," you are
nevertheless alone with your book. Again, like "now in the aeroplane,"
circumstances produce the necessity and possibility of a new way of seeing.
In this case, what was doubled sight now becomes literally singular; "your
glasses" are transformed into "a magnifying glass" and this singular sight,
focused through one lens, "makes the writing that is not anything be something." Stein's final repeating and accumulating series affirms her visual
and visionary achievement: "one at a time, oh one at a time is something
oh yes definitely something." Reading one word at a time enables seeing
a space that is rhetorical and textual and that holds the possibility of an
abstraction sufficient to the task of representing "something" as definite
and defining, as expansive and cumulative as (her) subjectivity.

Significantly and paradoxically, this "one at a time" that Stein achieves
is not an uninteresting "whole thing"; her "oh yes definitely something" is
"one" but not "whole," complete and definite and potentially multiple (a
series of ones), but not "whole." Myra Jehlen describes how Emersonian
ideology resolves contradictions through paradox:

> in the context of Emersonian pluralism, diversity connotes not difference
> but instead avatars of the universal. Such a concept of diversity tends in

fact to deny difference precisely by expressing it, as yet another facet of the enlarged whole.

In general the concept of nonantagonistic opposition implies the possibility of an energy untaxed by dialectical friction and, indeed, multiplied by the broadening sphere of its exercise. If in a dialectical setting contradiction signifies either-or, as paradox it ultimately means both-and. Its productivity is an endless reproduction, a multiplication, an increase essentially without costs. In this way, the paradoxical nature of American ideology—its celebration of the single self and simultaneous apotheosis of an all-encompassing "America" . . . —has functioned as a dynamo. Paradox generates not only good poetry but also goods.[5]

We might follow Jehlen's thinking here to argue that, for Stein, each "one at a time" is complete and separate, different but not consequentially, multiple but "an increase essentially without cost," cumulative but not an accumulated total. Each "one" is an "[avatar] of the universal," through the productive energies of the composing, representative human mind that makes "definitely something" from what was "not anything." In this way, the "one" who can see "one at a time" participates in what Jehlen calls "an endless reproduction."

Importantly, Stein's self-assertion as "I" quickly shifts to a second-person address that incorporates her readers into the productive act of reading, or the reading act of production, in which the complex relations of words with all their dependence on difference one from another become simply "one." The starting point of personal experience and identity—"I found"—leads to a speculative dialogue—"if you read"—and seemingly effortlessly to a demonstration—"so that shows to you"—that culminates in the resolution of these distinctions of different persons in relation, an apotheosis in which the "I" addresses a "you," in order to become "one." Reading *The Geographical History of America*—experiencing it as a book and on the page—necessarily will implicate "you" in acts of (re)production analogous to learning to see "one at a time." Moreover, on a figurative level, Stein will play through the performative possibilities of saying "I," gradually displacing them with her preferred representation of a subjectivity not entirely congruent with identity, the indefinite pronoun *one*. With its grammatically and referentially indefinite possibility, *one* can become Stein's subjective, even idiosyncratically personal "avatar of the universal."

Stein's title emphasizes the extent to which her text participates (indeed, extends and celebrates) the American ideology and founding myth that

5. Myra Jehlen, *American Incarnation: The Individual, the Nation, and the Continent* (Cambridge: Harvard University Press, 1978), 12.

America is out of time, out of history, a new start in a new world. In the late seventeenth century, the Puritan historian Cotton Mather, in *Magnalia Christi Americana*, his effort to write "the Ecclesiastical History of New England," calls on the traditions of classical and Christian historiography for support in writing a history that he insists must be, in this new and particular case, a geography:

> geography must now find work for a Christianography in regions far enough beyond the bounds wherein the Church of God had, through all former ages, been circumscribed.[6]

Precisely because it is seen from the vantage point of the "new world," Mather's "new [American] age" is "geographical." In "all former ages," Christian history was circumscribed, contained within time's limits, but now in America new "regions far enough beyond the bounds" will require new acts of imagination, new geographies to replace the older historiographies, to map the infinite expansions of Christ into America.

What for Mather had been the geographical progress of a singular but divine individual, Christ incarnate in Puritan claims on America, became—at least in a general sense—over the next two centuries the representative American laying claim to his manifest, geographic destiny, his place on the continent and in his/story. For instance, Jehlen locates a certain triumph of eighteenth- and nineteenth-century ideologies of liberal self-possession in Ralph Waldo Emerson's visionary possession of the American continent, whose landscape is defined "not through its actual farms but through his vision of them, which was permanently safe from time, tide, and man. Paradoxically, this idealization completed the work of the incarnation, embedding the historical United States in an idea of the physical American continent." Like Stein's discoveries when "somebody is cutting your hair," or "now in an aeroplane," Emerson, in *Nature*, manages to turn the world of matter before him into an abstract "idea" nevertheless embedded in what lies before him; he links "idea" to land and continent. Emerson claims a new way of seeing that constitutes a "new" way of being both "nothing" and "all":

> Standing on the bare ground,—my head bathed by the blithe air, and up- lifted into infinite space,—all mean egotism vanishes. I become a transparent eye-ball; I am nothing; I see all; the currents of the Universal Being circulate

---

6. Cotton Mather, *Magnalia Christi Americana, or The Ecclesiastical History of New England*, ed. and abr. by Raymond J. Cunningham (New York: Frederick Ungar, 1970), 16.

through me; I am part or particle of God. . . . I am the lover of uncontained and immortal beauty. In the wilderness, I find something more dear and connate than in streets or villages. In the tranquil landscape, and especially in the distant line of the horizon, man beholds somewhat as beautiful as his own nature.

Here we have the characteristic Emersonian move that Stein continues in *The Geographical History of America.* His position—simultaneously "on the bare ground" and in "infinite space"—represents an apotheosis of what Jehlen calls "American incarnation"; the self-possessed individual becomes incarnate in the continent and, consequently, all-encompassing, at once singular and individual. "With Emerson, [the conviction that the national destiny was inherent in the continent] achieved its full potential by projecting outward to a vision of the entire universe and inward to a universal definition of self."[7]

By becoming "nothing," or rather by becoming complete perception, the human subject sees all, an all that ultimately is both "the distant line of the horizon" and "his own nature." Stein likes to exploit this paradox, simultaneously asserting and negating an "I" that becomes all precisely through its capacity to be nothing. If the subject can transcend "his" own locations, through expansive acts of composition, it is in order to return to (to have) the "uncontained" beauty of precisely "his own" acts of seeing. In *The Geographical History of America,* Stein works with the same puns that Emerson uses so paradoxically and effectively here. Emerson's "I" shifts to an "eye" that, making the "I" nothing, sees "all." I have already discussed two such representative acts of looking, of visionary visualizing: "now from an aeroplane," and when "somebody is cutting your hair."

These locations for subjectivity in *The Geographical History of America* are spaces where the human mind emerges as at once fundamentally constitutive of *a* human subject and as representative, a universal generalization of *the* human mind. Stein the writer represents her acts of composition—all that comes into the locating and composing acts of the human mind as it writes—and this text represents for Stein a kind of celebration, an embrace, even in the face of limits, of what the human mind does and is. As Jehlen argues more generally for American writing, "it is only through possession of a physical universe that self-possessive individualism fulfilled itself as individualist universalism."[8]

7. Jehlen, *American Incarnation,* 111; Ralph Waldo Emerson, *Nature,* in *Essays and Lectures,* ed. Joel Porte (New York: Library of America, 1983), 10; Jehlen, *American Incarnation,* 89.
   8. Jehlen, *American Incarnation,* 14.

Stein's visionary possession of America is so complete that she not only can but must occupy America from outside. Given the difficulty of her relatively marginal status in hegemonic forms of American self-possessive individualism as a woman, Jew, and lesbian, taking America with her and occupying her abstraction is a sign both of the power of the visionary tradition she extends and of her own relentless rhetorical insistence on her place within it. Indeed, for Stein it is precisely her physical distance from the continent that enables her self-placement in America. Since America created the twentieth century in America during the nineteenth century, she argues, "the generation living as contemporaries . . . are occupying themselves to continue America by being outside of America."[9] She inhabits a concept, rather than a country. Her "geographical history" records and maps a conceptual, rhetorical, and grammatical space. She constructs a geography where words are places and where "the human mind cannot be displaced" (92), and a history of relations that are more syntactical and grammatical than they are temporal. In this text, time is structured in small ways: Stein shifts the idea of history from the large canvas of peoples and nations to the small, more particular shifts of her story. History is immanent in experience, in the everyday experiences against which her conceptual abstractions emerge and against which they are tested. This text abounds with references to everyday, daily, even intimate life and with references, which are often rejections, of a larger public life of government, propaganda, and war. Written in the middle of the 1930s, *The Geographical History of America* enacts a claim on a conceptual and rhetorical "America"; as her text wanders forward, this claim, situated in the concerns and political tensions of her time, increasingly raises the threat of European war, as the historical ground that American transcendence aims to rise above.

In a climate of polarized political options—the right or the left—Stein tries to lay claim to an American Republicanism that emphasizes self-reliance and self-realization. "Money" emerges as an area for the full operation of the human mind, as a conceptual *and* material value that Stein sees as foundational to the particularly American genius of entrepreneurialism. Money and language are abstract, purely symbolic signifying systems that, in their clear ties to one's material well-being, reenact the ahistorical, yet immanent, relations of the human mind to reality. The human mind engages in a system of exchange in which "money" or "words," commodities

9. Gertrude Stein, "Thoughts on an American Contemporary Feeling," in *Reflections on the Atomic Bomb: Volume I of the Previously Uncollected Writings of Gertrude Stein*, ed. Robert Bartlett Hass (Los Angeles: Black Sparrow, 1973), 159–60.

or language are indifferently exchanged: "And the human mind can live does live by anybody being able to sell something to somebody. This is what money is not give but sell" (102). William James articulates the "usual question" of Pragmatism this way: "What, in short, is the truth's cash-value in experiential terms?"[10]

Perhaps Stein's clearest, and most uniquely succinct, representation of the link between using and gaining money and trafficking in words and ideas is the following single-sentence "Autobiography number one": "I am writing all this with an American dollar pen" (191). This particular "autobiography number one" occurs in a series of six sections with the same title. The present-tense writing is possible because of the commodity, itself no doubt reproduced serially, and the commodity carries the signifier of its cost. Stein writes her self, her "I," which is both "autobiography" and "all this" (the entire text), with an instrument that, produced by American capital and American ingenuity, reproduces her articulation of self. The yoking of the most seemingly banal, "an American dollar pen," with the largest expansions of her human mind, "all this," recurs throughout this autobiographical and geographical history. Like Emerson, whose feet are "standing on bare ground," while his head floats in "infinite space," Stein insists on the relation of material and transcendent, of quotidian and universal.

In his discussion of "place identity as a component of self," Theodore R. Sarbin notes how grammatical, syntactical, and environmental locations give referential meaning to pronominal self-representations. " 'I' and 'me' take on their meanings from the predicates in uttered or implied sentences":

> To the proposition that the abstraction "self" is construed from uttered or tacit "I" and "me" sentences, I add another grammatical notion. In the course of dealing with problematic situations, people employ pronominal questions, questions beginning with who, what, where, when, why, etc. When the problematic situations place the actor at risk for survival, he/she must engage in epistemic actions that locate self in the relevant world of occurrences. Such actions include asking pronominal questions, such as *who am I?* and *where am I?* Not a blooming, buzzing confusion (as William James suggested), the world of occurrences is a set of loosely-organized environmental systems or ecologies.[11]

10. William James, "Pragmatism's Conception of Truth," in *Pragmatism, a New Name for Some Old Ways of Thinking;* and *The Meaning of Truth, a Sequel to* Pragmatism (Cambridge: Harvard University Press, 1978), 97.
11. Theodore R. Sarbin, "Place Identity as a Component of Self: An Addendum," *Journal of Environmental Psychology* 3:4 (1983): 337, 338.

Writing—and especially writing *I*—is such a problematic situation. The pleasures and perils of self-representation in the nonpresence of written text, for Stein, "place the actor at risk for survival." Once I have articulated "I," I am no longer that "I." Stein's predicate, "am writing all this with an American dollar pen"—drawn from her immediate and hence eminently relevant world of occurrences, the composing process—works as "an epistemic action" that locates her "I" in an ecology of writing.

Stein understood that writing is neither immediate nor present. It is precisely because it is not that she argued so strongly for the need to write as if it were immediate and present, or, better, for the need to push language to represent immediacy and presence. Stein's texts often achieve their discursive immediacy through an insistence on the spatial dimensions of language—the sentence, the page, the book—and the locations of contact between writer and reader, where one writes and where one reads. To be a careful reader of Stein requires that one place one's secure, comprehending self—all the old narrative and referential coherences—at some degree of risk. Her reader necessarily works to locate herself as a maker of meaning in relation to Stein's difficulties. One of the effects in Stein's texts is that we are always aware of language itself, of the medium of representation, of the immediate presence of language in our reading.

Granted that we are willing to become her readers, her book and her sentences "guide" us into their "reality's whole setting," which William James claims as the test of truth:

> Any idea that helps us to *deal*, whether practically or intellectually, with either the reality or its belongings, that doesn't entangle our progress in frustrations, that *fits*, in fact, and adapts our life to the reality's whole setting, will agree sufficiently to meet the requirement. It will hold true of that reality.[12]

In the rhetorical and cognitive space, the "geographical historical" space, the "America" claimed by Stein in this text, we are required to reconceptualize the "setting" of reality, especially what we take as the setting for the abstraction "self." Stein's experiments with figures, organization, and repetition figure a multiple, heterogeneous subject position for the human mind that writes, or, in other words, for the one who does the important literary thinking. Her language aims to put us into the cognitive space that her geographical history claims.

Over and over, she announces her theme in these meditations: "That is what I mean to be I mean to be the one who can and does have as

12. James, "Pragmatism's Conception of Truth," 102.

ordinary ideas as these" (57). For Stein, here, *ordinary* takes its common-place meaning of "belonging to the regular or usual order" (OED). She announces in her second sentence: "These are ordinary ideas. If you please these are ordinary ideas" (53). She means, then, to be the one who can and does have ideas belonging to the usual order. She writes of daily life, using domestic detail and commonplace phrases. She aims to locate her self in a tradition of powerful human minds ordering reality. If we attend to her insistence on the word *ordinary*, a deep structural meaning emerges. *Ordinary* devolves from the late Latin adverb *ordinalis* (in English, the adjective *ordinal*), referring to that "denoting order or place in a series (as a number)" (OED). We know Stein's interest in "one at a time" and in the series: "a rose is a rose is a rose." A series is a repetition, an order, an "ordinary" idea. Here she explores that interest in terms of how we understand and how we represent subjectivity in language; grammar, too, is an order.

How do we mean the ordinary idea "I" when we say "I mean to be I"? Her repetition produces a parallelism that suggests both her insistence on her meaning (her signifying act) and her solution to the problem of identity: "I mean to be I mean to be the one who can and does have as ordinary ideas as these" (57). Let me represent some of the semantic possibility of her syntax graphically:

"I mean to be I"

parallels another possibility,

"I mean to be the one who,"

thereby replacing the pronoun "I" with the pronoun "one." Throughout *The Geographical History*, Stein consistently renders problematic the saying of "I," displacing "I" sometimes into "I I" and often into "one."

Stein leads us playfully into her subjective space, as she numbers and arranges her chapters. Immediately following her assertion that "what I mean to be I mean to be the one who can and does have as ordinary ideas as these," she gives us our first indication that this text is to be organized into chapters:

End of chapter one.
If you stop to think about chapter one you will know that any one has had to die so that there is room for any one to be, that is if every one who had lived had not died where would we be. (57)

The numbering of chapters slips into her subject "any one," her figure of order into a trope of grammar. Since in what follows she mostly uses Roman numerals to mark chapters, we can see in her interest in numbering the pun on "one" as number and "one" as indefinite pronoun. Stein writes a series of ones, showing how the ones in a series shift between representation of number and subjectivity. Numbering chapters and subjectivity is, in any case, a matter of aesthetics and pleasure, of satisfying the desires of the human mind: "The thing about numbers that is important is that any of them have a pretty name" (114).

Any reader of Stein knows her use of repetition. In this text, repetition, or "insistence" as she preferred to name it, is a crucial aspect of her representation of the human mind thinking about identity and difference. Identity is "the sameness of a person or thing at all times in all circumstances; absolute sameness; recurrence of the same" (OED). As Stein repeats the same words and ideas over and over, we begin to understand that there is no identity in repetition. Rather, repetition with its inevitable variations of order and with her deliberate variations of syntax and complex word-plays is about difference, the inevitable and pleasurable heterogeneity of language that characterizes the human mind at play. Her insistence on a continual reworking of key terms, words, phrases, and thoughts results not in sameness, but in an accumulation of almost infinite semantic plenitude that begins to enrich all words, especially those that we had perhaps assumed to be simple. Stein's expansive repetition enacts on a rhetorical level what Jehlen has claimed for Emersonian paradox: "productivity [of] an endless reproduction, a multiplication, an increase essentially without costs."[13] I, one, and ordinary seem infinitely reproducible—flexible signifiers without cost.

With her rhetorical investigations of how we articulate our subjective locations, she rejects identity as it had been conventionally understood, affirming an abstracted, multiplied, heterogeneous subjectivity, "one," lifted out of historical constraints and not tied to traditional (gendered) notions of identity. In one of her little dramas, Stein plays through various possibilities of saying "I," writing:

Act III

No one knowing me knows me.
And I am I I.
And does a little dog making a noise make the same noise as a bird.
I have not been mistaken.

13. Jehlen, *American Incarnation*, 12.

Chorus. Some kinds of things not and some kinds of things.
Scene I

    I am I yes sir I am I.
    I am I yes Madame am I I.
    When I am I am I I.
    And any little dog is not the same thing as I am I.
Chorus. Or is it.
    With tears in any eyes oh is it.
    And there we have the whole thing.
    Am I I.
    And if I am I because my little dog knows me am I I.
    Yes sir am I I.
    Yes Madame or am I I.
    The dog answers without asking because the dog is the answer to
    anything that is the dog. But not I. Without tears not I. (113)

Stein revises the Descartian *cogito ergo sum* ("I think therefore I am"). The assumed proposition "I am" must be explored and questioned. She asserts definitely to "sir" the closed assumption: "I am I." When addressed to a feminine gendered interlocutor, named with the French of her expatriate home, her assertion becomes question merely by reordering the simple words: "am I I."

In her play, we can see a tension between her confident assertion of identity, of an assured, stable subject position, the "I," and her more tenuous, questioning, open-ended representation of subjectivity, "am I I." To question "I" is to say it still, but her questioning of the stable, unified self, the single, identical "I," leads to a subtle undermining of that unified identity in her assertion, and moreover, her affirmation, of a multiplied "I I," a compounded subject who speaks herself as both question and assertion. Moreover, it is her address to a feminine gendered interlocutor that enables that questioning. "Madame" ("My Lady") hints that her relationship with Toklas enables her revision of self. Interestingly, this bilingual interjection conflates her transatlantic move with the feminine gendering of her interlocutor. She links her expatriate American point of view with her address to her lover. Stein never innocently uses gender references as categories, especially in this text, which is celebrated for her confident claim, as "a woman" and "one," of literary genius.

In her lecture, "Poetry and Grammar," she describes the question mark as "the most the completely most uninteresting [of all punctuation marks]. . . . It is evident that if you ask a question you ask a question but anybody who can read at all knows when a question is a question as it is written in writing."[14] Clearly, for this reason, she is uninterested in the question mark. In *The Geographical History of America*, another reason is evident. Without its mark, and without the "servile" comma (218), an "evident" question might also be an assertion, however attenuated by questioning. When she asks "When I am I[,] am I I," she might as likely be asserting "When I am[,] I am I I." Such semantic plenitude recurs throughout this text in this favored syntactical strategy of maintaining question and assertion simultaneously. Indeed, it is the very questioning of unified subjectivity, of identity, that both allows and affirms a multiplied, heterogeneous subjectivity.

In the second line of this "Act III" (one of many in this text), Stein announces: "And I am I I": this seems to be a clear assertion of her denial of the unity of the self, of the enunciated "I." Her question/assertion "And I am I I," puns aurally on "eye eye" (seeing, both as vision and as understanding, is important). "I I" also suggests "aye aye"; later I will be arguing for the strongly affirmative tone of Stein's representation of the human mind and of writing as multiple, nonidentity based, and heterogeneous. "I I" also puns graphically on "one [and] one," so that here, as elsewhere, we might read "Act III" as a description of the multiple subjectivity that she is representing in this play (the genre and the puns) *and* as an imperative to act "III" or as if one were "I, I, I."

Judith Butler argues that:

> the "I" only comes into being through being called, named, interpellated, to use the Althusserian term, and this discursive constitution takes place prior to the "I." . . . Indeed, I can only say "I" to the extent that I have first been addressed, and that address has mobilized my place in speech. . . . The "I" is thus a citation of the place of the "I" in speech where that place has a certain priority and anonymity with respect to the life it animates: it is the historically revisable possibility of a name that precedes and exceeds me, but without which I cannot speak.[15]

Butler is interested to see both the discursive conditions for (gendered) subjectivity and the possibility of their revisions. When one speaks as "I," one is called into being, into a rhetorical space that precedes and forms the conditions for one's subjectivity, but also one cites the place of the subject, and in so doing, potentially revises it. Stein's articulations of "I," "I I,"

14. Gertrude Stein, "Poetry and Grammar," in *Lectures in America* (1935; reprint, Boston: Beacon, 1985), 214–15.

15. Judith Butler, *Bodies That Matter: On the Discursive Limits of "Sex"* (New York: Routledge, 1993), 225–26.

and "one" perform these citations and their revisions. In *The Geographical History of America,* the shifting "place of the 'I' " pushes against the "priority and anonymity" of the discursive constitution of the subject, even as it dramatizes it. Through her playful displacement of "I," Stein insists on her invention and revision of subjective possibilities to the point of risking not being understood, of being rejected as nonsensical and trivial.

As I have suggested, her most important strategy in this effort is her extended play on "I" as both first person pronoun and as number, and her displacement of "I" with the indefinite pronoun, "one." "I" as pronoun graphically puns on "I" as number, which in turn aurally puns on "one" as pronoun. These three repeat and shift throughout the text as Stein plays on the permutations of identity, number, and the subjectivity of the human mind. Identity means being single (that version of "one"), unified, same: yet, even the signs that we traditionally use to represent the identity of subject and the identity of number are unstable, as Stein shows in her grammatical tropes. Bringing this instability into play represents the human mind as it thinks, as it writes.

In the inverted syntax and passive voice of her first sentence, Stein announces "I" as her subject: "In the month of February were born Washington Lincoln and I" (53). She links her represented self, her "I," to a lineage of American leadership; Washington and Lincoln are mythic, heroic figures for America's birth in revolution and America's rebirth in civil war and reconstruction. By association, her "I" is also mythopoeic, larger than life, a representation and citation, historical and American, representing her reinvention of America. Out of its customary place at the beginning of the sentence, we hear it especially. Her syntax also suggests a sense of "I" as part of a series, as number, as an "ordinary" idea; it is as if she might have said "Washington Lincoln and one" or "one one and one."

Stein's rejection of traditional conceptions of identity repeats bluntly in her assertion: "Any dog has identity" (142). "Identity" is a property, then, not only of human nature, but of other life forms in nature. As such, it is not interesting as a defining characteristic of the human mind, of human subjectivity. In contrast, "being one" seems to be something that goes beyond (human) nature:

Number I
Every time any one can come to be one then there is no human nature no not in that one.
Human nature has to do with identity but identity has nothing to do with any one being one.
Not not anything in any one.

No no no. (167)

"One" is something "one can come to be"; as a potential, it differs from "identity," which is a common property of all, from "any dog" to any person in whom there is human nature. Again, a double negative multiplies the meaning: "Not not anything in any one" insists on the earlier idea that when "one" is "one" then there is no longer human nature "in that one." The phrase also introduces a new word, *anything,* and by doubly negating it, asserts that there is indeed something in "one." In other words, there is not nothing in one. "One" *is.*

"Being one" differs further from having identity in that it allows for difference: "If you are one then now and then you are not that one. That can happen at any time. It does happen when any one is a little one and any one, any one is then one" (181). "Being one," for Stein, is neither same nor unified nor stable. "One" becomes so much a figure *for* the human mind that it can represent the human mind alone (it is too irresistible not to pun, al/one):

> Part II
> I am coming to what the human mind is and I have one.
> Part III
> One. (177)

In *The Geographical History of America,* Stein resolves her own struggle for identity by rejecting the concept as less interesting than human mind.[16] It is as if she discovers that concerns about identity were, indeed, digressions, not that in which she is really interested. Rather, she is interested in constructing a rhetoric and grammar of subjectivity that goes beyond the

16. In the midst of all these assertions, rejections, and displacements of identity, we might remember that some critics delineate connections between problems that Stein was having with her own identity and her rejection of the concept in *The Geographical History of America.* For Gass, issues of (personal) identity recur throughout Stein's career and texts. In describing Stein's career following *Q.E.D.,* he argues that: "The problem of personal identity, which is triumphantly overcome in *The Geographical History,* would occupy her henceforth" (7). Cynthia Secor ("Gertrude Stein: The Complex Force of Her Femininity," in *Women, the Arts, and the 1920s in Paris and New York,* ed. Kenneth W. Wheeler et al. [New Brunswick: Transaction, 1982]) sees Stein's "problem" of (personal) identity in her attempts to reconcile her gender with her role as a serious writer. For Secor, Stein's struggle with the issue of personal identity results in her search for a modern voice; Secor describes the emergence of a voice that is authorial without being "masculine" and of a pattern of mind that is more interested in what she takes to be fact than it is in patriarchal myth.

limits and restrictions of the universal (male) unity of self. Her problem spreads out before her: how to write the geographical history of American self-possession in different gender terms; how to articulate the experience of difference insistently constituted by the gender terms of compulsory heterosexuality while simultaneously claiming an ungendered human mind; how to be "the only one that is the one that makes writing that goes on" (153). Confronted with a confidently masculinist and universalist tradition of American self-possession that, even with Emerson's and James's revisions, articulated a confidently individualist and universal *and* masculine subject, Stein wants in, but as herself, on her own terms. Stein wants to "ungender" the human mind by articulating it as "one." She questions stable identity and its grammatical fabrications, works through a variety of gendered performative possibilities, including her self-representations as "a woman," aiming to emerge with a reasserted ungendered identity, the human mind.

We can see awareness of gender as category when Stein writes "so he and she and she and he do know what the human mind is" (67). She will not stoop to the masculine pronoun as representation of the abstract, universal, human subject. Nor is it sufficient merely to include both genders; she re-orders the pronouns in her insistence. Furthermore, she compounds her representation of gender; it is as if each pronoun in the series were slightly different from the others. As a result, while she achieves insistence on gender, she also manages to suggest that one "she" or "he" does not represent all others. Paradoxical "individualist universalism" with its nonantagonistic opposition of sameness and difference, which Jehlen analyzes, recurs here with her insistence on a plurality of different subject positions that nevertheless "do know what the human mind is," a plurality that manages to overcome the differences that make it plural in the epistemological apotheosis that can "know what *the* human mind is."

Catharine Stimpson, writing of Stein's "transposition of gender," posits the possibility of reading Stein as a writer of "flexible texts that address both the heterogeneity that is one of gender's most fertile foes and the binarism that is one of its most rock-bound friends." Stimpson argues that Stein's poetic strategies lead her to juxtapose reconstitution and repudiation of gender in one of three ways: a preference for reconstitution over repudiation, a balance of reconstitution and repudiation, or a preference for repudiation over reconstitution.[17] Although the two remain in tension,

17. Catharine R. Stimpson, "Gertrude Stein and the Transposition of Gender," in *The Poetics of Gender*, ed. Nancy K. Miller (New York: Columbia University Press, 1986), 16, 11–14.

as elsewhere in Stein, the rhetorical force of *The Geographical History of America* points toward a preference for repudiation over reconstitution of gender. In this text, Stein reconstitutes the theoretical and grammatical and essentialist terms of gender in order to repudiate them, by pointing beyond them, with her theory of the human mind as subjectivity, and with her grammatical figure, the abstract, indefinite pronoun, *one*.

The representation of gender as a category, as a possible order for human experience, allows her to reject it in favor of what interests her:

> Part II
> I think nothing about men and women because that has nothing to do with anything.
> Anybody who is an American can know anything about this thing. (214)

Stein's blunt assertion seems a little disingenuous given her gendered references throughout the text. Here, at a relatively late point, as part of her complicated and heterogeneous representation of the human mind, she begins to move away from gender, and sex difference, as constraints on the human mind. Sex/gender categories are uninteresting, yielding "nothing" for the human mind as it does what it does (thinking and writing), limiting "anybody" who would "know anything about this thing." Another category of subjectivity, being an "American," enables her rejection of the contingent categories "men and women." Thinking and knowing, as activities and as possibilities, are understood here as attributes of an "I," paralleled with "anybody who is an American."

Stein accomplishes her repudiation of the terms of heterosexual gender through an assertion of the categories as topics, as "this thing" that shapes our thoughts. Her repetition of variations on "nothing" and "anything" resolves into a qualified assertion of "this thing" as something "an American" can know. The vagueness of the demonstrative adjective, "this," seems to suggest that the thing that "an American can know anything about" is the rejection of the sex/gender categories as "anything." The play on *nothing* and *anything* might lead us to observe that the first sentence does not assert "I do not think about." In contrast, "I think nothing about" could be read as an assertion of the thinking of "no/thing," a positive assertion of the contingency of such categories. "This thing," which is also the "nothing" that is thought about, is, of course, heterosexuality as a sex-gender system, the elaboration of sex difference as fundamentally constitutive of reality. For Stein, from the vantage point afforded her by "geographical history," heterosexuality is constituted precisely in the moment in which it is named, rejected, displaced.

The Geographical History of America makes evident that it is the idea of America, a conceptual space, that allows Stein her vantage point on the crucial differences between mind and nature. The figure *America* offers Stein what Emerson, in "Circles," claims for "literature . . . a point outside . . . to afford us a platform whence we may command a view of our present life, a purchase by which we may move it."[18] With her insistent claim of a "point outside" and her equally insistent claim of her centrality, Stein writes to get out from under gender; her escape, though, is a movement through, a process of displacement whereby the human mind and her figures for it, especially the ungendered "one," gain strength and loosen the order of gender. This text suggests that gender offers a grammatical and rhetorical geography that makes an interesting place to visit (or to think about), but one wouldn't want one's human mind to live there.

In "The Mark of Gender," Monique Wittig argues that:

> Sex, under the name of gender, permeates the whole body of language and forces every locutor, if she belongs to the oppressed sex, to proclaim it in her speech, that is, *to appear in language under her proper physical form and not under the abstract form*, which every male locutor has the unquestioned right to use. The abstract form, the general, the universal, that is what the so-called masculine gender means, for the class of men have appropriated the universal for themselves.[19]

For a "woman" to say "I," then, she says "woman" or "she," an attenuated, nonuniversal subjectivity. Stein reappropriates the abstract—the human mind, itself—and also the abstract form in grammar, "one." She does speak as "woman," as "she," under "her proper physical form," establishing the order of gender in language. But, simultaneously and, as I have been arguing, in a gradual displacement, she asserts the abstract form as her own subjective ground, as a representative human mind.

Here, as in her literary autobiographies and in her writing on writing from the same period, she confronts the central dilemma of reconciling her gender and her genius: "Also there is why is it that in this epoch the only real literary thinking has been done by a woman" (218). This question shifts to her assertion that she, sometimes "a woman" and sometimes "I," is the one who does the important literary thinking, an assertion, sometimes taking the form of an assertive question, that she repeats variously eight

---

18. Ralph Waldo Emerson, "Circles," in *Essays and Lectures,* ed. Joel Porte (New York: Library of America, 1983), 408.

19. Monique Wittig, *The Straight Mind and Other Essays* (Boston: Beacon Press, 1992), 79–80; emphasis added.

times throughout the last twenty-five pages of the book. Even as she asserts her own gendered genius, we can see this displacement at work: "It is natural that again *a woman should be one* to do the literary thinking of this epoch" (228, emphasis added). In her repeated assertions of literary genius, Stein asserts both the available categories of identity—the first person "I" and the heterosexual gender category "woman"—and what puts those categories into question, namely her being "one," her representative status as the human mind. In a triumph of paradox (or nonantagonistic contradiction), her vernacular phrasing reclaims "nature"—elsewhere so carefully distinguished from writing—as the ground for her reinvention of gendered experience as universalist genius: "It is natural that again a woman should be one to do the literary thinking of this epoch" (228).

Wittig describes her own choice of the indefinite pronoun as a representational strategy:

> A massive effort was needed to break the spell of the captured subject. I needed a strong device, something that would immediately be beyond sexes, that the division by sexes would be powerless against, and that could not be coopted. There is in French, as there is in English, a munificent pronoun that is called the indefinite, which means that it is not marked by gender, a pronoun that you are taught in school to systematically avoid. It is *on* in French—*one* in English.

The indefinite pronoun *one* is a strategy to represent outside of gender, for Gertrude Stein, as it is for Wittig. Her grammar of subjectivity, consequently, aims to represent a subject position located grammatically and rhetorically "outside" of gender. Furthermore, grammatically, *one* is beyond number. *One* as indefinite pronoun is merely conventionally singular in English grammar, since it can be said to represent any number, any indefinite number, of persons. As Wittig asserts, *one* "can represent a certain number of people successively or all at once—everybody, we, they, I, you, people, a small or a large number of persons—and still stay singular." Beyond number and gender, *one* is the perfect sign for Stein's representation of the heterogeneous, multiple, yet simultaneously self-possessed, subjectivity of the human mind. Unlike her other alternative, "And I am I I," *one* has the benefit of already being found in English grammar. Furthermore, "And I am I I" might imply two, rather than one, and again, one. Stein is interested in destabilizing the unity of identity, but in ways that necessarily assert its displacement by the human mind, her category of "individualist universalism."[20]

20. Ibid., 82–83, 83.

I want to suggest a further, somewhat strange-bedfellow political connection between the very conservative Stein and Wittig's late-twentieth-century, lesbian repudiation of the "totalitarian" category of sex. Given how she perceived her political choices in the 1930s, Stein is clearly on the right, even sympathetic to fascism in her fear of collectivist politics on the left. In "One Is Not Born a Woman," Wittig, however, given our very different political context, argues for the necessity for progressive (that is, left, materialist, Marxist, dialectical) politics to articulate a liberatory theory of the individual:

> to become a class we do not have to suppress our individual selves, and since no individual can be reduced to her/his oppression we are also confronted with the historical necessity of constituting ourselves as the individual subjects of our history as well. . . . For once one has acknowledged oppression, one needs to know and experience the fact that one can constitute oneself as a subject (as opposed to an object of oppression), that one can become *someone* in spite of oppression, that one has one's own identity. There is no possible fight for someone deprived of an identity, no internal motivation for fighting, since, although I can fight only with others, first I fight for myself.

Wittig's emphasis on solidarity amongst individuals clearly sets her politics apart from Stein's emphasis on being "alone," "one at a time." However, given recent academic practices of celebrating and advocating the death of the subject—with relative indifference to the historical difficulties of having subjectivity—and given a certain "progressive" disdain for individualism in all its forms, Wittig's insistence on the necessity of practices of individual subjectivity if we are to fight against oppression is instructive. We might understand Stein's acts of cultural revision as efforts both to claim her own abstract and subjective individuality and to claim a space that affords a purchase on the "nature" that oppressed her as a "woman." Her efforts—especially as they are constrained by the Emersonian paradox of "individualist universalism"—elaborate, articulate, and map an individual act of cultural engagement and revision.[21]

Stein's doubleness—in and beside heterosexuality, a "woman" and "one"—repeats her doubled continuation and revision of an American tradition that she must shift out of its masculinist universalism, in order to construct herself as representative, an "America" that she continues and occupies "by being outside." Stein's movement through and beyond gender should be understood as a movement beyond the ideological terms of heterosexuality. Teresa de Lauretis argues that "the terms of a different

21. Ibid., 8, 16.

construction of gender also exist, in the margins of hegemonic discourses. Posed from outside the heterosexual contract, and inscribed in micropolitical practices, these terms can also have a part in the construction of gender, and their effects are rather at the 'local' level of resistances, in subjectivity and self-representation."[22] Stein's explicit rejection of the larger spheres of politics and history, in *The Geographical History of America*, does not mean that she surrenders what de Lauretis calls "micropolitical practices." For Stein, such practices are her grammatical and rhetorical self-representations.

Earlier I mentioned how Stein's assertion of the multiple subject, "And I am I I," puns on "aye aye," or, in other words, "yes yes." "Yes," both stated bluntly and coded in double negatives and puns, runs through this long text working to affirm her fiction of a multiple subject, who is nevertheless "one." Other modernists may have been bemoaning the so-called fragmentation of modern life and of the (universal and masculinist) subject; Gertrude Stein embraced and affirmed the possibilities of a heterogeneous subjectivity, freed from the constraints of identity: "The human mind yes the human mind can say yes./ Human nature cannot say this human nature cannot say yes" (135). Again, utterance, affirmation, and the human mind converge. Furthermore, in her linking of the human mind with being one, there is affirmation: "It has nothing to do with anything but is one yes well yes that is what the human mind is" (160). Affirmatively and playfully, Gertrude Stein invented her subject position in the grammatical and rhetorical space of her American writing. This American lesbian writer inhabits an America of grammatical and conceptual space; writing her geographical history "from outside" allows this woman to be "the one."

22. Teresa de Lauretis, *Technologies of Gender* (Bloomington: Indiana University Press, 1987), 18.

Notes on Contributors

DEEPIKA BAHRI teaches postcolonial literature and theory at Emory University. She has coedited *Between the Lines: South Asians and Postcoloniality* (1996) and has published articles in *Ariel: A Review of International English Literature, Studies in American Humor, Postmodern Culture,* and *College English.*

TOM BERNINGHAUSEN is an Assistant Professor of English and the codirector of Women's Studies at Clark University. He has published essays on Shakespeare, Blake, and Melville. He is currently working on a comparative study of the representation of the American Revolution in historical and fictional narratives circa 1790–1835.

PETER CACCAVARI is an independent scholar living in Cincinnati. He has published articles on regionalism, pedagogy, and Reconstruction. He has recently completed writing "Reconstructions of Race and Culture in America: Violence and Knowledge in Works by Albion Tourgée, Charles Chesnutt, and Thomas Dixon, Jr."

MONICA CHIU is an Assistant Professor of English at the University of Wisconsin–Eau Claire, where she specializes in Asian American Literature. She earned her Ph.D. degree from Emory University in 1996, writing a dissertation on illness and self-representation in Asian American literature by women.

JACQUELINE DOYLE is Associate Professor of English at California State University, Hayward, where she teaches American Literature and Women's Literature. Her recent and forthcoming publications on contemporary ethnic women's writing include articles in *MELUS: The Journal of the Society for the Study of the Multi-Ethnic Literature of the United States;*

Frontiers: A Journal of Women Studies; Women's Studies: An Interdisciplinary Journal; Hitting Critical Mass: A Journal of Asian American Cultural Criticism; and *Critique: Studies in Contemporary Fiction.* Her article in *MELUS* won the Katherine Newman Award in 1995.

HUGH ENGLISH is Director of College Writing and Assistant Professor of English at the University of Southern Maine. He is at work on a longer study of Gertrude Stein, currently titled *"By Being Outside": Gertrude Stein's Continuation and Re-invention of America and Self,* while pursuing related questions about subjectivity and writing in his research on rhetoric and college composition.

CAROLINE GEBHARD is an Assistant Professor at Tuskegee University, having earned her Ph.D. degree in English from the University of Virginia in 1991. She has published essays on nineteenth-century American women writers such as Harriet Beecher Stowe and Constance Fenimore Woolson. Her most recent work includes "Reconstructing Southern Manhood: Race, Sentimentality, and Camp in the Plantation Myth," in *Haunted Bodies: Rethinking the South through Gender,* edited by Susan V. Donaldson and Anne Goodwyn Jones, forthcoming from the University of Virginia Press.

KATHERINE JOSLIN is Professor and Director of Graduate Studies in the Department of English at Western Michigan University. She is the author of *Edith Wharton* (1991) and the editor, along with Alan Price, of *Wretched Exotic: Essays on Edith Wharton in Europe* (1993). Her work on late-nineteenth- and early-twentieth-century writers includes essays on Dreiser, Cather, Chopin, Percy Lubbock, and Jane Addams. She is currently writing a literary biography of Addams.

GIAVANNA MUNAFO is the Director of the Women's Resource Center and an Adjunct Assistant Professor of Women's Studies at Dartmouth College. Her contribution is taken from a study in progress entitled "Properties of Whiteness: Contemporary American Women Novelists and the Figuring of White Womanhood."

SUSAN ROBERSON teaches English at Auburn University. She is the author of *Emerson in His Sermons: A Man-Made Self* (1995) and has published articles in *American Transcendental Quarterly* and *ESQ: A Journal of the American Renaissance* and has essays in the *Biographical Dictionary of Transcendentalism* and *The Stowe Debate: Rhetorics in Uncle Tom's Cabin.*

BARBARA RODRÍGUEZ is an Assistant Professor of American Literature at Northeastern University. Her book, *Autobiographical Inscriptions: Form, Personhood, and the American Woman Writer of Color,* is forthcoming from Oxford University Press.

RACHEL LEE RUBIN is an Assistant Professor of American Studies at the University of Massachusetts–Boston. Her book, *Reading, Writing, and the Rackets: Jewish Gangsters in Modern Narrative* is forthcoming from the University of Illinois Press. She is presently working on a book about the Bakersfield sound in country music.

KAY FERGUSON RYALS is currently a graduate student at the University of California–Irvine completing her dissertation on the discourse of manners and its configurations of race and gender in late-nineteenth- and early-twentieth-century realist writing.

Index

Credits

Acknowledgment is made as follows for permission to quote from copyrighted material:

The article "Haunting the Borderlands: Sandra Cisneros' *Woman Hollering Creek*," originally published in *Frontiers: A Journal of Women Studies*, 16:1 (1996).

Lines from "Malinchista, A Myth Revised" by Alicia Gaspar de Alba, from *Three Times a Woman: Chicana Poetry*, copyright 1989 Bilingual Press/Editorial Bilingüe, Arizona State University, Tempe, Arizona.